Michael Smith served for nine years in the British Army's Intelligence Corps as a latter-day codebreaker. He then worked for the BBC Monitoring Service. He has written for a number of newspapers, including the *Financial Times*, the *Sunday Times* and most recently the *Daily Telegraph*, where he is Defence Correspondent. He also covers espionage and intelligence matters for the *Telegraph* and is a member of the editorial board of the Bletchley Park Trust.

Michael Smith is the co-editor, with Ralph Erskine, of *Action This Day: Bletchley Park from the breaking of the Enigma Code to the birth of the modern computer*. Smith's previous books include *Odd Man Out: The Story of the Singapore Traitor* (with Peter Elphick); *New Cloak, Old Dagger: How Britain's Spies Came in from the Cold*; the number one bestseller *Station X: The Codebreakers of Bletchley Park*; and *Foley: The Spy who Saved 10,000 Jews*, which led to Israeli recognition of Frank Foley, the so-called British Schindler, as Righteous Among Nations, the highest award the Jewish state can make.

www.booksattransworld.co.uk

Also by Michael Smith

ODD MAN OUT (with Peter Elphick)

NEW CLOAK, OLD DAGGER

STATION X

FOLEY: THE SPY WHO SAVED 10,000 JEWS

ACTION THIS DAY (ed. with Ralph Erskine)

THE EMPEROR'S CODES

BLETCHLEY PARK AND THE BREAKING OF JAPAN'S SECRET CIPHERS

MICHAEL SMITH

BANTAM BOOKS

London • New York • Toronto • Sydney • Auckland

THE EMPEROR'S CODES
A BANTAM BOOK: 0553 81320 X

Originally published in Great Britain by Bantam Press,
a division of Transworld Publishers

PRINTING HISTORY
Bantam Press edition published 2000
Bantam Books edition published 2001

1 3 5 7 9 10 8 6 4 2

Set in 11/12pt Sabon by
Falcon Oast Graphic Art Ltd.

Bantam Books are published by Transworld Publishers,
61–63 Uxbridge Road, London W5 5SA,
a division of The Random House Group Ltd,
in Australia by Random House Australia (Pty) Ltd,
20 Alfred Street, Milsons Point, Sydney, NSW 2061, Australia,
in New Zealand by Random House New Zealand Ltd,
18 Poland Road, Glenfield, Auckland 10, New Zealand
and in South Africa by Random House (Pty) Ltd,
Endulini, 5a Jubilee Road, Parktown 2193, South Africa.

Printed and bound in Great Britain by
Cox & Wyman Ltd, Reading, Berkshire.

For Ben, Kirsty, Louise, Leila and Levin

CONTENTS

ACKNOWLEDGEMENTS

I am extremely grateful to all those former codebreakers and wireless operators who wrote to me or agreed to be interviewed for this project. Whether or not they are quoted in the book, their contributions played a major part in providing the information and encouragement I needed to complete it. I am particularly grateful to a number of people who went out of their way to help and encourage me. These include Geoff Ballard; Edith Becker; Geoff Day; Joan Dinwoodie; Joe and Barbara Eachus; Robert Hanyok; Margaret Henderson; Phil Jacobsen; Dennis Moore; Joe Richard; Harry G. Rosenbluh; Hugh Skillen; Joe Straczek; Jimmy Thirsk and Dennis Underwood. I am also grateful to Steve Kelley for sharing his expertise in Japanese machine ciphers with me and to Hilary Jarvis for her advice on the Japanese language. Special thanks are due to Hugh Melinsky; Norman Scott; Alan Stripp and Maurice Wiles for allowing me to quote from their own works and for their generous help and advice. I must also thank Ron Bonighton, Director of Australia's Defence Signals Directorate, for kindly sending me a complete set of the Technical Records of the Central Bureau (a uniquely generous example of openness from a signals intelligence organization); Margaret Nave and the Australian War Memorial for allowing me to quote from Eric Nave's original manuscript; the Library and Department of East Asian Studies of the University of Sheffield for permission to quote from the diaries of

Malcolm Kennedy; Christine Large and the staff of the Bletchley Park Trust for their assistance and dedication to keeping the memory of the codebreakers alive; and last but certainly not least Ralph Erskine whose willingness to share his unrivalled knowledge of wartime codebreaking operations with me provided a constant lifeline.

I should also like to thank Charles Moore, Editor of the *Daily Telegraph*, for generously allowing me to take a sabbatical to write *The Emperor's Codes*; Sally Gaminara, Katrina Whone, Simon Thorogood and Sheila Lee at Transworld for their painstakingly professional work on this project; my agent Robert Kirby for his constant enthusiasm; and my wife Hayley for her patience and encouragement.

'I believe most experienced cryptanalysts would agree with me that cryptanalysis is much closer to art than to science, and this is what makes the personal factor so important.'

John Tiltman, Chief Cryptographer at
Bletchley Park 1940–5

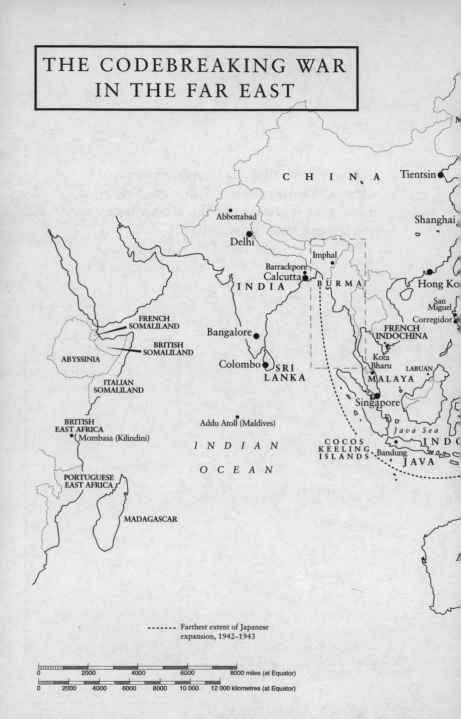

THE CODEBREAKING WAR IN THE FAR EAST

China

Tientsin

Abbottabad

Delhi

Shanghai

Imphal

Barrackpore

Calcutta

INDIA   BURMA   Hong Ko

FRENCH
SOMALILAND

San
Miguel

Corregidor

FRENCH
INDOCHINA

BRITISH
SOMALILAND

Bangalore

ABYSSINIA

Kota
Bharu   LABUAN

ITALIAN
SOMALILAND

Colombo   SRI
LANKA

MALAYA

BRITISH
EAST AFRICA
(Mombasa (Kilindini)

Singapore

Addu Atoll (Maldives)

Java Sea

INDO

I N D I A N

COCOS
KEELING
ISLANDS   Bandung   *JAVA*

PORTUGUESE
EAST AFRICA

O C E A N

MADAGASCAR

- - - - - - Farthest extent of Japanese
expansion, 1942–1943

| 0 | 2000 | 4000 | 6000 | 8000 miles (at Equator) |

| 0 | 2000 | 4000 | 6000 | 8000 | 10 000 | 12 000 kilometres (at Equator) |

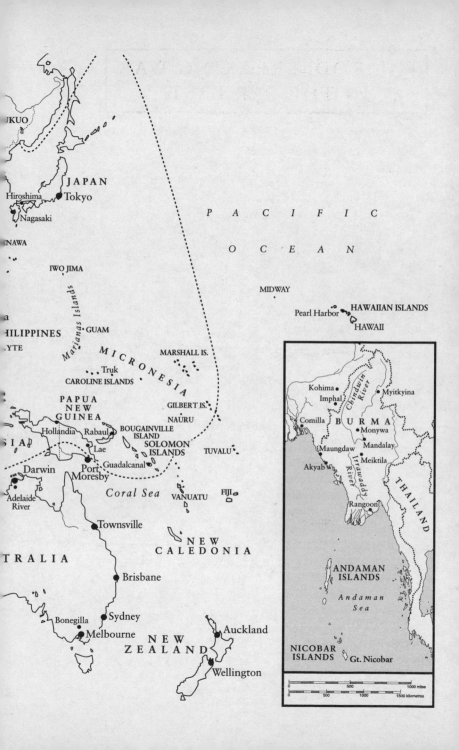

INTRODUCTION

The extraordinary achievements of the British code-breakers based at Bletchley Park in cracking Nazi Germany's 'unbreakable' Enigma cipher are now widely known. This initially oddball collection of mathematicians, classicists and musicians performed unexpected miracles in the hastily constructed huts scattered around the grounds of an ugly mock-Tudor mansion in the small Buckinghamshire market town of Bletchley. The location had been selected in part because it was just far enough outside London to escape the threat of German bombs. But perhaps more importantly, it was midway between the 'glittering spires' of Oxford and Cambridge, from where most of the leading codebreakers had come.

The apparently amateurish nature of these early beginnings was epitomized by the actions of the codebreakers' boss, Admiral Hugh Sinclair. His power over the Government Code and Cipher School, as the codebreaking operation was known, came from his role as 'C', the head of MI6. Perhaps surprisingly, this was in fact no secret within the limited confines of what was then described as 'polite society'. But Sinclair was far better known among his immediate circle of friends for his reputation as a man with a taste for the high life. They christened him Quex after the title character in Arthur Pinero's popular play *The Gay Lord Quex*, who was described as 'the wickedest man in London'.

This passion for the high life, and the fact that he had the personal wealth to fund it, dominated Sinclair's dealings with the codebreakers – an earlier headquarters had been based in the Strand in central London, apparently for no other reason than that it was close to the Savoy Grill, one of his more favoured haunts. Unable to persuade anyone in government to pay for the codebreakers' new country mansion, he dipped into his own pockets to buy it, immediately moving his favourite chef from the Savoy Grill to Bletchley Park to ensure that the codebreakers were well fed.

The result was an atmosphere at the highly secret Station X not unlike that of a weekend party at an English country mansion. The initial number of codebreakers in what was known for security reasons as 'Captain Ridley's Shooting Party' was little more than 200. They lived in hotels in the surrounding towns and all initially worked either in the mansion itself or in a neighbouring boys' school that had been commandeered for the purpose. When not breaking codes, or if simply seeking somewhere to contemplate their cryptographic puzzles, the codebreakers could wander through the lawned grounds of Bletchley Park, which included a maze, a lake and a number of rose gardens.

This brief idyll was shattered in part when the chef, unable to cope with the sometimes unusual demands of the more idiosyncratic 'guests' at Bletchley, attempted to commit suicide. But other factors were far more crucial in the transformation that was about to take place. As the Phoney War drew to a close and Hitler turned his attention to Western Europe, Britain's back was very much against the wall. The need to break Enigma and to obtain a permanent source of high-grade intelligence on German movements was paramount.

Bletchley Park was soon swamped by new recruits, some of whom had experience within those British companies which were adopting more efficient business practices pioneered in America. By the time the pre-war British codebreakers such as Dilly Knox made the first

British breaks into Enigma, Bletchley Park's operations were already turning into a production line. The grounds increasingly resembled a building site. The maze and rose gardens disappeared to be replaced by prefabricated wooden huts in which worked thousands of people, the vast majority of them women.

The popular view of Bletchley Park, as an organization manned by brilliant but amateurish eccentrics, is misleading. Certainly early on the organization was dominated by eccentrics such as Knox and Alan Turing, but the incredible progress made by some of them not just with Enigma but also with the development of Colossus, the world's first programmable electronic computer, gives the lie to suggestions of amateurism. The vast majority of those working at Bletchley Park were in fact neither amateurish nor eccentric, although many were indeed brilliant.

The work they did to unravel the intricate workings of the Enigma cipher machine is estimated to have cut around two years off the length of the war in Europe. But that is only part of the story. The British codebreakers were not just working on German codes and ciphers, they were breaking those of all of Germany's allies in Europe: Italy; Hungary; Romania; Bulgaria; and initially, of course, the Soviet Union, as well as those of neutral countries such as Sweden, Spain and Portugal. The codes and ciphers of a number of non-European countries were also coming under the scrutiny of the British codebreakers, and the most important by far of these was Japan.

Almost a year before Pearl Harbor, the British and the Americans had agreed in principle to share their codebreaking resources. The two most important items on the agenda were the major machine ciphers of Germany and Japan. Bletchley Park handed over a paper version of the Enigma machine, providing the Americans with the start they needed to read the Wehrmacht's messages. In return, the US Army gave the British its most precious piece of codebreaking equipment. The Purple machine had been built to decipher the messages passing between the

Japanese Foreign Ministry, the *gaimushoo*, and its major embassies abroad.

Although it was nowhere near as difficult to solve as Enigma, or the later German enciphered teleprinter systems known collectively as Fish, the breaking of the Japanese 'Type B' diplomatic cipher machine, by a team led by the American mathematics teacher Frank Rowlett, was one of the great cryptographic achievements of the Second World War. The Americans christened the Type B system Purple and the intelligence derived from it was given the codename Magic, probably because William Friedman, the head of the US Army codebreaking operation, routinely referred to his cryptanalysts as 'magicians'.

The amateurish eccentricity of the Bletchley Park operations is not the only myth to have grown up over the years. Enigma had originally been read not by the British but by the Poles. A team of Polish mathematicians, Marian Rejewski, Henryk Zygalski and Jerzy Rozycki, had managed to break it initially in 1933. While this was a brilliant achievement in its own right, it came at a time when German security procedures were very slack and the machines in use were at their most basic. Nevertheless, it provided the springboard that allowed the British to break the far more complicated systems put in place when the Second World War began.

Quite why the British had not attempted much earlier to break the Enigma machine, which was first introduced within the German armed forces in the late 1920s, is difficult to understand. It may be, as Josh Cooper, one of their number, said, that they really believed that, having had their codes broken easily by the British during the First World War, the Germans would never allow it to happen again. At any event, it was not until shortly before the Second World War broke out that the Government Code and Cipher School made any serious efforts to break the Enigma cipher. During the inter-war years, the British codebreakers had concentrated on what were regarded as the three main threats: Bolshevik Russia, widely perceived as being the biggest danger not just to the Empire but to civilized life itself; the upstart United States, still an uncertain force in world affairs; and the main threat to British colonies in the Far East – Japan.

This brings us to the other main myth: that the Japanese codes and ciphers were broken by American codebreakers. When Britain and the USA agreed to collaborate on breaking the codes of the Axis powers, a year before Pearl Harbor brought America into the war, the British were determined to keep control of the operations to break the Enigma cipher machine. It made sense that the Americans with their dominance of the war in the Pacific should likewise control the breaking of Japanese codes and ciphers, and a natural division of labour built up.

At the end of the war, details of how the US Army broke the Purple cipher were swiftly made public, to the horror of the British codebreakers. Almost certainly as a result of the rivalry between the two American services, news also leaked out of how the US Navy had broken the main Japanese naval code JN25, allowing its aircraft to shoot down the Commander of the Imperial Japanese Navy's Combined Fleet, Admiral Yamamoto Isoruku. This publicity led to the lasting impression that the Americans had broken the Japanese codes.

By contrast, the British clamped down on any mention of the remarkable achievements of their own codebreakers, determined to ensure that they could continue to intercept the communications of other countries with impunity. It was not until the mid-1970s, with the publication of Frederick Winterbotham's book *The Ultra Secret*, that sketchy details of how Bletchley Park had broken the Enigma ciphers began to leak out. News of the construction by Tommy Flowers, a British Post Office engineer, of the programmable computer Colossus only emerged much later, displacing the claims of ENIAC, an American computer which had until then been regarded as the world's first.

The official files, still in the possession of Bletchley Park's secretive successor GCHQ, did not begin to filter into the archives of the British Public Record Office at Kew, in south-west London, until the 1990s and those on the British codebreaking efforts against the Japanese were among the last to be released. Only now has evidence begun to emerge of how much work on Japanese codes and ciphers was done by the British codebreakers, not just during the Second World War but long before it even began.

During the inter-war years, several of the leading members of the Government Code and Cipher School became expert at breaking Japanese codes and ciphers: John Tiltman, an infantry officer who had won the Military Cross in the trenches of the First World War; Eric Nave, a Royal Australian Navy officer seconded to work with the British; and Hugh Foss, one of the true British codebreaking eccentrics, were breaking Japanese military, naval and diplomatic codes and ciphers long before the equivalent American codebreaking operation saw similar success. Nave was reading all of the early Japanese naval codes in the late 1920s; British codebreakers led by Foss were the first to break a Japanese diplomatic machine cipher in 1934; and it was Tiltman who first broke JN25, a few weeks after it was introduced in the summer of 1939.

The Americans, working independently, later came to make their own breaks into the Japanese codes and ciphers. But they were hampered by their lack of experience; the occasional refusal of the government to accept the necessity of their work (one inter-war Secretary of State, Henry Stimson, later declared that 'Gentlemen do not read each other's mail'); and an intense rivalry between US Army and US Navy codebreakers. It was not until Rowlett's breaking of Purple, at a time when all the British machine cipher experts were concentrating their energies on the German Enigma machine, that the American codebreaking operation really came into its own.

None of this is to deny the dominant role played by the Americans in the interception of Japanese messages. At the start of the war, the British were forced to throw all their efforts into breaking the German ciphers. They had neither the resources nor the incentive to pay as much attention to Japanese codebreaking as it undoubtedly deserved. The main Royal Navy codebreaking establishment in the Far East had been forced by the Japanese threat to move first from Hong Kong to Singapore, then to Colombo and swiftly on to Mombasa, where its very remoteness from the battle crippled its ability to receive the Japanese radio messages on which the codebreakers depended. The Americans, by contrast, had immense resources both in terms of manpower and the mechanical tabulating machines that were indispensable to the operations to break the Japanese codes. The US Navy station at Pearl Harbor in particular was second to none in its efficiency and capability.

The British understandably assumed that since they were willing to provide the Americans with all the intelligence they gained from breaking the Enigma ciphers, the Americans would do the same when it came to material gathered by breaking the Japanese codes. The US Army codebreakers proved as helpful during the war in the Far East as they had with their provision of the Purple machine. Sadly, the same cannot be said of some of the administrative officers controlling their naval counterparts.

The refusal of certain sections of the US Navy to share intelligence with the British seriously hampered operations in eastern waters and led the Admiralty to suggest that the fledgling exchange agreement on codebreaking with the Americans should be scrapped. Given that this was to form the basis for the UK–USA Accord which played such a vital role during the Cold War and still links the two countries' intelligence services, the potentially disastrous effects of the lack of co-operation are not hard to imagine.

The record of the US Navy on co-operation, not just with the British but with their own Army, was not merely lamentable, it was shameful. But it was not the only problem faced by the codebreakers. The very nature of the

21

Far East War, spread as it was over many thousands of miles, made communication between the main codebreaking centres extremely difficult. If Bletchley Park and its US counterparts had problems exchanging information with the various outstations that stretched from East Africa to the West Coast of America, the stations themselves found it almost impossible to co-ordinate their own operations during the early years of the war.

Yet while the codebreakers were only rarely to enjoy the same influence they exerted on the war in Europe and North Africa, their achievements were many. The existing literature credits this almost entirely to the US codebreakers. In fact, with the exception of Purple, only one of the key codes was broken by an American alone and that in Australia. It was British and Australian codebreakers who led the way in breaking the majority of the Emperor's Codes. Here for the first time is their story.

1

SINGAPORE, DECEMBER 1941

The old Cathay Cinema opposite Fort Canning military base in Singapore was packed for the matinée showing of the latest Rex Harrison film, a screen version of George Bernard Shaw's play *Major Barbara*. For weeks the talk among the city's expatriate community had been of the threatened war with Japan. But any suggestion that the Japanese might manage to invade Malaya or, heaven forbid, even succeed in capturing the 'impregnable fortress' of Singapore was ridiculed by the authorities.

Air Chief Marshal Sir Robert Brooke-Popham, Commander-in-Chief Far East, had told a press conference only two days earlier that there was nothing to worry about. 'There are clear signs that Japan does not know which way to turn,' he said. 'Tojo is scratching his head. There are no signs that Japan is going to attack anyone.'

There had in fact been some very clear signs, all of them pointing to a conclusion directly opposite to that expressed by Brooke-Popham. For the past month, a wireless intercept station at Kranji on the north of Singapore island, an offshoot of the British codebreaking organization based at Bletchley Park, had been picking up radio signals indicating the movement south of a large Japanese armada which was now crossing the Gulf of Siam towards the north-east coast of Malaya.

The intercept operators at the Kranji listening post included a batch of Wrens, four of whom had 'gone ashore' – naval parlance for leaving the base – to see *Major Barbara*. 'In the middle of the showing, the film suddenly stopped running and a big sign came up on the screen in two-foot-high letters,' one of the Wrens recalled. 'It read: "All British service personnel to report back to barracks immediately."' The cinema emptied quickly. But few of those leaving were particularly worried. It was just another security scare. Brooke-Popham had set the popular mood. The Japs were hopeless. There was no chance of them winning anything.

John Burrows, an Intelligence Corps sergeant on Brooke-Popham's staff, had just arrived in the colony and found the complacency impossible to believe.

> It was Cloud Cuckoo Land and to someone like myself who had come from Britain it was unbelievable. There were some who had their doubts, but the planter society as a whole was very comfortable. They had always been able to depend on the British to defend them and they totally underestimated the Japanese military threat. All the able generals were collected in the Middle East at this time and it was the duds who were shipped out to the Far East, some of them with no understanding of reality at all. There were one or two staff officers who were the exception but they hadn't any power to do anything about it.

The Wrens' bosses at the Far East Combined Bureau, the British joint service codebreaking and intelligence centre, were among those who were not underestimating the Japs. For the past two months, the airwaves had been full of Japanese radio transmissions and the codebreakers had identified every ship in the Japanese armada. They had also deciphered a message from the Japanese Ambassador in Bangkok to Tokyo revealing that the ships were to land an invasion force at Kota Bharu in north-eastern Malaya. But the British commanders were dismissive of their 'defeatist' warnings. The British officer class was reluctant

24

to believe that the good life was about to come to an end.

Until now life in Singapore had been very relaxed, even for the ordinary servicemen and women. The Wrens were in specially built wooden quarters, two sharing a 'cabin', each with the luxury of an ensuite bathroom; some even had a cabin to themselves. All the British service personnel had locally employed servants, recalled Lance-Corporal Geoff Day, one of a number of British Army intercept operators working alongside the Royal Navy, WRNS and RAF personnel at Kranji:

> Our life was one of relative luxury. We had native Malay boys to wait on us hand and foot, make our beds, do our washing and serve us excellent meals. We slept in dormitories built on stilts because of the heavy seasonal rains, and our beds were provided with mosquito nets which were attached to copper wires stretching from one end of the building to the other. During electrical storms lightning would run along the wires, frightening but harmless.

The work could be tiring, often requiring long periods of intense concentration, said Day.

> During our evenings off we played contract bridge or we would go into Singapore City to see the movies, to service clubs, of which there were many, or to the three amusement parks: New World, Great World and Happy World. Some of us attended recitals at the Gramophone and Music Society. The city was a very smelly place, particularly near the water. The street stalls selling all kinds of Chinese and Malay food added to the aroma – or should I say stench. Washing was hung on the lines between buildings, across streets. But the young Eurasian girls were truly beautiful. On one occasion some friends and I ventured across the causeway to the north to Johore Bharu to visit a brothel, but drank too much and left without sampling the goods.

Single British women were at a premium in Singapore and some of the Wrens soon found boyfriends. Lillie Gadd fell in love with her instructor at Kranji. 'Archie was in the Navy,' she said. 'We were learning the job alongside the naval operators who had been there for a while. We had to double bank, sit by the side of the operator who was training us, and Archie was watching over me to make sure I did the job right. So we saw each other day and night. We used to go "ashore" together to the pictures or to do a bit of shopping. Archie and I did all our courting in Singapore. We had quite a good time. We always say it was the best time of our lives.'

But things were about to change. The day after the servicemen and women were called out of the Cathay Cinema, Geoff Day went on the 'middle watch' at the Kranji intercept site. 'Since we were on a naval wireless station, we observed navy watches and middle watch meant you were on duty from midnight until a minute past four, when you were relieved.'

John Burrows had already begun the night shift as Duty Intelligence Reporter at GHQ Far East in the Selatar naval base, seven miles east of Kranji. 'I was working in what was more or less a Nissen hut collating intelligence from all sources, heading up the intelligence support for the Commander-in-Chief.' Shortly after one o'clock in the morning, Japanese troops began landing at Kota Bharu. It was some time before the first report came in by telephone, Burrows said. 'I remember one of my superior officers telling me at the time that there was only one telephone line from Kota Bharu to Singapore. That may not actually be true but as an indication of the un-preparedness it is quite vivid.'

At twenty-five minutes past three, the wireless operators at the intercept site were ordered to black out their windows in preparation for a raid by bombers flying in from Saigon. 'At three forty-one, the sirens went off,' Geoff Day noted in his diary. 'At ten past four we were sent "on post" which was considered safer than the accommodation and setroom buildings. At four forty-five, the all-clear sounded. Then, two minutes later, there was another warning siren and the final all-clear went at five fifteen.'

The military bases had been alerted by Fighter Control Operations Room. But the civil Air Raid Precautions Unit was unmanned and no-one could be contacted to sound the sirens. As a result the lights stayed on in Singapore, guiding the Japanese bombers into the skies above the city. 'I remember sitting there and seeing Japanese aircraft flying overhead and dropping bombs on parts of Singapore which were still brilliantly lit up,' John Burrows said. 'You would not believe it but that was how unprepared Singapore was.'

As the Japanese pushed rapidly down the Malay Peninsula, meeting little opposition from the retreating Allied troops, the intercept operators were warned that they were to be evacuated to Colombo with the Far East Combined Bureau's codebreaking section. Realizing they might never see their boyfriends again, three of the Wrens decided to get married.

Hettie Marshall and her fiancé John Cox, a major in the Indian Army, were married in St Andrew's Cathedral on 30 December 1941. 'We were engaged when the Japanese attacked,' Hettie recalled. 'At the time, everyone was escaping. The Indians were dashing back off to India. So we just decided to hasten it on. John's colonel threw a party for him and we had it with a marquee in the gardens of the brigadier's house.'

A day later, Lillie Gadd married Archie Feeney, also in St Andrew's Cathedral.

The fighting was coming, we might get separated, anything might happen, so make the best of it while you can, we thought. I had to keep my wedding a secret because in the Navy if a Wren married a sailor they split you up straight away. Archie and I went ashore on the same coach. There was one of the male operators to give me away, the best man and a few of the girls from my watch. I'd had a blue chiffon dress made up in Singapore for my wedding

27

but because the war had begun I had to wear uniform.

We came out to bells but you weren't allowed to take photographs. Then we just went across the road into the café. We had a bit of a celebration back at the camp with some of the girls but it had to be kept secret. The men slept in a different part of the camp, of course, so we would have to spend our nights apart. But we didn't that night. We spent our wedding night in my cabin.

On New Year's Day Rene Skipp married her fiancé, John Watson, a Royal Navy chief petty officer from another unit. 'It was very much a last-minute affair,' she recalled. 'There was no wedding as such. We were married in the registry office and the only other people there were the witnesses.'

Four days later, Lillie and Archie Feeney were evacuated to Colombo with the bulk of the codebreakers and intercept operators. Hettie Cox and Rene Watson were forced to leave their husbands behind. Geoff Day was one of a small party of intercept operators who stayed in Singapore to continue monitoring the Japanese radio messages.

When Singapore finally fell on 15 February 1942, many thousands of Allied servicemen would be captured, spending the rest of the war amid the horrors of Japanese prisoner-of-war camps. But by then John Cox had already been safely evacuated to Java, as had Geoff Day, while John Watson had sailed for Colombo. John Burrows had also escaped, having been recalled to England to work at Bletchley Park. But not before being asked to brief the generals on the complacency that led to the fall of Singapore and on how the codebreakers' warnings had been ignored.

2

BORROWING THE CABLES

The British had been busy intercepting the diplomatic communications of their enemies, and on occasion their friends, since 1324 when King Edward II ordered that 'all letters coming from or going to parts beyond the seas be seized'. After a brief period, during the second half of the nineteenth century, when Victorian morality and Foreign Office penny-pinching led to Britain's codebreakers being declared redundant, the onset of the First World War brought them more work than they might previously have imagined possible.

The British Army was the first organization to realize the potential intelligence to be garnered from 'censoring' the German diplomatic communications sent on the cables of the international telegraph companies. The War Office set up a special section, MI1b, inside military intelligence, recruiting a number of eminent academics, a mixture of classicists and Egyptologists, to break the German codes. Shortly afterwards, the Royal Navy followed suit on the orders of Winston Churchill, then First Lord of the Admiralty.

The army and navy codebreakers had little time for each other during the war, competing rather than co-operating in their own petty turf war. Following the Armistice, the moral imperative for 'censoring' the private communications of other countries' ambassadors and the strong desire within the Treasury for a 'peace dividend' put their role under renewed threat. But so successful had they been that every other government department was clamouring for more.

The army and navy codebreaking organizations were combined into a single civilian operation of just twenty-five people based in London's Berkeley Square and known as the Government Code and Cipher School. 'It was a very small organization for the Treasury had, throughout the negotiations, been insistent on cutting down the expense,' recalled William 'Nobby' Clarke, one of the old Room 40 codebreakers.

With the Foreign Office reluctant to fund its operations, GC&CS was placed under the control of Admiral Hugh 'Quex' Sinclair, Director of Naval Intelligence, who moved its offices to Watergate House on the Strand.

But when the lease on Watergate House ran out, it was transferred to a new headquarters at Queen's Gate in London's fashionable Kensington district where day-to-day operations were run by Alistair Denniston, a former Royal Navy education officer who had been in charge of codebreaking in Room 40. 'The public function was "to advise as to the security of codes and ciphers used by all government departments and to assist in their provision",' he recalled. 'The secret directive was "to study the methods of cipher communications used by foreign powers".'

The War Office's decision to close its censorship department caused major problems for Denniston and his codebreakers. Britain was a central point on the international cable network and messages from all over the world passed through London on their way to their ultimate destinations, so the censorship system had produced large amounts of intelligence on the activities of a wide variety of foreign governments.

'Temporary unofficial arrangements were made with the moribund censors which provided the cable traffic for some further months,' Denniston recalled. However, this was not enough to keep the supply of cables going indefinitely. Tapping the cables themselves was deemed to be too expensive. But although unwilling to fund the operations, the Foreign Office insisted that there was no question of not obtaining the information they carried.

'The deciphered telegrams of foreign governments are without doubt the most valuable source of our secret information respecting their policy and actions,' said Lord Curzon, the Foreign Secretary. 'They have proved the most accurate and, withal, intrinsically the cheapest means of obtaining secret information that exist.'

The easiest solution was for the codebreakers to take over the role of 'censorship'. So the cable companies were approached to hand over all their traffic to GC&CS, which would copy it before returning it to them. This presented no problem with one of the companies, Cable and Wireless, which was British-owned. But the other two, the Commercial Cable Postal Telegraph Company and Western Union, were American. They would need some persuasion before they handed any cables over to the British.

The Official Secrets Act already gave the Government the right to scrutinize cable traffic for purposes other than censorship, Denniston recalled. 'A clause was inserted authorizing a secretary of state to issue a warrant to cable companies operating in the UK requiring these companies to hand over all traffic passing over their systems in the UK within ten days of receipt.' The maximum punishment for refusing to hand over the cables was only a £100 fine or a three-month prison sentence so the Government still depended heavily on the goodwill of the cable companies. The last thing it wanted was for the procedure to become public knowledge. 'Secrecy is essential,' Lord Curzon told his cabinet colleagues. 'It must be remembered that the companies who still supply the original messages to us regard the intervention of the Government with much suspicion and some ill-will. It is important to leave this part of our activity to the deepest possible obscurity.'

It was not to be. The British practice of 'borrowing' the cables became the focus of an investigation by the US Senate. Western Union's president, Newcomb Carlton,

31

was forced to describe how his company connived with the intelligence service of a foreign power, but defended himself by pointing out that most of the telegrams were encoded. 'Messages in their original form – ninety per cent of them are in code – are taken to, I think, the British Naval Intelligence Bureau,' he said. 'They hold them not more than a few hours and then return them. They do not hold them long enough for anything like deciphering.'

This somewhat weak defence was ridiculed by the chairman of the investigation, who pointed out that it only took a few seconds to make a copy which could then be decoded at leisure. Nevertheless, the cables continued to flow into the Government Code and Cipher School where they were sorted in a department run by Henry Maine, one of the First World War codebreakers. Despite the implicit coercion, the relationship with the cable companies was handled in a thoroughly gentlemanly, and typically English, fashion. 'It was our aim to make this procedure work smoothly with the companies,' Denniston said. 'It was undoubtedly a nuisance for them to have to send all their traffic in sacks to an outside department and I have always considered that the credit for smooth working and no questioning should go to Maine.' The cablegrams were sorted and copied by a small group of workers borrowed from the Post Office, he added. 'Our aim was to inconvenience the companies as little as possible and throughout we tried to let them have their traffic back within twenty-four hours, though many million telegrams must have passed through their hands.'

The telegrams handed over by the cable companies were to provide the mainstay of the codebreakers' work. Although GC&CS came under the control of the Admiralty, the interest in naval intercepts had ended with the war. The codebreakers' main work was deciphering diplomatic messages, Nobby Clarke said. 'To give some idea of the change: in the early days of 1920, the strongest section of the GC&CS was the United States section.' The other most important priorities were the diplomatic ciphers of France, the Soviet Union and Japan, a former wartime ally but now increasingly regarded as a major threat to Britain's colonies in the Far East.

Fortunately, Maine was not content with obtaining the cables passing through London; he also made arrangements with Cable and Wireless to receive those available at other points on the international network, in particular Malta, a move that was to prove crucial to the interception of Japanese diplomatic telegrams. The Cable and Wireless repeater station on the island handled all the traffic between Europe and the Far East, including the telegrams from Tokyo to the Japanese embassies in London, Paris, Rome and Berlin. On Maine's instructions, Cable and Wireless had copies of all the telegrams sent to London for 'accountancy purposes'.

The GC&CS Japanese expert was Ernest Hobart-Hampden, a former senior official at the British Embassy in Tokyo and co-editor of the leading English–Japanese dictionary. So easy were the Japanese codes that 'the cryptographic task was for the first ten years almost non-existent', Denniston said. 'For the language, which was the main difficulty, we were lucky enough to have recruited Hobart-Hampden, just retired from thirty years' service in the East. For a long time, he was virtually alone. But with his knowledge of the habits of the Japanese, he soon acquired an uncanny skill in never missing the important.'

The first big test of Hobart-Hampden's uncanny skill came with the 1921 Washington Conference of the nine major powers. The Japanese had emerged from the First World War as the third largest naval power behind Britain and America and were determined to expand their influence in the Far East, particularly in China. Britain and America were determined to curb these ambitions and planned to use the conference to limit the ratio of their own naval ships to ten for every six Japanese vessels.

Both GC&CS and its US equivalent, the Black Chamber, were able to monitor the Japanese attitude to the Washington Conference, giving them a valuable advantage in the negotiations. During the first few weeks of the conference, the Japanese stuck out for a much tougher deal than the 10:6 ratio wanted by the British and Americans. But on 28 November 1921, with the talks reaching their conclusion, the codebreakers intercepted a message from Tokyo to the Japanese delegation. 'We think it necessary to avoid any conflict with England or the United States,' it said. 'If it becomes absolutely necessary, make it clear that this is our intention in agreeing a ratio of 10:6.' From that point on, the US and British delegations could hold out for the required ratio safe in the knowledge that the Japanese would eventually agree to it.

Herbert Yardley, the head of the US Black Chamber, later published his memoirs, revealing the success of the American codebreakers covering the conference. But the full scale of the information provided by GC&CS to the British negotiators, which no doubt included intelligence on the position of the Americans as well as that of the Japanese, is still shrouded in secrecy. 'No-one will ever tell how much accurate and reliable information was made available to our Foreign Office and service departments during those critical years,' said Denniston. However, he made it clear that Hobart-Hampden's contribution was critical. 'Throughout the period down to 1931, no big conference was held in Washington, London or Geneva in which he did not contribute all the views of the Japanese Government and of their too verbose representatives.'

Although virtually all the messages decrypted by GC&CS were diplomatic, the Foreign Office still appeared happy to allow the Admiralty to continue to control, and perhaps more importantly to fund, the cost of the codebreaking operations, Clarke recalled.

Things went on in a fairly peaceful way until in March 1922 a curious thing happened. Lord Curzon, at that time Foreign Secretary, had an interview with the French Ambassador in London at which he expressed certain views which did not coincide with the views of his colleagues in the Cabinet; at any rate he impressed on the Ambassador the desirability of keeping them secret.

The Ambassador duly reported the interview to the French Foreign Minister, as was his duty. His dispatch went by wireless, was intercepted by our stations and decoded by us. The decode was duly circulated to the usual recipients, the War Office and others. Curzon was furious. His reaction was immediate and he at once persuaded the First Lord that he might just as well hand GC&CS to the control of the Foreign Office, the very department which had refused to have anything to do with it three years before. The change made little difference, except that our new heads had only a vague idea of our possibilities.

A year later, Admiral Sinclair was made 'Chief' of Britain's Secret Service, which was also controlled by the Foreign Office, and was again placed in charge of GC&CS. Sinclair was a man of considerable means who was fond of fast cars and even faster living. But the Treasury's demands for a post-war peace dividend had forced him to run MI6 on a shoestring, recruiting former army officers because they already had pensions and paying them Christmas bonuses out of his own pocket. 'I liked him very much,' said Clarke. 'He was an extremely able and shrewd man, and during the next seventeen years I got to like him more and more. He trusted his subordinates and would take one's word as to the advisability of a certain course and give one the utmost help.'

With Sinclair's support, Clarke spent a great deal of time trying to persuade the Royal Navy that more attention should be given to intercepting foreign naval messages. 'There was no naval cryptography done and the Admiralty wireless stations were all engaged in diplomatic traffic. I tried to get the Fleet interested in interception as I thought it would be useful one day. A large quantity of useful material could be got if sufficient interest in the work could be aroused.' Clarke gave lectures on the exploits of Room 40 and eventually managed to build up interest in codebreaking with a number of enthusiastic officers working in their spare time to produce a steady stream of French and Russian naval messages.

'A greater problem presented itself in respect of Japanese, which it was recognized quite early on was of great importance,' said Clarke. 'The first difficulty was that the Japanese Morse code consists of about twice as many signs as the English.'

The advent of the telegraph had brought problems for the Japanese, whose written language was based on pictorial characters or ideographs, called *kanji*, and around seventy phonetic symbols called *kana*. The sound of words depicted by *kanji* can be represented using *kana*. However, this can lead to ambiguity since the Japanese language has a large number of different words which, while having distinctive written forms, sound the same (much like principal and principle in English). So a system of transliteration known as *romaji* developed which allowed the *kana* syllables to be spelled out in Roman letters. The Japanese created their own Morse code which contained all the *kana* syllables plus the *romaji* letters and was totally different from the standard international system that the Royal Naval wireless intercept operators were used to taking, Clarke recalled.

Ordinary wireless operators were faced with a number of Morse signs which were new to them and early intercepts from HM ships in Eastern waters (which of course took a long time to reach London) were quite unintelligible. Operators had to be trained to take this down in some form or other and then the messages so received had to be transformed so as to represent the actual Japanese messages. The initial stages were very difficult and many an obstacle had to be surmounted, but directly it had been proved that progress was possible the authorities at last recognized the importance of our work.

Clarke was appointed to head a small naval section within GC&CS. The Admiralty sent the best officer from its most recent three-year Japanese-language course,

Paymaster Lieutenant-Commander Harry Shaw, to assist Hobart-Hampden with the telegrams sent by Japanese naval attachés, but there was a desperate shortage of Japanese interpreters in the navy and it was difficult to find suitably qualified officers to work on other naval messages.

The Royal Navy set about increasing the incentive for officers to learn Japanese, but with the course requiring a minimum of two years to be spent in Tokyo, this was bound to be a slow task. 'Owing to the extreme difficulty of the language, we have very few officers who could be relied on to read an intercepted "en clair" Japanese message,' the Naval Intelligence Department complained. 'This state of affairs might be disastrous in the event of a war in the Far East.'

Clarke discussed the problem with Harold Parlett, co-author with Hobart-Hampden of the leading English–Japanese dictionary and the latter's replacement as Japanese Counsellor at the Tokyo Embassy. Parlett, who was the head of the board which tested the Royal Navy interpreters, told him of a brilliant young Australian linguist who had received even higher marks than Shaw and whose knowledge of Japanese was 'on a higher plane of practical utility than is usually obtainable in two years'.

Paymaster Lieutenant Eric Nave had joined the Royal Australian Navy in 1917 at the age of 18 and hired a private tutor to teach him Japanese after hearing that proficiency in the language would entitle him to an extra five shillings a day. He did so well in the official language test that, in February 1921, he was sent to Japan to study as an interpreter. After two years' intensive study, Nave's language skills were tested at the British Embassy. 'My examiner was Sir Harold Parlett, an accomplished scholar and to me a respected figure,' Nave said. 'He was after all the Japanese Counsellor, the senior post at the embassy for one with language knowledge. He came from the Consular Corps, a small band, all specialists in Japanese who spent their service in Japan, Korea, or Manila, with an occasional stint at the Foreign Office in London. I was quite delighted when given my examination result, a pass with over ninety per cent, the highest ever achieved by any service language officer.'

On his return to Australia, Nave was posted to HMAS *Sydney*, the RAN's flagship, where he began setting up an operation to intercept Japanese messages. 'I would suggest that all ships in the Fleet be instructed to intercept as many messages in Japanese as possible, these messages to be sent to me for decoding,' he said in a memo to his superiors in October 1924. 'Telegraphic messages in Japanese are more difficult than in English, as the Japanese ideographs are not easily abbreviated. After reading plain-language messages, I propose attempting to decode ordinary Japanese economic code messages, with a view to later breaking down the ciphers.'

It is not clear if Clarke was aware that Nave was already working on intercepted Japanese messages or was simply going on the recommendation of Parlett and Shaw, but he seems to have decided that the Australian was just the man he needed to help him break the Japanese naval codes. Denniston saw the fact that Nave was Australian as an insurmountable difficulty, Clarke recalled: 'So I short-circuited him and went to Admiral Sinclair, who listened patiently and went off straight to the Admiralty whence I was rung up two hours later to ask what was the exact type of officer I wanted.'

The RAN received a message from the Admiralty asking them for the loan of Nave's services.

My appointment was to be in HMS *Hawkins*, the flagship of the Commander-in-Chief, China Squadron, to act as a Japanese interpreter. The Naval Board had asked for further information and whether it was for duty on Admiral's staff. In a few weeks, we were told: 'Admiralty pressing for appointment of Nave for interpreter's duties on Commander-in-Chief's Staff. Naval Board consider Admiralty wishes should be met and propose embarkation in *Mishima maru* 26 June.' The die was cast, but I could have no idea of the effect of this appointment on my career and indeed my whole life.

Nave arrived in Shanghai in July 1925. 'The admiral on whose staff I was to serve was Sir Edwin Sinclair Alexander-Sinclair, a dour character from the north of Scotland. He had received advice from Admiralty, London, that "Lieutenant Nave is not to be employed in the Admiral's Office nor on ship duties, details will be forwarded by safe hand bag." This was intriguing and when they arrived the Admiralty instructions were noteworthy for their complete lack of information and directions.' The orders did in fact lay out precisely what the Admiralty wanted, albeit with a firm instruction that there were to be no additional funds to pay for it.

Their Lordships have had under review the question of interception of foreign wireless telegraphy messages – a subject to which they attach the greatest importance. The extent to which this method of obtaining intelligence can be utilized in war largely depends on a plentiful supply of naval cipher messages in peacetime. Owing to the necessity of economy, it is not possible to provide any special organization for this purpose on the China Station. The material must, therefore, be provided by HM ships under your command. To enable this to be done, ships should be specially detailed for the duty when opportunities arise. Up to the present, only a small number of naval cipher messages have been received and a great many more are required.

Their Lordships are of the opinion that the difficulty of passing intercepts from such places as Shanghai to Singapore rules out the latter as a deciphering centre. Nor does Hong Kong appear to be suitable for this purpose, for owing to its distance from Japan, it would have to be supplied from other areas and its liability to attack is an additional objection. The use of a ship as a combined intercepting and deciphering centre appears to offer the best solution.

The orders included a stern security warning: 'Their Lordships attach great importance to secrecy in this matter, for although the Japanese may be doing the same thing, they may not credit us with an equal degree of intelligence.' In order to restrict the number of people who knew about the interception of foreign messages it would henceforth be known as 'Procedure Y' and all reports or correspondence on the subject were to be addressed direct to the Director of Naval Intelligence.

There was, however, no indication in the Admiralty orders as to how the messages were to be intercepted or the codes broken. Nave said, 'I had to organize this interception myself. Success or failure depended on me alone.'

He was allocated a wireless-trained petty officer, Gordon Flintham, to help organize the interception operations and together they began to unravel the mysteries of the Japanese Morse system. 'When we started we could not even read Japanese Morse,' said Nave. Eventually they intercepted a practice message in which the operator had run through the entire Japanese Morse code symbol by symbol. 'This was our start. Instructions could now be issued to all ships on the China Station to intercept Japanese naval traffic and forward the messages to the flagship.'

Nave used the intercepted Japanese naval messages to build a picture of the make-up of the Japanese fleets and began attempting to break the *tasogare*, the basic naval reporting code used by the Japanese to announce the sailings of individual ships.

We started with watch on Tokyo radio and found it changed from the Commercial Call Sign 'JJC' to the Naval Service Call Sign 'AB' at hourly intervals. [Station AB was the main Tokyo naval control which was communicating with all the major Japanese naval bases.] This immediately led to identifying the main naval bases of Yokosuka, Kure and Sasebo and to the lesser bases under their umbrella. Yokosuka repeated signals at times for Chichijima, Kure for Maizuru, Sasebo for Bako, etc. The addressees of messages were spelled out at the beginning. This could be called a self-evident code with '*da*' for *daijin* – the Minister of Marine; '*shichi*' for *shireichookan*, or Commander-in-Chief. Ships themselves were abbreviated and could readily be identified. This step led me to identifying many call signs of commands, battleships and other vessels. Moreover, it had further value in showing a great deal of the naval organization and the extent of authority of the main naval bases. I had excellent co-operation from wireless operators, particularly those in gunboats in isolated ports. The volume of traffic kept me working at my desk six to seven hours each day, often Sundays as well, extracting and collating a vast amount of information. I certainly had no shortage of material for my regular reports to London.

All the information Nave managed to produce, together with any messages he was unable to break, were to be sent back by bag to the Admiralty in London which passed them straight on to the codebreakers. 'From then onwards,' Denniston wrote, 'there was a flow of traffic by bag to London where the various codes were segregated and broken as far as possible and a return flow of officers with skeleton books to carry on the work locally.'

When the messages began arriving back in the naval section, Harry Shaw was moved across to take charge of the London end of breaking the Japanese naval reporting code. 'A system of rotation arose,' Denniston recalled. 'Officers still on the active list came to us for two years and then joined the China Squadron in a ship where there were facilities for local interception. Thus a first start was made on Japanese naval traffic.'

The British codebreakers were assisted by the Japanese belief that their language was impregnable to others. Communications security was lax and many messages were sent in clear rather than encoded. When the receiving station had trouble deciphering a message, the other operator often provided assistance. Even where the Japanese stuck strictly to the codes, their insistence on using flowery preambles was a great help to the codebreakers. Messages to a superior tended to begin with the predictable phrase:

41

'I have the honour to report to your excellency that', providing Nave with an easy 'crib' of what was likely to be in the first part of the message and a way into the code itself.

When the Japanese Emperor Yoshihito died at the end of 1926, the official report of his death and the succession speech of his son Hirohito were relayed to every Japanese diplomatic, naval and military outpost around the world. Nave knew that the Japanese love of ceremony and obsession with predictable courtesies would ensure that every message was exactly the same. It was a simple task to follow it through the Japanese codes, breaking each in turn.

The codebreakers in London concentrated on the standard cryptographic technique of examining the statistical peculiarity of the Japanese language to work out the probability of each individual character appearing. The first step in breaking any cipher is to try to find features which correspond to the original plain text. Whereas codes substitute groups of letters or figures for words, phrases or even complete concepts, ciphers replace every individual letter of every word. They therefore tend to reflect the characteristics of the language in which the original text was written. This provides the codebreaker with a relatively easy entry point. For example, the most common letters in the English language are E, T, A, O and N. If a reasonable amount, or 'depth', of English text enciphered in the same simple cipher were studied for 'letter frequency', the letter that came up most often would represent E. The second most common letter would be T and so on. Writing out the letters recovered in this fashion will reveal obvious words with letters missing, allowing the codebreaker to fill in the gaps and recover those letters as well. They can in turn be filled in, producing other obvious words and so the process goes on until the whole message can be read.

Another basic weapon used by the codebreaker, 'contact analysis', takes this principle a step further. Some letters will appear frequently alongside each other. The most obvious example in the English language is TH, as in 'the' or 'that'. So, by combining these two weapons, the code-breaker could make a reasonable guess that, where a single letter appeared repeatedly after the T which he had already recovered from letter frequency, the unknown letter was probably H, particularly if the next letter had already been recovered as E. In that case, he might conclude that the letter after the E was probably the start of a new word and so the process of building up the message would go on.

The Japanese diplomatic messages were sent using *romaji*, where the syllables were spelled out using the letters of the Roman alphabet, and were particularly susceptible to contact analysis, one codebreaker recalled.

The orthographic structure of the Romanized Japanese used by the Japanese Foreign Office in its telegraphic communications worked to our advantage. In this form of Japanese certain limitations applied to the letter Y. It was [nearly] always followed by A, and almost never by E or I. Pairs of vowels frequently occurred, and the most common were the combinations OO, UU, AI and EI in about that order of frequency. YUU and YOO often occurred, preceded by a consonant, in combinations such as RYOO, RYUU, KYOO and KYUU. It was our hope that we could use these characteristics of the Japanese language to make accurate assumptions for plain text.

Nave made swift progress with the Japanese naval codes. 'Using our own reporting messages as background information, I was able to decode all Japanese naval reporting code traffic towards the end of my first year,' he said. He also made considerable inroads into the more complicated General Operational Code used for most major messages, which was sent in groups of nine letters.

He soon built up a complete picture of the Imperial Japanese Navy, with every ship and its base recorded and every call sign and frequency they used for their radio messages carefully logged. As a result, the British were able to keep track of Japanese naval movements and managed to read a considerable proportion of the messages passing between the Japanese ships and their bases.

At the end of each month, Nave sent a summary of the month's work back to London, adding the newly broken parts to each code, new additions to the Japanese order of battle and translations of key messages, as well as any material he had been unable to decipher, still on the red forms on which the Royal Navy wireless operators took them down. 'The daily batch of messages kept me constantly busy – it was seven days a week – and I was adding to the code groups in my reporting code as well as constant additions to the list of call signs. I had complete understanding of their abbreviated addresses and, with additions to the call-sign list and with inter-flotilla and intra-flotilla information, I had a regular supply of information for my reports to the Admiralty.'

The success that Nave and Hobart-Hampden enjoyed in breaking the Japanese codes and ciphers helped to encourage more interest in Japanese radio traffic. The Royal Australian Navy also intercepted Japanese messages and passed them on to Nave, and, in London, Harold Parlett, who had retired from his post as Japanese Counsellor in the British Embassy in Tokyo, was added to the GC&CS diplomatic section. Meanwhile, the British military based in Shanghai, the so-called Shaforce, set up its own interception facility as part of the Shanghai Army Intelligence Office, which operated from the British Consulate-General in the city.

By the end of 1927 Clarke had decided that Nave's expertise was now such that he should be recalled to London to concentrate on breaking the Japanese Navy's General Operational Code.

3

A SPY BASE IN THE FAR EAST

Nave arrived in London early in 1928, still totally unaware of the existence of Denniston's codebreaking operation. The Royal Australian Navy officer reported to his only contact in London, Rear-Admiral Sir Barry Domville, the Royal Navy's Director of Naval Intelligence. 'He explained that I would be working outside Admiralty in an organization which operated under the pseudonym of the Government Code and Cypher School,' Nave recalled. 'At this time the entire staff of GC&CS totalled not much more than forty and they handled the breaking and translation of telegrams from all the leading countries.'

Domville walked with Nave across Horse Guards Parade to the codebreakers' new office in Broadway Buildings, Victoria, which they shared with MI6. They were taken up in the lift to the fourth floor where they were met by Denniston who told Nave that, partly as a result of his work, Whitehall was 'beginning to take the Far East situation more seriously'.

The Washington Conference had provoked a great deal of anger among the Japanese over their treatment and the apparent determination of Britain and America to keep them from achieving what they saw as their rightful place at the head of the world table. There was particular resentment at the British decision, under pressure from the

United States, to terminate its treaty of alliance with Japan in favour of the far less comprehensive Four Power Treaty between Britain, America, France and Japan.

Throughout the 1920s, the diplomatic telegrams deciphered by Hobart-Hampden and Parlett had shown a marked increase in Japanese militarism and a determination within the Imperial Japanese Army to expand its country's interests in China, where Japanese troops had been garrisoned as 'advisers' since the First World War. Japan was also pursuing aggressive trade policies, 'dumping' its own textiles on to the market in the British Empire, in direct competition to the Lancashire cotton industry.

Whitehall was split over how to react to Japan's determination to flex its muscles as the leading power in the region. There was a considerable lobby for a more conciliatory approach towards Tokyo, but concern that if Britain backed Japan it risked antagonizing China and losing a substantial export market. Any intelligence that Nave and Harry Shaw could provide would be of immense assistance. The Japanese naval section was housed in a small shabby office containing an old desk, two chairs and a 'secure' cupboard. Within a few months, Shaw went out to the China Station and Nave was left on his own.

My main task was to decipher and translate the telegrams to and from Admiralty Tokyo to Japanese naval attachés in Europe. These cables passed through British hands somewhere and I had copies of them on my desk every day. The daily pile of telegrams ensured I would have no spare time. The naval attachés had their own code and a codebook required building before this became readable. I also had a steady research task as we had amassed quite a volume of messages in the General Operational Code. It was fortunate for me that I had available in the next room two eminent Japanese scholars, Hobart-Hampden and Sir Harold Parlett, who were always willing to come to my assistance when needed.

By the end of 1928 Clarke was able to report that the

Japanese Navy's General Operational Codebook was 'quite legible', thanks to Nave. 'Over 800 messages in this book have been decoded during the year and the degree of legibility attained can be gauged from the specimen messages circulated to the Admiralty,' Clarke wrote.

The Admiralty had the Australian transferred into the Royal Navy and in July 1931 he and Shaw were rotated, with Nave going out to the China Station while Shaw returned to London. At the end of that year the Japanese Navy introduced a new 4-*kana* General Operational Code. It had a totally random order and there were two codebooks in use, one to encode the messages and another to decode them. But the codebreakers soon realized that, despite its apparent differences from the 9-*kana* system, it used the same basic codebook and they began to break it with relative ease.

Two months after Nave arrived back in the Far East, Japanese troops based at Mukden in northern China staged a bomb attack, supposedly by Chinese dissidents, as an excuse to take over the province and create the puppet state of Manchukuo. The so-called Manchuria Incident provoked outrage not just around the world but in Tokyo itself, where the civilian government had been totally unaware of the army's plans.

It also provided the first 'live' target for the British codebreakers since the end of the First World War. The Shanghai Army Intelligence Office and the China Fleet flagship party sent many bags of the 'red forms' on which the intercepts were taken down to London, where Clarke's naval section had been joined by a small military section. With Japan the only major military power actively threatening British imperial power, the intelligence the codebreakers produced was examined with increasing anxiety within Whitehall.

The international condemnation of the Manchuria Incident led Japan to leave the League of Nations, further isolating it. By the end of 1934 it had occupied still more of northern China and abrogated the arms limitation treaties it had signed at the Washington Conference. Its foreign policy was now totally dominated by the Imperial Army, which held a virtual stranglehold over successive civilian governments and was determined to increase Japan's empire in the Far East regardless of what damage this might do to relations with the West. The extent of the danger posed to their interests in the Far East was brought home to the British in July 1934 when the codebreakers uncovered a major Japanese spy network centred on Singapore.

Eric Nave had now returned to London and Harry Shaw was working in Shanghai as the head of intelligence and chief codebreaker for the Royal Navy's China Squadron. He deciphered a telegram from the Japanese Consul-General in Singapore to his bosses in Tokyo which revealed that the Japanese had two 'top agents' at the heart of the British Government in Singapore. They were apparently providing their masters in Tokyo with details of all the secret plans to build up the colony as a bulwark against Japanese expansionism, a 'Gibraltar of the East'.

Although enciphered inside the Japanese Consulate-General, the telegram had been transmitted by the British-owned Eastern Telegraph Company. Like all the cable companies operating on British territory, the company was obliged under the Official Secrets Act to supply drop copies to the authorities on request. By coincidence, it had been asked only three weeks earlier by naval intelligence to pass on any messages from the Japanese Consul-General, whom the British believed to be in charge of Japanese intelligence-gathering for the whole of the Malay Peninsula. It was immediately clear to Shaw that the request had paid dividends. The Consul-General's secret telegram to the Japanese Foreign Office, the *gaimushoo*, described what he claimed was a brilliant piece of espionage by 'a very secret intelligence agent'.

The deciphered message contained the main points made by Admiral Sir Frederic Dreyer, the commander of the China Fleet, to a conference on the construction of the Singapore naval base which had been held on board HMS *Kent* earlier that year. They included details of a secret submarine base, RAF trials for landing aircraft on the base's slipways, a military fort that was to be constructed on the island and the decision to set up a new, independent Royal Navy squadron based in Singapore.

'England was extremely perturbed by the attitude of the Imperial Japanese Army and Navy towards the Far East,' the Japanese spy reported Dreyer telling the conference. There was 'absolutely no hope' of the Japanese agreeing to a reduction of their naval strength. Given the strength of the Japanese forces in the region, and the state of the Royal Navy in the Far Eastern waters, the British could not afford to neglect their defences for a day longer. Work on the base was to be speeded up so that it would be completed within three years.

At the end of his report the Consul-General explained how this explosive information had come into his hands.

> This was due to a secret person who had previously acted for me and who for a suitable reward obtained the minutes from a friend, who is a shorthand typist for personal confidential documents of civil Governor-general. This person took down the shorthand minutes of the conference. Hitherto, the shorthand notes this person has brought have been on the whole authentic. In this case, in addition to the bestowal of a large reward, I interrogated her. But she maintains there was no mistake. Actual date and names of those attending the conference will be obtained within a few days. The intelligence agent mentioned is said to be specialist in cartography and to be serving in public works department. He is now procuring a plan of the completed base very secretly. As I believe him to be amply reliable and it is necessary to pay him the reward that was agreed to, please telegraph me 1,000 dollars as special secret service fund.

Shaw took the deciphered telegram to Dreyer who immediately forwarded it on to London, to Admiral G. C. Dickens, the Director of Naval Intelligence. Dreyer expressed his concern, but, while he curiously made no comment on the contents of the Japanese report, he doubted that it could have come from the naval conference itself since only commissioned officers were present.

A preliminary inquiry decided that either the agents or the Consul-General must be inventing their intelligence reports for financial gain. MI5 was called in to investigate the affair 'to be on the safe side'. But there was general agreement that British officers were scarcely likely to have allowed their female typists and secretaries to pass secrets to the Japanese.

Dickens was not so sure. There was no doubt in his mind that Japanese espionage operations had increased dramatically over the past year. He had been complaining for some time at the decision to allow the Japanese to set up a 'Naval Centre' just a few yards away from the Broadway headquarters of Britain's own Secret Intelligence Service. The twenty-one officers based in the centre were known to be gathering intelligence 'presided over by the Japanese Naval Attaché and thus to all intents and purposes sheltered by diplomatic privilege'.

The increase in Japanese espionage operations was confirmed by the naval attaché messages being decoded by Nave. They revealed that a British Army officer, Major Frederick Rutland, had been recruited by the Japanese. 'This sorry story commenced with a meeting, using assumed names, at a hotel in Manchuria,' Nave said. Rutland was told to make contact with the Japanese Naval Attaché in London on his return to Britain. 'We were unable to listen in to the plans made with the Attaché in London at their meeting in Richmond Park. However, the report made to Tokyo gave us the complete picture.'

Rutland was to go to California to spy on the Americans. Nave passed the deciphered report to Sinclair and was called to a meeting with the head of MI6 and his deputy, Colonel Stewart Menzies. 'The colonel asked if we were now to hand the matter over to MI5, to which he received the answer, "No, they will only make a mess of it, we'll handle this ourselves."' Sinclair said the only evidence was the decoded messages and these could not be made public for fear the Japanese might change their code. An MI6 officer was detailed to tail Rutland across the Atlantic where he was handed over to the FBI.

The Japanese had also infiltrated a large number of spies into Malaya, bribing locally employed staff and even British servicemen to provide details of the naval base and the RAF facilities in Singapore. Both Dickens and Sinclair were concerned that the British, who still believed that there was something not quite gentlemanly about spying, were losing out in the intelligence war.

The British attempts to break the Japanese codes were sufficient for peacetime operations but it was increasingly looking as if they might need to be ready for war. 'The situation in the Far East has completely changed and left our intelligence arrangements high and dry,' Dickens said. 'The more I see of the cryptographic side of naval intelligence the more I recognize its vital importance and, further, that the nucleus we have at present is far too weak on which to build up rapidly an organization such as we would require in a war with Japan.' He had begun recruiting new potential Japanese linguists and had only recently sent his deputy, Captain Campbell Tait, to the Far East to investigate the situation on the spot. It was Tait who had arranged with the Eastern Telegraph Company for copies of all cables from the Japanese Consul-General to be passed to Shanghai for Shaw's attention.

'Shaw was specially sent to his present appointment because he is a trained cryptographer and a Japanese interpreter and therefore might be useful for occasional Japanese cryptographic work,' Dickens said. 'If it had not been for this and Captain Tait's initiative we should never have heard anything of this occurrence.'

It was unlikely, in the circumstances, that Japanese espionage in the Far East was limited to Malaya, he added. 'There is probably some interesting matter coming from the Japanese Consul-General at Hong Kong and it is proposed that the former's cables should be intercepted and sent to Shaw.'

Dickens was determined to ensure that there was a

substantial increase in British intelligence operations against the Japanese and persuaded the Admiralty to send an extra cryptographer to Hong Kong together with a dozen trained wireless operators to intercept any Japanese radio messages they could find. 'It will be necessary to go on increasing the number of Japanese cryptographers, as it is essential now to create a strong centre on the China Station as well as in London,' he said. 'Unless we can have a good grip of Japanese wireless, our intelligence will be quite inadequate and we may find ourselves critically at fault.'

In the meantime, Dickens said, he was asking MI5 to be discreet in its investigation of the Singapore spy scandal. 'Unless great care is taken,' he added, 'there is, of course, a danger that the Japanese will discover that we are intercepting their Consul-General's cables.'

The Japanese were already showing increased awareness of the need for more security, upgrading the naval attaché system by introducing a machine cipher. The success of the British codebreakers during the First World War had made foreign governments aware of the ease with which relatively complex ciphers could be solved using basic characteristics of the language, such as letter frequency. Machine ciphers were developed to try to protect against this, changing the system of encryption with each letter to ensure that the codebreakers could never build up sufficient depth to break the keys.

The new naval attaché system, which enciphered the *kana* syllables rather than *romaji* letters, was broken by Hugh Foss, a tall, gangly, red-haired eccentric who was the main Japanese systems-breaker, and Oliver Strachey, a former First World War military codebreaker. This was the codebreakers' first experience of machine ciphers, Nave said.

> There were two wheels, one containing twenty consonants and the other the six vowels, V being a vowel. The first trial was made in the office using a brown foolscap file cover with a collar stud retrieved from a returning laundry

52

parcel, a piece of string and slots cut in the cover for the letters. This worked, so we asked the Signal School at Portsmouth to help and received some expertly finished models in Bakelite. To find the starting point or key, the Japanese language provided good assistance. Japanese is not constructed like most European languages on a consonant–vowel basis, but is monosyllabic: YO KO HA MA is four syllables. The word *oyobi* [and] was a great help, giving a sequence of three vowels and at times four or even five on the smaller wheel. Then when one of these vowels represented itself we could have a zero position necessary to place the enciphered text underneath each other in sections of sixty symbols to establish the order of letters.

This first naval attaché machine was not solved by the Americans, who called it Orange, until February 1936, and then apparently only with the aid of a 'pinch', or theft, of information, possibly even a machine, from the Washington apartment of the Japanese Naval Attaché. By this time the Japanese had introduced a number of additional security measures which hampered the British codebreaking effort. 'Firstly, the machine could be set to jump certain positions,' said Nave. 'But this proved a minor nuisance. More tiresome was the subsequent monthly change of the order of letters on the wheel and introduction of one hundred keys based on the message serial numbers.'

Shortly after the British broke the naval attaché system, in November 1934, Admiral Sinclair chaired the annual meeting of an obscure Whitehall committee. The Committee of Co-ordination, or the Y Committee, as it was known for security reasons, was in charge of the interception of foreign communications. It met on the fourth floor of Broadway Buildings. Those who attended included Denniston and the directors of the three service intelligence departments. Since the threat from Japan was at the top of the agenda, Nave was also asked to take part.

The committee considered Captain Tait's report of his

visit to the Far East to investigate Japan's 'provocative' activities in the region. Admiral Dickens insisted it showed that the British had no choice but to counter the massive increase in Japanese espionage activities in the Far East with their own substantial intelligence-gathering operation.

Since the navy was responsible for the collection of 'special intelligence' in the Far East, it had strengthened the Japanese naval section at GC&CS, providing Nave with two other Japanese-speaking officers, while Shaw in Shanghai had been given another officer to assist him. Dickens had also sent a further naval codebreaker to Hong Kong with around a dozen wireless operators to set up a small intercept and codebreaking unit. But despite these moves to strengthen the British intelligence effort, more was needed.

There was general consensus around the table that Admiral Dickens was right. Japan constituted a major threat to British interests in the region. They would be shirking their responsibilities if they did not take the necessary steps to ensure there was early warning of any fresh Japanese moves. They needed their own spy base in South-east Asia and Hong Kong was ideally placed.

'The present trouble between Russia and Japan will provide a first-class rehearsal for interception and cryptography in the Far East,' Sinclair said. The committee agreed that in order to disguise its real role, the new organization should have a 'fairly bland' title, the Far East Combined Bureau (FECB). But its activities would be far from bland. It would collect intelligence from every possible source: spies, informants and, of course, the secret Japanese messages, 'the decipherment of which affords the most valuable source of information – especially in time of crisis, emergency or war – it is possible to conceive'.

The expansion of intelligence operations against the Japanese was hampered only by a lack of anyone with the necessary linguistic ability to staff the new bureau, most particularly in the army and RAF. All three services approached Denniston for assistance. Initially, he insisted that he was unable to help. 'It is not possible to deal with such traffic in the GC&CS in London owing to the distance and the delay in sending such material home. Nor are there any Japanese cryptographers at present available here to send out to the Far East as when the numerical peacetime establishment of the Code and Cipher School was arrived at the question of the provision of cryptographers for duty overseas was not contemplated.'

As a result of the difficulty finding the necessary language specialists, the Far East Combined Bureau was not set up until March 1935. It was housed in part of a block of offices on the Hong Kong naval dockyard, separated from other parts of the building by iron grilles which were manned permanently by armed guards carrying loaded revolvers. The guards excited a great deal of local curiosity, rendering useless any attempts to keep the bureau's presence secret.

The move to a more comprehensive intelligence-collection role led to the new organization having 'a somewhat shaky start', one former officer recalled. It now consisted of three main components. The first, and the part that was to cause the problems, was an intelligence-reporting section, made up of naval and army staff officers. It was headed by the Chief of Intelligence Staff (COIS), who was also the bureau commander. The department's task was to evaluate material from a variety of sources, ranging from the deciphered messages and MI6 agent reports to 'local gossip', in order to keep the authorities both in London and in South-east Asia informed of what the Japanese were doing.

The second component was the Special Intelligence, or codebreaking, section, also known as the Y Section, which consisted of a number of Japanese, Chinese and Russian interpreters, initially at least all naval or former naval officers. They mainly worked on Japanese messages but also on Chinese and Russian naval communications, deciphering any messages they could, and passing translations of anything interesting to the intelligence section. When they were unable to decode the messages, they sent them back to London, along with all enciphered army and air material, in the diplomatic bag.

The final component was a team of a dozen wireless intercept, or Y Service, operators, who lived and worked on Stonecutters Island, about four miles across the harbour from the naval dockyard. The operators, initially a mixture of Royal Navy ratings and RAF airmen, faced a number of problems. Their watchroom was ramshackle, with some of the wireless receivers located in a former washroom. They were located alongside the main Royal Navy radio transmission station, which interfered with their signals. The intercepted messages had to be carried to the bureau offices by courier on a steamboat ferry which took around an hour at a time. The only telephone link went through the local public exchange and was therefore insecure. During the summer months the area was buffeted by a series of typhoons which not only led to the suspension of the steamboat service, and therefore the courier operation, but forced the interceptors to take down their aerials until the storm had passed. To compound the difficulties of working there, the island was plagued by 'a plethora of winged and other insects'.

The codebreaking section was placed under the command of Harry Shaw, who had now retired with the rank of captain. He was assisted by two other Royal Navy Japanese cryptographers, Paymaster Lieutenant-Commander Dick Thatcher, who had been working with Nave in London, and Lieutenant Neil Barham. They concentrated on three Japanese naval codes and ciphers, Shaw recalled:

> The main commitment was the Japanese Naval General Cipher which was being worked up from an embryonic stage. This was a basic book of about 90,000 4-*kana* groups, with a simple transposition which was changed at intervals. Fortunately the book was alphabetical and was not changed for three years. This, and continuity of work, enabled the changes in transposition to be followed with comparative ease. Later, when Japanese naval codes and

ciphers were upgraded, this earlier experience afforded a useful background. Second priority was the Flag Officer system used by Japanese naval staff officers stationed in China. The book was rather smaller than that of the general system and the transposition was of a higher grade. Limitation of personnel restricted work on this system until staff was increased in 1937.

They also decoded the small number of messages sent in the *tasogare* reporting code originally broken by Nave. Any enciphered army messages were sent back to London, Shaw said. 'Special Intelligence translations were passed to the Chief of Intelligence Staff. If he and his colleagues thought the contents warranted it, a précis was drafted, usually in consultation with the Head of Special Intelligence. A comment was added and it was signalled to C-in-C China, then repeated to DNI, Admiralty, who was asked to pass it to the War Office, etc.'

But the need to pass messages through the Intelligence Department led to a great deal of tension between Shaw and the COIS and head of bureau, Captain John Waller. Shaw arrived expecting to be able to act much as he had in Shanghai, dealing direct with GC&CS with regard to the codes, and to the Commander-in-Chief Far East and the Admiralty on matters of intelligence. But despite being in charge of a much bigger operation, he found his hands tied by the creation of the Intelligence Department. Waller insisted everything went through him and appeared to pay scant regard to the need to protect the source of their material from becoming public knowledge, Shaw recalled.

Dissemination of Special Intelligence to local authorities was for long a bone of contention. The fact that some of the intelligence staff officers had no Far Eastern background militated against a proper appreciation by them of items of intelligence. None of them knew the implications of cryptography and security mindedness was inclined to be sacrificed to the desire to make definite use of Special Intelligence, particularly in dealing with civilian authorities. There were instances of leakage of information thus passed, and after one case of leakage the Admiralty ordered that Special Intelligence was not to be communicated to the head of government.

With the bureau's two most senior naval officers barely on speaking terms, morale suffered and divisions between the codebreakers and the intelligence-reporting section, and between the three services, became accentuated. The absence of any army or RAF codebreakers and any army intercept operators also caused problems, recalled Colonel Valentine Burkhardt, who arrived in the spring of 1936 to find the bureau embroiled in a series of petty turf wars. 'No great intimacy existed between the heads of the naval and military sectors. Each service ran its own work on its own, though all were under the same roof. Visits to the Y room were distinctly discouraged and very little information was handed out to the army on the grounds that it did nothing to contribute to production in this line. To overcome this monopoly of Y, four army signallers were sent by the War Office to assist with reception on Stonecutters.'

In an attempt to break down the 'atmosphere of mutual suspicion', Burkhardt obtained a grant of £1,500 a year from the Army Entertainment Fund. He used the money to set up a series of social gatherings, including a weekly 'Chinese dinner' at his own home for all the bureau staff, which 'did much to break down inter-service rivalries'.

Gradually, Shaw said, the codebreakers began to accept, and live with, a situation where they had no control over what intelligence reports were issued.

No intelligence records were kept in the Special Intelligence (codebreaking) department. The translators used their register and vocabulary indexes to refer to previous messages and private notebooks for matters of current interest. The translators generally had better local background than the Intelligence Department and they were expected to insert explanations of matters which called for local knowledge. Usually translations with notes appended were taken personally to the Chief of Intelligence Staff by the head of Special Intelligence who gave any further explanation asked for. The Chief of Intelligence Staff then distributed the sigint with comments of his own.

The arrival of the army signallers and increasing tension in the region led to more interest from the War Office in the work of the Far East Combined Bureau, Burkhardt recalled.

Japanese hatred of all foreigners made an outbreak of war, particularly against Great Britain, an imminent possibility. Responsibility for keeping track of political trends in Japan, of military and strategic developments, and of any secret preparations for a military blow to be delivered without warning, therefore devolved upon FECB.

During the summer of 1936 a murder in Peking, involving accusations of complicity against a British soldier by the Japanese Secret Service, led to the discovery that the interception of Japanese consular and military messages had lapsed. Two of the high-speed army operators who were then functioning on Stonecutters were moved to Tientsin [in northern China] to intercept Japanese Army traffic which was out of range of Hong Kong. The army code was far more complicated than either the naval or the consular and just when it was becoming readable the reciphering table would be changed. The preliminary work proved, however, extremely valuable.

The Tientsin listening post, staffed by around two dozen wireless intercept operators, was known as the North China Signals Section. At one stage it had its own codebreaker, but most of the intercepted material was sent back to London to Captain John Tiltman, the head of the GC&CS military section, which included an RAF Japanese interpreter.

John H. Tiltman was arguably one of the best codebreakers, if not *the* best, working during this period. Born in London on 24 May 1894, he was so obviously brilliant as a child that, at the remarkably young age of thirteen, he was offered a place at Oxford. He served with the King's Own Scottish Borderers in France during the First World War, winning the Military Cross for his bravery, and was seconded to MI1b shortly before it merged with Room 40 to become GC&CS. Although Tiltman spoke very little Japanese, he later recalled that his main work as head of the military section during the mid-1930s was on the material sent back from Hong Kong and Tientsin.

> I learned what I know of the written form of Japanese the hard way! We had a British intercept station at Hong Kong which from about 1935 forwarded to us considerable quantities of Japanese military intercept. The major part of the traffic was in a succession of military systems used for transmission of intelligence reports from China. During this period, the cipher systems used seemed to be changed quite drastically about every nine months and I had a hard time keeping up with the changes.

There were no Japanese interpreters working in the military section. Tiltman could occasionally call on the expertise of men like Hobart-Hampden and Parlett. But they were sometimes resentful of any forays Tiltman made into breaking Japanese codes and ciphers.

> In 1933, I solved the Japanese military attaché system which had been in use since 1927. There was a small basic code-chart of, I think, 240 units which meant that a large part of the plain text had to be spelled out in syllables. I don't remember the details of the system except that the code-chart had to be reconstructed and forty different sets of lines and column co-ordinates recovered. There were at the time two very distinguished Japanese scholars in the office who had each retired as British Consul-General in Japan. One of them partially reconstructed the code-chart for me from the material in one of the forty keys, and I set about recovering the other keys. Shortly afterwards the

other expert came and said he had heard I had some interesting work in progress and that he would like to help. So I gave him the material in one of the keys in which I had then recovered most of the syllabic values, numbers and so forth. He returned it to me three weeks later unchanged, saying my solution was 'plausible'. This should have warned me that I was treading on hallowed ground.

4

DIPLOMATIC SECRETS

With the Japanese threat increasing, Denniston applied to the Treasury for more funding to take on additional Japanese-language experts for the diplomatic section.

Normally, the Code and Cipher School recruit their cryptographers from men of nineteen to twenty-four years of age from the universities. They are untrained and have no special language qualifications. This entails considerable time spent on the study of oriental languages followed by a cryptographic course at the Code and Cipher School. Obviously, such a method of recruitment would not provide the necessary cryptographers for some years to come. Such delay cannot be accepted. It is suggested therefore that such individuals should be sought for amongst retired service or consular officers who have the necessary language qualifications for four additional appointments as Junior Assistants in the Code and Cipher School at say a fixed salary of £500 per annum.

The first two retired officers taken on were J. W. Marsden, a former assistant military attaché at the British Embassy in Tokyo, and N. K. Roscoe, a former consular officer who had served in Japan. They were followed by Captain Malcolm Kennedy, who during his military service had been seconded to the Imperial Japanese Army.

After a spell in military intelligence, Kennedy had returned to Japan as the Tokyo correspondent of the Reuters news agency. He was now a leading member of an influential clique of ex-officers who, while working in Japan during the 1920s and early 1930s, had become confirmed Nipponophiles.

None of this group was a natural codebreaker; they normally worked alongside the more experienced members of GC&CS translating and offering tips on the language structure. All of them were dismayed by what they saw as the anti-Japanese attitude prevalent in Britain, none more so than Kennedy who continually railed against 'the mistake we made in scrapping the Anglo-Japanese Alliance in order to please America, thereby leaving Japan with a feeling of grievance'.

When Denniston first offered him the post, Kennedy was attracted to the idea of 'getting to grips with the Far East question' and of working with Marsden and Roscoe, both of whom he knew well. But he openly admitted his distaste for spying on his Japanese friends, saying that while the work was 'more in my line' than anything else on offer, 'there are aspects of it which I would dislike intensely'. Nevertheless, he accepted the post, noting in his diary on 1 October 1935: 'Started work in my new job at the FO where working with a number of old friends – Marsden, Hobart-Hampden, Nave, Roscoe, etc.'

The diplomatic section received its raw material from two separate sources. The Royal Navy codebreakers based at the Far East Combined Bureau continued to obtain drop copies of Japanese telegrams from the Cable and Wireless offices in Singapore and Hong Kong, and, as Shaw recalled, also had surreptitious assistance from MI6 in obtaining others. 'Copies of Japanese diplomatic and consular codes in use in the Far East were supplied from GC&CS. Very little diplomatic material was taken at Stonecutters. But arrangements were made semi-officially with Cable and Wireless to supply the bureau with copies of Japanese Government telegrams passing over their lines in Hong Kong and with SIS [the Secret Intelligence Service,

MI6] in Shanghai to supply copies of those which were handled by the Chinese Post Office.'

Much of the Japanese diplomatic material had to be sent back to London where it supplemented the codebreakers' main source, the diplomatic telegrams obtained by Henry Maine. As international tension rose throughout the mid-1930s, he persuaded the international cable companies to be even more co-operative, Denniston recalled.

Maine's excellent liaison proved of the greatest help. When the state of unrest in the world became intense, from 1935 onwards, it was found that the ten days' delay granted by the warrant became intolerable. Maine was able to cut it down to twenty-four to forty-eight hours in the case of foreign companies, and to instant service, where necessary, in the case of the Central Telegraph Office and Cable and Wireless. The Japanese traffic to France and Germany always went via Malta. All Italian cable traffic passed there. Thus we were, throughout, enabled to watch the growth of the Axis combination.

Increasingly, diplomats began to use wireless transmissions. The three services had their own intercept sites but were reluctant to use them for diplomatic traffic. So Admiral Sinclair co-opted a small Metropolitan Police wireless intercept unit which had been operating from the attic of Scotland Yard, tracking the operations of Soviet spies. Harold Kenworthy, the unit's chief engineer, later recalled how Sinclair agreed to fund the unit which was moved from Scotland Yard to the grounds of the Metropolitan Police Nursing Home at Denmark Hill in south London. 'In the middle 1930s, secret government stations were set up by various foreign powers. These various groups were mainly covered by our own intercept set up in Denmark Hill. The services were disinclined to intercept diplomatic wireless to any extent as it would lead to curtailment of the examination of their particular service channels. The Commissioner came to an agreement and SIS paid a lump sum a year for the service and a number of police operators.'

The increased use of wireless transmitters was not the only new development the codebreakers had to face. Their success during the First World War had led to the development of a number of machines designed to encipher messages more securely. The most famous of these was the Enigma machine used by the Germans to encipher their most secret communications. But by the early 1930s there were a number of others in operation and there were clear signs that the Japanese were using one for some of the messages that had previously produced the most important intelligence.

While most of the diplomatic codes and ciphers employed by the Japanese were relatively simple to unravel, the codebreakers had found difficulty making an entry into a five-letter system introduced in the early 1930s. The traffic, which like other Japanese diplomatic messages was sent using the *romaji* characters, was being passed on two separate sets of links. The first was the Far East network including the Singapore, Hong Kong and Shanghai cables received in the Far East Combined Bureau. The other was the main diplomatic network connecting the *gaimushoo* in Tokyo to the embassies in the major international capitals such as London, Paris, Berlin, Rome and Washington.

It was immediately obvious to the codebreakers that the Japanese diplomatic links had gone over to a machine cipher for all of the most important 'State Secret' communications. If the British were to have any chance of predicting and countering the Japanese machinations behind the scenes in the Far East, the five-letter cipher had to be broken.

The machine was known to the Japanese as the *angoo-ki taipu A*, the Type A cipher machine, or as the *91-shiki oo-bun inji-ki*, Alphabetical Typewriter 91. The 91 was derived from the year of its development, 1931 being 2591 in the Japanese calendar. The Type A machine was similar to the Japanese naval attaché machine broken by Foss and Strachey, although it used *romaji* letters instead of the *kana* syllables. It had two typewriters, one to input the plain text, the other to type out the enciphered message; a standard telephone exchange plugboard; and the encipherment mechanism. This last comprised two so-called 'half-rotors' on a fixed shaft, each of which had twenty-six electrical contacts wired around the circumference of one of its sides, and a forty-seven-pin gearwheel which moved the half-rotors either one or two positions at every stroke of the typewriter keys.

The operator connected the two typewriters to the machine through the plugboard using a daily changing setting. Each message was preceded by a five-figure indicator group which told the receiving station the starting positions for both the rotor and the gearwheel, as well as the pins which were to be removed from the gearwheel.

He then typed the plain text into the input typewriter. The depression of each key sent an electrical impulse through the socket on the plugboard to which it was wired, then on through an endplate and into the circuitry of the two half-rotors. This reflected it back out via the endplate to the output typewriter which typed the enciphered letter. The decipherment was thus determined largely by the plugboard settings and the fixed wiring of the half-rotors, and only varied by the movement of the gearwheel. This normally moved the rotor forward by one contact for every letter inputted, but where a pin had been removed it jumped a contact.

Basic cryptographic analysis of the messages enciphered on the machine, almost certainly carried out by Foss and Strachey, found that the frequency patterns of the letters seemed to change every ten days and that six of the letters in use stood out as occurring either more or less often than the other twenty.

The first piece of evidence obviously indicated that the cipher machine's predetermined positions or 'keys' were changed every ten days. The six letters that stood out were more interesting and seemed to offer the means of making an entry into the system. They were all the vowels plus V. If, as seemed likely, they represented Japanese vowels, the vowel–consonant patterns in the enciphered text would exactly reflect those in the original plain text.

Using the common associations between the Japanese vowels, particularly the *yoo* and *yuu* sequences, the British codebreakers soon found that the cipher was vulnerable to attack, and by November 1934 they had not only found a way in but had discovered that the ten-day key periods operated on a predictable cycle.

The codebreakers realized that recovering the messages was likely to prove a tedious, time-consuming task if it were done by hand. So they turned to Kenworthy and his Metropolitan Police wireless staff who were intercepting diplomatic and commercial traffic for GC&CS and had become its advisers on virtually any technical matter. Kenworthy recalled being asked to produce a machine that would allow the codebreakers easy access to the Japanese diplomatic cipher.

> As codes and ciphers became more advanced the cryptographers required mechanical aids. In November 1934 our branch was asked to help as we possessed a small workshop. The particular project was a Japanese decoding machine on a mechanical hand-operated system where a number of geared wheels were made to revolve in a certain order. This process was quite slow as the answer had to be written down for every movement of the wheels against the keys. It occurred to us that this could be done electrically with relays and coupled to a keyboard such as used on a teleprinter. The first machine was working by August 1935. It was very successful and was known as the J machine.

This was spectacular progress. The American codebreakers of the US Army's Signal Intelligence Service led by William Friedman are always fêted as the pacesetters in the race to break the Japanese codes and ciphers. But it was not until late 1936 that they attacked and broke the Type A machine, which they designated the Red machine, and a further two years before they built a similar device to Kenworthy's J machine.

The mid-1930s had seen the appearance of a new threat to the British Empire that more than rivalled that from Japan. The rise to power of Adolf Hitler and the establishment of the Third Reich had created another state that was not only, like Japan, keen to expand its territory at the expense of its neighbours but was uncomfortably closer to home. Even more worryingly, both the diplomatic telegrams deciphered using Kenworthy's J machine and the military attaché messages broken by John Tiltman provided clear evidence that the Germans and the Japanese were preparing to form an alliance which would threaten peace not just in the Far East but throughout the world.

The British codebreakers had virtually ignored German radio traffic after the end of the First World War. Germany was thought to have been 'crushed never again to rise', recalled Clarke. Added to this, its diplomatic ciphers used the theoretically unbreakable one-time pad system while its armed forces employed the Enigma cipher machine, which the British initially assumed was too difficult to break.

'Considering what Room 40 had achieved in 1914–18, it seems extraordinary that anyone should believe this,' recalled Josh Cooper, another of the interwar codebreakers. 'But it was generally assumed that no civilized nation that had once been through the traumatic experience of having its ciphers read would ever allow it to happen again and that, after the wide publicity given to Room 40's results, it would be a waste of time to work on German high-grade systems.'

But the codebreakers did not need to read the German diplomatic traffic to build up a good picture of the new closeness between Germany and Japan. The enciphered telegrams of the Japanese Ambassador to Germany and, in particular, the messages that Oshima Hiroshi, the Japanese Military Attaché in Berlin, was sending back to Tokyo told their own story. Oshima was a key member of the group within the Imperial Army that was leading the drive to expand Japanese territory in the Far East. He was also an ardent advocate of closer ties with Germany. He had been born in Japan's Gifu prefecture in 1886, the son of a former Japanese War Minister. Oshima's father Kenichi was a keen Anglophile who had stayed at Windsor Castle as a guest of Queen Victoria. His period as War Minister had come during the First World War when Japan was allied with Britain against Germany. The younger Oshima had no such affection for the British. After graduating from military academy in 1905, he served with distinction as an army officer and was first posted to Germany in 1921. He returned to Berlin in 1934, speaking perfect German and determined to build up closer relations with the new regime. Within a year, he had gained a private audience with Hitler and was a friend and confidant of Joachim von Ribbentrop, then Hitler's Ambassador-at-Large. He was also close to a number of leading members of the German general staff, as one British military attaché noted in a report to London.

> Gen Oshima is a typically courteous and polite Japanese officer of undoubted intelligence and considerable personality. The German War Office have a high opinion of his attainments. Unlike many of his countrymen, he is a gregarious creature and enjoys society. This is probably mainly due to the fact that he drinks like a fish. He is very rarely sober in the evening and the more he drinks the more he talks. On the other hand, his discretion seems to increase under the influence of alcohol and I have often seen him surrounded by a circle of his colleagues, all hoping that he will produce some pearl of information, and all invariably disappointed at getting absolutely no return for their outlay of Kirsch, which is his favourite tipple. During the recent manoeuvres in East Prussia, he finished off a bottle of brandy in his car every day and after General Beck's dinner on the last night at Koenigsberg, he drank himself into a state of extremely noisy intoxication on a mixture of Cosacken-Café and Pillkaller.

Oshima's discussions with the Nazi leaders frequently

centred on the possibility of a pact between the two countries. By August 1935 the codebreakers' reports of traffic passing on the diplomatic circuits between Berlin and Tokyo had convinced the author of a British military intelligence report that an alliance was inevitable.

> The Japanese and German nations have many traits in common. Both have strong leanings towards nationalism. In both the military caste have traditionally been – in Japan they still are – the real rulers of the country. Recent events have served to accentuate this resemblance. Both countries have left the League of Nations, for not dissimilar reasons. While the Japanese, whose thirst for a safe source of raw materials has led to their annexation of Manchukuo and forthcoming annexation of North China, view with sympathy Germany's aspirations for the return of her colonies and for expansion into the Ukraine.

The diplomatic telegrams and the messages of both Oshima and his Imperial Japanese Navy counterpart revealed that, as part of the rapprochement, Berlin had said it would not be seeking the return of its Far Eastern colonies seized by Japan during the First World War. They also showed that the two countries' armed forces had begun exchanging technical know-how.

By early 1936 indications of an imminent German–Japanese pact, engineered primarily by the Imperial Japanese Army, were increasing. Oshima was one of its chief architects, leading Malcolm Kennedy to note that the evidence suggested it would be 'more in the nature of an understanding between the naval and military staffs of the two nations than a binding agreement between the two governments'.

The Anti-Comintern Pact was eventually signed in November 1936. Taken at face value, it was little more than an agreement to exchange information on the spread of communism. But a secret protocol to the pact went much further, effectively aligning the two countries against the Soviet Union.

The Foreign Office appears to have had no definite proof that the secret protocol existed, but Kennedy noted that, according to the Soviet Ambassador to Britain, 'Moscow has obtained a complete copy of the J–German agreement and, despite official denials to the contrary, it includes certain secret protocols. One wonders just how much the Soviet does know and how much is insidious gossip on its part.'

Meanwhile, the staff of the Government Code and Cipher School, like the rest of Britain, were in thrall to a different kind of gossip, concerning King Edward VIII's love affair with Wallis Simpson, an American divorcee. The very future of the British royal family seemed threatened by the scandal, as Kennedy recorded in his diary entry for Thursday, 3 December 1936.

> The King's affair with Mrs Simpson, about which the US press has been talking so freely for some time past, has now been brought to light in our own press, which hitherto has shown a laudable readiness to keep silent on the subject. The US press, of course, has been simply gloating over the whole thing and publishing columns and columns of the most sordid and sensational details. A most ghastly business and likely to do untold harm to British prestige in general and to the prestige of the Throne in particular. I heard of it first from Roscoe some three or four weeks ago and, of course, knowledge of it was spreading gradually in this country; but to the general public it has come like a bolt from the blue and most people are naturally horrified.

A week later the newspapers reported that the King was expected that afternoon to announce that he was abdicating. The staff of the Government Code and Cipher School were as interested in the events as everyone else in Britain, Kennedy noted.

> Knowing that the final decision was to be broadcast at 4 p.m., I went along with Marsden to a room which had

imported a wireless set for the occasion. Found most of the office congregated there – a curious, almost uncanny gathering, with everyone doing his or her best to appear calm and collected, though all present were clearly in a state of nervous tension. A low, subdued chatter. Then complete silence as the announcer began to speak, the tense silence continuing until the announcement was finished, when everyone dispersed quietly and returned to work. A most tragic ending to a reign which had seemed to hold out such great prospects. But in view of all that has come out, the King's decision to abdicate may perhaps prove all for the best. And even though his successor may not, at first sight, appear so well-fitted as his brother and may be lacking his magnetic personality, he seems likely to prove a far more conscientious, steady-going monarch, and his wife has all the qualities of a most popular Queen.

By now the codebreakers had not only obtained proof that the secret protocol existed; there was a good deal of evidence in the decrypts that the Japanese and the Germans were looking to extend the pact to include Italy. An alliance of Germany in northern Europe, Japan in the Far East and Italy, whose navy was capable of dominating the Mediterranean, was a major threat to world peace.

When Sir Eric Drummond, the British Ambassador in Rome, asked his Japanese counterpart Sujimura Yotaro if the reports in the Italian press of an imminent agreement between the two countries were true, Sujimura denied it. But the Japanese telegrams deciphered in Broadway Buildings told a different story. Nevertheless, Sir Eric was kept blissfully ignorant of the real facts for fear of compromising the codebreakers' activities.

A subsequent visit by Ribbentrop to Rome was played down in Rome and Berlin as being inconsequential. But again the deciphered Japanese telegrams kept the Foreign Office informed of what was really going on. 'We have more than a shrewd idea that the object of the visit is connected with the possibility of Italy adhering to the German–Japanese anti-Communist pact,' one official noted.

The Foreign Office had no need of codebreakers to interpret many of the Japanese and German moves towards a grand alliance with Mussolini's Italy. Sujimura was regarded as a moderate in Japanese terms, but in an interview with the Italian newspaper *Corriere della Sera*, he spoke of an 'identity of ideas' between Japan and Italy: 'We consider ourselves to be in the same condition. Overpopulation creates for obvious reasons the right to occupy more territory and the rights of civilization demand that people install themselves in those areas where the inhabitants stand in need of human evolution.'

One of the codebreakers helping to decipher the Japanese diplomatic telegrams was the eccentric Hugh Foss. 'He was a great six-foot-five Scot,' recalled one of the codebreakers' secretaries. 'Very bright, very shy and a great Scottish dancer with his long legs and kilt.' Foss's cousin Elizabeth Browning would later work alongside him in GC&CS's Japanese naval sub-section. But at this stage she was one of the Foreign Office staff handling the diplomatic intercepts. They arrived in blue-jacketed files and as a result became known as BJs, Browning recalled.

I first knew of the existence of GC&CS in 1934. I had begun work at the Foreign Office as a shorthand-typist in January and after a few weeks became one of the two girls assigned to the American Department. One of our jobs was to file what were called the Red and Blue papers. The Reds were SIS reports and the Blues were decrypts from GC&CS which at that time was located in Broadway. These Most Secret papers had to be housed in appropriately coloured folders with a typed précis of their contents on a sticky label outside while a corresponding card went into a sort of box-file which was kept in a locked cupboard. The locked cupboards were a bit bogus. When one was moved out from the wall, because the room was being decorated, it was found to have no back to it.

Browning had no idea that her cousin was one of the codebreakers producing the BJs.

A colleague had herself once previously worked in Broadway and when I said to her one day that I was meeting my cousin Hugh Foss for lunch she said: 'Oh I know him. He works there too.' This was the first I knew of Hugh's job. During the next two to three years I saw a lot of Hugh and his wife Alison. One day they suggested that I might join the Chelsea Reel Club. They had belonged to it for some time and they said they had a friend who wanted a female partner as his wife didn't care for country dancing. The club met in Cheyne Walk not far from my base in Pimlico and it offered a cheap and amusing form of exercise (FO typist pay at that time was forty-eight shillings and sixpence, £2.42, a week). Hugh's friend turned out to be a quiet little man called Commander Denniston and for a year or so we 'reeled' together once a week. When I later joined GC&CS, I encountered Commander Denniston and said, 'Hello, have you been roped in here too?' But so tight was security that I did not discover my faux pas for some time.

5

PREPARING FOR WAR

The Japanese military now began their expansion into China in earnest, protected from the Soviet Union to the north by the Anti-Comintern Pact. What was to become known as the China Incident began in July 1937 with a routine exchange of fire between Chinese and Japanese troops across the Marco Polo Bridge near Peking. The Japanese claimed one of their soldiers was missing and attempted to force their way into a small town where they alleged the man was being held – in fact he had simply wandered off looking for a woman. The Japanese force was repelled and with neither side prepared to back down for fear of losing face the incident escalated into full-scale war.

The Japanese were oblivious to the international, and in particular the British, reaction to their behaviour in China. This included the notorious Rape of Nanking, where as many as a quarter of a million Chinese, the majority of them civilians, died. They strafed the British Ambassador's car, bombarded British enclaves in Chinese cities and, in an attack specifically designed to draw Britain into the war, shelled HMS *Ladybird* and HMS *Bee* as they lay at anchor on the Yangtze River. But with one eye on Hitler and Mussolini in the West, the British Government declined to respond with force.

Neville Chamberlain, the British Prime Minister, believed

that the only possible military solution to the Japanese problem lay in joint Anglo–US action but President Roosevelt rejected the idea and the British were not prepared to go it alone. 'In the present state of European affairs with two dictators in a thoroughly nasty temper, we simply cannot afford to quarrel with Japan,' Chamberlain said. 'I very much fear therefore that after a lot of bally-hoo the Americans will somehow fade out and leave us to carry all the blame and the odium.'

If the situation in China filled Whitehall with gloom, the codebreakers were at least able to practise on the never-ending stream of Japanese intercepts it produced. Six weeks before the Japanese troops landed, Hong Kong intercepted and decoded a long message to the Japanese 3rd Fleet providing full details of which forces were to be used and when they were to arrive. John Tiltman recalled that the plethora of military messages that followed kept him fully busy throughout the second half of 1937.

> My time was almost entirely taken up with research on the intercepts from Hong Kong. The major part of the traffic was in a succession of military systems used for transmission of intelligence reports from China, especially detailed as to the characteristics of key personalities. The small basic code-charts used at the time necessitated the spelling of most of the plain text in *kana* syllables and each character of a Chinese name had to be precisely described by giving the native Japanese reading for the character or, in some desperate cases, an elaborate description of the way in which a rare character was put together.

Tiltman travelled to Hong Kong in the hope of persuading the Far East Combined Bureau to take over the military codebreaking. But the naval codebreakers had enough on their plate with the Japanese naval codes and the mission was a failure, leaving him with little choice but to continue with the Imperial Japanese Army codes and ciphers at the expense of other research.

During this period the cipher systems used seemed to be changed quite drastically every nine months and I had a hard time keeping up with the changes. I had no Japanese interpreter attached to me and the other members of my military section were otherwise engaged. There was an underlying thread of continuity in all the systems, this being irregular switches from one substitution to another within messages. It was here that I first came across 'bisection', which remained the Japanese practice from that time until the end of World War Two. This is the practice of dividing the plain text into two portions irregularly and placing the second portion first, with the intention of shifting the stereotyped preambles into undefined positions in the bodies of the messages.

At the end of 1937, the Japanese military began using a different system, a combination of a code and a cipher, Tiltman recalled. The message was encoded into blocks of figures using a codebook which gave numerical equivalents for all the main Japanese characters, phrases and *kana* syllables. The resultant code was enciphered using an additive system with predetermined groups of figures, taken from a cipher table or book, added to the code groups using the 'addition modulo 10' or Fibonacci system of addition in which no figures are carried over. Seven plus eight therefore becomes five rather than fifteen.

The first cipher which was intercepted in sufficient quantity for attack had a two-part, four-figure code book in which the cipher groups were limited to multiples of three and the additive recipher consisted of ten thousand four-figure groups arranged on a hundred pages, each containing ten lines and ten columns. Both the starting and ending points in the additive were indicated in each message and these were reciphered each by one of a hundred four-figure additive groups controlled by a particular dinome of the first cipher group for the starting point indicator and the last cipher group for the ending point.

It was not until the late summer of 1938 that Tiltman managed to make the vital breakthrough into the new Japanese military cipher. But by now the attentions of GC&CS were being concentrated elsewhere. With war looming in Europe, they were making frantic efforts to unravel the German Enigma cipher machine and were preparing for the seemingly inevitable confrontation with Hitler.

Admiral Sinclair had bought a mansion at Bletchley Park, fifty miles north of London, in the spring of 1938 as a 'War Station' for both MI6 and GC&CS. He was acting entirely on his own initiative. Having realized that, if it came to war, he would need to protect his staff from the inevitable air raids, Sinclair had asked the Foreign Office to pay for a 'War Station'. Its response was that the War Office was responsible for war: the generals should pay. The generals told Sinclair that as a former Director of Naval Intelligence he should go to the admirals, who told him he was part of the Foreign Office and the mandarins should pay.

Frustrated by his inability to get anyone to pay the £7,500 asking price for Bletchley Park, Sir Hugh dipped into his own pocket to buy it. 'We know he paid for it,' said one former intelligence officer. 'We're not sure if he was ever repaid. He died soon afterwards so he probably wasn't.' The Park itself was given the covername 'Station X', not as might be assumed a symbol of mystery but simply the tenth of a large number of sites eventually acquired by MI6 for its various wartime operations and designated using Roman numerals.

Shortly before the Munich Crisis of September 1938, some of the codebreakers and a number of MI6 sections moved to Bletchley Park briefly for 'a rehearsal'. It was while they were there that Tiltman made the breakthrough into the main Japanese military cipher, working out how the Japanese operators indicated which part of the additive book they were using. 'By the end of the year it seemed to me that we were sufficiently advanced to shift the responsibility for Japanese cryptanalysis to the Far

East. At the beginning of 1939 I went again to Hong Kong.'

Tiltman took with him two of his military codebreakers, Captain Peter Marr-Johnson, a Royal Artillery officer who had studied in Japan for a number of years and was immersed in both the language and codebreaking, and Lieutenant Geoffrey Stevens, a straightforward codebreaker. They would lead the FECB's efforts against the Japanese army codes and ciphers. Now at last Tiltman was successful in persuading the bureau to take on military as well as naval codebreaking.

At the same time, the RAF had decided to step up its own presence within the bureau. There was no separate Japanese air force: both the Imperial Japanese Navy and the Imperial Japanese Army operated their own aircraft. But although there were seven RAF wireless intercept operators at the Stonecutters Island site and an RAF officer in the bureau's intelligence section, there were no RAF codebreakers. Squadron Leader H. T. 'Alf' Bennett, who was an experienced Japan expert, having spent three years as British Air Attaché in Tokyo, was sent on a codebreaking course at GC&CS, arriving in Hong Kong in March 1939.

'As far as Air sigint was concerned no Japanese aircraft normally operated within 600 miles of Hong Kong and therefore traffic was mainly inaudible,' wrote Nigel de Grey, one of the leading codebreakers at GC&CS. 'On the other hand, the Japanese Naval Air Arm figured to a considerable extent in the naval messages that could be decrypted.'

Eric Nave had now returned to Hong Kong and under his leadership the naval codebreakers exercised a fair degree of control over the Japanese naval traffic, Shaw recalled.

Book-building on the 4-*kana* General Code went on steadily and progress was made with the Flag Officers' Code, which mainly concerned local politics in China. A new naval *kana* code came into use between Japanese naval bases and hence was known as the Dockyard Code. The book was alphabetical but the vocabulary, being largely technical, was slow to build up. In the early stages of the *kana* codes, when transposition was fairly simple, messages were decrypted by two selected and trained Y operators at Stonecutters.

By the end of 1938 Japanese communications security had been stepped up and this was no longer possible. New codes and ciphers were constantly being introduced and they were so complicated that trained cryptographers were required to unravel them. Nevertheless, according to Denniston, the codebreakers in London and Hong Kong remained 'reasonably fluent in their reading of all main Japanese naval ciphers and knew quite a lot about Japanese army ciphers used in China'.

They had also set up a separate section in London, under G. L. N. Hope, one of the First World War codebreakers, to decipher Japanese commercial codes and ciphers which Naval Intelligence was hoping to use to track supply convoys, Denniston recalled.

Some time in 1938, the Admiral [Sinclair] and the newly appointed Director of Naval Intelligence [Admiral John Godfrey] formed the opinion that, in the event of a troublous political situation in the Far East, the Japanese might take steps to render their diplomatic and service material illegible, and that the communications of the big Japanese firms, particularly as to shipping, might be the only available source of intelligence. Therefore, Hope started a very small section to investigate commercial traffic, more especially the telegrams of the big Japanese firms.

The concerns of the intelligence chiefs soon proved justified. At the end of 1938 the codebreakers began to read messages enciphered on the Type A diplomatic cipher machine referring to a new device *angoo-ki taipu B*, the Type B machine. It made its first appearance on 20 March

1939 and while the Type A machine continued in service for most messages, it was clear that it was being gradually replaced for the secret messages sent between the Japanese embassies in the major world capitals and Tokyo.

In November 1938 the Imperial Japanese Navy replaced its codes, introducing a new 4-*kana* system for its main General Operational Code. Then the codebreakers began to find messages referring to yet another system to be called *kaigun angoo-sho D*, or Navy Code D, which was introduced on 1 June 1939 as the new General Operational Code. The recently introduced system it replaced was now reserved only for the use of Flag Officers. The Japanese also introduced yet another Dockyard Code.

Nave concentrated on trying to break the Dockyard Code while all intercepted messages in the new five-figure General Operational Code were sent back to GC&CS in London for investigation. Nobby Clarke called in Tiltman, who immediately recognized a number of similarities to the Japanese army codes he had been working on.

Barbara Abernethy was one of those working in the naval section at the time. A fluent German-speaker, she had been plucked out of the Foreign Office and sent to Broadway Buildings.

Nobby Clarke was the most delightful man, very quiet, but very bright. I know he spent a lot of time fighting with the Admiralty for more staff. But it was a most civilized office. I was posted over there for a week not knowing what I was doing and told that it was strict secrecy. I was there for a week and they apparently approved of me because I was kept on and I stayed there. Life was very civilized in those days, you know, we stopped for tea and it was brought in by messengers. We had our own cups. I was very impressed by this, first job I'd ever had and it seemed paradise to me. I thought: 'Well this is the life, isn't it? Thank God I'm not back in the Foreign Office.' The head of the Japanese naval sub-section, Lieutenant-Commander Bruce Keith, and one of his sidekicks, Lieutenant Neil Barham, used to come into our office to have tea but we rarely saw John Tiltman. He was head of the military section, a very nice, good-looking guy who always wore tartan trews. Very bright.

Since many of the messages sent in the General Operational Code were reporting ships' positions, they used a lot of figures and this was one of the ways into the system. Tiltman noticed that the code groups representing figures were stepped in a similar way to the army codes. Each code group for a figure differed from the ones below and above it by 102. The most common figure in longitude and latitude positions is zero and the most common group in the encoded positions was also the lowest. Clearly it was zero. The next lowest, just 102 on, was found to be one and from then on it was a simple task to work out the other figures. Within the space of a few weeks Tiltman had broken the new code.

Tiltman's breakthrough into the new General Operational Code, brilliant though it undoubtedly was, did not mean that the British could now read the Japanese messages. The code, which would later become known to the Allies as JN25, was typical of the combinations of codebook and cipher additive that were to become common throughout the Japanese armed forces. The codebook contained more than 30,000 words or phrases designed to cover every contingency faced by the Imperial Japanese Navy, with the most frequently used repeated a number of times to enhance security. Alongside each was a five-figure group which the operator used to encode his message.

Having encoded the message into a series of five-figure groups, the operator then used an additive table book containing pages of randomly selected five-figure groups to encipher the encoded message, adding a second level of security. These additive groups were set out on each page on a 10 × 10 matrix. There were two-figure indicators at the top of each column and alongside each row so that both the starting and ending points of the additive could be easily identified to the Japanese station that was to receive the message. The operator sending the message now used the Fibonacci system to add the first of the five-figure groups he had selected to the first of the five-figure groups previously encoded. Each of the additive groups in turn was added to the next code group until the entire message had been disguised from anyone who might have obtained a copy of Navy Codebook D.

What Tiltman had done was first to identify how the system worked and, second, discover how to 'strip away' the cipher additive to reveal the encoded message. But although the groups for encoding numbers were known, only a few of the words and phrases represented by the five-figure code groups had been recovered.

As for the new Japanese diplomatic cipher machine, the British machine specialists were now far too busy attempting to break the Nazi Enigma cipher. War was fast approaching and both GC&CS and FECB were pre-occupied with evacuating their staffs to safer quarters.

'In view of the apparent imminence of war, my particular branch of the FO received orders this morning to pick up all our secret documents etc. and to proceed to "war stations" tomorrow,' Malcolm Kennedy recorded in his diary for 24 August 1939. The next day he drove to Bletchley Park where the Japanese diplomatic sub-section was to be accommodated in the neighbouring Elmers School.

Left by road for war station, arriving there a bit before noon after a 60-mile run. Find that no arrangements have been made for providing us with lunch and the school which is to serve as our office building is still occupied, so we won't be able to get in our stuff and settle down to work till tomorrow at the earliest. Find too that we are to be billeted in Northampton, 23 miles from our work, so thither I took Roscoe in my car in the evening and now I am sharing a single room with him at the Angel Hotel, a 19th Century coaching inn, as accommodation is limited. Ostensibly we are now engaged in 'Civil Air Defence' but this cover is wearing a bit thin and why we can't admit that we are a branch of the FO heaven alone knows.

While the FECB was not threatened by the Germans, there had been concern for some time that the Japanese might attack Hong Kong, and contingency plans had been put in place for a move to Singapore, where there was already a small group of intercept operators. During the summer, the bureau's staff had been warned that they should be packed to move at a moment's notice.

On 25 August, the same day that the Japanese diplomatic sub-section left for Bletchley Park, the FECB staff, together with twenty lorries full of secret files, were loaded on to HMS *Birmingham* and sailed for Singapore. They arrived three days later, setting up their offices in Selatar barracks, in the north of the island, while the intercept operators bolstered those already in place at the Kranji wireless station seven miles away. Within two days it was in full operation, although it was some time before teleprinter links could be set up between Kranji and Selatar and messages had to be carried by motorcycle dispatch riders.

A small team of four intercept operators, supported by one Special Intelligence officer, Squadron-Leader Alf Bennett, was left in Hong Kong. Links were also established to a number of other intercept operations on Royal Navy and Royal Australian Navy ships, at a Royal Navy site in Bombay, at a Royal Canadian Navy Base on the Pacific coast and in Melbourne.

The FECB was given responsibility for gathering intelligence for an area stretching from the Suez Canal to the Panama Canal and for keeping track of all enemy and Allied vessels in that area, one of the bureau's officers recalled. 'This was a very different picture from that of FECB Hong Kong, when the output had been limited to periodical summaries and a few signals.'

The main Special Intelligence contribution to this new enlarged role came from traffic analysis, the use of routine radio communications between the units being intercepted to work out their order of battle, location and method of operation. The study of the call signs used by the stations, the subordination of each station, preambles to messages and operator 'chatter' provided a wealth of information about the Japanese networks the codebreakers were monitoring. This traffic analysis was aided significantly by the process of direction-finding (DF) which had been practised intermittently in Hong Kong but now became common practice whenever a new Japanese radio station appeared on the air.

The DF stations at Kranji and Stonecutters Island were part of a network of British-controlled DF stations across the region from Canada through New Zealand and Australia to India and East Africa. Each station had an array of radio masts set up in a circular formation. From the way in which a given signal was picked up by the various aerials it was possible to produce a bearing on the enemy transmitter. By using two or more DF stations against the same target, a number of different bearings could be plotted on a map to determine the precise location of the enemy radio station.

A few weeks after the codebreakers arrived in Singapore, Nave was married in St Andrew's Cathedral to Helena Gray, whom he had met while she was working as a nursing sister at Queen Mary's Hospital, Hong Kong. One of his close friends from GC&CS, Lieutenant-Commander Malcolm 'Bouncer' Burnett, who had just flown out to Singapore with the code groups Tiltman had recovered from the new General Operational Code, was the best man. Nave only had two days off for his honeymoon and shortly afterwards managed to break the new Dockyard Code.

The bureau's vastly expanded role and the need to intercept a large depth of the new General Operational Code, in order to recover more code groups, led to increased attempts to recruit new staff, particularly Japanese linguists and intercept operators capable of taking *kana* Morse.

The Japanese naval and military sections at Bletchley Park, which had each contained only four codebreakers when the European war broke out, were slimmed down still further to find experienced officers for Singapore. By

May 1940 the penetration of the codebook used as the basis for the main General Operational Code had progressed to the stage where stereotyped messages such as convoy schedules and individual ship movements could be decoded, although it was still not possible to read detailed operational orders.

Extra intercept operators were obtained by retraining Royal Malayan Navy signallers. But demands made on manpower by the outbreak of war in Europe meant that finding good intercept operators was difficult and as a result the navy began training Wrens to take *kana* Morse so they could be sent out to Singapore. They were trained as wireless telegraphists at King's College, Campden Hill Road, Kensington, in west London. Joan Sprinks, from Norwich, was twenty-three when she joined the course.

It was expected to take six months and the weekly payment was to be 33/6d [£1.67], of which £1 a week was to be deducted for board and lodging. I had no experience at all at this sort of thing but some of those on the earlier courses were already trained telegraphists and two had actually served in the same job during the First World War. Life at the depot was a mixture of Morse, drill, PT, assorted lectures, and 'darkening the ship' for the blackout.

The need for intercept operators was now so urgent that the *kana* Morse course was cut down from six months to three. The Wrens were then sent out to one of the main Royal Navy intercept sites at Flowerdown, near Winchester in Hampshire, or Scarborough in Yorkshire. Joan Sprinks was sent to Scarborough.

We were given brass buttons and rated as Chief Wrens so as to be equal in status to the civilian men's trade union. At Scarborough we were billeted in boarding houses and walked or cycled to go on watch in a room that was below ground. The night watch took a lot of getting used to – from 11.30 p.m. to 8 a.m. sitting at a bench with a number of ex-naval personnel who all seemed to consume very strong tea and to smoke endless 'ticklers', which were hand-rolled with very strong navy-issue tobacco. There was no fresh air at all, although the watchroom was occupied for the whole of the twenty-four hours and in addition there was of course a total blackout. Everything was so secret that we were trusted not to breathe a word about the work we were doing, which was intercepting the messages of German ships.

A few months later Sprinks and her fellow Wren wireless intercept operators were asked if they were prepared to serve overseas.

We learned later that this was to be in Singapore – at the wireless telegraphy station at Kranji. We reported to the Royal Naval College, Greenwich, for a special course under civilian instructors and met the officer who was to be in charge of us – Second Officer Betty Archdale, who had been a barrister and captain of the Women's Cricket Team to tour Australia in the 1930s.

Kirk Gill was one of the service instructors allocated to teaching *kana* Morse to new recruits. An RAF sergeant instructor, he was well aware of the difficulties they faced, having been thrown in at the deep end himself.

Air Ministry decided that we should concentrate on teaching Japanese *kana* Morse. It did not matter that we hadn't any idea what it was all about. Just do your duty and the devil take the hindmost. Frantic swotting was the order of the day to combat this mammoth task. We not only had to memorize the code but to be able to transpose it into Japanese language which was a very formidable task.

The *kana* Morse Code had seventy-five different characters. It employed a mixture of the standard Morse symbols to which the wireless operators were accustomed plus a number of 'barred' letters, combinations of two standard symbols run together. But neither the standard symbols nor the barred combinations of letters represented the same thing in *kana* Morse as they did in the international code. The standard Morse code symbol − . . ., for example, which is B in the international code, was HA in the Japanese code. A dash on its own, T in the international code, was MU in the *kana* code, while the barred letter BT, ie −. . .−, was ME in the *kana* code. In addition, the operators had to cope with a system of suffixes, Hanigori or Nigori, designed to provide an inflection to the character: Hanigori, sent as ..−.−, denoting a soft sound, and Nigori, sent as .., denoting a hard sound.

The British intercept operators took the characters down Japanese style, in columns, rather than working left to right. But in order to ease the process of learning the Japanese system, they wrote them initially as if they were standard international characters and then transcribed them into the *kana* versions afterwards using a table.

Having mastered the complicated Japanese Morse code, the new Wren operators set off for Singapore, leaving from Greenock in Scotland. They sailed on board the Blue Funnel ship SS *Nestor* in a convoy of about fifty ships protected by the aircraft carrier HMS *Argus* and its escort vessels.

'A few days out of port a lone Focke-Wulf Kondor attacked the convoy, dropping several bombs without apparently scoring a direct hit,' said Joan Sprinks. 'But they were close enough for two of us to finish a whole box of Black Magic chocolates, very precious in those days, just in case we, and they, went to the bottom.'

6

PURPLE MAGIC

The increasing use of the Japanese Type B machine had restricted the amount of high-grade Japanese enciphered diplomatic traffic the British were breaking. But there had been enough indications in the Type A traffic of what was to come to ensure they were not caught out by the signing in September 1940 of the Tripartite Pact, binding Germany, Italy and Japan together in a full-blooded military alliance.

The three Axis powers agreed to recognize each other's expansionist claims in Europe, Africa and Asia. More importantly, they promised to come to each other's assistance in the event of military intervention in either Europe or South-east Asia by any power not already involved, a transparent allusion to the USA.

Malcolm Kennedy was dismayed by Japan's decision to sign the pact. 'Though the announcement of this alliance has not come as a complete surprise to those in the know it is nonetheless unwelcome,' he noted in his diary. 'One cannot but feel that Japan herself will live to regret what she has done as, compared with Germany and Italy, she has precious little to gain by it and the Dickens of a lot to lose.'

Although the Type A machine would not be totally replaced for another year, Kennedy's diplomatic section was struggling. It managed to intercept messages ordering all Japanese missions abroad to co-operate with their Italian and German colleagues in collecting intelligence on the movement of British and American warships, aircraft and troops because the message circulation was so large that the Type A machine had to be used. But the main Japanese diplomatic cables between Berlin, Rome, London, Washington and Tokyo were now being sent on the Type B machine and frequently the latest Japanese moves were clearly as much 'a complete surprise' to Kennedy as they were to anyone else.

As the Japanese diplomatic section had found to its cost, the bombing of British towns was in full flow. On 21 November 1940 Kennedy had arrived at the office in Elmers School to find that it had been bombed overnight.

Typists' room and telephone exchange blown to bits by a direct hit and the Vicarage next door damaged by another bomb which landed in the garden. A third bomb exploded in the road outside, while two more landed over at the Park, one of them bursting a bare half-dozen paces from Hut 4. By great good fortune there were no casualties. We however have been moved to the room used by the South American section, who in turn have been transferred to the Park.

The decision to move Kennedy's section is a reflection of the low priority accorded to Japanese material at Bletchley Park at the time. Its research section was completely pre-occupied with breaking German machine ciphers. With their backs very firmly against the wall, the British could only concentrate on one problem at a time and the battle to break Enigma took first place. All over Bletchley Park, prefabricated huts were being put up, but none of them was to work on Japanese radio traffic.

That was considered the sole prerogative of the Far East Combined Bureau. It was concentrating the bulk of its resources on the Japanese Navy General Operational Code, which made very heavy demands on manpower. The Type B machine was simply not regarded as a high enough priority to throw resources at it. The British code-breakers in Singapore did at one point come close to obtaining a 'pinch' of a Type B machine, Harry Shaw recalled. But they were prevented from doing so by bumbling bureaucracy.

> A Tokyo cipher message gave the date of arrival, and name of ship, in which Cipher Machine B was being sent to the Japanese Consulate in Singapore under diplomatic immunity. The police were approached to obtain their connivance in engineering an 'accident' while the cases containing the machine were being hoisted out of the ship, enabling a technical officer to view the contents. The police refused to co-operate without the tacit support of the Colonial Secretary, Singapore, who strongly opposed the scheme, and the project was dropped.

If the British had decided to place the breaking of the Type B traffic on the back burner, the Americans had not. The US Army codebreaking organization, the Signal Intelligence Service, had been concentrating on it since it first appeared in late February 1939. On 27 September 1940, the day the Tripartite Pact was signed, they succeeded in making the first break into the Type B machine.

The new machine was also known as the 97-*shiki oo-bun inji-ki*, Alphabetical Typewriter 97, indicating that it was first developed in 1937, the Japanese year 2597. Like the Type A machine, it was electro-mechanical and had two typewriter keyboards and a plugboard. There were, however, a number of fundamental differences between the two machines. The principal difference was that the encipherment circuits on the Type B machine ran not through a rotor, as on its predecessor, but through a series of telephone stepping switches of the same type as those used by Harold Kenworthy to produce the J machine with which the British were deciphering the Type A traffic.

A single main switch controlled the encryption of six letters which, unlike the Type A machine, were not the vowels but changed daily. The other switches were organized in banks of three and controlled the remaining twenty letters. The switches were designed to simulate the action of the rotors on a standard cipher machine such as the German Enigma machine, moving to change the method of encryption as each letter is typed in. The single main switch stepped one level every time a letter was keyed in. The other three banks moved at different speeds, much like the rotors on an Enigma machine. The first bank of switches was the 'fast' bank, stepping once for the first twenty-four key strokes. When the twenty-fifth character was typed in, the fast bank stayed where it was and the second 'medium' bank of switches stepped once. The second bank also only moved twenty-four times before the third or 'slow' bank came into play. At the end of the next full 'rotation' of the fast bank of switches, the 625th operation of the machine, both the fast and medium banks remained where they were while the slow bank stepped once.

The result was a much more complex encipherment process where the substitution produced at each point was completely unrelated to any of the others, unlike a rotor system where all the substitutions produced by the wheel follow each other in rotation.

Although this appeared to make the Type B machine far superior to the German Enigma machine, it was paradoxically much less secure. The Enigma had a number of differently wired rotors which could be changed and shuffled through a wide variety of permutations. But the Type B's stepping switches were all fixed into the machine, drastically cutting the number of encipherment options. The real difficulties generated by the machine lay in the tangled web of wiring connecting the banks of stepping switches. If any potential codebreaker were to work out the wiring of the Type B machine, the enciphered traffic would be broken with ease.

The Japanese cipher clerk operating the Type B machine used a specific letter sequence listed in a book of 1,000 daily changing sequences to plug the connections from the input and output typewriters into the cipher machine's plugboard. He then selected a five-figure indicator group at random from a list of 120, each of which had different settings that should be applied to the banks of stepping switches and to the main switch which controlled the encryption of the 'sixes'. This five-figure indicator group was enciphered using an additive and sent immediately before the enciphered text in order to tell the receiving station what settings to use.

To encipher the message, the cipher clerk first encoded it using a basic commercially available substitution cipher known as the Phillips Code. He then typed the enciphered text into one of the electric typewriters, generating an electrical current which ran though the machine's internal wiring and typed out the enciphered text, letter by letter, on the second keyboard.

The eighteen-month operation to break the Type B machine, which the Americans designated Purple, was based in the SIS headquarters in rooms 3416 and 3418 of the Munitions Building opposite Seventh Avenue on Constitution Avenue, Washington. It was led by William F. Friedman, America's leading codebreaker.

Friedman was born in Kishinev, the capital of Moldavia, in 1891. When he was still a baby, his parents had emigrated to the United States where he studied genetics and was offered a job in the laboratories of the wealthy textile manufacturer George Fabyan. It was here that he first began to take an interest in ciphers, as a result of Fabyan's obsession with proving that Shakespeare's plays were written by Francis Bacon. After doing some code-breaking work for the US Government during the First World War, Friedman became head of the US Army's small cryptography unit. He set up a special team to break the new Japanese cipher machine. The 'Purple Section', as it was known, was led by Frank Rowlett, a small, bespectacled mathematics teacher from Rocky Mount, Virginia, who had been one of Friedman's earliest recruits. 'The salary offered with the position was two thousand dollars a year, which was more than both my wife and I were making as schoolteachers and we decided we would give it a try,' Rowlett recalled. He was called to Washington to be interviewed for the job.

It was during this first exchange with Friedman, when he got through inquiring if I had a place to live and had I been to Washington before, just sort of simple conversation, that I found an opportunity to ask him what a cryptanalyst was supposed to do and he said: 'You mean you don't know what a cryptanalyst is?' and I said: 'I never heard the word before.' Then he looked out the window and said: 'Well, that's not strange. I just invented it.' We were collaborating with the navy at that time and both of us were very anxious to get an insight into this new machine, which we early on named Purple, and we had some success with it in the first weeks but not enough to allow us a close solution of it. All we had was pen and paper and a calculator, one of those desktop things with nine keys and ten columns wide.

Rowlett's section found that, just as in the traffic enciphered with the Type A Red machine, six of the *romaji* letters stood out as appearing either more or less frequently than the other twenty. It was not difficult to isolate and recover these six letters, Rowlett recalled.

While we had no idea of what sort of enciphering mechanism the Japanese cryptographers were using, we were able to design a 'pen and paper' analogue which enabled us to decipher the sixes wherever they appeared in the intercepts. This analogue was essentially a deciphering chart six columns wide by twenty-five rows deep representing a polyalphabetic substitution system of twenty-five differently mixed alphabets composed of the same six letters. Recovery of this chart enabled us to decipher the sixes of any key period by the straightforward process of relating each of the six letters to its proper position in the chart.

The ability to identify six letters wherever they occurred in a message meant that a number of other letters could sometimes be guessed. The Japanese had not only made the mistake of enciphering the message numbers but had incorporated them into the same series used for traffic sent on the Red machine. The message numbers, spelled out in letters, were therefore instantly recoverable. Once again the Japanese tendency towards flowery, long-winded, stereotyped introductions such as the phrase 'I have the honour to inform your excellency' assisted the code-breakers, Friedman recalled.

When the 'sixes' in a given message were deciphered, the plain text value of cipher letters scattered here and there throughout the text became available, so that the skeletons of words and phrases offered themselves for completion by the ingenuity and the imagination of the cryptanalyst. For example, suppose that on a given day the six letters forming the 'sixes' were E Q A D R H and the following text was at hand:

Cipher:	B	R	A	X	E	F	Q	C	E	V	Q	O	O	X	H	E	C F
Plain:	–	H	E	–	A	–	A	–	E	–	E	–	–	–	E	R	– –
Cipher:	D	L	N	H	Q	R	V	Q	P	P	L	C	E	R	P		
Plain:	E	–	–	R	E	Q	–	E	–	–	–	–	H	A	–		

It is not difficult to imagine that the missing letters are those shown below:

Cipher:	B	R	A	X	E	F	Q	C	E	V	Q	O	O	X	H	E	C F
Plain:	T	H	E	J	A	P	A	N	E	S	E	G	O	V	E	R	N M
Cipher:	D	L	N	H	Q	R	V	Q	P	P	L	C	E	R	P		
Plain:	E	N	T	R	E	Q	U	E	S	T	S	T	H	A	T		

The codebreakers also had access to a number of helpful 'cribs' of the plain text. Messages sent on the Purple machine had often also been sent on the Red machine. Japanese diplomats were usefully unwilling to cut anything from US State Department communiqués, copies of which the codebreakers had no difficulty in obtaining.

But while all this could help to break a number of individual messages, it did not provide any continuity of decryption. The American codebreakers were only able to take one message at a time with only the position of the deciphered letters from the day's 'sixes' and the context in which the message was being sent to assist them, Friedman recalled.

It speedily became apparent that any cryptographic relationship between the plain text and the constantly shifting cipher text values in the case of the letters constituting the group of 'twenties' had been most carefully eliminated, disguised, or suppressed. In several cases, after a few words had thus been obtained by pure 'guessing', a clue was afforded as to the general nature of the message. This led to a frantic search for a complete document which might be available either in our own files or in the files of other government agencies.

In all the plain texts for parts of some fifteen fairly lengthy messages were obtained by the methods indicated above, and these were subjected to most intensive and exhaustive cryptanalytic studies. To the consternation of the cryptanalysts, not only was there a complete and absolute absence of any causal repetitions within any single message, no matter how long, or between two messages with different indicators on the same day, but when repetitions of three, or occasionally four, cipher letters were found, these never represented the same plain text.

In fact, a statistical calculation gave the astonishing result that the number of repetitions actually present in these cryptograms was less than the number to be expected had the letters comprising them been drawn at random out of a hat. Apparently, the machine had with malicious intent – but brilliantly – been constructed to suppress all plain-text repetition. Nevertheless, the cryptanalysts had a feeling that this very circumstance would, in the final analysis, prove to be the undoing of the system and mechanism. And so it turned out.

The US codebreakers soon realized that what they needed was an immense 'depth' of enciphered text sent on the same day and using the same indicator. But although by now they had managed to reconstruct, at least in part, around one thousand messages, only in a very few cases were there any messages sent on the same day with the same indicator and even then there were only ever two messages that coincided in this way. There were, however, a number of messages sent on different days but using the same indicator and, ingeniously, by working out how the machine treated each of those different messages, the codebreakers managed to deduce how it would have enciphered them on one single given day. They now had a depth of six different messages all notionally sent on one day's keys.

Their attempts to find any links between the way the plain text in the messages was enciphered in the various messages that would let them into the machine were hampered by the need to find extra space in the crowded Munitions Building. Workmen had begun adding a fourth floor directly above their office, Rowlett recalled.

> Our ears and minds were filled with the distracting sounds of hammering, banging and shouting. When the construction cranes hoisted heavy materials to the workmen above us, we could feel the building shake as the loads were dropped on the roof. Worst of all was the incessant vibration from the jackhammers overhead which started early in the morning and continued all day long. This took place while the heat of the late summer was still on us, long before the days of air-conditioning. When we closed the windows to cut down on the noise, we sweltered. When we opened them to get relief from the heat, the racket was unendurable. At times it was impossible to communicate.

The codebreakers were understandably jubilant when on 20 September 1940 Genevieve Grotjan, one of the key members of Purple Section, found similar sequences of enciphered and plain-text letters in a number of the messages she was studying. When she called out to her colleagues to tell them what she had found, one of them became so excited that he started dancing around Grotjan's desk holding his hands in the air like a victorious boxer. Another codebreaker, normally among the most studious members of the team, was yelling, 'Hurrah, Hurrah' at the top of his voice, Rowlett recalled. 'I could not resist jumping up and down and waving my arms above my head and exclaiming: "That's it! That's it! Gene has found what we have been looking for." '

The Purple Section celebrated its success rather modestly by sending out for bottles of Coca-Cola. But the strain of the eighteen-month operation had been too much for Friedman, who suffered a nervous breakdown and as a result was off work for several months.

The US Army codebreakers used the relationships between the like sequences of enciphered and plain text to work out the wiring of the machine, and Leo Rosen, a young electronics engineer, began to construct a customized machine that would simulate its operations.

The most urgent priority, once the machine was built and the Purple traffic could be broken regularly, was to go back over the messages sent before the signing of the Tripartite Pact to uncover the fine detail of the negotiations. The diplomatic signals intelligence produced by deciphering the Purple traffic, codenamed Magic by the Americans, was to be of inestimable value to the Allies as the war progressed and none was to prove more valuable than the messages passing between Tokyo and its Ambassador in Berlin, Oshima Hiroshi.

After being promoted to Ambassador in 1938, Oshima had been recalled to Tokyo in the wake of the German invasion of Poland in September 1939. Joachim von Ribbentrop, now German Foreign Minister, had made strenuous efforts to persuade the Japanese Government to leave him in place, but to no avail. Nevertheless, Oshima maintained his close contacts with the Germans and was one of the leading advocates of the Axis alliance. In the wake of the signing of the Tripartite Pact, he was sent back to Berlin as Ambassador.

In a speech given at Oshima's farewell party in Tokyo, Matsuoka Yosuke, the Japanese Foreign Minister, praised the newly appointed Ambassador. 'His thorough knowledge of German affairs far exceeds one's imagination,' Matsuoka said. 'He has developed the highest personal trust among the leading members of the German Government, thus he can have heart-to-heart talks with them.'

It was the product of those heart-to-heart conversations that the Allies were anxious to hear and it was not just the Americans who were to have access to them. For the breaking of the Purple cipher was just the bargaining chip the US Army needed as part of the tentative negotiations that were already in place for a codebreaking alliance with the British.

A few months earlier, the Bletchley Park codebreakers had succeeded in breaking the Enigma machine cipher used for all high-level communications throughout the German armed forces. Armed with their own bargaining chip, they had approached the US Navy in June 1940, offering an exchange of cryptographic information, but they were rebuffed.

However, a direct approach to President Franklin D. Roosevelt succeeded in winning his backing for an exchange of technical information. At a meeting in London with the British armed forces chiefs of staff, a month before Friedman's team broke Purple, the Americans suddenly suggested 'a free exchange of intelligence' on the breaking of the Japanese diplomatic ciphers.

Although Captain Laurance Safford, the commander of the US Navy's codebreaking operation OP-20-G, was still very much opposed to any major exchange of information, Friedman and Colonel Spencer B. Akin, the civilian and military heads of SIS, were both very keen. Despite the US Navy's reservations, Roosevelt approved a deal under which Britain and America would 'exchange complete technical information re Japanese, German and Italian codes and cipher systems' but which excluded an exchange of actual intercepts.

The cryptographic exchange accord was agreed by senior US and British representatives in Washington in December 1940. The following month, nearly a year before the Japanese attack on Pearl Harbor brought the Americans into the war, a four-man American delegation – comprising two US Army officers, Captain Abraham Sinkov and Lieutenant Leo Rosen, together with two US Navy officers, Lieutenant Robert Weeks and Ensign Prescott Currier – set sail for Britain carrying 'certain packages'. The presence in the party of Rosen, the technical expert who had constructed the so-called Purple machine, was significant. At least one of the 'packages' the Americans brought with them to Bletchley was a Purple machine.

'It was early in 1941,' said Barbara Abernethy, who was then working as Denniston's personal assistant. 'Commander Denniston told me he had something important to tell me. "There are going to be four Americans who are coming to see me at twelve o'clock tonight," he said. "I require you to come in with the sherry. You are not to tell anybody who they are or what they will be doing." '

Currier described landing at Sheerness dockyard on the afternoon of 8 February, and being met by a small delegation from Bletchley Park which included Tiltman. The crates containing the precious top-secret 'packages' were loaded on to lorries and the convoy headed west towards London en route for Bletchley, Currier recalled.

It soon became dark and the countryside was pitch black with rarely a light showing except for the faint glow emanating from a small hole scraped in the blacked-out headlight lens of the cars. When we arrived at BP, the large brick mansion was barely visible; not a glimmer of light showed through the blackout curtains. We were led through the main doors, and after passing through a blacked-out vestibule, into a dimly lit hallway, then into the office of Commander Denniston RN, chief of GC&CS. Denniston and his senior staff were standing in a semicircle around his desk and we were introduced to and greeted by each in turn. It was truly a memorable moment for me.

Barbara Abernethy served each of the American guests with a glass of sherry.

It came from the Army & Navy Stores and was in a great big cask which I could hardly lift. But Denniston rang the bell and I struggled in and somehow managed to pour glasses of sherry for these poor Americans, who I kept looking at. I'd never seen Americans before, except in the films. I just plied them with sherry. I hadn't the faintest idea what they were doing there; I wasn't told. But it was very exciting and hushed voices. I couldn't hear anything of what was said but I was told not to tell anybody about it. I guess it wasn't general knowledge that the Americans had got any liaison with Bletchley. It was before Pearl Harbor, you see, and presumably Roosevelt was not telling everybody there was going to be any liaison at that stage.

The British kept to the precise letter of the agreement, providing detailed information on how they had broken the Enigma cipher and on their work on a number of other codes and ciphers, including Tiltman's studies of the main Japanese Army system. But in line with the Washington discussions, no details were provided of any of the actual messages they had intercepted. Even if this had not been an American condition, it seems likely that the British would have raised it since they were concerned over the Americans' lack of a secure system for the dissemination of the 'Special Intelligence'.

Denniston told Stewart Menzies, who had taken over as 'C' in September 1939 when Sinclair died, that Currier and his colleagues had been 'informed of the progress made on the Enigma machine'. The Americans were given a 'paper model of the Enigma machine', detailing its wiring and how it worked, together with details of the Bombes, the primitive computers designed by the British codebreaker Alan Turing to break the Enigma keys. This was as much as, if not more than, the Americans provided.

Without a shadow of doubt, the most significant contribution on the American side had been the ability to break Purple, provided generously from the outset by the US Army codebreakers. The British were again able to read all of the 'State Secret' communiqués passing between the main Japanese missions and Tokyo, just at the point when Oshima was returning to Berlin to continue his close relationship with the Nazi leadership and the German High Command.

Safford complained at what the Americans received in return, horrifying the British, and doing nothing to assuage their concerns over US security, by writing an unclassified letter to demand that the Americans be given an Enigma machine. Safford later claimed that the British reneged on their side of the deal and had 'double-crossed us'.

The false perception that the British were holding back on the exchange deal, largely the result of the US Navy codebreakers' initial failure to understand the 'paper Enigma machine' the British had handed over, was to become endemic among a number of senior US officers. Yet, at the cutting edge, US codebreakers said there was nothing the British held back. Currier recalled an atmosphere of 'complete co-operation' and said the members of the American delegation were shown everything they wanted to see.

All of us were permitted to come and go freely and to visit and talk with anyone in any area that interested us. We watched the entire operation and had all the techniques explained in great detail. We were thoroughly briefed on the latest techniques applied to the solution of Enigma and in the operation of the Bombes. We had ample opportunity to take as many notes as we wanted and to watch first hand all operations involved. Furnishings were sparse, a desk with a chair for each of us, a pad of paper and a few pencils. The rooms were a bit cold and uncarpeted and a bit dusty but we soon found out that this was a condition common to all work spaces, including the Director's.

The British codebreakers also did everything they could to make the Americans feel at home, Currier recalled.

During lunch hour on one of the many days at BP, we were introduced to 'rounders', a game resembling baseball played with a broomstick and a tennis ball. It was a relatively simple game with few complicated rules; just hit and run and keep running. It was not long before I could hit 'home runs' almost at will and soon wore myself out running around the bases. Many of our evenings were spent at the home of one or another of our British colleagues. Food and liquor were both rationed, especially liquor, and it was not easy for them to entertain. Whisky and gin were generally unavailable in the pubs and most people had to be satisfied with sherry.

7

WORKING WITH THE AMERICANS

Two days after the American delegation arrived at Bletchley Park, Admiral John Godfrey, the British Director of Naval Intelligence, authorized a full exchange of Japanese signals intelligence between the Far East Combined Bureau and the US Navy's 'Cast' codebreaking and intercept site, on the island of Corregidor in the Philippines. The Cast site was based in an underground tunnel at Monkey Point, so called because of a colony of monkeys that had once inhabited the area.

Lieutenant Jefferson R. Dennis, head of the Cast codebreaking section, spent a week in Singapore setting up the procedures for the routine exchange of all information on Japanese codes, ciphers and intercepts. Dennis wore civilian clothes throughout his mission in order to disguise what was going on. He handed over a 'pinch' – a stolen version of the Japanese merchant shipping code; a naval personnel code; a new diplomatic hand cipher called 'Hagi'; and details of how to tell the various types of Japanese naval unit from their call signs.

But the primary target for both Shaw and Dennis was the Japanese Navy's General Operational Code, known to the Americans as JN25. In return for the material Dennis had brought with him, Shaw gave him 'a current JN25 book and the indicator and subtractor tables up to 31 January, on all of which the US Navy had no information'.

Prescott Currier had taken an 'almost empty' JN25 codebook with him to Bletchley Park, perhaps unsurprisingly given that the Japanese had introduced a completely new book only two months earlier. The new book, designated JN25b, was larger than the first. There were also several differences in the way in which the keys were generated. But this had not deterred the British codebreakers. Tiltman's early break into the superenciphered code and the fact that the Far East Combined Bureau had around forty people solely employed on JN25 put them in a distinctly advantageous position.

By May 1940, the original JN25 codebook had been sufficiently rebuilt for simple messages to be translated. This success and a bad mistake by the Japanese ensured that the introduction of the new codebook, JN25b, on 1 December 1940 was nowhere near as bad a blow as it might have been, said one of the naval codebreakers working in Singapore at the time. 'The Japanese introduced a new codebook but, unfortunately for them, retained in use the current reciphering table and indicator system. These had already been solved in some positions and new code groups were discovered immediately. But for this mistake on the part of the Japanese the form of the book might have taken a matter of months to discover.'

The JN25b book given to Lieutenant Dennis already had 500 of its 33,333 code groups recovered. He was also given 4,000 cipher additive groups and 290 indicator additive groups, all of which were from the old system in use before the codebook changed, which was now known as JN25a.

Although these additive groups were no longer in use, they covered the two-month window given to the codebreakers by the Japanese mistake. They were vitally important for the research into that period which was still producing new JN25b code groups. These in turn allowed sustained recovery of the new additive and further recoveries of other groups from the JN25b codebook.

The British in turn were grateful for another source of JN25 messages to supplement their own intercept sites. They were unable at Singapore to receive any messages by day from the Combined Fleet, based in the Japanese Home Waters, and reception of traffic from the Japanese Mandated Islands in the western Pacific was intermittent. The smaller sites at Hong Kong, Esquimalt, in Canada, and Auckland in New Zealand helped, but the Cast station was in an ideal site for reception of both the Home Waters and the Mandated Islands traffic.

The British were not co-operating just with the Americans. They set up an exchange arrangement with a Dutch codebreaking unit, known as *Kamer 14* (Room 14), which was based at the Bandung Technical College, in Java, part of the Dutch East Indies. A retired Royal Navy officer, Commander Burroughs, who was living in Java, was called up and appointed as Liaison Officer to *Kamer 14*. The technical exchange was restricted by London to information on diplomatic ciphers because the Dutch were deemed not to have made enough progress on the military and naval codes and ciphers. There was, however, a limited exchange of decrypts and intelligence on military and naval material, particularly where it had a direct importance for the other side.

Nave was meanwhile diagnosed unfit for service in the tropics and sent back on leave to Australia. Since he was flying via the Dutch East Indies, he travelled in civilian clothes and was issued with a civilian passport describing him as an 'accountant'. But once there, the doctors refused to let him go back to Singapore and he had to be loaned to the Royal Australian Navy to head up a new Australian codebreaking unit.

Captain F. J. Wylie, the head of the FECB, flew to Australia to discuss the setting-up of the new 'Special Intelligence Bureau' and co-operation with the Australian intercept units. There were two RAN intercept sites in operation, at Canberra and Townsville, and a small Royal Australian Air Force site at Darwin. Wylie toured all three sites and held a series of meetings with senior RAN officers, including Commander Jack Newman, the Director of Signals and Communications. He also briefed the Australian Prime Minister Robert Menzies and his Defence and Finance ministers on the British codebreaking operations.

The RAN agreed to provide the British with additional coverage of Japanese Navy, consular and commercial traffic, as well as Russian Navy traffic, which Singapore was now too busy to cover. Wylie agreed that Nave should be allowed to set up the new Australian codebreaking section, conceding that 'in wartime there are certain advantages in avoiding having all eggs in one basket and, in view of the necessity for Commander Nave to remain in Australia, considerable value should be obtained from a subsidiary organization'. But he insisted that its operations would have to be controlled by Singapore.

Wylie also flew to New Zealand to talk to the small Royal New Zealand Navy unit which had been formed in 1940 and as a result two senior RNZN wireless experts were attached to the Kranji intercept site.

The Australian Army had intercept operators and traffic analysts attached to Allied forces in the Middle East working with the Combined Bureau Middle East, a Bletchley Park offshoot based in the former Egyptian Flora and Fauna Museum at Heliopolis, near Cairo. There was no central signals intelligence organization in Australia itself, but Australian military intelligence had intercepted a number of Japanese messages which it had passed on to a four-man 'unofficial group' set up at Sydney University to examine enemy codes and ciphers. The group included Thomas G. Room, Professor of Mathematics, and Dale Trendall, Professor of Greek, a knowledge of mathematics being regarded as evidence of the necessary aptitude to understand codes and ciphers and the ability to master unusual languages an assumed prerequisite for mastering Japanese.

Nave's Special Intelligence Bureau was set up at HMAS *Canberra* in April 1941 to work on material provided by the RAN wireless operators at Canberra and Townsville, the RAAF intercept section at Darwin and a similarly sized military operation in an attic at the Victoria barracks, in Melbourne. Using GC&CS as a model, Nave began recruiting a small number of RAN officers with knowledge of Japanese and in June 1941 absorbed the four academics of the Sydney University cipher section.

> The military intelligence people had told me that Military Intelligence Sydney had a small group at the university who were studying Japanese cable messages. This showed most commendable planning by the army and also an excellent spirit on the part of the university staff who gave their time in the interests of the country. I met the gentlemen concerned. All agreed to come to Melbourne and the necessary arrangements were made by the army.

An exchange of information on a number of codes and ciphers was agreed between Shaw and Nave. As part of the exchange deal, Professor Room and one of Nave's RAN codebreakers flew to Singapore to 'pick up tips' while a Royal Navy Japanese interpreter, Paymaster Lieutenant-Commander Alan Merry, was sent to Melbourne to act as British Liaison Officer.

The British were still well ahead of the Americans on JN25 at this point and the additional traffic from the Philippines, Australia and New Zealand was helping them speed up the breaking of both additive and code groups. By April 1941, they had recovered 30 per cent of the new additive book, although it is not clear how many more of the code groups had been recovered at this point.

A full agreement on exchange of material was completed in May 1941. The Americans appointed a liaison officer, Commander Jack Creighton, to ensure that the exchange worked smoothly, Shaw recalled. 'To avoid duplication, a mutual signal was sent every three days, giving date and first three groups of JN25 messages received by each party; both would then send copies of the traffic which the other had not received.'

Hard copies and any correspondence on codebreaking methods were sent by safe-hand bag in the weekly Pan-American Airways 'Clipper' between Manila and

Singapore, securely stashed away in a strongbox specially built into the hull of all the Pan-American Clippers specifically to carry secret government documents.

Since it was 'well ahead with JN25 results', the Far East Combined Bureau was initially the 'controlling unit' for the deciphering of the JN25 messages, making the vast majority of the recoveries. An improvised one-time pad system was brought in to allow daily exchange of information. The increased co-operation allowed both stations to surge ahead with their recoveries. The Americans had developed a highly mechanized system of using punch-card tabulating machines to sort the code groups and they soon began to catch up with their British counterparts.

There was also collaboration on Japanese military systems between the British codebreakers and the US Army's 'Station 6' intercept site at Fort McKinley, near Manila. Two US Army codebreakers were sent to Singapore, where Peter Marr-Johnson, the chief British Army cryptographer, handed them partial solutions of two Japanese Army codes, and Lieutenant Geoffrey Stevens, the FECB's other military codebreaker, was posted to Washington to liaise with the US Army codebreakers.

By now Joan Sprinks and her fellow Wrens had arrived in Singapore and had been integrated into the watch system in operation at the Kranji intercept site.

Kranji was a very happy ship. We all mixed very happily together, except in the station swimming pool where no mixed bathing was permitted. Our mess and quarters had been built specially for the Civilian Wireless Service Personnel but were reallocated to us. The buildings were on six-foot concrete pillars and six of us were accommodated in each block, each with a well-furnished room, bathroom and small veranda. A Chinese 'amah' was provided for each block for cleaning and dhobying. The space under the block was a happy hunting ground for frogs and was presumably to discourage snakes and to keep out the flooding caused by sudden tropical downpours.

The Wrens were divided among the four watches alongside the British servicemen and Malayan naval wireless operators who had been drafted in to bolster the bureau's limited resources. George Gamlin, one of the British Army 'Special Operators', or Spec Ops, as they were known, recalled.

> The Kranji radio sets were rigged in banks of two, one tuned to the transmitting station, the other to the receiving station. Each operator grew to recognize the 'fist' or sending technique of the Japanese operators they were monitoring. If required, they could pick out a particular 'fist' from dozens of others. This ability became a valuable asset when Japanese units began changing their transmission frequencies and call signs. When this was reported to Kranji, an intense search of the air waves was undertaken, a gruelling task around the clock, not knowing where or when the lost Japanese Army transmitters would be discovered. Y operators searched through so-called 'banks' of frequencies. The operators who would recognize the missing 'fists' would hurry from set to set, to listen to any strange Japanese signal. Usually a head shake was the answer. Eventually, an exultant cry of 'That's him' would be followed by the search for the other end.

Regardless of which service they were in, the intercept operators all worked Royal Navy watches of four to eight hours on and four to eight hours off. With daytime temperatures inside the concrete watchroom often unbearable, the time off came as a welcome relief, said Joan Sprinks.

> Working in the watchroom was the hottest thing I have ever known. You had to be there to believe the heat. We were in a concrete building with no windows, no air-conditioning, constantly manned so that it was never aired, additional heating from the sets and a haze and smell of smoking that could almost be cut with a knife. We went on watch armed with giant flasks of iced 'ayer lima'

110

[lime water] and small towels to wrap around our necks to absorb as much as possible of the constant sweat. The tropical heat outside seemed almost cool by comparison.

The female operators were reinforced by a further ten Wrens in July 1941. But the third overseas draft of WRNS wireless intercept operators which was sent to Gibraltar met with disaster, Joan Sprinks recalled. 'They had sailed on the SS *Aguila* and had been torpedoed by the U-201 in the waters to the west of the Bay of Biscay, the ship sinking in less than a minute with very few survivors. We could hardly believe it. Some of those girls had been on watch with us at Scarborough. They were all really nice girls and first-class operators.'

Although the joint British and American efforts against JN25 did not allow them to break detailed operational messages, they were able to track the Imperial Japanese Navy and to build up a good picture of its activities through a combination of those messages they could decode and traffic analysis. The latter technique had been greatly helped by improvements in the British direction-finding network and by the introduction in early 1941 of radio-fingerprinting. This was a method of identifying transmitters by recording their individual idiosyncrasies on film which ensured that once a transmitter was identified to a ship or location, it could always be recognized, whatever call sign it used.

Despite America's new-found enthusiasm for intelligence co-operation with the British against Japan, it continued throughout the latter part of 1940 and well into 1941 to show remarkably little interest in supporting Britain's attempts to rein in Tokyo's expansionist ambitions in China and South-east Asia. But as the deciphered Purple messages began to establish a clearer picture of Japan's real intentions, the American attitude was to change dramatically.

The Japanese signalled their intentions from the very start of 1941, informing all their missions abroad that all future intelligence and propaganda must be directed at aiding the expansion of Japanese territories southward 'in order to secure supplies of war commodities'. Attempts to undermine and subvert the position of the British, American, Dutch and French authorities in South-east Asia and the gathering of military and naval intelligence were to be intensified 'so that the new order in Greater East Asia may soon reach fruition'.

Nevertheless, there was a good deal of disagreement within the Japanese Government of Prince Konoye Fumimaro over the extent to which it should go to achieve regional dominance. The Imperial Japanese Army, War Minister General Tojo Hideki and Foreign Minister Matsuoka Yosuke were quite prepared to provoke war with America and Britain but the navy was far more cautious. Admiral Yamamoto Isoruku, Commander of the Japanese Combined Fleet, had warned Konoye on the signing of the Tripartite Pact that Japan should at all costs avoid a conflict with the United States. The initial element of surprise and Japan's better preparedness for war would allow it to make early gains over the short term but it could not hope to win a sustained conflict against US economic might.

As a result of this conflict within the Japanese Government, a series of mixed messages emerged from Tokyo during the early part of 1941. The British codebreakers intercepted one telegram from the Japanese Military Attaché in Stockholm which spoke of the possibility of using the predicted German invasion of Britain as an opportunity to occupy French Indochina, but insisted that Japan had no wish to be drawn into a fresh war in the region.

The Bletchley Park report on the contents of the intercepted message was heavily disguised to protect its source:

We have learned through a very reliable channel that the Japanese Military Attaché in Stockholm has recently – on or about 24 February – made remarks to the following effect in the course of an intimate conversation.

The German General Staff has assured the Japanese

112

General Staff that the United Kingdom will be invaded this spring. The Japanese General Staff have hitherto believed this but have recently begun to have doubts. As a result the Japanese Military Attachés in Europe have been instructed immediately to investigate the possibility of a German invasion of the UK as Japan wishes to co-ordinate her actions in the Far East with such an invasion. Japan does not wish to be drawn into a new war in the Far East but hopes to exploit conditions in Europe with a view to occupying French Indochina. If Japan receives information that Germany is not, or not yet, in a position to undertake a direct attack on the UK she will proceed with greater caution in regard to French Indochina.

Very few people outside Bletchley Park were aware at this time of the work going on there and of the origins of some of the remarkable intelligence they were producing. As a result the 'Most Secret Source' reports were often treated with extreme scepticism, even by many British intelligence officers. The disguised nature of this particular report led one disbelieving member of MI2, the department of military intelligence covering the Far East, to say that if it were true 'the Japanese Military Attaché in Stockholm is indiscreet to the point of imbecility'.

Despite the suggestion that Tokyo was not interested in being drawn into a fresh war, Japanese officials in London were ordered to restrict their dealings with the British and to be ready to leave for home at a moment's notice.

Purple messages passing between Oshima in Berlin and the *gaimushoo* in Tokyo also provided the codebreakers with some of the earliest evidence that Hitler was about to turn on Stalin, his ally of convenience in the early days of the European war. They revealed in February 1941 that Matsuoka would be travelling to Europe, via Moscow, to have talks in Rome and Berlin with both Mussolini and Hitler. The Japanese Foreign Minister was reticent in his messages back to Japan, but he revealed that Hitler had hinted that he was preparing to invade Russia.

Although Matsuoka was in the process of negotiating a

neutrality treaty with the Soviet Union, the Japanese Foreign Minister told Hitler that 'it would be practically impossible to foretell what attitude the government of Japan would take at the time of such an eventuality'. But he added that in his opinion, he 'could not imagine that Japan would not attack the Soviet Union, via Manchukuo, if war were declared between Germany and the Soviet Union'.

The Purple intercepts also revealed Matsuoka's request for Japanese access to 'all Germany's inventions and lessons from the war'. It was immediately met, with Oshima reporting that four representatives of the Junkers aircraft company were travelling to Tokyo to set up a joint military aircraft factory, and adding that Germany was willing to loan Japan a number of ships. Oshima was told to inform the German Government that in return Japan was prepared to send it rubber acquired from Thailand.

The Führer's hints of the forthcoming German attack on Russia were confirmed in April, again through the Purple messages passing between Oshima and Tokyo. One US Army codebreaker who worked on the key message – broken in both London and Washington – said it described a meeting between the Japanese Ambassador and Hermann Goering, Hitler's most senior lieutenant. 'Goering was outlining to Oshima Germany's plan to attack Russia, giving the number of planes and numbers and types of divisions to be used for this drive . . . I was too excited to sleep that night. It was the liveliest news for many a day. We and the British informed the Russians about it but they were too dumbfounded to believe it at first.'

In fact, the British codebreakers working on the Nazi Enigma ciphers had been reporting German preparations for Operation Barbarossa for some time. But the warnings to Stalin did not come until later. Even the meeting between Goering and Oshima had failed to convince many in Whitehall that Hitler was about to turn on his Russian allies. The Germans were simply trying to intimidate Moscow, British military intelligence argued.

114

The codebreakers were not believed until 10 June, twelve days before the invasion, when the Japanese diplomatic section in Elmers School translated two messages from Oshima. One reported that Hitler had told him personally that war with the Soviet Union was now inevitable. The other suggested to his bosses in Tokyo that 'for the time being I think it would be a good idea for you, in some inconspicuous manner, to postpone the departure of Japanese citizens for Europe via Siberia. You will understand why.'

Two days after Operation Barbarossa began, Oshima reported that Ribbentrop had asked him for as much help as Tokyo could provide. The Japanese Ambassador described the German successes on the Eastern Front in glowing terms. More than 2,000 Soviet aircraft had been destroyed already, he said: 'Thus the Soviet air forces were completely annihilated and the German Air Force has gained, already, mastery of the air.'

Matsuoka's response seemed to offer the Germans what they, and Oshima, wanted. 'Japan is preparing for all possible eventualities as regards the USSR in order to join forces with Germany in actively combating the communist menace,' the Japanese Foreign Minister promised.

But although extending Japanese influence by attacking north into the Soviet Far East was still regarded as a feasible option even by some elements within the army, the predominant view was that Japan should strike towards the south, with an attack on Malaya through Thailand seen as the most likely starting point. One Cable and Wireless 'drop copy' supplied to the FECB in late April 1941 was an ominous message to the Consul-General in Singapore from the Japanese Military Attaché in Bangkok, asking for regular weather reports and the names of 'suitable residents' who could be used as observers.

Confirmation that the favoured expansion was southwards came with a telegram resulting from an Imperial Conference held on 2 July 1941. An Imperial Conference was a plenary meeting of the Japanese Government called only when decisions of great moment were to be taken and held in the presence of the Emperor himself. Hirohito looked down on the proceedings from a raised throne in front of a gold screen. Prince Konoye and his ministers were suitably placed below the imperial presence, seated around a rectangular brocade-covered table.

The *gaimushoo* telegram to Oshima informing him of the conference decision, which was deciphered in Bletchley Park's Japanese diplomatic section on 4 July, made it clear that Japan was intent on expanding its empire into Southeast Asia. The first step was the occupation of the whole of French Indochina, by force if necessary, to provide bases that would allow it to launch attacks against Malaya and the Dutch East Indies. Should Britain or America attempt to interfere, the Japanese would 'brush such interference aside', Oshima was told.

The Japanese intentions did not remain secret for long. 'Judging from confidential information and newspaper reports alike, Japan appears to have given up the idea of joining in against the Soviets – anyway for the time being,' Malcolm Kennedy noted in his diary a few days later. The Japanese were 'preparing for a showdown in Indochina, the idea apparently being to obtain naval and air bases so as to be in a position to strike at Malaya later'.

As alarm bells began to sound around Whitehall's corridors and across the Atlantic in Washington, the British Government ensured that the full import of what the Japanese were doing was made clear. 'There seems to have been a pretty good "leakage" to *The Times* about Japan's intentions to occupy bases in Indochina,' Kennedy noted. 'In order to prepare our own people for the coming shock it has apparently been thought advisable by HMG to indicate to the press what is about to happen.'

On 24 July Bletchley Park read a Purple message confirming that Vichy France had agreed to allow the Japanese to occupy southern Indochina, ostensibly to protect it from a possible British attack, a suggestion that infuriated Kennedy. 'Anything more contemptible than this attempt on the part of Vichy to hide up its own supineness is difficult to conceive,' he wrote in his diary.

The Americans were in the process of negotiating with the Japanese in an attempt to find a peaceful end to the tension building up in South-east Asia. As a result, there had been a dramatic increase in the number of messages between the Japanese Embassy in Washington and Tokyo, all of which were read by the US codebreakers. The perfidious Japanese attitude evident in the messages and Tokyo's privately dismissive attitude to the talks left US officials furious. Under pressure from the powerful China lobby in America, Roosevelt finally agreed to take firm action, imposing large-scale trade sanctions against Japan in tandem with the British and the Dutch. At a stroke, Japan's foreign trade was reduced by three-quarters and its oil supplies by 90 per cent.

The British, who had earlier been so frustrated by the Americans' lack of action, now became concerned at the extent to which Washington was prepared to go. The BJ (blue jacket) decrypts showed that Japan was already ordering businessmen and non-vital consular and diplomatic officials home from various points in the British Empire. The Foreign Office feared that the Japanese would now be forced to invade the British and Dutch Far East colonies simply to obtain the raw materials upon which the Japanese economy depended, and that war was therefore inevitable.

8

EAST AND WEST WINDS

The Purple decrypts of Oshima's reports to Tokyo were now providing the Allies with a good deal of useful intelligence on the war in Europe. The Japanese Ambassador had unique access to the thinking of the High Command and even of the Führer himself. As Hitler sought to draw the Japanese into the war with the Soviet Union, he had Oshima flown to his Eastern Front field headquarters in Rastenberg, East Prussia, for private briefings on the progress of Operation Barbarossa. By August, the Japanese Ambassador's telegrams to Tokyo were speaking of staggering Soviet losses 'estimated at between five and six million'.

The Purple decrypts also revealed the extent of the pressure exerted by Hitler and his lieutenants to get Japan to declare war on the Allies. Oshima reported that 'the Führer was not at all satisfied with Tokyo's attitude, particularly with regard to the continuation of Japanese–US negotiations'. This campaign culminated, in mid-August, in Hitler promising that 'in the event of a collision between Japan and the United States, Germany would at once open hostilities with America'.

Winston Churchill had just returned from a conference in Newfoundland with President Roosevelt at which they had cemented their special relationship and agreed jointly to warn the Japanese against any aggression towards

Malaya or the Dutch East Indies. The British Prime Minister received all the most important Bletchley Park decrypts each day, delivered in a yellowing leather box by Colonel Stewart Menzies, the head of MI6. When Churchill read the Oshima report of Hitler's promise to attack America, he sent it back to Menzies immediately. 'In view of the fact that the Americans themselves gave us the key to the Japanese messages it seems probable the President knows this already,' he wrote beneath the decrypt. 'But anyhow it is desirable he did know it. WSC.'

Two weeks later, on 6 September, Churchill went to Bletchley Park himself to thank the codebreakers for the unprecedented flow of intelligence he was receiving, both on the war in Europe and the increasingly tense situation in the Far East.

'Winston made us a very nice speech of thanks and went off to lunch at Blenheim,' noted Nobby Clarke. 'He had arrived in the usual cortège of cars with flags flying and must have been spotted by the local inhabitants. For lunch, the BP staff crowded out into the town and no doubt talked about the visit to all and sundry. Late that afternoon, an order came round to say that his visit must be kept secret.'

Earlier that day, at an Imperial Conference in Tokyo, the Japanese Government had been told by Tojo, in the bluntest terms possible, that there were only three alternatives open to them. They could back down in the face of American pressure and withdraw from Indochina, and eventually from China; they could stall for more time and continue negotiating with the Americans; or they could prepare for war.

The wind was taken out of the Japanese War Minister's sails by the Emperor, who reminded those present of the awesome consequences of what they were discussing. Tojo had hoped to railroad the Japanese Cabinet into authorizing an attack on Malaya and the Philippines, effectively declaring war on Britain and America. In the end, he was forced to agree that Japan should continue to negotiate for peace. But in return for this temporary compromise, he secured the Emperor's sanction to prepare for war.

This was to be only a minor setback for Tojo, but it was confusing for those attempting to interpret the Purple intercepts. Although the messages between Berlin and Tokyo were full of indications of the Japanese preparations for war with Britain and America, they lacked any conclusive evidence that the threatened confrontation was imminent. With Oshima under pressure from Hitler and Ribbentrop to persuade his political masters to open a second front against Stalin, he was as irritated by the lack of information as the codebreakers.

'It is an indispensable condition that envoys serving abroad should be kept apprised of the Government's policy,' the Japanese Ambassador in Berlin complained to Tokyo. 'One can only assume that the lack of clear instructions from you in these matters is from considerations of secrecy or because no definite policy has yet been formulated.'

The difficulties the codebreakers faced in 'rebuilding' the new JN25 codebook meant that the evidence from Japanese naval traffic was sketchy. Although Tiltman had broken JN25, he was now more concerned with Japanese military codes, and Bletchley Park's small Japanese section was limited in its ability to assist. Nor were the US Navy codebreakers at OP-20-G in Washington any help, having placed all their emphasis on diplomatic ciphers. During a visit to Washington in the late summer of 1941, Denniston was unimpressed with the priorities of the American codebreakers who had failed to read a single JN25b message. 'They have done very well, but only in one thing – Japanese diplomatic. Japanese naval and Japanese military are still behind,' he said. The veteran British codebreaker was particularly critical of OP-20-G's allocation of resources.

I feel they have really neglected the naval work. The staff there is interested in the solution of the cryptanalytical problem and the contents of the results do not concern them. The finished document based on the translation of

120

the cypher telegram is not always of the standard we aim to maintain. It might nearly be said that they wish to find mathematical formulae or mechanical methods to solve their problems while we aim to provide the various intelligence services with a clear and accurate text.

Denniston persuaded OP-20-G that since America was supposed to be taking the lead on Japanese codes and ciphers, leaving Bletchley Park to concentrate its resources on the German Enigma machine, it should do more work to help the Far East outposts in Singapore, Corregidor and Hawaii on Japanese naval material and in particular JN25. 'The section dealing with Japanese diplomatic is well staffed by cryptanalysts and translators and has a priority claim on the Hollerith machine room. This section has undertaken collaboration with BP and Singapore in investigation of the Japanese naval ciphers and they now regard this, as we do, as one of their most important research jobs.'

Fortunately, the exchanges between the British codebreakers in Singapore and their American colleagues in Corregidor had doubled the number of code groups recovered. Many routine messages and stereotypical movement reports could now be read if not immediately at least within a day or two. Those parts of the JN25b codebook that had been rebuilt were still no help in deciphering detailed operational messages. Nevertheless, even routine messages when combined with traffic analysis, direction-finding and radio-fingerprinting were capable of providing enough information to build up a substantial picture of what was going on.

Two days after the Imperial Conference gave the go-ahead for war preparations, the British codebreakers in Singapore reported, probably from the Dockyard Code broken by Nave rather than from JN25, that all naval vessels of the Japanese Combined Fleet, under Admiral Yamamoto Isoruku, had been recalled to base for the annual reorganization. Since they would normally have remained at sea for two more months, the British

121

codebreakers concluded that it seemed likely that the Combined Fleet was being prepared for war.

Meanwhile, Tojo was cranking up the screw at home, petitioning the Emperor to approve a military offensive. Konoye's determination to avoid war with America at all costs had led him to offer to meet Roosevelt for peace talks, a move seen within the army as a loss of face for Japan. With Konoye still arguing that the negotiations with America be allowed to run their course, Tojo let it be known that the army would withdraw its support for his government if he did not back war. No Japanese Government could hope to survive without the army's support. Konoye was now dead in the water. He resigned on 18 October and Tojo took over as Prime Minister while retaining the War Minister portfolio. The outbreak of war with Britain and America was simply a matter of time.

Bletchley Park now deciphered a circular to all Japanese consular posts abroad that ordered them to provide 'prompt and detailed reports of the movements of British, American, French and Dutch warships, aircraft and troops'.

The Far East Combined Bureau began picking up almost daily messages from the Japanese Consul-General in Singapore relating to subversion and intelligence gathering. He reported on the precise strength and location of defensive forces and anti-aircraft guns in the area around Singapore itself together with full estimates of the time it would take to knock them out. He described RAF organization and tactics; dispatched 'fishermen with a knowledge of surf conditions on the east coast of Malaya' to Bangkok to brief the Japanese Military Attaché, and reported that members of the anti-British Young Men's Malayan League KAME would act as guides for Japanese troops if they invaded Malaya.

Oshima was gung-ho at the prospect of a full-blown Axis military alliance against Britain. The successful attack on the Soviet Union suggested the Wehrmacht would have no problem occupying the United Kingdom, he reasoned. Japan should synchronize an attack on Malaya with the launch of the German invasion force across the English Channel, a move he believed would provide an answer to those concerned over the dangers of becoming embroiled in a conflict with America. 'Germany is not considering any compromise with Britain and is sure that after the occupation of the British Isles – even if an attempt is made to carry on the war from a dominion with American help – the British Empire will break up, after which a compromise peace with the Americans can be easily arranged.'

By the end of October the naval intercepts had left no doubt that the Combined Fleet had been mobilized. Given the strict Japanese attention to radio security, traffic analysis backed by direction-finding and radio-fingerprinting still remained the codebreakers' most effective means of tracking the movement of the Imperial Navy. By early November, although Singapore was still locating the bulk of the Combined Fleet in its home port of Kure, it had begun to detect large movements of Japanese transport ships south.

'There are increasing indications that Japan is preparing for further advances southwards with . . . the Dutch East Indies, Siam, Malaya or Burma, or any or all, as her objectives,' wrote Malcolm Kennedy in his diary. 'As she is feeling the pinch of economic strangulation seriously now, as a result of the freezing orders and of her inability to obtain oil, it should cause no great surprise if she had a crack at the Dutch East Indies before long.'

A firm indication that one of the key targets was actually Malaya came a few days later. The Far East Combined Bureau deciphered a message from Tokyo to the Consul-General in Singapore informing him that the *Asamu maru*, which was leaving in just over a week's time, would be the last Japanese ship to call there. An RAF 'Y' interception unit, 52 Wireless Unit, arrived in Singapore in early November to reinforce the British codebreakers, but resources remained stretched.

Meanwhile, the Japanese preparations for war escalated. Yamamoto formally concluded a 'Central Agreement' with General Count Terauchi Hisaichi,

Southern Army Commander, setting out Japanese plans to turn the whole of South-east Asia into a Japanese-controlled Greater East Asia Co-Prosperity Sphere.

None of these plans were available to the codebreakers at Singapore, Corregidor and Pearl Harbor. But despite the problems with JN25, the preparations for the initial phase of the Japanese offensive were clearly reflected in the naval traffic. Over the next two weeks, the codebreakers continued to record the movement of elements of the Combined Fleet south towards Hainan.

The Purple messages remained the best source of detailed intelligence on Japanese intentions. On 19 November the *gaimushoo* warned the Japanese Embassy in London that the international situation was 'tense' and told it to await a coded weather message on Japanese overseas radio that would indicate the opening of conflict with Britain, America or Russia. 'With America, the words: *higashi no kaze, ame* [Easterly wind, rain]. With Soviet, the words: *kita no kaze, kumori* [Northerly wind, cloudy]. With Britain, including invasion of Thailand, the words: *nishi no kaze, hare* [Westerly wind, fine]. On receipt of these code words all confidential books are to be burned.'

On the same day, Yamamoto sent a message to all his flagships ordering them to test 'the communications set-up required upon opening hostilities'. It was followed a day later by a second Yamamoto message to Fleet Commanders informing them that 'the second phase of preparations for opening hostilities' would begin at midnight that night. Both these messages from Yamamoto were intercepted by the British and the Americans, but the limited reconstruction of the JN25b codebook did not allow either to be deciphered.

Nevertheless, November provided the codebreakers with their most productive period so far on JN25b, recalled Neil Barham, one of the leading codebreakers at the Far East Combined Bureau. By now they had recovered more than 3,000 code groups, a tenth of the book, and although the recoveries they had made so far were still largely confined to routine messages, the General Operational Code produced 'intelligence covering a wide field'.

The Singapore codebreakers had worked out from a mixture of traffic analysis and codebreaking that the Japanese aircraft carriers had been reorganized into five squadrons. They had also deduced that a large number of passenger liners had been incorporated into the Combined Fleet as auxiliary cruisers, although in London 'this was not regarded as entirely reliable or authentic'.

The American 'Hypo' communication intelligence research unit at Pearl Harbor was not working on the JN25 code and as a result had become highly skilled at traffic analysis. On 26 November it produced detailed evidence of the formation of a special task force consisting of 4 Kongo-class battleships, 4 aircraft carriers, 2 seaplane carriers, 8 heavy cruisers, 13 light cruisers, 56 destroyers and 19 submarines. The task force was believed to be moving south. Singapore confirmed that 'a special force has been organized for an operation' and that large numbers of Japanese vessels of varying sizes were now known to be moving southward.

Despite the heavy movement of Japanese vessels, there had been a drop in the amount of Japanese radio traffic as Yamamoto ordered all units to maintain radio silence. Among those messages which were intercepted but could not be deciphered were two speaking of plans for 'exhaustive conscription' and the need to prepare extensive medical facilities. There was also a signal from Admiral Prince Fushimi Hiroyasu, the retired Chief of the General Staff, to his successor Admiral Nagano Osami, in which he said: 'I pray for your long and lasting battle fortunes.'

The most intriguing, with hindsight, were a report from Imperial Headquarters on the identity of any ships operating in the North Pacific and another that spoke of a 'northern force' as well as the southern task force that was being monitored. Had either of these last two been deciphered, they might have pointed to the fact that there was an additional target apart from Malaya, the Philippines and the East Indies. But they were not.

While the codebreakers remained completely unaware of the Japanese plans to attack Pearl Harbor, there could be little doubt they were about to go to war. Meanwhile, the Japanese team continued to negotiate in Washington as if nothing was happening. But the Purple messages made it clear that Tojo did not expect, or indeed want, the talks to succeed and that once they failed 'things are automatically going to happen'.

Fully aware of the Japanese preparations for war, Cordell Hull, the US Secretary of State, presented the Japanese negotiating team with an ultimatum. Japan must withdraw not just from Indochina but from China. No-one in the Washington administration could have seriously believed that the Japanese would accept these terms.

When the US demands reached Tokyo, both the army and the navy were furious. It was clear once again, as it had been during the drafting of the 1921 Washington Naval Treaty, that the Anglo-Saxon nations did not regard Japan as an equal and were determined to keep her down. Now at last Oshima was told what was happening. 'Breakdown of the Washington talks is inevitable,' the *gaimushoo* said in a signal sent to Berlin on 30 November and deciphered at Bletchley Park. Oshima was to brief Hitler immediately. 'The British and American attitude has been provocative and they have continued to move troops in all parts of East Asia,' the message said. 'Japan is therefore compelled to make corresponding movements and armed collision with British and American forces is feared. This may happen sooner than expected.' A day later, Japanese diplomats in London were ordered to destroy their codes and ciphers. They were issued with a limited number of special codewords to receive their remaining messages from Tokyo and began making preparations to leave. It was not until the next day that Washington received a similar series of messages, Rowlett recalled. 'As I look back at all the messages and other information available to us at that time regarding the Japanese

126

intentions, it becomes crystal clear to me that this message ordering the destruction of certain of Washington's codes provided the necessary evidence that the Japanese unquestionably intended to take some action which would make war between the United States and Japan a certainty.'

The Purple messages from Tokyo to Berlin also revealed the Japanese anxiety to ensure that Germany would support it in any confrontation with America. Oshima's problems in confirming this beyond a shadow of a doubt were exacerbated by Hitler's absence at Rastenberg, controlling events on the Eastern Front. The Japanese Ambassador managed, however, to secure a firm promise from Ribbentrop. 'Should Japan become engaged in a war against the United States, Germany, of course, would join the war immediately,' the German Foreign Minister said. 'There is absolutely no possibility of Germany's entering into a separate peace with the United States under such circumstances. The Führer is determined on that point.'

Meanwhile, the Allied intercept operators stationed around the Far East were reporting that the Japanese Navy had changed all of its call signs. Since these would normally remain in use for six months and had only been changed three weeks previously this was yet more evidence that a Japanese offensive was imminent.

By now more detailed analysis of the deciphered messages and radio traffic associated with the Japanese 'special task force' had allowed the British codebreakers to name most of the vessels involved and to state that it had been put together 'to carry out an operation in the south. Indicators are an attack on Siam, including possibly a landing on the Kra Isthmus [the narrow strip of land north of the Thai–Malay border].'

A diplomatic telegram from the Japanese Minister in Bangkok to Tokyo revealed that the Thai Cabinet was hoping Britain could be made to strike the first blow at Thailand to give Japan an opportunity to intervene. Landings at Singora and Patani, the most suitable places along the eastern Thai coast, and at Kota Bharu, the most northerly town on Malaya's north coast, would induce the British to attack the Japanese forces through Thailand, which would then declare war on the British 'aggressors'.

The British had accurately predicted the Japanese landing sites five years earlier and had devised plans for Operation Matador, under which British and Indian troops would occupy the Kra Isthmus to oppose the landings. But with continuing uncertainty over the American position and its forces stretched by the war with Germany, Britain could not afford to make a pre-emptive strike. The authorities in Malaya were ordered to hold the start of Operation Matador until the American position became clear.

Churchill sent a naval task force to the Far East to provide a deterrent against Japanese attack. Force Z arrived in Singapore on 2 December to a tumultuous welcome. It was led by the brand-new battleship HMS *Prince of Wales* and the battle-cruiser HMS *Repulse*. It was also due to comprise the aircraft carrier HMS *Indomitable* and four destroyers: HMS *Electra*, HMS *Express*, HMS *Tenedos* and HMAS *Vampire*. But *Indomitable* had run aground in the West Indies, leaving Force Z with no air support of its own and dependent on the RAF's Malaya-based Brewster Buffaloes, which had a very limited operational range.

The main question now was when precisely would the attack take place? The codebreakers guessed that the departure of the Japanese task force from Hainan would be preceded by a change in the JN25 additive. It came on 4 December with the introduction of a new table. While this robbed them temporarily of their limited ability to break the naval messages, it was not as bad as it might have been had the codebook itself changed. They now had nearly 4,000 code groups recovered, allowing them to get out additives on many of the most common messages and make further inroads into the codebook itself.

Meanwhile, Oshima was making frantic efforts to firm up Hitler's promise of support against America. The Japanese Ambassador told Tokyo he had negotiated a 'secret agreement' with Germany and Italy, adding that 'should a state of war arise between Japan and the United

States, Germany and Italy for their part will consider themselves at war with the United States'.

The British codebreakers at Bletchley Park, Singapore and Hong Kong were now on full alert, waiting for the 'Winds' code message. 'Owing to the critical situation was on duty at the office from 9 a.m. yesterday until 9 p.m. today,' noted Malcolm Kennedy in his diary for 6 December.

> From now on, for the time being, we are to take turns about at night in case anything calling for immediate action comes in.
>
> Incidentally, the All Highest [Churchill] is all over himself at the moment for latest information and indications re Japan's intentions and rings up at all hours of day and night, except for the four hours in each 24 [2 p.m. to 6 p.m.] when he sleeps. For a man of his age, he has the most amazing vitality. His chief form of recreation, I gather, is to get out onto the Admiralty roof whenever there is a raid on London and shake his fist at the raiders! As there have been no serious raids on London now for six or seven months he must be missing his recreation.

It was late on Sunday 7 December local time when Hong Kong reported having heard the coded Winds message. It had said: '*higashi no kaze, ame; nishi no kaze, hare* [Easterly wind, rain; Westerly wind, fine]. This was the signal that Japan was about to declare war on both Britain and America.

A few hours later, in the early hours of Monday 8 December, Singapore time, the first Japanese troops began landing on Kota Bharu beach in northern Malaya. It was the first in a carefully co-ordinated series of attacks against Malaya, the Philippines, Hong Kong and the only real surprise, Pearl Harbor.*

*Although the attack on Pearl Harbor took place on Sunday 7 December, the relative location of Hawaii and Malaya on either side of the international dateline meant that in 'real time' the attack on Malaya occurred first.

The inability to decipher any detailed operational orders sent in the JN25 naval code had prevented the code-breakers from noting the existence of the 'northern force' that was to attack Pearl Harbor. Persistent references to training by the Japanese 1st Air Fleet in the use of torpedoes in shallow water were also intercepted but not deciphered as a result of the difficulties with JN25. These messages would also have pointed to an attack on Pearl Harbor, where the US ships moored in Battleship Row were protected by waters too shallow for conventional torpedoes.

The surprise air attack on the US Navy's Pacific Fleet on the morning of Sunday, 7 December 1941, left 18 ships, including 7 battleships, destroyed or badly damaged, 164 aircraft destroyed and 2,341 US servicemen dead. Roosevelt denounced it as 'infamy' and promptly declared war on Japan.

That the attack on Pearl Harbor had come as much as a shock to the British codebreakers as to their American counterparts is shown by Malcolm Kennedy's diary entry for 7 December. 'A message received just before leaving the office this evening had indicated that the outbreak of war was probably only a matter of hours. But the news on the 9 p.m. wireless that Japan had opened hostilities with an air raid on Pearl Harbor more than 3,000 miles out in the Pacific came as a complete surprise.' Kennedy's incredulity remained undiminished the next day. 'That Japan, if she struck, would strike swiftly and heavily was only to be expected but the widespread nature of the attacks has come as a surprise and shows extraordinary audacity,' he wrote.

Nave, whose Australian operators had also been monitoring the Japanese preparations for war, said the Japanese Navy had mounted a massive deception exercise to prevent anyone realizing that Pearl Harbor was a target. 'One step which undoubtedly deceived the US Navy was the transfer of the wireless operators from aircraft carriers taking part in the Pearl Harbor attack to other ships in the Inland Sea,' Nave said. Since the Allied intercept operators were using the 'fists' of their Japanese counterparts to identify the various enemy radio stations, this move completely threw them, leading them to place the carrier force that was to attack Pearl Harbor in Japanese home waters. The JN25 additive change on 4 December meant 'there was no help from the codebreakers,' Nave said. However, wireless traffic to the Philippines and South-east Asia not only continued but increased with the intention of focusing interest on that area.'

The entry of America into the war was of little use to the British in Malaya. The Japanese, with far better aerial power, destroyed all but ten of the RAF aircraft within two days. Without air support, the retreating British troops had no hope of holding up the advancing Japanese. They were forced into a long, ignominious retreat down the Malay Peninsula.

Defeat followed upon defeat. One of the earliest and most demoralizing was the demise of Force Z on Wednesday 10 December, only a few days after the Japanese onslaught began. The British codebreakers monitored the Japanese aircraft messages reporting the sighting of HMS *Prince of Wales* and HMS *Repulse* but it was too late. Caught out in the open in the Gulf of Siam with no air cover, they were sitting ducks for the 33 high-altitude bombers and 53 torpedo-bombers of the Japanese 22nd Air Flotilla which attacked and sank them.

At a stroke, the Royal Navy's only two capital ships in Eastern waters had been destroyed. 'Something like a gasp went round the dining room at BP when the 1 p.m. news opened with the announcement that the *Prince of Wales* and the *Repulse* had been sunk off Singapore by J air attack,' Malcolm Kennedy wrote in his diary that day. 'A terrible blow just at this time when with the US Pacific Fleet so severely hit at Pearl Harbor we are so badly in need of every ship we can get.'

Three days later, one of the Far East Combined Bureau's outstations, a direction-finding unit at Penang on the west coast of Malaya, was forced to pull back. On Christmas Eve another team of direction-finders at Kuching, in northern Borneo, had to destroy their equipment and flee by sea. The detachment left at Stonecutters Island was not so lucky. Despite having been warned by the codebreakers that a Japanese army division was preparing to take Hong Kong, the military authorities preferred to believe the Japanese would not bother with the British colony. It was forced to surrender on Christmas Day. The four intercept operators destroyed their direction-finding and wireless equipment, but they and Alf Bennett were captured by the Japanese and spent the next four years in Japanese prisoner-of-war camps.

This was a fate that could not be risked for the members of the Far East Combined Bureau itself. They knew far too much about the breaks into the Japanese ciphers to be allowed to fall into enemy hands. Some of the family members had already been sent by ship to Australia and it was initially suggested that the unit should re-form there, but eventually it was decided to evacuate the naval section to Colombo, the new headquarters for the Royal Navy's Eastern Fleet, where it was thought reception would be better.

The army codebreakers were to go to Burma and mainland India while the army and RAF wireless operators stayed behind to monitor the Japanese air attacks. Arthur Cooper, a Foreign Office codebreaker who had lived in Japan for some time and whose brother Josh was head of Bletchley Park's air intelligence section, volunteered to stay behind. The Cooper brothers were both known for their brilliance: Arthur was the younger of the two and was rumoured to be able to complete the *Times* crossword in his head. When working at Bletchley Park, later in the war, he was said to have watched colleagues playing tennis each day for several weeks, analysing their technique. Then, never having played before, he borrowed a racket and performed like a veteran. Cooper was joined by a Royal Navy interpreter, Lieutenant-Commander E. H. M. Colegrave, four Royal Army Service Corps clerks and Lieutenant Norman Webb, who had worked for a Japanese subsidiary of Shell in Tokyo before the war.

Webb had been commissioned into the army on the outbreak of the war in Europe.

The radio security of the Japanese naval bomber aircraft attacking Singapore was not high, Cooper recalled. The codebreakers were soon able to work out that specific units, recognizable by the nicknames they used, specialized in certain targets. 'Thus when the unit airborne was recognized its probable target could be foretold, while from counting the number of individual calls and acknowledgements the strength of the forces airborne could be assessed. Results were telephoned to the local RAF defence and several successful actions were fought. The RAF became enthusiastically appreciative.'

Cooper, Colegrave and Webb were assisted by the capture, from one of the Japanese aircraft downed as a result of their work, of a codebook for the *kuuchi renraku kanji-hyoo 1-goo* three-figure air–ground liaison code used for air–ground communications. They stayed in Singapore until almost the last moment, getting out on a ship to Java on 11 February 1942, just four days before Singapore finally fell to the Japanese.

The fall of Singapore was a disaster of immense proportions for the British. The island was supposed to be an 'impregnable fortress', defending the Empire against all attackers – 'the Gibraltar of the East'. Its capture by the Japanese was described bitterly by Churchill as 'the worst disaster and largest capitulation in British history'. He was not to know that within weeks, the codebreakers would have sown the seeds of revenge, turning the tide of Japanese victory and putting them continuously on the defensive for the rest of the war.

9

THE AMERICANS TAKE THE LEAD

The news that the naval codebreakers were to move to Colombo sparked a series of weddings and a rush to crate up the unit's records. On 2 January, the day after Rene Skipp's wedding, they began loading the crates and boxes of personal belongings on to lorries and taking them to Keppel Harbour, where the troopship HMS *Devonshire* was waiting. The Temporary Women Assistants were given the option of going to Colombo with the codebreakers but most decided to stay with their families. Some of the staff took their cars with them to the docks in the hope of shipping them to Ceylon on board the *Devonshire*. The captain initially refused but finally agreed to take twelve of the codebreakers' cars as deck cargo.

'We left Kranji on 5 January 1942, on board the *Devonshire*, accompanied by HMT *Lancashire*, two destroyers and two cruisers,' Joan Sprinks recalled. 'As the Japanese had by this time driven a long way down the Malayan Peninsula, we were unable to take the usual route through the Straits of Malacca and headed south through the Banka and Sunda Straits. The food was pretty grim, the bread and porridge being full of weevils, but who were we to complain about such a minor detail?'

The voyage caused something of a problem for Lillie Feeney's attempts to keep her marriage secret and ensure the navy did not split her up from her new husband. 'When we got on to the ship to Colombo you had to say if you were married or single and so I had to tell my senior officer. She said, "I know." The best man had asked for leave and had to explain why. But we were very lucky, I think; because of the shortage of *kana* Morse operators, they were very good, they let us live out together.'

The codebreakers arrived in Ceylon on 14 January and moved into Pembroke College, an Indian boys' school about two miles inland from Colombo which had been requisitioned as a combined codebreaking and wireless interception centre.

The officers stayed in hotels while the clerks, wireless operators and Wrens were in hostels and boarding houses. All but the Wrens were free to find their own alternative accommodation. 'We were quartered in Galle Road, Colpetty, near Colombo, very near to the sea,' said Joan Sprinks. 'The kitchens were most unhygienic with piles of raw meat covered with flies lying on the floor.'

Aerials were draped over palm trees, wireless sets installed, and within five days the intercept station was up and running. The codebreakers started to try to rebuild the JN25b codebook using messages collected before departure from Singapore and what messages were being intercepted currently. They re-established communication with the codebreakers at Corregidor and began exchanging results. 'Working conditions were quite good,' recalled Joan Sprinks. 'One of us would leave half an hour before the change of watch to "shake" the relieving operators and this involved walking past long lines of rickshawmen sleeping near their vehicles, with only their coconut oil lamps to light our way.'

But while the personnel themselves had arrived safe and sound, some of the equipment had not. The bulk of the Hollerith tabulating machine was eventually traced to the dockside but a key part was missing and an officer had to be sent to Bombay to borrow one from the Indian State Railways.

More worrying was the non-arrival of a Purple machine

promised to the codebreakers several months earlier by Bletchley Park. Shaw sent an urgent signal to London enquiring as to its whereabouts.

> It was learned from Admiralty that the case containing the machine had left England in a warship and was transshipped at Durban to the freighter *Sussex*, although ordered to be conveyed only in a warship or military transport. At the time of the enquiry the *Sussex* was at an Australian port and in reply to a wireless message the master said that he had landed the case in question at Singapore at the end of December 1941 and obtained a receipt from the Naval Stores Officer.

A frantic signal to Singapore failed to find any trace of the crate containing the Purple machine. The Naval Stores Officer denied all knowledge of it. The Master of the *Sussex* insisted he had left it in Singapore. 'By this time the situation in Singapore was chaotic and it could only be hoped that if the case were there it had been destroyed or dumped in the sea by a demolition party.'

The alternative was too awful to contemplate. Had the Japanese found the Purple machine, the Allies' insights into the intentions of both Tojo and, through Oshima, Hitler would have been lost and the fledgling exchange of signals intelligence between Britain and America stifled at birth. Sadly, it would not be the last time that the precious secret of the extent to which the Allies were reading the Japanese codes and ciphers was to be put at risk.

By now Singapore had fallen and the three codebreakers left behind had gone to join the army operators who were at *Kamer 14*'s base in Bandung on Java, Geoff Day recalled:

> We arrived on Monday 2 February to a very heavy storm. The streets of Batavia were flooded and we took a three-and-a-half-hour train ride to Bandung. Fourteen of the seventeen-man rear party arrived on Tuesday 17 February. These boys were given quarter of an hour to get to a boat,

the *Wang Chow*, which was loaded up with high explosives and which they themselves had to stoke. It took them four days to reach Batavia. Six of the rear party had been sent to work as a mobile DF section at Serangoon village on the north-east shore of Singapore island and three of them were left behind. Another man went missing in Batavia, but turned up later, having been 'jugged' for alleged desertion and failure to destroy secret papers.

Two days after the attack on Pearl Harbor, the US Navy's Hypo codebreaking unit at Hawaii was ordered to forget the Flag Officers' code and join the attack on JN25b. At the same time, both Corregidor, in tandem with the British codebreakers at Colombo, and OP-20-G, the US Navy's codebreaking headquarters in Washington, had increased their own efforts to reconstruct the codebook, leaving the US Army codebreakers to provide the main effort on Purple and other diplomatic ciphers. By the end of January there was a marked increase in the additive recoveries.

As competition built up between the various Allied intercept sites to produce operational messages, Colombo found itself left behind. Their very closeness to the Japanese theatre of operations alone meant that the US Navy codebreakers on Corregidor led the way in breaking messages, Shaw recalled. 'Corregidor's output increased at an amazing rate. The telegrams from Corregidor were coming in such numbers that, even with augmented staff, we had difficulty in keeping pace with decoding them and applying the recoveries.'

The move from Singapore crippled the British attempts to break the Japanese naval codes. The number of messages they were able to intercept dropped dramatically. The loss of the Temporary Women Assistants caused problems; so too did the initial British reluctance to embrace machine technology. Breaking JN25 by hand was extremely labour-intensive. Although contact with their US counterparts at Corregidor had made the British codebreakers realize the potential of the Hollerith tabulating machines, the Admiralty did not, and continued to ignore their repeated urgent signals requesting a replacement for the missing part. The final straw was an outbreak of dengue fever that laid low the whole of the JN25b code-breaking section shortly after the arrival in Colombo.

The British codebreakers had managed to penetrate the new additive cipher before they left Singapore. But the move had broken the all-important continuity and, despite a number of crucial successes, it would be another two years before they would fully catch up with the breaking of JN25, said John MacInnes, one of the GC&CS code-breakers based in Colombo.

> The original work on this had all been British but from the start of co-operation with Corregidor in 1941, the burden was carried more and more on the broad shoulders of the US stations. Work on the British side was badly dislocated by the move to Colombo. The loss of depth on the cipher table caused by the break in interception during the move, and the subsequent reduction in volume, greatly hampered stripping in bulk.
>
> It was at this time that the US Navy first took the lead in cryptanalysis. The unit at Corregidor had, in return for its small size and its physical discomfort in the bowels of the fortress, the advantage of a very large intercept of clean messages, as it was at the geographical centre of the main Japanese operations. The unit made full use of this and the volume of cipher recoveries received from it in Colombo was very large.

As Corregidor began to evacuate its staff in the face of the advancing Japanese, the Hypo site at Hawaii took over its mantle as the lead station in breaking JN25. Hypo had just moved into the cellar of the Naval Headquarters at Pearl Harbor, dug deep into the volcanic rock. It was a completely open-plan office apart from one dividing wall to protect the codebreakers from the noise of the tabulating machines. The officer in charge was the 'tall, thin and humorously caustic' Commander Joe Rochefort, the leading Japanese expert in US naval intelligence for more than a decade. Born in Dayton, Ohio, he had served as an ordinary enlisted man during the First World War. He was commissioned in 1919 and six years later put in charge of the US Navy's cryptologic section.

Rochefort took over the Pearl Harbor Hypo site in June 1941, inheriting around fifty intercept or DF operators and an intelligence staff of twenty codebreakers and analysts. He transformed the station, turning it from a sedate peacetime organization into a bustling twenty-four-hour operation. But the decision from on high that it concentrate on the Flag Officers' code and traffic analysis, leaving JN25 to Corregidor and the British, seriously hampered its ability to produce intelligence. Let loose on the new JN25b, the Hypo codebreakers soon showed their true worth. For the next three months, Rochefort rarely left the office. He slept there and ate there, kept going by US Navy-issue amphetamines, and even when working was invariably to be seen wearing a silk smoking jacket and slippers. Rochefort insisted that there was a logical explanation for this eccentric attire.

I'd spend all of the time in the office, putting in around twenty or twenty-two hours a day. I would only leave when I had to leave and that was just about all. This went on for about forty-eight hours at a stretch. So it was a very fantastic operation down there. I started to wear a smoking jacket over the uniform. It was a sort of reddish smoking jacket somebody had given me. The main reason for wearing it besides keeping me warm was that it had pockets where I could keep my pouch and pipe. Then my feet got sore from the concrete floor we had down there. So I started wearing slippers because the shoes hurt my feet.

Long-term research was dominated by Washington with its larger resources both in terms of personnel and access to tabulating machinery. But while OP-20-G led the way in reconstructing successive JN25 codebooks, and in building up the necessary database on which the out-stations would come to rely, it was Rochefort and his Pearl Harbor codebreakers who dominated the race to break messages in real time.

By mid-February Malaya, including Singapore, Hong Kong, much of the Philippines, Guam, Wake and Sumatra were in Japanese hands. On 19 February, the 1st Air Fleet, the force that had attacked Pearl Harbor, struck a crippling and demoralizing blow against the northern Australian town of Darwin. A few days later the Allied codebreakers reported a build-up of Japanese naval forces in the Java Sea, apparently preparing to land troops on Java itself. On 27 February a joint US, British, Dutch and Australian naval force under the Dutch Rear-Admiral Karel Doorman intercepted the Japanese ships. Doorman made an audacious but ultimately unsuccessful attempt to outsmart the Japanese, going down with his flagship RNNS *De Ruyter*. The Allied force lost two cruisers and several destroyers. Japanese control of the sea and air around Java was now total; within days their troops were pouring on to the beaches with little or no effective opposition.

Two weeks later, General Douglas MacArthur, the com-mander of the US forces in the Philippines, pulled his men out, famously vowing to return. But some of the Cast codebreakers remained in the tunnel at Monkey Point until the very last moment, when they were taken off by submarine and ferried to Melbourne, where Lieutenant Rudi Fabian, the Cast unit's commander, had already set up a new intercept operation. Fabian had been born in Butte, Montana, in 1908. After a year spent at the Montana School of Mines he had entered the US Naval Academy. Known to his men as an often unreasonable 'hard charger', Fabian was a purely administrative head, in charge of a number of codebreakers with more senior rank. He was to create a number of ripples within the as yet undeveloped Australian sigint community and the greater field of Anglo-American collaboration.

The Cast codebreakers recommenced work on rebuild-ing the JN25b codebook, in conjunction with Eric Nave's

'Special Intelligence Bureau' and Newman's naval intercept operation which had now also moved to Melbourne,
Nave recalled. 'To accommodate the US party we had to
move from the navy office and a new block of flats,
"Monterey", was taken over by the Government, a section
being allocated to our activities: Commander Newman
and party on the ground floor, the US unit on the first
floor, and my party on the top floor.' New doors were cut
in the walls between the apartments in the Monterey
complex and members of the Women's Royal Australian
Naval Service were detailed to work as clerical assistants.
'A special site was chosen and an interception station
established. The US operators were reinforced by
WRANs, specially trained in a crash course to receive
Morse and the Japanese *kana*. They performed
magnificently.'

Nourma Gascoine was one of the first WRANs to arrive
at the new intercept station in Moorabbin, a south-eastern
suburb of Melbourne.

A signal was sent to pick up nine ratings and as this was
the first draft of WRANs to a US naval station, the powers
that be had expected sailors. Our conveyance arrived – an
open truck. We clung to each other for our trip through
wintry Melbourne and its suburbs, all the way out to
Moorabbin, arriving stiff with cold, tired out after sitting
up all night on the train, not even knowing where we were
going, and our welcome was just as frigid: two solitary
Americans to get us off the truck and take delivery of us.
With our luggage we tramped across the windswept open
spaces to our quarters, a seventy-five-year-old cottage
which looked as though it had not been cleaned since it
was built; with two beds in each of the enormous six
rooms. For the first few days, newspapers were at a
premium for protecting our possessions from the filthy
floors.

The naval station was manned by US Petty Officers who
had escaped from the Corregidor Tunnels in the
Philippines, where they had existed on a steady diet of rice

for some months. Arriving in Australia in just what they were wearing, the last thing they needed was to work with 'a bunch of girls' and in no uncertain manner we were made aware of this. The five telegraphist WRANs had three weeks to be taught to adapt to the USN methods. We worked day and night – went on watches within that time, and were so busy we could not look sideways, let alone communicate with the Yanks. We just worked, ate and slept around the clock, adapting to the eight-, nine- and ten-hour watches. These hours were even increased during the battle operations.

When later we finally swung into full watches, we were delighted with the longer time off between the three watches, enabling us to leave the station, get to know Melbourne and enjoy our other WRAN friends stationed at Monterey. Gradually we took our places, alternating on all the frequencies, and slowly the antagonism disappeared towards us.

At no time were there more than sixteen WRANs at Moorabbin, with seventy-five to one hundred Americans coming and going for the three years, so you can imagine that each of these WRANs has many memories that she cherishes. It is true that eight of us lived through the hell of typhoid fever, but the happy moments of building three marriages and friendships with the Americans that still exist overshadow the grim realities of those eventful days.

General MacArthur, who was appointed Allied Commander-in-Chief in the Far East and Pacific, also set up his base in Melbourne. He created his own army and air force signals intelligence facility, Central Bureau, with a mixture of Australian and US codebreakers, including Abe Sinkov, who had led the first US delegation to Bletchley Park.

Central Bureau was set up in Cranleigh, a large ivy-clad house in the Melbourne suburb of South Yarra. It was staffed by the Australian Army, the Royal Australian Air Force and the US Army. The intention was for the bureau to control a number of forward intercept stations in order to drag in as much Japanese air and military traffic as possible. The codebreaking staff in Melbourne itself consisted of eight officers and thirty enlisted men, of whom all but two were involved in full-time cryptanalysis. There was a fairly even split of Americans and Australians, plus Lieutenant Norman Webb, the British Army codebreaker who had escaped from Singapore with Arthur Cooper and Lieutenant-Commander Colegrave, both of whom were attached to Nave's Special Intelligence Bureau, which also included the British liaison officer, Lieutenant-Commander Alan Merry, Nave recalled.

> Arthur Cooper became a useful addition. Particularly so when we received a request from the Director of Naval Intelligence for assistance in drawing and making a facsimile of a Japanese pass used by them in New Guinea. The plan was to infiltrate a man into Rabaul, the HQ of the invading Japanese Army, and DNI had a man of partial Greek extraction who was willing to return to the area in which he had lived and traded. We were to produce the drawing from which a convincing stamp could be made. Arthur Cooper entered into it enthusiastically but I didn't fancy my life hanging on its successful use and suggested it be slightly smudged when used.

Neither the Americans nor the RAAF had been fully prepared for signals intelligence and initially it was the Australian soldiers, with their experience against the Germans, who dominated the Central Bureau operation. They were assisted by the British representatives and by Eric Nave. Although still running the Special Intelligence Bureau, Nave assisted in the establishment of the new unit, teaching Central Bureau's cryptanalysts how to break the Japanese naval air codes and ciphers, recalled Geoffrey Ballard, an Australian codebreaker who had seen service in Crete and the Middle East, breaking low-level German ciphers.

One of my indelible memories of those early days in Central Bureau was of the scene in Captain Nave's room upstairs in Cranleigh with the winter sun slanting through the lead-paned windows. There, in a class-like atmosphere, Captain Nave taught a small group of us how to unravel the Japanese naval air codes so effectively that, when we were posted to field sections, we were able to read them continuously and, when the codes changed, we were able to reconstruct them with the minimum of delay.

The military intercept operators included some of the British operators who had escaped from Singapore, among them Lance-Corporal Geoff Day. They were sent to the army's Park Orchards intercept site in Melbourne and formed into the Australian Special Wireless Group, he recalled.

Initially the ASWG consisted of returned soldiers from the Middle East who had been engaged in interception of German Morse signals enciphered using the German Enigma machine. Some had had a short introduction to the Japanese *kana* alphabet but our job was to make experts of them. My main personal memories of this time were of the dreadfully cold wet weather, and the fact that we were under canvas. The ground was a sea of mud, and I had six blankets to keep warm at night, and still went to bed with my clothes on. Talk about a change from tropical Singapore.

The group was gradually split up into a number of sections, the majority of which were to be sent north closer to the front line to intercept the Japanese military traffic. Day found himself assigned to 51 Section, bound for Darwin, a journey that involved a five-day train journey to Alice Springs followed by another five days travelling by road to Darwin itself. 'My main memory of the road trip, apart from the dust, was the hordes of flies one had to battle in order to eat,' he said. 'We finally set up camp at a place called Winelli, seven miles from Darwin.

Eric Nave (*second from left, front row*), the Australian codebreaker who pioneered the breaking of Japanese codes during the inter-war years, acting as interpreter during a visit by the Japanese Navy to Australia, January 1924.
Margaret Nave

John Tiltman (*right*) with Alistair Denniston, the original head of the Government Code and Cipher School (*left*), and Professor E. R. P. Vincent, later one of the Japanese naval codebreakers, before the move from Broadway Buildings to Bletchley Park. National Archives, Washington DC

Members of 'Captain Ridley's Shooting Party' arriving at Bletchley Park, the country mansion bought by the head of MI6, Admiral Hugh 'Quex' Sinclair, from his own funds as the codebreakers' wartime home.

Barbara Eachus

The GC&CS diplomatic and commercial codebreaking operations at No 7–9 Berkeley Street, London.

National Archives, Washington DC

The accommodation for the operators of the Far East Combined Bureau at Kranji Royal Naval base, Singapore, 1942. Geoffrey Day

A cartoon of Ernest Hobart-Hampden, whose 'uncanny skill' ensured that GC&CS kept on top of the Japanese codes during the 1920s and whose behaviour was frequently likened to that of Lewis Carroll's White Rabbit.
Hobart-Hampden Family Collection

Hugh Foss, the British codebreaker who broke the first Japanese machine cipher, the Japanese Naval Attache's cipher Orange and whose red beard and eccentric behaviour led the Americans to dub him 'Lend-Lease Jesus'. Foss Family Collection

Wren wireless telegraphists based at the Kranji listening station on Singapore. Joan Sprinks is second from left in the back row. Lillie Feeny is at the far right of the back row. Lillie Feeney

The British intercept and codebreaking base outside the North-West Frontier town of Abbottabad, where British codebreakers monitored Russian radio transmissions in the pre-war years. Dennis Underwood

An American Purple machine designed to decipher messages enciphered by the Japanese Type B diplomatic cipher machine, also known to the Japanese as *97-shiki-oo-bun-inji-ki*.

National Archives, Washington DC

Frank Rowlett (*back left*), who broke the Purple machine, Abe Sinkov (*right*), who took the Purple secret to Bletchley Park, and William Friedman (*seated*), the 'father' of the US Army codebreaking organization.

Oshima Hiroshi, the Japanese Ambassador to Germany, whose reports from Berlin, sent in the Purple cipher, kept the Allies informed of what was going on inside Germany. Oshima is seen talking to a Wehrmacht general in the foyer of the Hanover Opera House.

© Public Record Office, WO208/4702

A cartoon by a Bletchley Park codebreaker depicting the variety of unusual people working there. © Public Record Office, HW3/171

Members of Hut 7 during a Japanese language course. Angus Wilson is pictured third from right, front row, Bentley Bridgewater on the extreme left, and Isobel Sandison fifth from left also front row. Isobel Sandison

攻撃	メイ	(ヲ)攻撃セヨ(地點)	フヨトウ	重砲
	ヌチ	(ノ)敵(…)ヲ攻撃セヨ	ロツヲホ	野砲
	ノロ	敵…ヲ…	レナヤチ	海岸砲
	ハチ	敵ノ…(方)ヨリ攻撃セヨ	マレオモ	指揮所
撃	ヌス	攻撃法第…法	ホレツヲ	無線電信所
	ニキ	展開セヨ	ケフウマ	兵舍(…車)
目	ノホ	攻撃目標(知ラセ)	ラキヌカ	格納庫
	ヌヘ		ツツノサ	飛行場
	ラヨ	攻撃[…]目標發見(位置…)	ロツテイ	滑走路
	キヲ	攻撃目標ヲ(…ニ)變更セヨ	ホレワハ	重油槽(タンク)
	ヌイ	攻撃[…]目標發見セズ「ナシ」(位置…)	ナホホシ	鐵道線路
	ノエ	順撃セヨ 目標分擔	ノマスロ	鐵橋
標	ホマ	目標[…]ヲ監視セヨ	ラツモタ	密集部隊
	ラツ		フラルヌ	A
	ヌア	敵(…)ヲ撃退[攪]セヨ	マレコリ	B
	ヤレ			
	ヌマ	(方面)(高度)…百米以下ノ爆撃可能(ト認ム)		
	ミウ	敵(…)附近下層雲高…百米同高度以上爆撃不可能ナリ		
	ハホ	敵(…)上空附近斷雲アルモ斷雲上方ヨリノ水平爆撃可能ト認ム		
	ヌネ	(方向)爆撃不可能(ト認ム)		
	ロク	(方向)爆撃困難(ト認ム)		
	マサ		レレホタ	C
	ミホ	(ヲ)搜索[偵察]セヨ	ネネマチ	D
雑	ムユ	(ノ)搜索[偵察]ヲヤメ	ヨレマソ	1
	ラシ	(ノ爲)搜索[偵察]困難ナリ	ケナトエ	2
	ランカ	(…ノ爲)(…ノ)狀況明ナラズ	フマルノ	3
	ハキ		キノルニ	4
	ミヌ	高度…百米ノ風向…風速…	ホマキラ	5
	ロヘ		ネマカモ	
	ニヲ		レキヒサ	
	ムヒ	(ハ)全力ヲ擧ゲ…ヲ攻撃[…]セヨ		
	ナル	(ハ)(第…次)攻撃ハ全力ヲ陸戰隊[…]當面ノ敵陣地[…]ニ指向セヨ		
	ヌセ			
	ワシ	本日戰鬪機[…]攻撃參加ヲ取止ム		
	モセ	本日戰鬪機攻撃參加ヲ取止メ攻撃隊ノミヲ以テ…ヲ攻撃セヨ(攻撃豫定時刻…)		
	ヒロ			
	ヌシ			
	ヒツ			
	ノヌ			
	ヒウ			

A page from a Japanese Navy air-ground codebook, designated 2867.

MOST SECRET

J.N.25C/13

June 06/130/1942   16.1 Mc/s   T.o.r. 0932

```
        To:-  TU WI 904    -
F/I. ⊙      MI YO RE      1st Sect. Naval Staff Imp: HQ
            I NU 804      Comb. Flt exclud: Subs.
            HI TI SO      -
From:       MA RA KI      C. of S. KURE Nav: Dist.
            MEDINISARI•KERAMA [?]
```

<u>TEXT</u>:-   Army Transport convoys (ships largely empty) leaving

Japan for the south and desiring special escort as follows:-

Leaving on 10th July for BATAVIA

ZENYOO MARU JKOL, KINUGAWA (鬼怒川) MARU JURM,
SHINNOGAWA (信濃)MARU JBTI, KANSAI (関西)MARU JPZO,
MAKO (邦古)MARU JRWZ. Speed of convoy about 13 knots. Leaving on
17th July for SINGAPORE SENKOSAN (洗香山) MARU JTNL, SOBO (相木莫)MAR
JWUN, HIROGAWA (宏川) MARU JJFO. Speed of convoy about 14 knots.
AKIURA (昭浦) MARU JMKM (for SAIGON), YAMABUKI (山吹) MARU JCO
(for [blank]). Speed of convoy 12•5 [knots].

A rare Bletchley Park decrypt of a JN25c message. Movement reports such as these were the most commonly read JN25 messages. © Public Record Office, HW23/1

Interception of *kana* traffic began two weeks later and searching to establish frequencies became the order or the day. The operators worked out of two "set trucks" and intercepted around the clock.'

The unit under Captain Ralph Thompson intercepted Japanese military and air activity to the north of Australia, tracking aircraft movements and establishing patterns of activity. High-level codes and ciphers were sent back to Central Bureau for processing, along with logs of all transmissions. Army intelligence analysts like Geoff Ballard working alongside the intercept operators broke low-level codes and did on-the-spot traffic analysis. They were able to predict the Japanese schedule of fighter and bomber movements and alert the RAAF, which sent its own aircraft to attack the Japanese on the ground in Timor before they had a chance to take off. When Japanese aircraft did manage to get through their numbers were greatly reduced and Australian Spitfires were already in the air waiting for them, Geoff Day recalled.

We were a close-knit group and formed close friendships between British and Aussies. Our campsite was simply an open-air affair; we literally slept under the stars (and a mosquito net). The chief danger was green ants, which infested the trees, and march flies. Both pests could inflict painful bites. There wasn't much we could do in leisure time; some went to Darwin's beach for a swim and sun bake but, as far as I know, there was no fraternizing with the locals or other troops. The need for secrecy was paramount.

A few months later Day was ordered back to the Special Wireless Group headquarters and training base at Bonegilla, around 150 miles north-east of Melbourne, where he was needed to help train the new recruits, who now included an increasing number of women. With able-bodied men wanted at the front line, the group had begun to recruit a number of members of the Australian Women's Army Service as intercept operators.

Joy Roberts, from Ballarat, sixty miles west of

145

Melbourne, was just eighteen when she joined up.

> As my eighteenth birthday approached I was repeatedly
> asked what I would like as a present. The only answer I
> could or would give was: 'Please let me join the army.'
> After four weeks of discussion and dare I say some argu-
> ment – in those days girls did not argue with their parents
> – my really wonderful gift, their consent, was given to me.
> I wrote enquiring if I might enlist. The papers came back
> within weeks, I replied, filling them in, went for a medical,
> and went into the 'rookie' camp at Balcombe, Victoria, on
> 29 December 1942.

They were sent to Heidelberg, near Melbourne, for
assessment and then posted to Bonegilla to be given signals
and wireless training. 'After we were taught to send and
receive the Morse code, sixteen of us were sent to
Australian Special Wireless Group where we had to forget
about sending and concentrate on receiving, at a very fast
speed, the Japanese *kana* Morse code. Some of those
signals I still recall. We used to work four-hour shifts.
How I enjoyed those days up there.'

By now the Special Wireless Group had moved to
Kalinga, just outside Brisbane, and it was while there that
Joy fell in love with one of the young British instructors.
'The army took every precaution to ensure that no
extracurricular activity took place between the men and
women,' said Geoff Day.

> There was a road through the middle of the camp – men's
> quarters on one side, women's on the other, and women's
> huts were guarded at night. However, there was a sheltered
> creek at the back of the camp which would have had a few
> tales to tell if it could have talked. I proposed to Joy there
> and she accepted. She was very pretty and we were very
> much in love. We bought our engagement ring in Brisbane
> and then as word got out she was transferred back to
> Bonegilla – about 1,000 miles to the south. Engaged couples
> were not allowed in the same camp, no matter what.

They arranged to be married in Ballarat on 18 December 1943, but since both of them could not get leave until their wedding, Joy's parents had to make all the arrangements, Day recalled.

Joy was aged nineteen, engaged to someone who was not only completely unknown to her parents but wasn't even an Australian. So it was with a certain amount of trepidation that I arrived at Ballarat a couple of days before the wedding, meeting Joy's parents for the first time. Well, I was greeted like a long-lost son. They couldn't have been nicer. Our engagement was about as long as our courting period. But it was a very long marriage, fifty-four years. Joy died of lung cancer on 30 March 1998.

Early in the war, the ASWG supplied intercept operators to help Eric Nave's Special Intelligence Section to monitor Japanese naval messages. They included a number of Women's Australian Auxiliary Air Force operators, among them Joy Linnane, who joined up in April 1942.

While on the rookies' course there was a call for volunteers for a special, interesting course. Since anything was better than learning to march and salute, I volunteered and found myself involved in a most extraordinary interview. I was accepted, not knowing for what, was sworn to secrecy and found I belonged to Central Bureau for the duration. The thirteen WAAAFs accepted for the job were among the first to learn *kana* Morse and we were sent first to Point Cook, in Victoria, where we operated from a building known as the 'Hush-Hush Hut' intercepting naval *kana* from submarines operating along our coast. Since we worked on Tokyo time, we were out of step with the rest of the station. During my six-month tour, I never ate in the mess. We collected what food was available and cooked it ourselves over a radiator in the hut. Rarely did we ever have more than two hours of sleep at one time. We had a brief course in unarmed defence and in the use of firearms. We worked behind bolted doors and shaded windows. A

Smith & Wesson revolver was always kept at the door and there was an emergency button near each radio set. It was a memorable experience.

The WAAAFs were later taken off naval tasks and posted to the RAAF's No. 1 Wireless Unit, at Townsville, on the Queensland coast. The building in which they worked was built of reinforced concrete but camouflaged as a farmhouse, with features such as windows, railings and a trellis painted on, Linnane said.

We lived in a bush camp under fairly rough conditions and worked from a wonderfully camouflaged operations room made to look like a farm. No. 1 Wireless Unit was the first of seven WUs that were formed during the war, all air force personnel. Since there was a large team of male operators already there, the workload on the thirteen WAAAFs was considerably improved. At Point Cook, we worked four hours on, four off around the clock, no stand-down. At Townsville, it was eight on and eight off and sixteen hours stand-down after a week or so.

The RAAF and WAAAF intercept operators played an invaluable role in predicting Japanese air raids, assisted by four experienced US Army operators who had escaped from Station 6 at Fort McKinley in the Philippines. The Townsville operation was frequently able to provide Allied air defences in Australia and New Guinea with up to seven hours' notice of enemy attacks, Linnane recalled.

We intercepted air-to-ground and air-to-air messages sent by enemy aircraft often on their way to bomb our bases. As each message was intercepted, it was quickly passed into the intelligence room. Enemy aircraft positions were fixed by DF and warnings forwarded to the targeted areas. It was always a great satisfaction to operators when enemy aircraft signalled 'I am being attacked', and we knew our warnings had got through. We were a dedicated group and gained great satisfaction from our work. We had lots of

148

fun, too – dances in the rec' hut, swimming trips to Magnetic Island, but always with our own unit. I soon learned not to accept invitations from outside casual acquaintances. Their interest was mostly not in me but sadly in what went on in our top secret ops room.

There were other local pests to put up with, Linnane recalled. 'I was on the dog watch one night and it was just sunrise. I was feeling drowsy and decided to take a few minutes' break in the fresh air and to splash some water on my face. The ablution block was some twenty yards away – a fragile hut offering a hand basin and two toilets with a timber divider, halfway to the roof.' While there Linnane decided to use the lavatory.

Then I looked up. Gazing down at me from the top of the divider was the speculative eye of a snake. It appeared to have a goodly length of body spread along the timber. I immediately lost all interest in using the toilet and all I wanted was out. The difficulty was that each time I moved to pull up my jeans and to open the door, the snake slid another couple of inches down the wall. I was almost frozen with horror, but knew I must get out immediately as the situation could only worsen.

Dragging on my jeans, I shouted for the guard to come in. He was young and replied that regulations prevented him from entering the female ablution block. Exasperated, I sent him off to get the sergeant of the guard. The snake and I were still having eyeball confrontation when he arrived and said: 'Oh gosh. What do you want me to do about it?' I suggested he dispatch it with the Owen gun he was carrying, at which stage I returned to work. As I left the building he called out to me: 'Hey, Sarge. Why were you so scared?' I wasn't scared, I said, I was terrified because the snake was eyeing me with so much interest. 'Don't kid yourself,' he replied. 'He wasn't interested in you. He was protecting his mate who was curled up behind your toilet.'

10

A TRICKY EXPERIMENT

Bletchley Park's Japanese naval section was now under the control of Hugh Foss, who had grown a wild straggly red beard which only served to accentuate his eccentricity. The section had been expanded slightly, but with only thirteen members, including clerks, and a severe shortage of Japanese-speakers it had no chance of making any headway against JN25. The only traffic it received in anything approaching real time came by motorcycle courier from the Royal Navy intercept site at Flowerdown, near Winchester in Hampshire.

Juliet MccGwire was one of eight Wrens posted to the Flowerdown station as Japanese intercept operators.

We worked in the 'Y Hut' with sailors who were taking down Morse signals in pencil as numbers and the alphabet plus signs to account for Japanese. We Wrens typed the coded signals on special typewriters with extra keys adapted to Japanese coding and the result was sent to Bletchley. We did watchkeeping in four shifts and the sailors in three so they never had a day off. One sailor regularly missed his sleep to go to London for the Proms. My colleagues were extremely pleasant as well as conscientious and everything was busy and so secret that sometimes it was hard to focus on a reason for having to work so mindlessly. I longed for a grain of information to sustain me. But senior people did not talk to or encourage us. We lived in our own world and in some ways were happily independent.

A reorganization of Bletchley Park, designed to make the operation more efficient, had seen Commander Edward 'Jumbo' Travis put in charge and Denniston moved sideways. He retained control of the diplomatic section, which was moved back to London to make room for the new codebreakers needed for the service sections. The decision infuriated Malcolm Kennedy, who complained in his diary that he had only just bought a new house in nearby Woburn Sands.

Orders definitely issued for our branch of the FO to return to London next week. Feel very sore about it as the move has been manoeuvred by certain 'interested parties' and by gross misrepresentation of facts while AGD [Denniston] is so utterly spineless that, on his own admission, he has made no attempt to point out all the serious snags and difficulties involved. No small portion of the personnel who, for one reason or another, are unable to go have had to resign and for many of us the move will entail 4 to 5 hours' travel daily to and from work. Yet AGD has the brass to contend that efficiency will be increased 'in the tenser atmosphere of London'!

The British naval codebreakers in Colombo had solved some of their manpower difficulties by recruiting an extra fifty Temporary Women Assistants from among the local military and expatriate communities. They had also acquired the services of one of *Kamer 14*'s codebreaking experts, Shaw recalled. 'When Batavia fell, the Dutch naval C-in-C with a few key personnel, including Lieutenant-Commander Leo Brouwer RNN, flew across the Indian Ocean and, failing to find Ceylon, landed in India with their last pint of fuel. They refuelled and flew back to Colombo. Lieutenant-Commander Brouwer, a Japanese linguist, joined our JN25 team where his Special

Intelligence experience and knowledge of the area around the Dutch East Indies were of great use.'

But there remained an acute shortage of Japanese linguists both at Bletchley and in Colombo. John Tiltman, the head of Bletchley Park's military section, consulted the School of Oriental and African Studies in London, which had already been training a small number of RAF Japanese interpreters. The SOAS experts told Tiltman that it took five years to train someone properly and two years was the absolute minimum required for any kind of decent standard. This was clearly far too long so Tiltman decided to set up an 'experimental course' of only six months using young men who had already shown aptitude for learning unusual languages as potential codebreakers. 'I was advised to recruit classical scholars of from eighteen to twenty years of age from Oxford and Cambridge,' Tiltman said. 'For a short but glorious period I achieved considerable personal popularity at both universities because I was the only person who wanted classical scholars because of their attainments in Latin and Greek.'

Jon Cohen was reading Greats at Balliol when the Japanese launched the attacks on Malaya and Pearl Harbor. Shortly afterwards, he was asked if he would like to learn Japanese.

A lot of the British people who knew Japanese in the Diplomatic, Consular, and Colonial Service and suchlike had been rounded up by the Japanese in places like Hong Kong and Shanghai. So there was a shortage of people who could translate Japanese in the Government Code and Cipher School. I was approached by the master of my college, Sandy Lindsay, who had no doubt been asked by Colonel Tiltman to recruit some people who might be capable of learning Japanese in a very short space of time. He didn't tell me anything about what I was to do and I don't think he knew.

The School of Oriental and African Studies said it would take two years to teach anybody Japanese. But Tiltman had taught himself in a few months and thought it would be possible with students like myself. So we were recruited and went first of all to Bedford to the Gas Showrooms at Ardour House where about two dozen of us, some from Cambridge and some from Oxford, were taught Japanese by an elderly captain in the navy. Oswald Tuck taught us, I think brilliantly, for a period of about four months.

Tuck, who had served in naval intelligence during the First World War and was now sixty-five, was brought out of retirement to run the course. Tiltman asked him if he felt he could manage to teach young students enough Japanese to break codes in six months. 'The idea sounded impossible but was worth trying,' he noted in his diary. Tuck had left school at the age of fifteen to go to sea. He had learned to speak fluent Japanese, of his own volition and very much against the mood of the time, during a spell on the China Station, and subsequently served as Assistant Naval Attaché in Tokyo.

There were about twenty-three students on the first course, most of them classicists and including only one woman. They studied from 9.30 to 5 on weekdays plus Saturday morning. Tuck was a natural teacher, able to instil his own enthusiasm for the Japanese language in his students and willing to employ a number of innovative teaching methods. The youngest student on the first course was Maurice Wiles, who had been recruited by his brother's tutor at Cambridge.

My elder brother Christopher had been up for two years at Christ's before the war and had won the Porson Prize for Greek verse two years running. When his tutor Sidney Grose recommended him to Colonel Tiltman, he recommended me too. So we started at this course in Bedford, above the noisiest crossroads in the town, and in walked Captain Tuck, who was a very small, very dignified ex-naval man with a neat white beard and this old-world civility which seemed old-world even in those days.

153

Tuck's opening gambit was to tell his new students that they had not greeted him properly. 'When I come into the room,' he said, 'you are all to stand up. I shall then say "*shokun ohayo*," which means: all you princes are honourably early. You will then reply, "*ohayo gozaimasu*," which means: honourably early it honourably is. I shall now leave the room and come in again and we shall do this.' Tuck's teaching methods were innovative. Every day the students moved back one row, with those in the back row moving to the front.

Prior to taking on the Bedford course, Tuck had worked at the Ministry of Information, censoring dispatches by Japanese journalists based in London, and these provided the students' texts. 'We did a lot of learning and practice on our own,' said Wiles, 'but Tuck was very effective in getting us into the language. The pressure of the war and the knowledge that many of our peer group were in circumstances far less comfortable than ours rather concentrated the mind . . .'

The students' spare time was spent in the pubs of Bedford and in privileged access to performances by leading classical musicians, recalled Jon Cohen. 'The BBC moved its classical music section to Bedford and they gave the services free tickets, so we had endless wonderful first-hand music.'

After about four months, Tiltman decided to send two of the students to the Japanese diplomatic section which had now moved back to London and was based with the rest of the GC&CS diplomatic and commercial sections in Berkeley Street, off Piccadilly. 'The question was whether the course was good enough,' Cohen said. 'So two of us, myself and another, were sent to work in this office in London for a short while to be tested by the people who were long-term interpreters into Japanese. We seemed to satisfy them.'

The success of the course sparked a mixture of disbelief and embarrassment at SOAS, which had suggested it could never be done, said Wiles. 'They had always said that the war would be over before anyone was anywhere near good enough at Japanese to be useful. When their experts tested two of the students at the end of the course, they were amazed.'

Bletchley Park's air intelligence section under Josh Cooper ran its own special short-term Japanese course since it required a different kind of linguist capable of listening to the clear speech passing between pilots and their ground controllers. Cooper was one of the more eccentric codebreakers at Bletchley Park, a fact reflected in the course he selected for his students of Japanese. It was described by Tiltman, with some understatement, as 'a rather more tricky experiment' than the Bedford code-breakers' course.

What the Royal Air Force needed were interpreters who could read air-to-ground and air-to-air conversations. For this purpose my counterpart in the air section, J. E. S. Cooper, started an intensive eleven-week course at which the students were bombarded incessantly with Japanese phonograph records, ringing the changes on a very limited vocabulary. The course was directed, not by a Japanese linguist, but by a phonetics expert. I remember taking a US Army Japanese interpreter, Colonel Svensson, round the course. Stunned by the volume of sound in every room, Svensson mildly asked the Director whether all the students made the grade and the reply he received was: 'After the fifth week, they're either carried away screaming or they're nipponified.'

The American codebreakers were also desperately trying to recruit new personnel to be sent to the various out-stations. Japanese-speakers were the obvious priority but they also needed more wireless operators to intercept and DF the Japanese Navy's radio stations. So urgent was the need for reinforcements, Rochefort recalled having to recruit navy bandsmen to operate his punch-card machines behind the dividing wall in the Hypo basement.

Our whole operation depended on IBM machines. We'd just assemble the cards and we would be able at any moment to pick out any group or two or three groups, or half-a-dozen groups, in a message. Suppose the message said, A, B, C, D, E. If we wanted to use this for some reason or another, all we'd tell the officer in charge of this operation, this IBM thing, 'Give me all the A, B, C, D, Es you have,' and he'd run this whole thing through the collators, through the tabulators, and he would then come up with printed forms where the use of this thing had ever been made together with the messages from the groups ahead of it and, of course, after it.

OP-20-G grew dramatically in size, with large numbers of young sailors straight out of college and Waves, the US Navy's female contingent. There was already a large pool of trained Japanese-speakers to draw on from among America's business community. They were sent on refresher courses set up at Columbia and Yale while a Japanese-language school was set up at the University of California at Berkeley, moving later to Boulder, Colorado, with new students being put through an intensive fourteen-month course.

The US operators were trained to take Japanese *kana* Morse on top of the Navy Building and as a result became known as the 'On the Roof Gang'. But after the attack on Pearl Harbor Hawaii was in urgent need of operators. Phillip H. Jacobsen was one of a number of standard US Navy radiomen in Hawaii who found themselves moved on to interception duties.

Near the end of March 1942, I and about seventeen others of those who were at the Transmitting Station were transferred to the Radio Receiving Station at Wahiawa, Oahu, to commence training in Japanese *kana* code and Japanese naval communications. This first class at Wahiawa was augmented by eight or so radio operators from the submarine base and a musician off the USS *California* who knew the Morse code.

As an attempt at security, we were all quartered in houses formerly used for married men. It was a bit crowded at first, but it was much nicer than living in the barracks. We had a reserve first-class radioman in our house to supervise us. Six men in double-decker bunks slept in the larger bedroom while I and three others slept in two double-decker bunks in the small bedroom. Having a bathtub was a bit of luxury as the navy only provided showers. Those of use who were still seamen second class were given the third-class radiomen's test and all eighteen of us passed. We bought out all the beer at the navy exchange and held a big party. Apparently, it got a bit out of hand because the Exchange Officer wouldn't let us do it again.

Tiltman travelled to Washington in March to discuss arrangements for joint coverage of Japanese Army and Navy communications with the Americans. His brief was 'to urge upon them the necessity of a division of labour, and that they should concentrate on Japanese, leaving the German and Italian to us'. Given that the British were way ahead on the breaking of Enigma and rapidly losing touch with the Americans on Japanese naval codes and ciphers, this division of responsibility made sense. A good deal of suspicion remained at higher levels over the burgeoning exchange of signals intelligence. But among those actually working on the Axis codes and ciphers there was little if any antipathy.

Tiltman agreed that OP-20-G should take the lead on JN25, with Fabian's Melbourne unit, the Hypo station at Pearl Harbor and Colombo sending all their messages and findings to Washington, which was to be codenamed 'Susan'. The British Chief Cryptographer, who was used to working by hand on his own, standing up at a custom-made desk, was impressed by OP-20-G's JN25 section but staggered by the number of tabulating machines in use. 'It is controlled by a psychologist, Dr Ford, and appears to be extremely well run, if somewhat over-mechanized. This section divides its work with Melbourne and Colombo and the general result is I believe quite satisfactory.' But the section dealing with all other naval codes and ciphers, which was run by Preston Currier, was not so efficient, Tiltman said. 'He is a very good man with experience of Japanese naval ciphers extending over at least ten years. But he is the only man in the section who knows Japanese and much of his time is occupied in trying to cope with un-reciphered codebooks to the possible detriment of research on the Flag Officer and Submarine ciphers.'

The Americans asked that Bletchley Park attempt to crack the Flag Officers' codes, JN16 and JN49, and to assist on the breaking of the Japanese naval attaché machine cipher, which had changed in September 1939, and was now codenamed 'Coral' by the Allies. In return, they would provide a complete six-month study of JN25 recoveries in order to help the British codebreakers to catch up. Both sides agreed to a full exchange of data.

Liaison with the Signals Intelligence Service was much less productive, largely because the US Army codebreakers had been concentrating on Purple at the expense of the army codes and ciphers. But they also agreed to exchange all their research.

The Royal Navy codebreakers at Pembroke College just outside Colombo were still struggling, but somehow managing to keep pace with the Americans in terms of breaking JN25b. But with the British intercepting far fewer messages and working largely by hand, while the Americans made extensive use of the tabulating machines, it was a 'long and laboured' process, said Lieutenant-Commander Neil Barham, one of the leading Royal Navy codebreakers.

The first step was to strip off the cipher additive that had been added to the coded messages. This depended on being able to line up messages that had been sent using the same portion of the additive table or cipher book. Each message had a preamble which told the receiving oper-ators the serial number and priority of the message, who originated it, who it was for, and how many groups it con-tained. The message itself began with a six-figure group giving the date and time of origin in clear. It was followed by a series of five-figure groups. The last five figures of the date–time group were repeated as the penultimate group and the last group was a repeat of the first five-figure group. Buried somewhere in the message was the five-figure indicator group, which told the receiving station the so-called starting point, the precise place in the additive table from which the originator had begun taking additive groups. In addition to the preamble notification of the number of groups in the message, the receiving station had a built-in garble check – the sum of every five-figure JN25 group was divisible by three. This was as invaluable to the Allied codebreakers as it was to the Japanese.

Finding repeated sequences could be very difficult, particularly with the limited number of messages being received at Colombo. But the insistence, common among most service radio operators, on sending routine messages at precisely the same time every day was invariably the way in. Once the format of these messages had been recovered, they could very often be predicted. A message sent at 0900 hours every morning by an isolated station and with the same low group count was almost inevitably to say that he had nothing to report. Such messages were often the easiest way into the code.

The Japanese mistake in changing codebooks and additive tables at different times meant that either the code groups or the additive in use could be recovered simply by subtracting whichever of these two values was known or could be guessed. Weather messages, which were invariably transmitted in a number of different codes and ciphers, some of which were already broken, were also a useful way in, as were low-level intelligence reports of enemy shipping movements. Since these messages were always sent in a stereotyped format and the Allies knew where their ships were, such messages were relatively easy to break. From this lowly start, other messages containing some of those known code groups or different parts of the same sequence of additive groups could be recovered.

The codebreakers had to find the indicators and identify

as many messages as possible that had been enciphered using additive sequences that were identical or overlapping, said Barham. 'The lining-up of these messages, or parts of messages, in their correct relative positions on the reciphering table may be termed "forcing".'

The messages were written out horizontally in rows on a large sheet of graph paper, known as a worksheet, and lined up under each other so that each vertical column provided a 'depth' of five-figure groups all enciphered using the same additive group, Barham said.

> Once it has been possible to force two or more messages into their correct relative positions on the reciphering table, it is not impossible to discover the subtracting figure common to all groups for a certain position. This becomes a definite possibility if groups in the underlying codebook are known. It is possible to break into the reciphering table, to subtract the group found from the textual group in the message and thus produce the corresponding unreciphered group. This process is known as 'stripping'.

There were a number of key code groups that the codebreakers would look for. The intrinsic difficulties of the Japanese language, in which one word can have a variety of different meanings depending on its context, meant that the Japanese operators had often to spell things out to ensure they were correctly understood. The only certain way of doing this was to use a commercial code known as the Chinese Telegraphic Code which provided a four-figure group for each ideograph. In order to warn the receiving station that the message was about to start using this system, all the main Japanese codes had special code groups that indicated its use was beginning or ending. This was also true of figures – which were frequently used in predictable places in the proforma sighting reports passed on the JN25 code – and a special code which had individual groups for each of the ships of the Japanese Merchant Navy, known by the codebreakers as the *maru*, from the suffix used after the name of each ship. So the codebreakers would look at the enciphered groups in their columns for ones that might be hiding the basic code groups indicating the start of the use of the Chinese Telegraphic Code, the *maru* code or figures. They subtracted the enciphered message group from this basic code group in the likely positions until they found one that fitted the pattern. The difference between the two must then represent the additive group. This could be added to all the five-figure groups in that column, providing yet more basic code groups. Some of these would already have been recovered and would provide a clue as to further basic groups in their own horizontally written message.

The next thing the codebreakers would look for would be the inevitable code group indicating that the use of the Chinese Telegraphic Code, the *maru* code or figures had come to an end. This would give them another additive group to be subtracted from all the enciphered groups in each column, providing yet more basic code groups, and so the process continued.

Figures were often easy to dig out, particularly in sighting reports which gave complete longitude and latitude for each ship spotted. Since the reporting station was routinely located by the direction-finders, the codebreakers knew the first two figures of the longitude and the latitude would have to be the same as that of the reporting vessel, while the last figure was invariably a zero. This recovered further additive groups that could be subtracted up the column, filling in more gaps.

By now the worksheet would have begun to resemble a massive crossword and a Japanese linguist could begin to suggest other potential basic code groups, providing more additive groups to be subtracted from other five-figure groups in the columns. This process of uncovering the meanings of new JN25 code groups was known as 'penetration', or rebuilding the book. 'The production of unreciphered groups leads to the last stage of cryptography which consists of "penetration" into the underlying book,' said Barham. 'Each group is listed and

161

the messages in which it occurred noted. From the varied contexts, guesses are made at its significance. It may easily be seen that the process of "book-building" is long and laboured and the speed with which it can be done varies with knowledge of types of messages and the number of complete messages which can be stripped from the re-ciphering table.'

As the codebreakers laboured away trying to break into JN25b, everything depended on the Japanese not changing the codebook or the cipher table, John MacInnes recalled. 'As the life of the cipher table [introduced at the beginning of December 1941] was extended, so more and more read-able messages became available. The table remained in force for nearly six months. The book-building was delayed at first by much new jargon unknown in peace-time but, as regards units, was much helped by the possession of a library of messages going back to early 1941, so covering a period when the call signs were well identified.'

Among the first messages the codebreakers were able to read, if only in part, were a number which indicated a direct Japanese threat to British assets in the Indian Ocean. The first, on 3 March 1942, was the news that the Japanese Navy was to base five I-boat submarines at Penang in Malaya to operate throughout the Indian Ocean. A few weeks later they began intercepting messages indicating a threat even closer to home.

The decoded JN25 messages had revealed that the Japanese were using letters as code for key areas and places. By mid-March, the codebreakers began noting repeated references to an operation by a Japanese carrier force, accompanied by another force, in the area of 'D' with an air raid planned for 2 April on something coded 'DG'.

George Curnock, one of the most experienced of those working on JN25, would later recount how on the after-noon of 28 March they were working on messages that were talking about plans for a major attack on 'DG'. Amid confusion over the location, one of the Japanese operators spelled out the name of the target in *kana* phonetics: KO-RO-N-BO. Curnock said an electric shock ran through what had been until that moment a very relaxed office. The Japanese were planning a major raid on Ceylon, with Colombo itself as the main target.

Admiral Sir James Somerville, the Commander-in-Chief of the Royal Navy's Eastern Fleet, summoned Shaw and asked him if the codebreakers were certain that 'DG' was Colombo. Told that they had not a shadow of doubt, he withdrew his fleet to 'Port T', its secret Indian Ocean hide-away at Addu Atoll in the Maldives, and sent the merchant shipping in Colombo Harbour to the south-western Indian port of Cochin.

When 2 and then 3 April came without any sign of a Japanese attack, the codebreakers' stock slumped, Shaw recalled. On Saturday 4 April a lone Catalina flying boat on patrol over the Bay of Bengal spotted ships of the Japanese Navy's 1st Air Fleet, commanded by Admiral Nagumo Chuichi, who had led the attack on Pearl Harbor. The Catalina got off a short radio message before being shot down. Then the codebreakers began to pick up Japanese air-to-ground messages, indicating aircraft were within 500 miles range. The plain-language messages made it clear that Nagumo had merely delayed his attack until Easter Sunday, when the Royal Navy might be less alert. But Somerville had already decided the codebreakers were wrong. The cruisers HMS *Cornwall* and HMS *Dorsetshire*, which were to escort an Australian troop convoy on its way back home, had been sent back to Colombo, while the aircraft carrier HMS *Hermes* and her destroyer HMAS *Vampire* were dispatched to Trincomalee. As the realization dawned that the code-breakers were right, the *Cornwall* and the *Dorsetshire* were ordered to leave Colombo immediately and Somerville set sail with his fastest ships immediately in the vain hope of intercepting the Japanese fleet.

Lillie Feeney was having her hair permed when the Japanese aircraft attacked. 'I was in the hairdresser's and someone said the Japs were bombing and I thought: Well, yes. I knew all about that. I remember being quite pleased with myself at the time because we had been reading all the Japanese signals about it.'

The codebreakers' warning had prevented British losses from being as heavy as they might have been. There was an exceptionally heavy mist with visibility restricted to about 200 or 300 yards, but the Japanese naval bombers still managed to sink the destroyer HMS *Tenedos* and the armed merchant cruiser HMS *Hector* while two other ships were damaged. RAF fighters shot down nineteen enemy aircraft and a further five were brought down by anti-aircraft fire. However, British air losses were just as high.

Somerville's scepticism that the codebreakers' prediction would be fulfilled was punished a few hours later when the *Dorsetshire* and the *Cornwall* were caught out in open seas as they raced to link up with the rest of the Eastern Fleet and were sunk.

That evening, a JN25 message gave the movements of the Japanese carrier force for the next day. There were no additive recoveries covering the page given in the message indicator, but within a few hours the British codebreakers had worked them out and were able to pass the details of Nagumo's plans to HQ Eastern Fleet.

Unfortunately, the intelligence report passed on to Somerville was garbled and he failed to find Nagumo's force. Three days later, a signal from the Japanese flagship *Akagi* was located by the codebreakers' direction-finding network. It appeared to be preparing an attack on Trincomalee. The *Hermes* and the *Vampire* immediately put to sea, leaving very little for the Japanese to attack in the harbour. Damage was slight and the Japanese lost a further twenty-four aircraft. But as the remnants turned away they spotted *Hermes* and her escort hugging the coastline and heading south.

The codebreakers heard the Japanese aircraft report the sighting and passed it immediately via scrambler to Eastern Fleet Headquarters but it was too late. They listened helplessly to the Japanese aircraft reporting the sinking of *Hermes* and *Vampire*. Had the codebreakers been fully trusted, the *Hermes,* the *Vampire*, the *Cornwall* and the *Dorsetshire* would probably not have been sunk. But the belated acceptance that they knew what they were talking about had dramatically cut British losses and Nagumo had received his first setback, however minor, in four months of rampage throughout the Pacific and Indian oceans.

For the first time since moving from Singapore, the wireless operators had been close enough to their target Japanese stations to pick up the messages without difficulty, said MacInnes. 'They intercepted every transmission from the Commander-in-Chief of the raiding force. The messages were immediately available to the translators and translations were made after a very short interval from first transmission. That no great victory, but only avoidance of defeat, could be claimed by sigint was due to the material inadequacy of the British forces, by sea and air alike.'

11

MIDWAY: THE BATTLE THAT TURNED THE TIDE

The Japanese raid on Ceylon and the growing concern that India itself might come under attack persuaded the British to withdraw the Eastern Fleet out of range of the Japanese. On 25 April Somerville sailed for Mombasa, in Kenya, taking the codebreakers with him.

'It was one of the biggest thrills of our service to be part of this fleet,' said Joan Sprinks.

> We embarked in the AMC *Alaunia*, surrounded by many ships of the Eastern Fleet: HMS *Warspite*, the flagship; the carriers HMS *Indomitable* and HMS *Formidable*; the cruisers HMS *Emerald* and HMS *Newcastle*; and many others. And as the voyage proceeded we took part in many naval manoeuvres. On deck one day, when the rum ration was being issued, we asked: 'What about us, don't we get any?' 'No love,' the Master-at-Arms said. 'You are on the ship's books as boys and while you're in the tropics you'll get your share of lime juice, same as the young lads.' We arrived in Kilindini Harbour, Mombasa, on 3 May 1942 to an accompanying welcome of wolf-whistles from HMS *Royal Sovereign* and were quartered in a small hotel in Mombasa – the Lotus.

The local authorities insisted that those members of the female clerical staff who were accompanied by their

166

children, most of whom were codebreakers' wives, must be sent up-country. Harry Shaw said the women were essential to the operation but the authorities, led by the District Commissioner, demanded that they be removed. The problem was solved by the women themselves, who refused to leave the Lotus Hotel, despite all attempts by the local authorities to have them evicted.

Meanwhile, Shaw and his officers had selected an Indian boys' school at Alidina, overlooking the Indian Ocean about a mile outside Mombasa. The formalities of requisitioning the school and arranging for an armed guard from the King's African Rifles took some time, Shaw recalled. 'It was a week before the Temporary Women Assistants could be brought in, during which time their all-day presence in the centre of town did nothing towards alleviating local resentment.'

It was scarcely a promising start, made worse by poor reception conditions and lack of equipment. One antenna mast had to be borrowed from a local RAF station, Shaw said. 'Frequently there were periods of "black-out" and no messages were received for hours.'

The civilian wireless operators had been left behind in Colombo with two codebreakers to attempt to keep continuity on the JN25 operation. With the reduced reception and half the number of operators, the codebreakers were receiving only a quarter of the JN25 messages they had done previously. 'Our watchroom was constantly plagued by bats and masses of flying insects, including praying mantises,' recalled Joan Sprinks. 'We cursed the Arab dhows that came in from the sea beating drums so loud that we couldn't read signals at times.'

For the British codebreakers, their work on JN25 already badly affected by the original move from Singapore, the transfer to Mombasa was a disaster, recalled John MacInnes. 'The moves from Singapore to Colombo, and Colombo to Kilindini, followed by the miserable volume of traffic which was intercepted there, caused an almost complete collapse in this field of work. When efforts were resumed the leeway was too great.

Signals frequently took up to a fortnight to be enciphered, transmitted and deciphered. There were several periods when even the task of absorbing additives from elsewhere was almost overwhelming.'

Despite the setbacks suffered by the British, the codebreakers left behind in Colombo were still able to make a major contribution to what was to become a vital stage of the war. A JN25 message decrypted at Colombo in early March had revealed that the Japanese had sent two aircraft carriers, the *Soryu* and the *Hiryu*, from the Indian Ocean to the naval base at Truk in the Caroline Islands. Over the following weeks the British and American codebreakers began to pick up repeated references to Japanese naval movements indicating a drive southwards towards Australia. As early as 3 April Hawaii intercepted a message indicating an offensive to be mounted from Rabaul, on the northern tip of New Britain, and a few days later OP-20-G reported that air-search patterns indicated an interest in the Coral Sea, off the north-east coast of Australia.

At the US codebreaking base in Pearl Harbor, Joe Rochefort became convinced that the Japanese were planning an operation against Port Moresby, on the south-eastern coast of New Guinea, and the neighbouring Solomon Islands. This would give them a base from which to mount attacks on Australia and threaten America's links with MacArthur's headquarters in Melbourne. His predictions were confirmed on 9 April when a JN25 decrypt revealed the existence of an 'Operation MO' strike force, based at Truk, and an RZP occupation force, to be launched from Rabaul.

The British and the Americans had already confirmed that RZP stood for Port Moresby and the designation Operation MO given to the scheme by the Japanese left little room for doubt. Five days later, Colombo identified the Japanese 1st Air Fleet as being 'concerned with an operation against RZP'. The following day, the British codebreakers reported that the Japanese aircraft carriers the *Shokaku* and the *Zuikaku* had been detached from

168

Admiral Nagumo's 1st Air Fleet and sent to Truk to lead the Operation MO strike force.

The amount of intelligence flooding in from the previously impenetrable JN25b was now immense. Only around 20 per cent of the messages that were being intercepted could be read and most of those only partially, but the codebreakers were now providing MacArthur and the Commander-in-Chief of the US Pacific Fleet, Admiral Chester W. Nimitz, with extensive intelligence on Japanese operations.

But this 'priceless advantage' was very nearly brought to an end by the first in a series of security lapses. On 27 April a story which appeared in the *Washington Post* under the dateline of 'Allied HQ Australia' spoke of a major concentration of Japanese naval vessels in the Marshall Islands 'apparently preparing for a new operation'. General George C. Marshall, the US Army Chief of Staff, sent a furious signal to MacArthur pointing out that if Japanese intelligence spotted the story it would be 'justified in believing their codes broken – which would be disastrous'.

By now the Japanese had at any event ordered a new codebook to be introduced on 1 May and, for the first time, the additive tables used to encipher the encoded message were to be changed at the same time, promising to hamper the work of the codebreakers severely. But for a few crucial weeks the Japanese naval operators did not receive their copies of the new book and were forced to continue using the JN25b codebook with the old additive cipher tables. 'The Japanese had the first of their many difficulties with distribution,' MacInnes recalled. 'The life of the table was extended and the total number of readable messages rose to over a hundred daily before the book and the table expired on 25 May 1942.'

Those messages were to be among the most crucial read by the codebreakers throughout the Pacific War. Led by Rochefort's men in Hawaii but with important contributions from both Colombo and Fabian's unit in Melbourne, the codebreakers could trace virtually every major movement made by the Japanese throughout the final days of the JN25b codebook.

Fully briefed by the codebreakers, who laid bare both the organization and plans of the Japanese forces preparing to occupy Port Moresby, Nimitz ordered Rear Admiral Frank 'Black Jack' Fletcher to prepare the aircraft carriers USS *Lexington* and USS *Yorktown* for action. The resultant Battle of the Coral Sea was the first naval battle in which surface ships failed to engage each other, relying entirely on carrier-borne aircraft to destroy the enemy.

It was to be a catalogue of errors by both sides. Large numbers of US and Japanese aircraft were launched against minor targets misidentified as being of much greater importance. The elements of farce were accentuated by the Japanese pilots' lack of night-flying experience. At one point the Japanese flagship sent out a homing signal, giving the American intercept operators stationed on board the *Yorktown* and *Lexington* the location, speed and course of the main Japanese strike force. A further Japanese force of twenty-seven aircraft set off in an abortive mission to find the American aircraft carriers. Having failed to find any sign of their targets, they jettisoned their bombs and headed back to the Japanese strike force, only to blunder upon the American force in the dark. Nine Japanese aircraft were shot down by American fighters sent up to intercept them and the pilots of a number of others became so confused they tried to land on the deck of the *Yorktown*.

The Americans did, however, succeed in sinking the Japanese carrier *Shoho*. The Japanese managed eventually to sink the *Lexington*. But they also thought they had sunk the *Yorktown* and a number of other ships, some of which had either existed only in the imagination of Japanese pilots or had not been hit, and as a result claimed a major victory. In terms of vessels and aircraft lost, it was more accurately described as a draw, the Americans losing more ships, the Japanese more aircraft. But overall the victory belonged to the Allied forces. The Japanese were forced to abandon their plans to occupy Port Moresby.

The threat to Australia and the supply lines with America was averted. The Japanese had lost their first major warship and for them the aircraft and pilots downed would be far more difficult to replace than any of the losses suffered by the Americans.

If the battle had been dominated by blunders, it had been won by superior intelligence, produced in Hawaii, Colombo and Melbourne. After the failure to predict the Pearl Harbor attack, Signals Intelligence had proved its worth. Nevertheless, there had been drawbacks for the Allied codebreakers. Fletcher had shown himself prone to ignoring intelligence provided by the Radio Intelligence Unit based on board the *Yorktown* and appeared to have totally failed to understand the potential and capabilities of tactical signals intelligence.

The codebreakers also made their own mistakes, in large part, the British believed, because the Americans were too quick to jump to conclusions. 'During the whole of the JN25b period it was apparent that the US Navy units had not yet learned the art of book-building, being too ready to adopt doubtful recoveries as confirmed,' MacInnes said. 'Two discrepancies whose origins can be traced directly back to JN25b were the wrong identification of the new Japanese aircraft carrier *Shoho* sunk at the Battle of the Coral Sea as the *Ryukaku* and the confusion as to whether prior to the outbreak of war the main Japanese fleet had assembled at Truk or at a port in Kyushu. The latter, however, was righted in good time for the Battle of Midway.'

The Battle of Midway, widely regarded as the turning point in the Pacific War, was the result of a calculated strategy by Yamamoto to draw the US Pacific Fleet *en masse* into an ambush. Despite the loss of the *Shoho*, the Japanese had a massive naval superiority over the Americans. But it could not last. The US Navy had huge numbers of ships under construction. If it was not beaten into submission now, it would eventually win control of the Pacific by sheer weight of numbers.

Yamamoto decided to pre-empt this by seizing Midway,

171

just over 1,000 miles west of Pearl Harbor, using an attack on the western Aleutian Islands, off the Alaskan coast, as a diversion. Japanese occupation of Midway, with its potential as a base for an attack on Hawaii, would leave the US Navy with little choice but to commit the bulk of the Pacific Fleet to a concerted counter-attack. The Japanese Combined Fleet would be waiting and its superior forces would prevail. Hawaii could then be taken with ease and with luck the Americans might even sue for peace.

The preparations for the Midway attack were being picked up by the codebreakers even before the Battle of the Coral Sea. There was frequent mention of a 'forthcoming campaign' in association with the cover designator AF, which Corregidor and Colombo realized was Midway as early as 7 March. Rochefort agreed but Washington did not accept this deduction, believing that the thrust of the Japanese attack might be Hawaii, Alaska or even the West Coast of America. More proof was needed if the codebreakers were to win the day and Hypo began taking wireless operators off the training courses and putting them straight to work, Phillip Jacobsen recalled.

> The need for operators on watch was dire so as they met the qualifications they were assigned to operations watch sections in the same building in Wahiawa. I think I was about the seventh or eighth operator to go on watch, to the best of my memory, just before the Battle of Midway. I do recall seeing those in charge poring over navigational charts in their office. They talked in hushed tones, but I could see the charts with two tracks from the Marianas Islands and the main Japanese islands eastward to a point somewhere around Wake Island. Some general knowledge filtered down to us operators that a large Japanese operation was pending and Midway was mentioned as the possible target. This probably came from Rochefort to Intercept Watch Supervisors to be vigilant on certain circuits to ensure their coverage and for immediate transmission of vital information to Rochefort's group by teletype.

By early May both traffic analysis and deciphered JN25 messages were indicating the massing of Japanese naval vessels, in preparation for the impending operation, in Saipan, the most logical base for an invasion of Midway or Hawaii. A message from Nagumo intercepted on 16 May revealed that the Japanese proposed to stage their air attacks from a point fifty miles north-west of 'MI' two days before the invasion. Hawaii, Melbourne and Colombo were all agreed. But still OP-20-G refused to accept that Midway was the target. So Rochefort and one of his senior analysts, Jasper Holmes, hit upon a plan to prove it beyond doubt.

Midway was ordered, via the secure submarine cable from Hawaii, to report in a low-level code that its de-salination plant had broken down and that it was short of fresh water, information that would of course be of vital interest to a potential occupation force. On 22 May Melbourne intercepted a message from Japanese naval intelligence reporting that AF had radioed Hawaii to the effect that it only had enough water to last two weeks. On the same day, Colombo reported that it had intercepted a message indicating that the Japanese were planning to invade Midway. Rochefort had proved Washington wrong, but at what would later prove to be an extra-ordinarily high price.

The change to the new cipher tables and codebook (JN25c) was only days away but the crucial message was already in the bag. On 20 May the Wahiawa station had intercepted a long message from Yamamoto to his commanders. It was his final operations order for the Midway and Aleutians attacks.

The Wahiawa operators had a teleprinter link with Rochefort's codebreakers but most messages had to be sent by courier to Pearl Harbor, recalled Phillip Jacobsen.

Our normal intercept positions had two high-frequency receivers elevated on a standard US Navy metal operating table with a typewriter well in the centre for the operator's chatter and watch log plus a side table for the typewriter

173

used to copy messages. Each watch had a courier who made two trips per watch to Pearl Harbor with accumulated messages. The windows had blackout shutters on them and although the temperature at Wahiawa was rather temperate, the heat from the radios and lack of air-conditioning made the operating spaces rather warm and uncomfortable at times. We stood three rotating eight-hour watches starting off with the evening watch, day watch and finally the mid-watch. The latter watch was a killer until you got used to getting some sleep in the short time between watches. In addition, the junior operators had to do clean-up work, burn classified paper, etc. and relieve the day watch for chow in the morning of their evening watch. One of the permitted harassments was to give a 'hot foot' to any operator who went to sleep on the mid-watch by putting paper matches in between the sole and top of his shoe and lighting the matches. Somewhere along the line someone complained and the practice was discontinued.

When the Yamamoto message arrived at Hypo, the codebreakers struggled to decode it. The attack was led by cryptanalyst Wesley 'Ham' Wright and Lieutenant-Commander Joe Finnegan, a Japanese interpreter who had seen service as a language officer at the US Embassy in Tokyo, Jasper Holmes recalled.

Finnegan barricaded himself behind a desk with two flanking tables, all piled high with IBM printouts, newspapers, messages, crumpled cigarette packs, coffee cups, apple cores, and sundry material, through which he searched intently, usually with success, for some stray bit of corroborative evidence he remembered having seen days or weeks before. He paid little attention to the hours of the day, or the days of the week, and not infrequently he worked himself into such a state of exhaustion that his head dropped into the rat's nest on his desk and he reluctantly fell asleep.

Although Finnegan and Wright led the attack, all the senior officers at Hypo were involved. They were able fairly quickly to decode the parts of the message in which Yamamoto described what he wanted his forces to do, Rochefort recalled.

We could tell them what was going to happen, such things as where the Japanese aircraft carriers would be when they launched their planes, degrees and distance from Midway. Then, of course, the rest of the dispatch would be the strength of the attack and the composition of the attack forces and so on. The only two things we lacked were 'where and when' and these were especially enciphered within the basic operation order by the Japanese in a separate little cipher system. Now, the 'where' was easily solved. There was no problem there at all. This was the AF. The date, time and hours – 'when' – we were unable to get this.

The separate internal cipher used to disguise the date and time of the attack had only been seen in use on three occasions, Rochefort said.

This was the third time it had been used and we, of course, had the other two instances available to us which we kept studying. But unfortunately one of them was garbled, so we had nothing in which to prove or disprove our assumptions as to 4 June, or 8 June or 10 June or whether it was 19 July. We had no way of knowing. But by concerted attack by everybody concerned we were finally able to restore or to rebuild the little system just based on these three particular little incidents and, admittedly, it was rather shaky, but it was the best we could do under the circumstances.

On the morning of 25 May Rochefort was summoned to report on Hypo's latest findings.

Admiral Nimitz had sent for me to arrive at a certain time at his headquarters and I was late. The reason I was late

175

was that we were still working on the final aspects of this dispatch and when I say that we were working on it, I mean that this would involve an agreement among the senior people at station Hypo and would probably have included Dyer [Hypo's chief cryptanalyst], Wright, Finnegan, the translator, Huckins, the radio intelligence officer and possibly Jack Williams, also radio intelligence officer, and this message that went out then was our consensus of what the dispatch meant and what the dispatch said and our reasons for it. Like everything else in station Hypo, any major decision of this nature would be the result of [what you might call a] staff conference. We never did call it things like that. We just said that we all agree with this. When I say 'we' I am always referring to the people who were most experienced and the most knowledgeable.

The threatened Japanese codebook change occurred as the Hawaii codebreakers were finishing off their report on Yamamoto's final operations order. But Rochefort was still able to brief Nimitz in full on the Japanese plans, giving details of the diversionary attack on the Aleutians on 3 June to be followed the next day by an aerial bombardment of Midway and two days later by a full-scale invasion.

This was an extraordinary achievement in its own right. For the vast bulk of the war, the only JN25 messages the codebreakers could break were those sent in stereotyped formats: sighting reports; convoy schedules; ships' movements; routine air moves; anti-submarine attacks; and reports of air and sea bombardments. Yet so detailed was Rochefort's version of Yamamoto's operational orders that Nimitz's staff officers could not believe it was genuine. They argued that it must be part of a deliberate Japanese deception operation. But Nimitz was convinced and positioned his forces for a surprise attack.

US Navy dive-bombers from the USS *Enterprise* and the USS *Yorktown*, the carrier the Japanese believed they had sunk in the Battle of the Coral Sea, were unleashed against the main Japanese carrier force at 10.25 on 4 June, scoring

176

immediate direct hits on the three Japanese aircraft carriers the *Akagi*, the *Kaga* and the *Soryu*. All three were sunk within five minutes. The fourth, and sole remaining Japanese aircraft carrier involved in the battle, the *Hiryu*, launched its aircraft in two waves against the *Yorktown*, finally killing her off, but was itself left crippled and ablaze by dive-bombers from the *Enterprise*. The Japanese were eventually forced to scuttle it, leaving Yamamoto with no carriers or air support and forcing him to retire, conceding defeat.

Within the space of five minutes, the tide had been turned in the Pacific. The unhindered Japanese progress had been brought to a juddering halt. The psychological effect on the hitherto victorious Japanese forces was immense and the initiative was handed to the Americans. It was Nimitz who gave the credit for his victory to the codebreakers who had provided him with 'a priceless advantage', ensuring that even the newest radio intercept operator was congratulated for his part in the battle.

'As soon as the attack was repulsed, the word was spread in our group of our successes in providing the early warning intelligence,' Jacobsen said. 'A commendation came down from Admiral Nimitz and we all were quite proud of our work and organization but realized that the details were top secret and we would not get any public recognition.'

Unfortunately, the codebreakers' contribution would not remain secret. Three days later, on 7 June, a dispatch by the *Chicago Tribune* reporter Stanley Johnston revealed that the 'US Navy knew in advance all about Jap Fleet'. Johnston's report was syndicated to a number of newspapers, most notably the *Washington Times Herald*.

Admiral Ernest J. King, the Chief of Naval Operations, apparently 'in a white fury while his staff frantically tried to discover the source of the leak', called an immediate press conference to deflect suggestions that the US Navy had known the detailed dispositions of the Japanese invasion force heading for Midway. But Johnston had published them in his article. The Japanese only had to read it to know that the information was right. It seemed the cat was well and truly out of the bag.

The British, whose worst fears about American security had been realized, protested to Washington and were told that Nimitz's operations order for Midway had been intercepted by wireless operators from the *Lexington* who had been on their way back to America after the sinking of their carrier during the Battle of the Coral Sea. Johnston, who was himself a British subject, was on the same ship and had managed to see the Nimitz order. What they did not tell the British was that the reporter had been shown it by Commander Morton T. Seligman, the *Lexington*'s Executive Officer.

The damaging situation was not improved by the subsequent Grand Jury investigation, which, while it failed to lead to a prosecution, managed to generate yet further publicity about a leak that in the words of the veteran columnist Walter Winchell in the *New York Daily Mirror* on 7 July, a full month after the original report, 'tossed security out of the window'.

There was nothing for the codebreakers to do but sit and wait, hoping that the Japanese had not picked up on the damaging leak and its attendant publicity. They did not have to wait long. In early August Nave's Royal Australian Navy intercept operators picked up Japanese messages telling stations to use an old, lower-grade code as emergency back-up on the orders of the 'Head of War Inquiry Bureau'.

A week later, at 1500 hours Greenwich Mean Time on 14 August, two months into the new JN25 codebook, it was changed. Neither the American nor the British codebreakers were in any doubt as to the reason behind the sudden change, which was swiftly followed by changes to the other codebooks and a major change in the call-sign system. This combination of changes seems to indicate that the Japanese had read the US reports but that the inquiry into the affair concluded that the Allies had either worked out the details of the Japanese fleet from traffic analysis or somehow obtained a codebook and additive tables. The Japanese simply could not believe that anyone, least of all a Westerner, could break their codes.

A post-war Japanese history of wartime naval communications makes no mention of the US media reports, suggesting that somehow Japanese intelligence may have missed them, although it does confirm that they were worried that a codebook had been secured by the Allies. The Japanese history said:

> With the failure of the Midway operation, it was feared that some of the codebooks lost were seized by the enemy. However, the staff of the Combined Fleet was of the opinion that if there were any codebooks lost, they would not cause an immediate danger. The Central Agency also held the same opinion and the only action taken was to apply the emergency regulations (using the old codebooks as the master code) as a temporary expedient. Subsequently, all the codebooks were revised in the order of their importance.

The change of the JN25 codebook led the British to protest a second time and to ask that no further public action be taken over the leak since 'preservation of this invaluable weapon outweighs almost any other consideration'. Five days later, the *Chicago Tribune* published a front-page story claiming that it had been 'cleared' by the Grand Jury. The US Navy barred Seligman from all further promotion and there, finally, the matter was allowed to rest.

But as far as Washington was concerned, there was one matter left to resolve. Laurance Safford had been replaced as head of OP-20-G some months earlier by Commander John Redman, the brother of the Director of Naval Communications, Rear Admiral Joseph Redman. The Redman brothers were determined to ensure that communications experts were in charge of naval codebreaking. John Redman also appears to have resented being made to look foolish by Rochefort over the Midway disagreement. Word began to spread within the naval hierarchy in Washington that the naval intelligence centre in Hawaii was not working well and Rochefort was to blame. The esoteric codebreaker with a penchant for wearing a silk smoking jacket over his uniform was never likely to go down well with the tub-thumping Redman brothers. In an extraordinary memo that never once mentioned Rochefort by name, John Redman complained to his superiors that the Hawaii codebreaking operation was in the hands of a man who was merely 'an ex-Japanese-language student'.

Rochefort was replaced and sent back to San Francisco where he was put in charge of the commissioning of a new dry dock. 'What a waste of a priceless talent for a political payback,' said Phillip Jacobsen. 'Nimitz's recommendation for the Distinguished Service Medal for Rochefort was twice denied, but given to political cronies of the Redmans in Washington.'

12

FRIENDS FALL OUT

The US Navy codebreakers may have been enjoying some of their best moments of the war but their Royal Navy counterparts had reached their lowest point. The new recruits were finishing the Bedford course just in time. After undergoing codebreaking training, Jon Cohen was sent to the Japanese naval section in Elmers School at Bletchley Park with five other graduates of the first Tiltman course, including Hugh Denham, who had been just nineteen when he was recruited from Jesus College, Cambridge, where he had been reading Classics. The section now had around forty members. Hugh Foss was still in charge with Lieutenant-Commander Bruce Keith as his deputy and chief intelligence reporter, Hugh Denham recalled.

We were introduced all round and then went in to Keith for instructions. He said that there were about a thousand encrypted Japanese naval messages intercepted every day, of which some seven hundred were in JN25. A fraction of these reached Bletchley within days – in fact under forty intercepted at Flowerdown [near Winchester, in Hampshire]. Some of the remainder were in due course forwarded by bag from elsewhere. Current material was handled expeditiously at Washington, Kilindini and Melbourne. The Bletchley party had, up to that point, he said, achieved nothing. Whenever they began to attack a problem, the solution arrived from another centre and they turned to something else.

Keith told the new recruits gloomily that there was no work in the section for six Japanese linguists. The new boys were squeezed into a small room, recalled Jon Cohen. 'At some stage a bomb fell on the building, purely an accidental target, as it were. We were sitting round the edge of this room and the whole ceiling fell down into the middle of the room. It was just fortunate that every one of us was sitting round the edges of this room and so we weren't hit by anything. We made some attempts to break the Japanese Merchant Navy Code JN40, though we didn't have much success.'

Hugh Foss may have been a brilliant codebreaker but his eccentricities were legion both at work and at home. His cousin Elizabeth Browning, who was now also working in the naval section, was a regular visitor to his home.

I saw a lot of Hugh and Alison Foss. They lived in a bungalow at Aspley Guise with their two small children, one of whom was my goddaughter. The house was always chaotic, as Hugh's wife was a darling but almost totally incompetent domestically. Hugh went home pretty well every day at four-thirty in order to put the children to bed, get supper, and do what he could to organize things. An example of their modus vivendi was the highly complicated arrangement for washing-up (dreamed up, needless to say, by Hugh). Every article was supposed to be washed in a particular order – saucers first (as least polluted by human lips); then teaspoons; then sideplates; then pudding plates; soup bowls; main-course plates; knives; glasses; cups; forks; pudding and soup spoons; and finally saucepans. As these were usually stacked on the floor the dogs were a great help. The theory of this procedure in the days before dishwashers may have been excellent but in practice one usually found two or three days' washing-up waiting to be done, with plates and

182

dishes piled around and in the sink. If one tried to help there would be shrieks of 'Oh you mustn't do the cups yet. Saucers first.' There was also in theory some weird arrangement so that things Hugh was supposed to put away were located at distances appropriate to his great height and long arms, while Alison, who was small and dumpy, had a shorter range. But in practice things ended up pretty well anywhere. I remember having lunch there one day with Hugh's muddy boots on the table beside me to remind him they needed cleaning.

Like most of the civilian codebreakers, Jon Cohen and Hugh Denham were billeted in a private house.

Hugh and I were in a village called New Bradwell, which was attached to the railway company. The house was run by a dear old lady who must have been about seventy and was the widow of somebody who had worked on the railway. It was just a two-up, two-down cottage. I was from an upper-middle-class background in London and this was far in the other direction. But Hugh and I got on very well there. It was wartime and during the war people did all sorts of things they wouldn't always think of doing.

There were also very considerable class differences at Bletchley Park itself. I took up with a girl who I was quite surprised to find was a countess's daughter, because with my middle-class Jewish background that wasn't the kind of person I would normally mix with. But it was a place where all sorts met and there were dances and parties and we enjoyed ourselves to a certain extent. But there was always the background and the need-to-know criteria, that is to say you didn't ask questions about what other people were doing or working on. You never went beyond your own narrow field.

Bletchley Park was full of eccentrics and there was a very informal approach to rank and the wearing of uniform, Cohen recalled.

One day the military police guarding the entrance to Bletchley Park saw two RAF sergeants walking down the driveway. They suddenly seemed to stop, look around them and walk very fast in the opposite direction. It was thought that this was suspicious behaviour and they were arrested and brought into the guardhouse. It turned out that they had a quite valid posting to Bletchley but they didn't like the look of it because people were there walking about, officers and ratings, people in uniform and people not in uniform, all sorts, all gesticulating and arguing and so on. So they thought this must be a services lunatic asylum. They said to each other: 'Well, knowing what postings are like in the armed forces, this is a mistake. We'd better get away quick or we shall be mistaken for a couple of the lunatics.' It was explained to them of course that it was safe and they came in.

Meanwhile, at Kilindini, poor reception, an acute shortage of personnel and the point-blank refusal of Fabian to exchange results meant that the British codebreakers had made no progress at all with JN25c.

A procedure had been set in place whereby Fabian's unit in Australia, now known as Fleet Radio Unit Melbourne (FRUMEL), and Kilindini would exchange results via Nave in Melbourne. But the veteran Australian codebreaker had fallen out with both Fabian and Newman, who had accused him of breaching security by helping the army codebreakers at Central Bureau. The belligerent Fabian blamed security concerns over Nave for his reluctance to exchange material with Kilindini. Given the American's admitted predilection for only exchanging material where his own unit was likely to gain from it, this may be only part of the truth. Starved of information by their US counterparts, the British codebreakers lost complete touch.

Meanwhile, through a combination of good organization, close co-ordination and extensive use of tabulating machinery, and no doubt boosted by the effect of codebreaking on the Battle of Midway, the US codebreakers forged ahead. The Kilindini codebreakers were devastated by a signal received from Bletchley Park in late July. It was an update from OP-20-G on US progress against JN25c which came only five weeks after Kilindini had estimated it would take six to eight months to begin to read messages in real time and stated that:

> Stereotype movement reports of small units and certain type of intelligence reports on our communications in Pacific area are already readable but these types only occasionally yield intelligence of any value. Convoy and shipping control reports should be sufficiently readable within a fortnight to disclose any important activities which may occur in that field. Difficult to estimate probable progress in reading traffic dealing with projected operational large-scale movements, etc. But believe within month general context of 30 per cent of such messages can be determined with perhaps 15 per cent yielding specific information. Forthcoming succeeding months should see 50 per cent increase over preceding months in each of the above categories.

Realizing how far behind they were, some of the British codebreakers, led by 'Bouncer' Burnett, suggested they would be serving Somerville better if they moved *en masse* to Washington. They believed Bletchley Park was only concerned with the European War and as a result was starving them of resources, while the Americans seemed uninterested in intelligence covering the Indian Ocean areas patrolled by the British Eastern Fleet. A British code-breaking presence at OP-20-G would ensure that Somerville received the information he required.

Shaw, who as head of the unit had a better grasp of the logistical problems – not least the major manpower crisis at Bletchley Park – agreed with the Admiralty that the answer lay in a separate, bigger British operation, but with a direct link to Washington. However, Burnett had Somerville's ear, and amid a damaging clash of personalities Shaw found his position undermined.

Somerville appears to have sought a rational compromise, sending Burnett to London in an attempt to sort things out, and in particular to press for the direct radio link between Washington and Kilindini which would have solved most of the problems. Somerville suggested sensibly that a British naval codebreaker should be attached to OP-20-G, adding that 'Burnett would be eminently suitable in a technical capacity as he has a brilliant brain and is 90 per cent responsible for any results we achieve at Kilindini. But he is somewhat intolerant and might not prove satisfactory if used for purely liaison duties.'

Although Somerville seriously overestimated Burnett's contribution to the British codebreaking operation, the assessment of his protégé's personality traits was prescient. Burnett's part in the subsequent debate was severely limited by an early clash with Commander Edward Travis, the head of Bletchley Park. The British had long pressed for America to take overall responsibility for Japanese codebreaking, leaving them to control the German and Italian operations. But they were not prepared to be entirely dependent on Washington for any area where British servicemen were fighting.

Travis had already ordered a major expansion of Bletchley Park's Japanese codebreaking operations. 'It became evident that a more vigorous policy was being pursued at GC&CS,' Shaw said. 'It displayed more practical interest in Kilindini's work, arranged communications via the RAF in East Africa, supplied Typex machines and offered more personnel.'

At the same time, the British codebreakers enjoyed their first major success since leaving Colombo. The Japanese Merchant Navy used its own special codes or ciphers to communicate with the Imperial Navy and to protect shipping movements. In May 1940 it had introduced a code which the Americans dubbed JN39. Within six months the Allied codebreakers had managed to crack the relatively easy code. But in February 1941 it was changed. 'The FBI, thinking that they were being helpful, had boarded a Japanese freighter in San Francisco harbour and stolen a copy,' said Joe Eachus, a former US Navy codebreaker. 'The first thing the Japanese did when they found out was change the merchant shipping code.'

Its replacement, JN40, was believed to be a code super-enciphered with a numerical additive in the same way as JN25. But in September 1942 a textbook error by the Japanese gave John MacInnes and Brian Townend, another of the civilian codebreakers sent to Kilindini by GC&CS, the way in.

The Japanese operator omitted a ship's position from a detailed message and instead of sending it separately in a different message, re-enciphered the original with the same keys, this time including the longitude and latitude that had previously been missing. A comparison of the two messages made it immediately clear that JN40 was not a superenciphered code but a transposition cipher. It was based on a daily changing substitution table, containing 100 two-figure groups or dinomes, each representing a *kana* syllable, a *romaji* letter, a figure or a punctuation mark. The operator wrote out the message in *kana* syllables and then substituted the relevant dinomes. This produced a long sequence of figures which was written into a 10 × 10 square horizontally and then taken out vertically, thereby splitting up the dinomes and making it more difficult to break.

Within weeks MacInnes and Townend had discovered that the substitution tables were formulated in a predictable pattern. By November the codebreakers were able to read all previous traffic and be confident of breaking each message in real time, allowing enemy supplies to be tracked and attacked at will by Allied submarines. What was more, since it was a cipher, there were no code groups to recover and therefore no gaps in any of the messages. 'This was the first time that any large body of non-coded naval Japanese had become available,' said MacInnes. Over the next fortnight, they broke two more systems. The first was the previously impenetrable JN167, another merchant-shipping cipher. The second was JN152, a simple transposition and substitution cipher used for broadcasting navigation warnings.

Meanwhile, the first steps towards resolving the problems with JN25 and the difficulty in getting anything out of Fabian were being taken by Edward Travis and Frank Birch, head of the Bletchley Park naval section. During a visit to Washington in September and October 1942, they thrashed out a co-operation agreement on naval interception and codebreaking with OP-20-G. This was dominated by the continuing dispute between the two sides over naval Enigma, in particular the British attempts to break the four-wheel version used by the German Navy's U-boats, dubbed Shark.

Motivated primarily by a determination to protect the Enigma secret, the British were anxious to keep control of the breaking of all Enigma traffic. The US Navy was equally determined to get to grips with the Shark traffic. Although OP-20-G had already begun working on Shark, an agreement on this had been put on hold. It seemed to be the obvious trade-off for full assistance on 'the Japanese problem'.

But the negotiations did not go as planned, with some very obvious 'stickiness' on the American side. Despite being head of the British codebreaking operation, Travis was treated in a very dismissive way and Birch was refused entry to the OP-20-G intelligence-reporting section. The US Navy codebreakers were deeply, and quite wrongly, suspicious that the British were holding back on them. No doubt stung by the British criticism over the lack of security evident in the Midway leak, they had found their own alleged evidence of poor British security in the shape of Fabian's claims against Nave.

The American delegation refused point-blank to allow the British codebreakers at Kilindini to have the secure cipher machines necessary for a direct link with Washington. Under an agreement between the US Navy and the US Army, the American ECM enciphered teleprinter machines could only be used if controlled by US officers. The obvious answer was for a US liaison officer to be posted to Kilindini, but despite the presence at

Bletchley Park of a US Navy liaison officer, Washington was adamant not only that none could be sent to Kilindini but that the US Navy representative at Bletchley could not deal with Japanese matters. 'It always struck me that the main reason why OP-20 would not send us representatives on the Jap side and forbade their European representatives to discuss Jap matters with us was just pride,' said Birch. 'On the European side we had led, and they had sent representatives to us, not we to them. Therefore, however different the Japanese problems, it would have been infra dig for them to send representatives to us on the Jap side.'

The inequities of this curiously one-sided 'co-operation agreement' did not end there. The Americans also insisted that the naval section of Nave's unit be totally absorbed by Fabian's FRUMEL; that Nave, an Australian, be sent 'back to Britain'; and that the British 'abandon naval cryptanalysis at Kilindini and retain there only an exploitation unit which will read traffic from recoveries supplied by other units and supply to these other units any code or other recoveries obtained in the course of this reading'.

Washington would assume responsibility for sending 'pertinent naval information' to GC&CS which could then pass it on to Somerville and Kilindini. The agreement made it clear that this would include all Japanese naval code and cipher key recoveries plus 'radio intelligence from Japanese naval communications indicating major strategic moves in any area and any details bearing upon operations in the Indian Ocean Area'. GC&CS would also be sent all intercepted Japanese material by pouch. 'The British will withdraw from active cryptanalytical work in the Pacific Area but will continue to intercept and read Japanese traffic at Kilindini. The British plan however to maintain a research and intelligence unit at GC&CS so as not to lose touch with the Japanese problem. With regard to German communications, the British accede to US desires to attack the submarine and naval problems.'

It was clear that the US Navy at least had a very different idea from the British of what constituted co-operation.

Birch was distinctly unhappy with the results of the negotiations. FRUMEL did take over the naval interception section in Melbourne, including the former FECB codebreaker Lieutenant-Commander Alan Merry. But the signal informing Shaw of what had been agreed was a much watered-down version, describing Kilindini's new role as 'to act mainly as book recovery and exploitation centre for C-in-C Eastern Fleet and any special problems such as JN167 which they can undertake'.

This left open a loophole through which Kilindini's operations would continue much as before, but with the added assistance of American recoveries, albeit through Bletchley Park rather than Melbourne. But even in its watered-down version it was a demoralizing blow to the British codebreakers who had hoped to be reintegrated into the US codebreaking network as an equal partner in the attempt to break JN25.

The dismissive, almost arrogant approach adopted by Washington towards the British codebreakers is difficult to understand given that without their greater experience in breaking JN25 it would have taken the Americans very much longer to get on top of the Japanese code. That the agreement came at the same time as the British were breaking JN40 and JN167 only added insult to injury. 'Unfortunately, it was difficult to get full confidence and co-ordination because the United States codebreakers had the idea that they were ahead of their British colleagues and were consequently very restrained in their co-operation,' one British codebreaker said.

Brigadier W. A. Jolly, Royal Marines, a member of British naval intelligence who visited Melbourne during a tour of the Pacific theatre, put it more succinctly. 'The most notable feature was the inability of the Americans to appreciate the full meaning of the word "co-operation",' he said. 'The atmosphere was "What is yours is mine, and what is mine is my own."'

Throughout 1942 and into 1943 British attacks on the Imperial Japanese Navy's codes and ciphers remained hampered by the lack of co-operation from the Americans and the emphasis at Bletchley Park on winning the war in Europe. While the latter was simply a reflection of the Allies' agreed policy of 'Europe first', the former had to be sorted out if the British codebreakers at Kilindini were to make any headway. More importantly, the limitations on the amount of signals intelligence being passed to the Admiralty for Somerville's Eastern Fleet under the agreement with the Americans was causing serious concern both in London and Mombasa. The British were supposed to receive all strategic intelligence on Japanese naval activity plus details of any Japanese movements in the Indian Ocean area, or more specifically west of 110 degrees longitude. In practice, the Americans showed little interest in sending anything. The co-operation still remained very one-sided. 'Granted they had the leadership, we were bound to help them where they needed help,' said Birch. 'By and large as time went by and they grew bigger and bigger they needed less and less help and would therefore be less and less obliging and more obstructive.'

The problem threatened to rip the fledgling intelligence co-operation arrangements between Britain and America apart since the Admiralty was rapidly coming to the conclusion that if the Americans were not prepared to share their intelligence, the British would be better off going it alone.

'The lack of US intelligence supply to C-in-C Eastern Fleet led the British to consider ditching the Americans on the Japanese side,' said Birch. 'Admiralty was not willing to be dependent on such small scraps as US were willing to provide and the only alternative to sharing all available intelligence between the two countries was for this country to build up independently an organization big enough to provide, without American help, as much intelligence as could be got with American help.'

The British set about building up their Japanese codebreaking efforts both at Bletchley and Kilindini. Shortly after arriving to replace Harry Shaw as the head of Kilindini in February 1943, Bruce Keith concluded that the problem lay in the inherent shortcomings of the agreement with OP-20-G. His report reflected the disappointment felt both at Bletchley Park and Kilindini at the lack of American co-operation and the resultant rows. The British were too dependent on the Americans taking an interest in matters that were essentially only of interest to the British, he said. Admiral Somerville was right: the only answer was to exchange liaison officers. British liaison officers inside OP-20-G would be able to pick out the messages that the Commander-in-Chief of the Eastern Fleet was interested in, said Keith.

This agreement depends entirely on the goodwill of the higher US authorities, and the efficiency of the US Japanese interpreters working on the cipher. Messages may contain information vital to the Commander-in-Chief [Eastern Fleet] but whether he gets this information or not is entirely beyond his control. It is not much good coming to an agreement in so vital a matter if you have no means of checking up that it is being efficiently carried out.

An American interpreter picking up a message may see that it affects the Commander-in-Chief, Eastern Fleet's area, but may say to himself that it is not important and anyway there are too many unknown groups to get anything out of it, so he passes on to the next message. If one of our interpreters were working in this room then this message would be passed to him and he, realizing its importance, would make every effort to find meanings for the missing groups and to extract as much information as possible. The US intelligence officer going through the translator's efforts may or may not pick out a message as being of interest to the Commander-in-Chief. If we had one of our people in this room, he would have a far better idea about this, and if there was a partly decipherable message which looked as if it might be of considerable interest, he would take the trouble to go back to the translator and ask for further elucidation. A US officer might not take this trouble.

192

This was the logical solution to the British problem. The difficulty was that it was just that, a British problem. The poor reception at Kilindini meant it could only intercept messages sent by the main stations using powerful transmitters and these were all easily accessible to both Melbourne and Hawaii. There was nothing that OP-20-G needed on the Japanese side from the British and as a result it had no incentive to co-operate. Its refusal to allow Birch access to its intelligence section emphasized the difficulty of implementing Keith's proposals. 'Bouncer' Burnett, who despite his poor relations with some of his British colleagues appeared to get on well with Commander Joseph Wenger, the head of OP-20-G, was keen to act as a Royal Navy liaison officer in OP-20-G. But Travis refused point-blank to contemplate Burnett's staying in Washington. 'Colonel Tiltman informed me that, although there was nothing personal in it, Commander Travis would in no circumstances agree to my appointment for liaison with US in Washington,' Burnett recalled. The official reason at least was that his ability at Japanese was too precious to be spared.

Burnett returned from his visits to Washington and London convinced that Bletchley Park was deliberately preventing Kilindini from having a direct link to Washington in order to bolster its own position. 'The Kilindini unit will suffer from malnutrition while BP grows fat on the pick of the food,' he said. This erroneous view, which was undoubtedly widely held among members of the East African station, remained a constant irritant in the relationship between Kilindini and Bletchley. It was reinforced by the fact that it often took six days for Washington's recoveries to reach Kilindini via Bletchley Park. But Burnett's claims were rebuffed by Commodore Edmund Rushbrooke, a former member of the Far East Combined Bureau who had now taken over from Godfrey as Director of Naval Intelligence. Rushbrooke pointed out that Bletchley Park had repeatedly asked for most of what Burnett was demanding but it had always been blocked by the Americans.

Several other senior naval intelligence officers had been dispatched to the various US Navy codebreaking operations and to Kilindini to report on what could be done. They included Captain H. R. M. Laird, Admiral Somerville's chief intelligence officer, who visited Melbourne to try to find some way of improving relations. His mission was not a success. 'Fabian was friendly,' said Laird. 'But when it came to producing a practical solution of our mutual problem he raised every sort of objection.'

13

BREAKING THE MILITARY
ATTACHÉ CODE

In the wake of the victory at Midway, both MacArthur and King urged that the Allies should build on the momentum with an offensive aimed at recapturing a number of the Pacific islands taken by the Japanese. MacArthur wanted a direct army-led thrust at Rabaul, the main Japanese base on the island of New Britain; King believed the US Marine Corps should be thrown into a series of island-hopping operations. The agreed compromise involved a pincer movement with US Marines moving north-west through the Solomon Islands towards New Britain, while MacArthur's joint US–Australian force seized control of New Guinea as a stepping stone for the assault on Rabaul.

The phased operation began on 7 August when the 1st US Marine Division landed on Guadalcanal, swiftly overcoming the small Japanese garrison and taking the neighbouring islands of Tulagi, Gavutu and Tanambogo. But the Japanese, anxious to prevent the Allies from gaining the upper hand, poured troops on to the island, with its navy making regular night-time forays down the 'Slot', the channel between the islands to the north-west, in a move dubbed the 'Tokyo Express'.

Despite John Tiltman's pre-war work on Japanese military codes and ciphers, the Allies were unable to read any of the high-level operational army messages during the bloody battle for Guadalcanal, and although low-level plain text was available, along with traffic analysis, much of the sigint assistance during this period came from decoded Japanese Navy JN25 messages. One high-level code was, however, available to the Allied commanders. Tiltman's roles as Chief Cryptographer, head of the Bletchley Park military section and troubleshooter on liaison with the US codebreaking operations kept him very busy. But throughout the first half of 1942, he had spent much of his spare time attacking a new code used by Japanese military attachés based in Japan's embassies abroad (the JMA code as it was dubbed at Bletchley Park). The codebreakers knew from past experience that this was likely to provide a wealth of useful intelligence on Japanese activities, filling in the gaps caused by loss of continuity on the high-grade army systems.

'About the end of 1941, I had to rescue the material from a party of French cryptanalysts who had remained with us after the fall of France,' said Tiltman. 'I had given it to them as a task when I and my research section were fully occupied with German problems and they had diagnosed it wrongly as a combined substitution and transposition system and had got the intercepts in a hopeless tangle.'

Tiltman took up the problem himself using messages sent back to Tokyo by the Military Attaché in Santiago and discovered that the JMA code was a digraph code in which the basic *kana* syllables stood for themselves and other two-letter groups stood for certain words or phrases commonly used in military communications: for example, AB stood for 'west' and AV for 'message continued'. The two-letter groups were then set out in a square grid in adjacent squares, sometimes horizontally and sometimes diagonally, and the letters were read off vertically to form the basis for the encrypted text. They were then enciphered using a pre-arranged 'literal additive', a series of letters that would be notionally 'added' to the letters taken out of the grid on the basis of a pattern laid down in advance on a separate table. Reading off the enciphered letter along the relevant horizontal line and the 'additive' letter down the appropriate vertical column would produce a superenciphered letter which would be transmitted by the operator.

'By the time I first went to Washington in March 1942, I and my section had partially recovered the indicating system and had diagnosed the cipher as a literal additive system with indicators which gave the starting and ending points for messages,' Tiltman recalled. 'It became clear that the normal practice was to tail successive messages rigorously through the additive tables: i.e., to start reciphering each message with the additive group following the last group of the preceding message.'

After returning from Washington Tiltman set to work on a large number of JMA messages emanating 'from some unplaced station in the middle of Europe'. The cipher clerk in this as yet unidentified Japanese embassy had used the additive table again and again, giving a large 'depth' for Tiltman to work on. 'It was clear from the indicators that the sender had tailed right round his additive table five times and it was this depth that I set myself to resolve.'

Tiltman found similarities were particularly strong in the first five groups of each message, where the same letters appeared frequently in the same position in different messages. 'From this it could be deduced that the system was a true additive system, addition being in normal cyclic alphabetic order,' he said. The solution took a lot of work, but with a depth of five on the cipher additive, he eventually managed to break the system. One of the first JMA messages deciphered revealed the Japanese intentions to construct a 'Burma Railroad'. It was not until several months later that it became clear from another Japanese military attaché decrypt that British prisoners-of-war would be used as slave labour to build the railway.

Tiltman set up a small Japanese military section at Bletchley Park in June 1942. It comprised a codebreaking sub-section and a traffic analysis team but its main purpose was to handle the JMA material, using some of the graduates of the Bedford Japanese course. These included Maurice Wiles, who was told he must join the army and then transfer to the reserves to ensure that he was not called up for another unit.

Three of us, Mervyn Jones, myself and Roland Oliver, were sent to the army recruitment office in Bedford where we were interviewed by this caricature of an old-style army colonel. He asked me which school I had gone to and when I said Tonbridge, he told me he knew the school secretary. 'We were fellow brigade commanders in Lucknow,' he said. He then asked me if I played cricket. 'Yes,' I said. He beamed. 'Were you in the first XI?' 'Yes,' I said. He beamed again. 'Did you bowl?' 'Yes.' He beamed again. 'Did you bowl left-handed?' It was at that moment that I fell from grace. He then interviewed Mervyn Jones who had been at Trinity, Cambridge, and had a starred first in Classics. 'Got your school certificate, eh?' he said to him. 'Well done. Well done.'

Tiltman explained to the new recruits that although he had broken the cipher, his knowledge of Japanese was not good enough for him to take it any further forward. That was up to them, he said. It was initially an intimidating task, Wiles said.

We were pretty ill-equipped. Knowledge of the language was essential to the task assigned to us, but it was no straightforward matter of translation. As yet there were no texts on which to exercise our newly acquired translation skills. None of the thousand or so characters that we had painstakingly learned were there on the page before us. Something much more was needed, for which we had no specialist training – an approach to problem-solving that our initial interviewers no doubt hoped had been ingrained in us by our interest in chess and crosswords.

But eventually the messages began to flow, producing a

good deal of intelligence and, on occasions, amusement. 'Foreign names were normally spelled out in *kana*,' Wiles recalled. 'Until one got used to them, they were not always easy to recognize: CHI-YA-A-CHI-RU does not obviously spell "Churchill" to the untrained eye. But once the principle was mastered, they offered plenty of entertainment as well as a quick guide to the subject matter.'

Thereafter, the codebreakers were able to read the messages of the Japanese military attachés without any problems, aided by the fact that each time the code changed, the difficulties of distributing codebooks dictated that some were forced to respond to messages from Tokyo in the new book using the old broken one. The messages provided a wealth of useful material on the movements and existence of Japanese military units. Much of the more valuable intelligence came from the so-called Tokyo Circular, which was sent to all military attachés around the world and contained a rundown of Japanese activity on all fronts.

The main British stations for intercepting Japanese military codes and ciphers were in India. There had been an intercept capability in India since the First World War, when the Indian Army set one up at its headquarters in Simla. In the immediate wake of the First World War, with Russia the main threat to British interests in India, an intercept site was constructed at Abbottabad on the North-West Frontier. Throughout the 1920s and 1930s the Indian codebreakers concentrated on Soviet codes and ciphers in an extension of the Great Game, the intelligence battle between the Russians and the British that had raged across the region from the late 1900s. Their work was given an early start by Tiltman, who recalled spending most of the 1920s in India.

I was a member of a section of the General Staff at Army Headquarters in Simla, India, consisting of never more than five persons. We were employed almost entirely on one task, to read as currently as possible the Russian diplomatic cipher traffic between Moscow, Kabul in

199

Afghanistan and Tashkent in Turkestan. From about 1925 onwards I found myself very frequently involved in all aspects of the work – directing the interception and encouraging the operators at our intercept stations on the North-West Frontier of India, doing all the rudimentary traffic analysis that was necessary, diagnosing the cipher systems when the frequent changes occurred, stripping the long additive keys, recovering the codebooks, translating the messages and arguing their significance with the Intelligence Branch of the General Staff. A cryptanalyst should take every opportunity of acquiring a general working knowledge of branches of Signal Intelligence other than his own. I realize that I was exceptionally lucky to have this opportunity and that very few others have had the chance of acquiring this kind of general working experience.

The experiment proved a success. The Wireless Experimental Depot moved briefly to Cherat but had returned to Abbottabad by the time the war with Germany broke out. As war with Japan loomed in 1940 and 1941, two more British Army intercept units were set up in Burma, at Rangoon and Maymyo, near Mandalay. Meanwhile, the main Indian Army station, now known as the Wireless Experimental Centre, had moved to a site at Anand Parbat, just outside Delhi, explained W. C. Smith, an Intelligence Corps sergeant who worked there.

The centre occupied the site of Ramjas College, an *Arya Samaj*, or Protestant Hindu foundation evacuated elsewhere, on the outskirts of old and new Delhi. Its hilly, isolated and self-contained position, accessible to the capital, made it very suitable for a wireless station. We were on the edge of the Thari or Rajputana desert, where the clear air perhaps aided reception, but where we lived with the continual terror of the *anhi* – the dust storm.

This was a nerve centre of intelligence from military wireless sources against Japan. Well over a thousand are believed to have inhabited it, at its height, made up of

Intelligence Corps (the real Wireless Experimental Centre, India Command); RAF, from 166 Signals Wing; Women's Auxiliary Corps (India); Indian airmen, many from the far south of India, perhaps with Malayalam or Tamil mother tongue; West African Signals, from what are now Ghana and Nigeria; occasional British ATS, and more than one WAAF officer; and, of course, a host of Indian Army NCOs and men. There were many civilians too, not least the Sikh postmaster, and Habibullah, the Pathan fruitseller, and last but not least the cycle shop at the gate, our lifeline off duty at a hire of one rupee eight annas a day.

The WEC was subordinate to the British authorities in India and was in theory independent of their counterparts in the UK. It was controlled by the Inter-Service Wireless Intelligence Staff which was in charge of signals intelligence in India. But effectively the WEC was an outpost of Bletchley Park. It was a joint RAF/army unit, ostensibly commanded by an RAF group captain but split into five sections, most of which came under the direct control of Lieutenant-Colonel Peter Marr-Johnson, who had flown to India when the FECB was evacuated from Singapore. He was in charge of A Section, administration; B Section, the intelligence collation and reporting section; C Section, which was the 'Special Intelligence' or codebreaking department; and D Section, which co-ordinated traffic analysis and DF results. E Section, interception and communications, was controlled by an RAF wing commander, Smith said.

My own B Section duties were partly concerned with ordering maps to cover the whole of the war in Asia, from Burma to the Pacific, for the adjoining Map Room in which were kept detailed maps of the situation in Burma and the parts of India subject to invasion. The real star of the Map Room was the huge map of the estimated Japanese order of battle. My main task was to make a card index of every place east of Burma under Japanese occupation or in which there were Japanese forces, to help in locating geographical places, and to enter the appropriate units. When I started there was nothing to go on, so I picked up the *Statesman* (Calcutta and Delhi) and looked at the war news in the East. Even in March 1943 they devoted far more attention to war in Europe than to Asia, except perhaps in the Arakan. However, that day our planes bombed Kavieng, New Ireland. So it was found, and the first card was made with the latitude and longitude and brackets (KABIEN) for the Japanese equivalent. By the end of the war there were many cards and WEWAK, HOLLANDEA, RABAUL (RABAURU) had many entries. Many were the puzzles in identifying BANPON, KANBURI and so forth, and from that began the tracking of the course of the Burma–Siam Railway. Hardest of all to identify were places in China with many variations in spellings – according to various readings of Chinese characters and translations – and the Japanese renamed many places. It was thrilling gradually to build up a picture of the whole area, although individually one knew that was a very small part.

Although communication with other signals intelligence centres was difficult because of distance, the WEC was at the forefront of breaking Japanese army codes. The first success was technically shared with Kilindini. Major John Figgess, one of the centre's codebreakers, was sent as a liaison officer in November 1942 to the Royal Navy unit, where he spent much of his time producing military intelligence from a simple substitution cipher, the WE code, which the Japanese Navy used when sending military traffic.

The system, introduced because the existing naval codes had no facilities to disguise the identities of recipients and senders of army messages, was known as WE because the transposed *kana* syllables it used were always bracketed by the syllable WE. Despite its lack of security, the WE code was mainly used for preambles of important messages between Tokyo and the main Japanese bases of Palau, Rabaul and Truk; it became a valuable source of information on the Japanese order of battle and provided a number of cribs for more secure code and cipher systems.

The WEC had two main outposts of its own: the Western Wireless Signal Centre (WWSC) at Bangalore in south-western India and the Eastern Wireless Signal Centre (EWSC) at Barrackpore, near Calcutta, in northeast India. The western centre was purely a fixed intercept site covering military operations in Malaya and further afield, but the eastern centre was much more substantial. It had its own intelligence operation, known as Intelligence School 'C', which reported to 14th Army at Calcutta. It also provided operational air intelligence to aid the city's air defences, and three mobile special wireless sections, which in April 1943 were deployed close to the front line at Imphal, Chittagong and Maungdaw.

Harry Beckhough, the then officer commanding Intelligence School 'C', said operations were hampered early on by inexperience.

Lack of sufficient knowledge of the Japanese language and radio dispatch system meant first tracking Japanese units by strength of radio traffic in different areas. Monitoring units were set up in the jungle and manned by Royal Signals and RAF radio operators, furnishing me with all possible intercepts of Japanese signals for decryption. These were courageous groups, glued to their radios, picking up enemy messages in difficult areas, often cut off from communications except ours.

Abbottabad was independent of the WEC, coming under the direct control of the Inter-Service Wireless Intelligence Staff. It was mainly concerned with diplomatic traffic, having taken over that responsibility from the Royal Navy codebreakers after the evacuation of Singapore. There was a large number of Indian civilian and service wireless operators at Abbottabad, but there were also Royal Signals and RAF intercept specialists, some of them training the Indian staff. Dennis Underwood volunteered to join the Royal Signals at eighteen and was sent to Douglas on the Isle of Man for his special operator training. With manpower desperately needed for the front-line regiments, the army was increasingly turning to members of its female equivalent, the Auxiliary Territorial Service or ATS, as a source for intercept operators. 'By the time I finished there was only our male squad left,' said Underwood. 'All the others were ATS. That might sound like a possible heaven but in fact it was just the opposite. We men were on one duty or another almost every night, guard duty, fire piquet, kitchen fatigues, etc., and when the occasional night off came we were too exhausted to take advantage of the opportunities!'

At the end of his training, he was sent to Abbottabad.

I recall it as being a fairly small mountain town. At that height the Japanese signals came in loud and clear. We had a bearer to whom we each paid one rupee a week. For this he kept the barrack room clean, the fires burning, our equipment clean, woke us in the morning with a mug of cha and then shaved us as we lay in bed. I have no re-collection of the food but can remember a canteen which served cha in glasses which were very difficult to carry because of the heat. In addition, a traditional *cha-walla* toured the camp charging one anna a glass. There were then sixteen annas to the rupee and twelve rupees to the pound.

There was a service club in Abbottabad run by, I think, the ladies of WASBI (Women's Services British India), where we gathered some evenings when I remember eating toast and drinking yet more cha. One lasting memory is of listening to Dvorak's *Symphony from the New World* via the BBC World Service. We also visited the local cinema on occasions. I can recall sitting on benches reminiscent of church pews but have no memory of any of the films we saw except that sometimes they were Indian. We played football in our spare time, although at that height it was rather exhausting. On one occasion a group of us travelled down to Rawalpindi to watch a match between a team of professional players and a services team. I can't remember who won, but I do recall the hair-raising journey there and back along a road with precipitous drops and no barriers.

Dorothy Ratcliffe worked at the Abbottabad Wireless Experimental Depot, sending the reports back to Bletchley Park via a Type X machine cipher link.

My husband was in the Indian Army and he was sent off to Iraq in 1941, leaving me behind in Secunderabad. A friend who was married to a Gurkha officer had said: 'If ever you're abandoned come and visit me in Abbottabad.' So I went to see her and while there stayed in the Abbott Hotel, which was a collection of chalets scattered over a fairly wide area. I was going over to the dining room one day when a man I didn't know stopped me and said: 'Can you type?' Well, I'd done a course of typing and book-keeping after I left school but I'd never actually had to work. He said, 'Why don't you come along to the mess tonight, have a drink and meet Colonel Kenneth Tippett,' who was the head of the Wireless Experimental Depot. Colonel Tippett asked me a few questions to make sure I was suitable – they didn't want anyone who drank, who might talk, you see – and then told me I should start the next day at a salary of 100 rupees a month. This was only about £7 but I thought it was marvellous. What did I know, I'd never had to work before in my life.

So I was picked up in a car the next day, along with four others, by one of the men who worked there and he took us a couple of miles outside Abbottabad to the Wireless Depot where I was given a typewriter and told to start typing these intelligence reports. After a while I was put on ciphers, sending the messages to Bletchley. First of all it had to be done by hand but then we got one Type X cipher machine and I was put on my own in a little side room where I didn't see anyone. There was a large notice on the door saying, 'Keep Out, This Means You', and there were all these young men coming up to the door to ask me for a date who read the notice and went away again. It was such a different life there. We were not normal people. We abandoned wives had a whale of a time. There were always chaps ready to take you out dining and dancing. But after a couple of years my husband was posted back from Iraq and I had to hand my notice in and join him in Lahore.

Central Bureau, the Australian-based military signals intelligence operation, had moved with MacArthur's headquarters to Brisbane. Its director was Brigadier-General Spencer B. Akin, the former military head of the Signal Intelligence Service, the US Army codebreakers, who was now MacArthur's Chief Signal Officer. The day-to-day running of the bureau was initially in the hands of an assistant director, Colonel Joe R. Sherr, the former commander of Station 6, the US military sigint unit at Fort McKinley in the Philippines, and an executive officer, later also assistant director, Lieutenant-Colonel A. W. 'Mic' Sandford, a member of the Australian Imperial Force (AIF), the Australian Army, and a veteran of mobile tactical sigint units in the Western Desert.

There were three other key senior officers within the headquarters operation: Major Abe Sinkov, the US Army codebreaker who led the first US delegation to Bletchley Park, was head of 837th Detachment, the US codebreaking component; Wing Commander Roy Booth, the former commander of the RAAF's Darwin intercept operation, was in charge of the air force contingent, eventually becoming a third assistant director; and Norman Webb, now a major, was the most senior British representative.

The bureau was organized in a remarkably similar fashion to Bletchley Park. Its headquarters was at 21 Henry Street, a two-storey mansion close to the Eagle Farm racecourse at Ascot Park. But this soon overflowed and a series of huts was erected on the racecourse itself. Surrounded by wire fences and patrolled by Australian military, it was to become home for the Central Bureau codebreakers, linguists and intelligence analysts working on the Japanese messages. As the bureau grew in size, the racecourse became covered in more and more huts, numbered much like those at Bletchley, each containing a particular section. Central Bureau was divided into four main sections: Traffic Analysis, employing six officers and sixty ORs under Captain Stan Clark, one of the Australian Army officers who had seen service in the Middle East; High-Grade Codebreaking under Major Sinkov, employing thirteen officers and sixty ORs (including a tabulating machine section), of which roughly a third were Australians; Air–Ground Codebreaking under Nave, with the naval air side led by a US Army major, the army air by an Australian major and a meteorological section under Professor Room; and Collateral Intelligence, employing four officers and six ORs, shared between the Australian Army and the RAAF. This last section was a purely Australian operation. It checked the transcripts alongside sighting reports and captured documents, provided intelligence reports to the Australian commands, built up a picture of the order of battle, and liaised with Bletchley Park and the WEC in Delhi. The US Army codebreakers at Central Bureau had no responsibility for circulation of the intelligence they gathered. Their transcripts were 'edited' for intelligence value and then passed direct to Akin and General Charles Willoughby, MacArthur's chief intelligence officer, to be disseminated to US customers.

Joe Richard, then a sergeant, was one of the first US Army codebreakers to arrive in Brisbane.

At Central Bureau, during 1942, the Americans contributed very little. They were attacking low-level Japanese Army messages that were sent in three-figure groups. These proved both hard to intercept and mostly unreadable (being mostly one-time pad). The Australian Army [AIF], led by experienced men who had returned from the Middle East, was doing the interception, starting the traffic analysis, and carrying out the field processing of the army air-to-ground messages in three-figure code and the naval air-to-ground messages in 3-*kana* and 4-*kana* codes. The Royal Australian Air Force was at

Townsville intercepting the Japanese naval air-to-ground 3-*kana* and 4-*kana* codes and sending them to Central Bureau. Due to the Europe-first policy, the US did not send many intercept army personnel to Australia until mid-1943. A handful evacuated from the Philippines by air worked with the RAAF at Townsville, teaching them to pick up the air-to-ground frequency. The training of Australian personnel in breaking and reading the Japanese Army and Navy air–ground messages was done by Eric Nave.

14

CENTRAL BUREAU'S BIG BREAK

Despite Fabian's efforts to have Eric Nave sent 'home' to Britain as part of the terms of the Anglo–US Agreement, the Australian codebreaker had been transferred instead to Central Bureau. Fabian was unapologetic over his refusal to share FRUMEL's signals intelligence with the Royal Navy codebreakers at Kilindini and the US and Australian Army codebreakers at Brisbane. He later recalled:

> Security was a paramount concern for me. I was relieved when Commander Nave, an Australian cryptanalyst, left FRUMEL for Central Bureau. He left because I reprimanded him for his lack of security. I also had to get my admiral to remind MacArthur about the need for security. As the commander of the South-west Pacific theatre, MacArthur informed Admiral Leary, who was set up at Brisbane, that he wanted information produced by FRUMEL. Admiral Leary told me that we had to give MacArthur information but asked my suggestion on the best way to supply such material.
>
> I felt that certain restrictions were necessary to ensure security. Admiral Leary issued the following requirements: (1) Fabian or one of his unit's representatives will report to MacArthur's headquarters each day at 1400 hours. The FRUMEL representative will never be kept waiting in MacArthur's outer office. (2) No-one will be authorized to

make copies of any material provided by FRUMEL. (3) During the briefing of FRUMEL material, only MacArthur and his chief of staff, General Sutherland, will be present. Everyone else, including General Willoughby, will be excluded from these briefings.

On one occasion Fabian actually burned a signals intelligence document in front of Willoughby to demonstrate that he was not allowed to see it. After the move to Brisbane FRUMEL transmitted a daily radio intelligence summary to the naval staff officer at MacArthur's headquarters and he conducted the daily briefing. But despite his security concerns, Fabian freely admitted that part of his reason for not co-operating with Central Bureau was that, in his opinion, it had nothing to offer FRUMEL since it was less advanced and had entirely different interests. 'FRUMEL was concerned solely with information on Japanese naval circuits,' he said. 'The Central Bureau was not.'

This was simply not true. Few wars had seen more need for complete co-operation between the army and navy. The Japanese Army was forced by the very nature of the campaigns it was fighting, cut off from its home bases by thousands of miles of ocean, to pass messages on naval communications circuits, often in naval codes and ciphers. Messages would be translated from one system to the other providing a wealth of potential 'cribs', if only they could have been followed through the system. There were also a number of joint navy–army codes and ciphers providing potential 'cribs'.

Naval systems such as JN25, JN40, the merchant-shipping code broken at Kilindini, and JN11, the auxiliary fleet system, all carried large amounts of important military intelligence, particularly on movements of troops. The raw JN25 messages intercepted by FRUMEL's mainly Royal Australian Navy operators, and by FRUPAC (Fleet Radio Unit Pacific) in Hawaii, offered an important insight into Japanese attempts to reinforce Guadalcanal and New Guinea in the face of the Allied advances. While they were available to MacArthur, they were not seen by the Central Bureau codebreakers, who needed any assistance they could get to 'cheat' their way into the Japanese Army codes.

Fabian's refusal to co-operate also affected Central Bureau's attempts to keep track of air-to-ground messages and inform the Australian air defences of enemy aircraft movements, since virtually all of the Japanese aircraft operating north-east of Australia were naval air force.

'Brisbane was in the position of needing material and traffic analysis results from Melbourne for the sake of the naval air problem, whereas Melbourne thought that it had nothing that it wanted from Brisbane and was disinclined to co-operate,' said Nigel de Grey, a deputy director of GC&CS and one of those attempting to mediate to solve the problem. 'Fortunately, Brisbane established a "black market" with 7th Fleet which, however gratifying at the moment, was entirely reprehensible in principle.'

Sandford had initially passed material produced by Central Bureau to Fabian but after failing to receive anything in return had set up a private link with the US 7th Fleet while at the same time asking Bletchley Park to intervene in order to get the material through the proper channels. The British, who were concerned both at the lack of co-operation and the insecure procedures it was encouraging, spent a good deal of time battling to get OP-20-G to persuade Fabian to pass information to both Central Bureau and Kilindini. His attitude represented a microcosm both of the sometimes obstructive attitude Bletchley Park itself faced in co-operating with OP-20-G on Japanese codes and ciphers and of the even more bitterly competitive relationship between the US Navy codebreakers in Washington and their US Army counterparts now based at Arlington Hall, a former girls' college at Arlington, Virginia.

There was at least one happy fallout for Central Bureau from all the rivalry and rancour. If Fabian did not want Nave, the US Army codebreakers were very happy to have him, said Joe Richard.

Fabian's dislike of Eric Nave was very fortunate for us. Nave became an indispensable person. Early in the war, Central Bureau found that reading air-to-ground messages containing the weather gave away the intended target for that day. The warnings of Japanese air raids gained from reading these air-to-ground messages saved the Allied air forces in New Guinea and Australia early in the war and made possible the destruction of the Japanese air forces in that area when Allied air force got better aircraft and became stronger. Since General George Kenney, commander 5th Air Force, used these messages to gain command of the air, just reading them would have made possible the eventual winning of the war in MacArthur's area.

The diplomatic section of Nave's Special Intelligence Bureau "remained in operation in Melbourne under the control of the Australian Assistant Director of Military Intelligence Lt-Col R A Little. The operation was run by Henry Archer, a former British Consul-General in Harbin, with the assistance of Hubert Graves, a former British Consul-General in Kobe, Japan; Professor Trendall; and Roland Bond, a young Australian soldier who had been one of Trendall's students. The majority of the small unit of intercept operators working for the SIB were AWAS.

By early 1943, the Australian Special Wireless Group had deployed 51 Wireless Section to Darwin where it was picking up a good deal of Japanese military traffic, particularly from Borneo and the Philippines, and 55 Wireless Section to Port Moresby, on New Guinea. At one point the Japanese were only thirty miles away from Port Moresby and Bob Edwards, one of 55 Section's operators, recalled seeing RAAF Spitfires and USAAF Thunderbolts doing victory rolls as they flew back from the front line.

There were occasions when bombers returned with gaping holes in wings or tail assembly, sure evidence of the activity they had been involved in. There were two sad occasions. Firstly when a Flying Fortress, returning at night from a raid, hit the top of the mountain behind the camp and

212

blew up with the loss of all its crew. The second tragedy occurred one night when a bomber crashed on take-off. As its bomb-load went up, it sounded like all hell had been let loose.

Despite their closeness to the front line, the Allied forces based at Port Moresby were well looked after, Bob Edwards recalled.

For entertainment, deck-tennis tournaments were a feature of camp life and the inevitable picture shows and USO shows, including one in which Bob Hope appeared. There was a lot of interest displayed when Australian girls made their appearance with an Australian concert party. Poker, five hundred and chess were also popular pastimes. On more than one occasion, Keith Walshe [a professional entertainer] organized good concerts with talent from our own section and some imported from our counterparts in the RAAF at Port Moresby. Those so minded joined a church parade of a Sunday evening and attended a service at St John's on the Hill at Port Moresby where Padre Hammond and a US Army padre officiated. The cup of tea and a yarn after the service were happy and interesting interludes in the routine. For a fortunate few, Padre Hammond organized a cruise round Port Moresby Harbour on a New Guinea pearling lugger. Fishing with hand grenades proved a dangerous and frustrating occupation.

Each wireless section now had an Australian Special Intelligence Personnel Section attached to it, providing a basic codebreaking, traffic analysis and intelligence-reporting facility. There was a wealth of information to be had from reading the operator logs. Procedural codes, designed more to help operators discern what was being said than for security reasons, often produced important material, frequently confirming DF fixes of locations. The procedural code CHI A, which stood for 'this station is located at', was normally followed by a simple *kana* equivalent of the name, while the times of transmission of HI KE, the code for an air-raid alarm, could be compared with times of Allied raids to provide locations for the stations concerned. Low-grade messages sent without the use of codes or ciphers included casualty lists and preparations for Allied attacks. Plain-language operator chat often gave names that could be tied to specific units.

The Japanese system of recruitment also provided the traffic analysts with an easy method of identifying individual units. Each infantry regiment was strongly identified with a local district. It recruited from that district through a home depot in its garrison town. The division it was subordinate to also had a home depot covering the area in which the district lay and the neighbouring districts from which the division's other infantry regiments came. If a member of the regiment, from the lowliest soldier to its commanding officer, did anything of note – was promoted; decorated; captured by the enemy; wounded; or killed – this had to be reported back to both the regimental and divisional home depots. So it was relatively easy for the traffic analysts to identify new units from the home depots they were in contact with.

Although the Japanese Army codes were still frustratingly difficult to break, traffic analysis of 55 Wireless Section intercepts provided an early success for Central Bureau. It very quickly built up a detailed picture of the Japanese troops attempting to cross the Owen Stanley Range, north of Port Moresby, allowing the Australian 7th Division and the US 32nd Division to defeat them at Kokoda and force them back to the northern coast.

It was JN25 messages picked up by FRUMEL's intercept stations in the southern Melbourne suburb of Moorabbin and at Adelaide River, two hours south of Darwin, which led MacArthur to deploy the Australian 18th Infantry Brigade to Milne Bay in eastern New Guinea in September 1942 to repulse an attempted Japanese amphibious landing. But traffic analysis provided by Stan Clark's E Branch provided the backbone of MacArthur's intelligence about Japanese military activity on the ground.

214

A detachment of the RAAF's No. 1 Wireless Unit was sent to Port Moresby in January 1943 to assist 55 Section in its coverage of air-to-ground radio networks. The Japanese followed set procedures that allowed the intelligence analysts attached to the intercept units to predict precisely when and where they would strike. Direct telephone links between the intercept sites and the fighter controllers ensured that Allied aircraft could be in the air to intercept the enemy bombers.

Enemy weather reconnaissance flights provided the first clues. Naval air-to-ground traffic always contained a high percentage of weather messages. The codebreakers soon realized that those broadcast by stations at Truk, Rabaul and Tokyo were always of weather over territory held by the Allies. They invariably mentioned the name of the target, which was sent using a simple and easily broken substitution cipher. The difference between the time the weather reports were issued and the time of the raids was so standard that it was a simple task to predict when the Japanese aircraft would be overhead.

Japanese aircraft maintained strict radio silence when about to take off for a raid but the tuning-up of radio sets located by the interceptors' DF units provided forewarning that the enemy mission was about to start. In addition, the Japanese usually dispersed their aircraft to rear bases, only moving them to a frontline airfield shortly before a raid. The staging movement was normally accompanied by much slacker radio security than the mission itself and Allied aircraft could frequently be dispatched to mount a pre-emptive attack against the aircraft on the ground at the forward base.

The Guadalcanal campaign provided the Allied cryptographers with two useful bonuses in the form of 'pinches' of Japanese codebooks. The first came when US Marines captured a JN25c codebook shortly after landing, although this was superseded a week later by the JN25d book. The second was a major haul of various different codebooks and signals instructions recovered in early 1943 from a Japanese submarine. 'The New Zealand ships

HMNZS *Kiwi* and HMNZS *Moa* surprised the *I-1* at Kamimbo and sank her by ramming on 29 January,' said Phillip Jacobsen, who was now serving with Station AL, a small US Navy radio intelligence unit based on the island.

> While fifty or so Japanese survivors buried some documents, including codebooks, a later salvage operation by the submarine rescue vessel *Ortlan* recovered many other codebooks, communications and other secret documents from the *I-1* and the surrounding waters. These were brought to Station AL and we carefully dried them out page by page, as we knew their value. Although the codebooks were mostly superseded, it was very useful to have these complete codes and fleet vocabularies to aid further code recoveries.

Australian troops captured a list of Japanese naval area designators and a book of Japanese call signs at Milne Bay. But by early February 1943, when the Japanese finally gave up their fight for Guadalcanal, the Allied codebreakers were still struggling to make the break into the high-level Japanese Army codes. A solution was, however, close at hand. The Japanese Army's Water Transport Code, or *senpaku angosho 2*, a four-figure super-enciphered code known as 2468 since this appeared as the first group, or 'discriminant', of each message, was under attack at a number of centres. The lead appears to have been taken by Wilfrid Noyce, a classicist from King's College, Cambridge, and a well-known mountaineer, who together with Maurice Allen, an Oxford don, realized that the first letter of the third group of each message was not random. The third group in the 2468 received at Delhi was the repeater group or indicator. As in the main naval systems, this gave the starting point of the additive which was added to the encoded message.

The lack of randomness was the entry point into the code that the Allied codebreakers had been seeking. Accounts of who subsequently broke it differ, with the earliest date being ascribed to Noyce and Allen in March

1943. But Arlington Hall also claimed to have broken it first, in April, and, according to John MacInnes, Kilindini was receiving enough 2468 messages for Brian Townend to break it 'about the same time as solutions were reached by Delhi and Washington'.

Since Delhi was already sending decoded material back to Bletchley Park in April 1943, it seems likely that it was at the forefront of the first break into high-level Japanese military codes. But it appears to have been joined there by Central Bureau, where Joe Richard had begun working almost obsessively on the 2468 code to take his mind off the death of a friend:

> I decided to do double work after the accidental shooting of my friend John Bartlet. After the traffic analysts had extracted all the data they needed from the four-figure traffic, it was simply filed unsorted. So I volunteered to Colonel Sinkov to come back evenings and sort it by system. Each day's intercept was contained in a manila folder and the day was based on Greenwich Meantime so that all the traffic wherever intercepted could be collated together.
>
> Colonel Sinkov agreed and sent me to Major Norman Webb, an English officer who escaped from the FECB at Singapore with some records and twelve intercept operators. Webb put an Australian soldier to work pulling the traffic and, being a careful man, had him number each message consecutively so that if necessary it would be returned exactly as stored.

Working on the basis of Tiltman's previous break into a Japanese military system, the Allied codebreakers had made the assumption that mainline army systems were still based on a codebook and a cipher additive. So Richard needed to find a way to strip off the additives. To recover additives, a depth of messages must be available for each set of additives used and the messages superimposed in proper relative order, as determined by the indicator. This might appear anywhere in the message but somewhere else it would be repeated, so it was relatively easy to find. But the problem with this type of system was that the indicator was disguised by the use of a second, separate additive system. It was this system that Richard had to uncover to have any hope of breaking the messages. 'We decided to start with traffic for 19 December 1942 in order to catch any changes that might occur on 1 January 1943. So on an evening in January 1943 in a second-storey room at 21 Henry Street with the blackout curtains drawn and working on a big table under a dim drop light, I started sorting the traffic.'

On the table in front of him, Richard had three separate types of message: the Water Transport Code; the Army Air Force General Purpose Code, *koku angoo-sho 3*, known to the Allied codebreakers by its discriminant group 3366; and the General Army Administrative Code, or *rikugunangoo-sho 4*, which they referred to as the 7890. He first sorted the messages by system. 'Then I sorted each system by the repeated text group – all four-figure systems repeated a group from near the beginning as the last group. I used the repeated group because I thought it would enable me to place fragmentary messages together. In the first few evenings, I made two discoveries.'

The first was in the 3366 where Richard found sixteen messages passing between Rangoon and Saigon in which the first twenty-one textual groups were identical. This seemed to indicate that they all used the same additive and contained large amounts of identical plain text. It should by rights provide a way into the system. But it came to nothing when in March 1943 the 3366 system stopped for ten days and returned in a changed form, Richard said.

The other discovery was in the Water Transport Code, the 2468. This system repeated the third group – the other two systems 7890 and 3366 repeated the fourth group. I noticed that when I sorted the messages by the first figure of the repeated group in 2468 the piles of messages stayed the same from day to day. For example, the daily piles for the figure three would have lots of messages in them

218

while all the nine piles would have only one or two or none. This was non-random behaviour and differed from the way the 7890 and the 3366 sorted. I reported this non-random behaviour to Colonel Sinkov some time late in February 1943 and I think he brought me a typed three-page letter from WEC also noting that the first figure of the repeated group in 2468 was non-random.

A few days later I saw a message from Arlington Hall to all centres saying they would make an IBM listing of 2468 messages to look for this non-random figure. About two weeks later Arlington Hall sent another message saying their listing did not show any non-randomness. This puzzled me until I remembered that the non-randomness changed in character about every four weeks and I decided Arlington Hall must have mixed up two or three months' traffic across these changes. I remembered that I had not told Colonel Sinkov that the non-randomness changed every few weeks. So I went to him and told him – he was not very happy.

That evening I came back determined to find the exact day and hour when the first change occurred. I pulled the 2468 folders for about three days before the day that I thought the first change had occurred and for about three days after and started to copy down the date and message number. I found three groups of every message. I soon found this was a long job and was about resigned to staying most of the night when I noticed that there was a relationship between the non-random figure and the first figure of the group that preceded it. For any given figure in this preceding group only three figures and always one of the same three figures appeared as the non-random figure. So I prepared a three-column table for the editors. If a message fitted on the table it would belong in that particular period. After I had constructed this ten-row, three-column table I left the office.

The next morning, Colonel Sinkov held a meeting to decide what to do with my table. It was logical to put it in our monthly progress report but that had been typed up and given to the courier so it was decided to send it by

219

radio to Washington, a most generous gesture by Colonel Sinkov because we felt it was only the first big step and that in a few days we would disclose a lot more. We also told them about four-weekly change dates.

When there was no immediate reply from Washington, Zach Halpin, the officer in charge of the Central Bureau IBM tabulating machines, had each message of the first period Richard had sorted punched up on IBM cards and they did their own run.

Captain Larry Clark, a veteran of both Rowlett's 'Purple Section' and the pre-war Philippines Station 6, examined Richard's findings and pointed out a number of other figures which appeared to relate to each other in some way. If the first and second figures of the fifth group were the same, the first and second figures of the fourth group were the same, too. Clark also noted that the third and fourth figures of these two groups were similarly paired in 'doublets'. But it did not work the other way round. So if the first and second figures of the fourth group were the same, it was not necessarily the case with the first and second figures of the fifth group. This led Clark to deduce, rightly, that the fifth group was used to encipher the fourth group.

Having made this discovery, Clark went off to lunch, Richard said, leaving the junior codebreaker alone.

I started to copy their list of doublets, hoping to study it later. I soon realized I could not hope to do this in one lunch hour so the thought came to me to try to condense the lists – there were one hundred of them – into one 10 × 10 square table. I remembered from my instructions in Fort Monmouth Cryptanalysis School how Mr Friedman said to recover an alphabet square. To my pleasure, the lists organized into a square which I had out almost completely when Clark returned. He then checked it for accuracy and said, 'That three-column table of yours should be in this square someplace,' and after some time and a lot of searching we found the three columns in the square.

By then it was time to leave the office for the evening meal, but after eating I returned determined to recover the column figures across the top of the square. We had the row or key figure but the column or plain-text figures we had not fixed. I was using the three columns from my table as book figures (either 0, 1, 2 or 1, 2, 3) and assuming that the figures of the repeated group with the non-random first figure were respectively the book in use, the two figures of the page number of the additive table and the sum of all three figures by non-carrying addition, since we had seen that order on a captured decoded message in another army system. But the final solution kept slipping away, and I was sleepy. Then Larry Clark called on the telephone and, finding I was there, came in. Together we managed to recover the top co-ordinates of the square. We finished the task begun in December 1942 on 6 April 1943. What a great feeling to have finally found the solution.

The next morning we sent telegrams to all centres giving the square and all other details. That afternoon we were somewhat deflated to receive a message from Arlington Hall saying they had the square, and proving it by sending the second period square together with instructions for co-ordinating the work on 2468.

Because Sinkov had kept Arlington informed at each step of the way, they had been able to follow in Richard's footsteps, but there was little doubt the credit for the American contribution belonged to him. He could now begin to decipher and decode the messages.

With the squares we could recover the additive starting places of all messages and immediately sorted them by book and page, but we found that the row and column co-ordinates on the additive pages were in mixed random order. This meant that in order to write out the messages with the enciphered groups in the correct position above each other, they had to find two or three that started with the same row and column. They slid one message along the top of a second until subtracting a known likely code group in one message gave an additive that, when it was added to the enciphered group below it in the second message, left them with another known and commonly used code group in the second message.

After several possible additives had been found other messages starting in the same row or column could be tried so that other row and column digits could be placed and more messages using them added. Even we non-linguists could start and recover much of a page, starting with the *dendai* or message number group followed by a number group, which always occurred at least one-third of the way into the message as transmitted. Since the Japanese Army knew that the beginnings of a message were its weakest parts, they cut them into several parts and sent them in a rearranged order. I think this procedure baffled Washington and gave the Japanese Army high-level traffic security for almost a year and a half after the war started.

Apart from the spelling-out of numbers, there was a variety of different cribs that the codebreakers would look for to get into a message, Richard said. 'There were the code groups for open and close parenthesis, begin repeat and end repeat, begin skip code or end skip code, and most useful of all to the book breakers, begin Chinese Telegraph Code and end Chinese Telegraph Code. I think it was Major Webb who told our linguists to look for that.'

Within weeks, Central Bureau was able to read the Water Transport Code without difficulty and did so until the end of the war. Perhaps more importantly, as a result of the work done by Richard, Noyce and Allen, the Allied codebreakers now knew how the Japanese signallers enciphered the additive indicators for their high-level codes and ciphers. Delhi was already producing decodes which provided details of military units embarking on troop transports for the various areas occupied by the Japanese, and the knowledge gained through breaking it was being used to attack the other high-level military codes.

15

THE YAMAMOTO SHOOTDOWN

The Japanese had made numerous attempts to build up a series of coastal enclaves in northern New Guinea throughout the latter part of 1942. The Japanese Army was forced to pass messages to its commanders on board the transport ships via the easily broken WE code, providing Central Bureau's codebreakers with access to 'intelligence of considerable operational value'. This and JN25 messages intercepted in Melbourne and Hawaii ensured that many of the convoys were disrupted, but a number did get through. Despite Central Bureau's difficulties in breaking the main army codes, its Australian traffic analysts, using skills honed in the Western Desert, were soon building up a detailed picture of the enemy garrisons at Madang, Wewak, Hollandia and Lae and their efforts to construct new air bases from which to attack MacArthur's US and Australian troops.

In early January 1943 Central Bureau picked up the first signs of a major Japanese attempt to reinforce the garrison at Lae as a prelude to striking south towards Port Moresby in order to capture the tiny Australian garrison at Wau. In response MacArthur and Major-General George C. Kenney, the commander of the 5th Air Force, began a campaign of sustained attacks on the Japanese convoys taking the Japanese 51st Infantry Division to Lae. American B-24 'Liberator' bombers supported by

Lockheed P-38 'Lightning' long-range fighters picked off large numbers of supply barges and troop transports, killing thousands of Japanese troops.

As the FRUMEL codebreakers struggled with the Japanese Navy's introduction of an additional codebook, JN25f, in early February, aerial reconnaissance picked up signs of a much larger attempt to reinforce New Guinea. It was not until 19 February that Fabian was able to tell MacArthur that a major reinforcement convoy was scheduled to arrive in Lae in early March. OP-20-G deciphered another message indicating that there would be three reinforcement convoys, the other two going to Wewak and Madang. But the Lae convoy was by far the largest. It was to contain at least six transports and a similar number of escort destroyers, throwing the Japanese 51st Infantry Division into the battle for New Guinea.

In order to disguise the source of their intelligence MacArthur and Kenney sent out reconnaissance aircraft to spot the Japanese convoy. Knowing that it would take five days to reach its destination, they bided their time. The convoy was attacked by a single Liberator bomber on 1 March, losing one troop transport. On the morning of 3 March the US bombers attacked in force in what was to become known as the Battle of the Bismarck Sea. Using a low-level attack technique called skip-bombing, designed to skim their bombs across the water into the Japanese ships, the B-24s sneaked in under the convoy's shield of escort fighters. As the ships caught fire the Japanese troops rushed up on to the deck, only to be caught in a hail of machine-gun fire. All eight Japanese transport vessels and four destroyers were sunk and more than 3,000 soldiers killed. Only 1,000 managed to make it to Lae; the rest were taken back to Rabaul by the remaining destroyers.

The Japanese response, devised by Admiral Yamamoto, was Operation I: concerted aerial bombing of the Allied positions in Papua New Guinea and Guadalcanal. Again, the Allies were informed by Ultra, as high-grade signals intelligence was now known, of what was going on and were able to make defensive preparations.

In mid-April 1943 a number of Allied intercept sites picked up messages referring to a proposed visit by Yamamoto to the Solomon Islands to boost the morale of the Japanese forces based there. It was first picked up in Hawaii, in a JN25 message from Combined Fleet to the outstations that Yamamoto was to visit. FRUPAC's chief linguist, Major Alva 'Red' Lasswell, began to work on it. 'Lasswell approached cryptanalysis like a chess player manoeuvring relentlessly to untangle his problem,' wrote Jasper Holmes. 'His desk was usually clear of everything but his current puzzle. He worked sitting upright at his desk, wearing a carefully pressed Marine Corps uniform of the day, his sole deviation being a green eyeshade for protection against the hours under the fluorescent lights.'

As Lasswell worked his way through the Yamamoto message and began to realize what it was about, he called out to his colleagues: 'We've hit the jackpot.' He laboured through the night to recover the itinerary. Then Lasswell and Holmes took it by hand to Commander Edwin T. Layton, the Fleet Intelligence Officer.

As the message filtered down to the Japanese lower echelons, it was relayed on in much lower-level systems and was picked up in Australia by both the US code-breakers in Melbourne and 51 Special Wireless Section in Darwin.

Lieutenant-Commander Gill Richardson decoded the message at FRUMEL: 'The message I worked on was in a Japanese Army code system. Although we were unfamiliar with Japanese Army codes, we got this message out in a hurry because it was a substitution system.'

Nobby Clarke was working at Central Bureau when a message about the visit was picked up by Australian Army operators using a very basic army-air code:

The signal was intercepted by 51 Wireless Section and translated at Central Bureau in Brisbane before being passed on to those thought to need to know. The implications of this message are so bizarre that they have remained clear in my memory to this day. They were sent in the familiar Japanese Army air–ground code they were obliged to use to communicate with their beleaguered outposts. The message was so larded with the *kana* spellers that anyone familiar with the book could read them on sight.

As the two Betty bombers carrying Yamamoto and his aides flew past the coast of Bougainville, a formation of sixteen Lightnings led by Major John Mitchell of the 339th Squadron USAAF was waiting for them. Four of the pilots were air aces specifically selected for the accuracy of their shooting. While Mitchell and the other aircraft kept the escort of Naval Air Force Zero fighters busy, the four aces attacked and shot down the two Japanese bombers. Yamamoto was found still strapped to his seat wearing a brand-new green tropical uniform and clutching his ceremonial sword. He was cremated and his ashes taken back to Tokyo for a state funeral. The Japanese ordered an investigation amid concerns that the JN25 code had been compromised but eventually concluded that the later use of the low-level code by a junior army commander was to blame. Once again the codebreakers' secret had survived.

The moves to encircle the Japanese garrison at Rabaul continued throughout the latter half of 1943 with US Marines, under the command of Admiral William F. Halsey but now subordinate to MacArthur's South-west Pacific Area, island-hopping their way through New Georgia, Vella Lavella and on to Bougainville, where they gained a toehold at Empress Augusta Bay. Meanwhile, the Australian and US forces, now under the Australian general Sir Thomas Blamey, took control of eastern New Guinea, capturing the Japanese coastal enclaves at Lae, Salamaua and Finschhafen.

The men of 55 Wireless Section at Port Moresby were monitoring divisional- and regimental-level army networks along the northern New Guinea coast and at Rabaul. But many of these operated on low power, and reception on the other side of the Owen Stanley Range was far from perfect, so a detachment was moved forward to Kaindi, some 7,000 feet above the frontline Australian outpost of Wau, an old gold-mining centre. Based in the deserted home of a former mine manager, the detachment was able to pick up large numbers of new radio networks, many of which used extremely lax security. There were a lot of plain-language transmissions and the detachment was able to report a good deal of intelligence, including details of troops being sent in to reinforce the Japanese garrison at Lae.

Traffic analysis of the operator message logs carried out by Stan Clark's section in Central Bureau built up an extremely accurate picture of the movement of barges down from Palau and along the northern New Guinea coast, allowing General Kenney's 5th Air Force to launch devastating attacks that cut supplies to the increasingly beleaguered Japanese outposts.

When Blamey's forces captured Lae on 16 September and the Japanese 51st Infantry Division began its retreat to Kiari, the Australian Army intercept operators at Kaindi were able to track its movements. Ripped apart during the Battle of the Bismarck Sea as a result of intelligence provided by Central Bureau and FRUMEL, the unlucky 51st now found itself under sustained attack yet again as a result of the codebreakers' efforts.

Meanwhile, the complete stranglehold enjoyed over enemy air activity by the RAAF operators at Port Moresby had played a major part in assisting General Kenney's aircraft to destroy the Japanese carrier air groups based in Rabaul. The Japanese had lost nearly 3,000 pilots in the struggle for the Solomon Islands alone. Their replacements were not so well trained, aircraft and spare parts were in short supply, and casualties mounted at horrific rates. Japanese naval air power in the region would never be the same again.

The breaking of the Army Water Transport Code led to renewed attacks on other mainline systems. The US Army codebreakers at Arlington Hall were concentrating on the main ground forces' codes, among them the General Army

Administrative Code, or *rikugun angoo-sho 4*, known as the 7890.

David Mead, a young army corporal at Arlington Hall, recalled how the first breakthrough came in April 1943:

I had asked the IBM unit on numerous occasions for printouts of messages sorted on specific code groups in selected positions in the text. One of these revealed a pair of messages sent on the same date from Tokyo and apparently beginning with the same additive numbers. This could happen by chance, but more likely a Japanese operator carelessly or inadvertently sent almost identical messages without shifting to a different starting point in the additive table. The number of hits or matching groups was much greater than random. Further IBM runs on these matching groups uncovered two more messages, neither sent from Tokyo, using the same table, but with different starting points.

Mead used the depth of messages on the same table to break his way into the 7890 indicator system. 'As I walked the two miles home that day, I tried to sort out my feelings about the breakthrough,' he said. 'Relief, quiet elation, even a tinge of disbelief all combined in a kind of emotional tangle. I wondered, of course, what influence the breakthrough would have on the solution of the code. Most of all, I felt a bond, a sense of community, with the Allied forces who were enduring the hazards and hardships of the war in the Pacific.'

Until now, Bletchley Park's attacks on Japanese military codes and ciphers had been in the hands of a small Japanese codebreaking section assisted by John Tiltman as and when his other responsibilities allowed. With manpower at a premium, Japanese military had been very much the poor relation of its European counterparts. But with the breaking by the Wireless Experimental Centre and Central Bureau of the Water Transport Code and Arlington Hall's promising assault on the Army Administrative Code in progress, Tiltman decided the time was right for a more sustained and better co-ordinated attack on the Japanese Army high-level codes.

The British called a conference of senior codebreakers from all the main organizations working on the Japanese Army high-level systems. Mic Sandford happened to be visiting Bletchley Park at the time, and he and Tiltman were joined by representatives from Arlington Hall and Delhi. It was agreed that Bletchley Park and the Wireless Experimental Centre should concentrate their cryptographic resources on the codes and ciphers of the Japanese Army Air Force. Arlington Hall would deal with the high-level systems used by the Japanese ground forces, leaving Central Bureau to concentrate on the low-level material produced by its forward field units and the Water Transport Code broken by Joe Richard.

The Bletchley Park Japanese military section was forced to expand rapidly to take on the new responsibility and to cope with the increased intelligence expected as a result of the recent successes. Italy was on the verge of defeat and codebreakers were becoming available for other tasks. The section acquired its own army air sub-section in May 1943, and some weeks later a military intelligence section, which reported to MI2, the War Office intelligence section covering the Far East.

The Japanese military section had been located in Hut 10, originally home to the Bletchley Park air section. Its expansion during 1943 forced it to take over rooms in Hut 4, the former location of the German and Italian naval section, which had moved into one of the new purpose-built blocks that were replacing the old wooden huts. But so many army messages were being sent over Japanese naval circuits, and in a number of cases using JN25 and other naval codes and ciphers, that it was eventually decided that all the Japanese sections needed to work together, and they were moved into Block F, the largest of the newly built blocks. This consisted of a number of wings jutting off a long, central corridor which, as a result of its length and the proliferation of various Japanese sub-sections in the block, became known as the 'Burma Road'.

229

Most of the sections dealing with Japanese Army material were a mixture of Intelligence Corps personnel, Foreign Office civilians and members of the Women's Auxiliary Territorial Service (ATS), many of whom did extremely repetitive work preparing messages for the codebreakers to tackle. Gladys Sweetland was sent to the mysterious 'Station X' as a young ATS corporal:

I went for an interview at a place in Praed Street, in London. We were there for several days being interviewed by lots of different people, most of them officers. Then finally we were told we were being transferred to Bletchley. It was really rather weird. I was taken to a billet in Bedford, dumped off on the door with all my kit, given a travel pass and told to report to an administration officer the next morning. I was taken into a hut and introduced to what I was supposed to do. An officer explained it to me in great detail and it sounded so complicated I thought: I'll never be able to do that. But after he'd gone another officer came over and said, 'Did you understand all that?' I admitted I hadn't understood a word of it and so he explained it to me in much simpler terms.

Teleprinter sheets of coded messages were handed to me and I had to copy each message out in different-coloured inks across one line on large sheets of graph paper, a bit tricky when some stretched across four different sheets. Each message was marked with a sign to indicate which colour ink I should use. When I had completed copying one batch of messages out they were collected from me by one of the codebreakers and I was given another batch to copy. There were about ten people doing this on each shift, 8 a.m. to 4 p.m. and 4 p.m. to midnight. There were only two ATS on my shift, most were soldiers who were either no longer A1 or were considered too old to fight. I know it sounds ridiculous but we never asked what they did with the sheets of messages. It was all so secret. Even with the other girls in the ATS we only ever asked, 'Where do you work?' And they'd say, 'Oh, Hut 6' or 'Block F' or what-ever. We never asked each other what we actually did.

We were given travel passes to come in by train during the day, which was similar to going to and from work in 'civvy street' and, provided one stayed clear of male and female Redcaps, it was fairly easy. When we finished at midnight there was a bus which would take a whole load of us home, dropping everyone off at the various villages where they were billeted and it depended on how many of you there were, and what route the bus took, how long it took you to get home. The first woman I was billeted with was rather peculiar. She had two young children and wanted me to stay in and look after them all the time so she could go out. The second was much nicer. She was middle-aged. She had a son who was in the RAF and her attitude was that if she could treat people billeted with her kindly, then perhaps other people would treat her son the same way. She would insist on bringing me breakfast in bed after I had worked the late shift.

When we moved into Shenley Road Camp at the end of 1943 life became more complicated. Shenley was a bit grim when we first went there because it had been raining. But eventually it dried out. The huts slept about thirty people and were heated by two old army stoves, one at each end, which didn't throw out much heat. We had to follow the rules of the camp and read daily orders, take part in marches, PE, etc. and stay in on Tuesday (called Barrack Night) for lectures, kit and hut inspection. One could only escape this if on evening shift. We were separated from the men's camp by the coal yard. We were allowed to walk through it but not to linger.

When we moved into camp, I bought a bicycle and spent many a pleasant time cycling round the countryside. Bletchley Park was a wonderful location and sometimes we just sat in the grounds in fine weather for our break. I had a boyfriend who was transferred into our office after being invalided back from the front line. But there was a whole group of us who used to go around together to pubs and concerts. There was an assembly hall just outside and it was there I got my love for opera and ballet because I saw the D'Oyly Carte touring company and the Ballet

Rambert. There were also discussion groups where people would play classical music records and then explain the merits of the various pieces. I shall never forget the comradeship and meeting all those different types of people who were there. I never thought, leaving school at fourteen and a half, that I would be able to have a proper conversation with a university professor.

As a result of the work done by young women like Gladys Sweetland, the codebreakers' task was made much easier. The main army air code under attack at Bletchley at this time was the Army Air Force General Purpose Code, designated 3366. It was a four-figure system with a numerical additive applied in much the same way as 2468. Although Joe Richard had hit a brick wall when trying to gain an entry via the identical Rangoon–Saigon texts, both Delhi and Bletchley Park had enjoyed more success and the Japanese military section at BP managed to break the code not long after the breaking of the Water Transport Code.

Maurice Wiles was moved from the Japanese military attaché section to the team decoding the 3366 material some time in the first half of 1943:

The main work was done by four of us. Alexis Vlasto, who was one of the few who had not come via the Bedford school, was in charge. He was a Japanese and Russian linguist. Very quiet, very relaxed, with a nice ironic sense of humour. George Ashworth, later Registrar of Manchester University, was the quickest mind among us. He had a wonderful memory. He would say, 'Oh, I remember something similar to that four months ago.' The other was Mervyn Jones. He was a more reserved character, but with a similarly lively mind and a delightful sense of humour. I remember the day the war ended and there was nothing to do, he came in and pulled out an Aristophanes text and sat there chuckling away to himself. Then he put that away and pulled out a musical score.

Despite Ashworth's brilliant memory, the section needed a record of code groups and information passed on the messages if it was to keep control of the system and rebuild the book. Elsie Hart, an ATS staff sergeant, was recruited to set up an index:

I was called up to an ATS station, I think in Northampton, where they sorted us out and a few of us were kept back. We had to go to London for interviews and an intelligence test after which we were told to report to Euston Station. Nobody knew where we were going but we were taken on a train to Bletchley where we were billeted in various villages in the surrounding area, fleets of buses ferrying us to and fro. I was billeted in a little village called Wolverton. It was a bit sparse and they were a nice couple but unfortunately her greeting was a bit off-putting: 'Of course, we had to have you,' she said. 'We had no choice.' I then went into one of the wooden huts where I was interviewed by a captain and a colonel and from then on I stayed in that department setting up an index.

It was an index of the *dendai*, which is the Japanese name for telegram. The messages came through on sheets of paper which had been decoded. I had to devise a scheme so I could sort it out. I think I must have filed them under the names of the officers. I hadn't been on a Japanese course but gradually I picked up what I needed to know and Maurice Wiles helped me. In the end we had a crypto-index as well as this military one. I used to get calls from other parts of BP about what I had noted in this index, usually on the name of an officer.

'Elsie's Index', as it became known, was an invaluable working aid to the codebreakers, Wiles recalled. 'She was a lesson to me coming from my public school background, the sheer ability. Her combination of high intelligence, dedication and unfailing good humour made Elsie's Index the hub around which the activity of the section as a whole revolved.'

While working at Bletchley, Elsie fell in love with

another young codebreaker, John Griffin, who was a close friend of Wiles. 'It was quite a small department and we all got to know each other quite well,' she said. 'John had a particular friend in my department and they were billeted together in what was then a little village called Newport Pagnell.'

John Griffin, George Ashworth, Mervyn Jones and Maurice Wiles were all keen table-tennis players and played against each other in their spare time, Wiles said.

Fiercely competitive foursomes were marvellous relaxation during times of intense work. As a civilian I belonged to the Home Guard, which was a bit like *Dad's Army*. We weren't very efficient. There was a good deal of competition between the two platoon commanders and we had night exercises. Alexander Aitken, the Scottish chess champion, was one of these people whose limbs are very unco-ordinated. Marching alongside him was often very comical. There were a lot of very good chess players at BP. We used to have evenings when Hugh Alexander and Harry Golombek, both members of the British chess team, would take on twenty boards.

I found the codebreaking a stimulating mental activity. I think, being a civilian, it was very easy for me to have an easy relationship with the senior hierarchy and the most junior person, although that was certainly true of many of those who were in the services as well. I felt it was a very relaxing way to work. There were certainly boring periods. It's a much longer-term thing than a crossword and it was vital in codebreaking to do the groundwork first, to read through the text first, because that can be how you begin to spot the patterns.

The Japanese military intelligence section received material from the Japanese military attaché section, the army air material decoded in Vlasto's section, enciphered intercepts from Brisbane, Delhi and Arlington Hall, as well as anything arriving in the Japanese naval section that related to the Japanese Army.

The JMA material provided valuable information on the movement and existence of military units, as well as detailed intelligence – through the Tokyo Circular, the briefing paper sent to all Japanese military attachés – on Japanese activity on the various fronts. The most valuable naval codes were: JN25, which provided material on a wide range of subjects and was commonly used by military units in the major naval bases to pass their own traffic; JN11, the auxiliary fleet system, which contained a great deal of information on the movement of troop convoys and the locations of various military units; JN40, the merchant-shipping code, which also provided very valuable information on the movement of troop convoys; and JN147, the minor operations code, which often contained quite useful intelligence on local troop movements. There were a number of joint army–navy systems specifically designed for liaison but these produced very little intelligence.

Many of the decrypts that the section was working on arrived by teleprinter or from neighbouring sections, but since a lot of the material from overseas stations had to be sent by bag, it could be several weeks old by the time it got to Bletchley Park. Nevertheless, even these decrypts could have a great deal of current operational value, largely because the great distances involved in any campaign in the Far East and Pacific regions meant that Japanese movements had to be planned well in advance; one Japanese division took four months to move from its base in Korea to Burma. Strategic plans were often discussed and rehearsed many weeks in advance.

The section was under the control of Don Parkin, a Foreign Office civilian who was popular with his staff of mainly ATS and Intelligence Corps officers and NCOs, among them John Burrows, who after escaping from Singapore had been commissioned and sent to Bletchley Park. Betty Vine-Stevens was one of the ATS senior NCOs producing intelligence reports on Japanese military activity:

I and some friends walked out of college in August 1941 because we thought we were wasting our time when we should be doing something for the country. One had to do one's basic training and then everyone was tested to see what job they would be best at. Because I spoke a bit of German, they sent me off to Devonshire House, the head-quarters of MI8 – the branch of military intelligence that dealt with Bletchley Park. The interview was conducted in German but was quite simple, so I could cope with that. One didn't know where one was going, no-one had heard of Bletchley at that time, but we were taken along in coaches and dumped outside civilian billets.

She was put to work on 'paraphrasing', turning the decoded messages into intelligence reports so that their source could not be traced and the secret of the broken codes remained intact.

One was given these messages and you had to put them into different wording so that it could be put out in this disguised form. Everything went out under a double-envelope system with different addresses. There were a lot of numbers on the outside one so that the dispatch rider could tell where it was supposed to go and then someone else opened it and sent it on to the address on the inside envelope. But as with everything we did, we knew very little of the next step. I decided in my own mind that the reports probably went direct to Churchill or to other Allied leaders.

It was a large section but I do remember a number of people: Captains John Burrows, John Humphries and John Brett-Smith; Sergeants Sandy Sanderson and Trixie Taylor; Lance-Corporal Jimmy Bentley; and Sergeant Mark Glover, whose wife and son were killed in London by a doodlebug. I shall never forget that poor man coming back on duty and saying, 'All I found was my boy's tie.'

Sergeant Glover's brother-in-law was the pianist Jack Byfield and he had been to BP to give us a recital. We were well blessed with recreational activities such as sport, drama, music, etc., and, despite much repetitive and sometimes rather boring duties, the atmosphere was happy and relaxed, with the usual services humour. While small fry like me did not fully understand the importance of our own input, we did understand that it was imperative that we kept at it and that we did so in the utmost secrecy.

The fact that much of the material that the Japanese military section worked on came from abroad, and in particular from Arlington Hall, also led to a great deal of competition between the codebreakers at Bletchley and their US counterparts to get material out first, to the extent that at times Arlington Hall was almost regarded as the enemy, said Maurice Wiles.

We felt very detached from the Japanese and there wasn't much feedback. We weren't really seeing the impact of what we were doing. But we swapped what we were doing with the Americans and there was a sense in which they were the 'enemy'. The word enemy has to be in inverted commas but research people are always very keen to get their research out first. When you're doing a crossword you don't like being told by someone else what the answer is. There were great cries of dismay when they told us something first and jubilation when we did it to them.

16

THE BLETCHLEY PARK STRIPPERS

By the spring of 1943, the British had become convinced that it was pointless if not foolhardy to rely on the Americans for Japanese naval material and were committed to building up their own codebreaking operations both at Bletchley Park and in the Indian Ocean area. The irritation and frustration over the US Navy's attitude towards co-operation had culminated in the discovery that the Americans were holding back a large number of 'pinches', captured codebooks that would have been of immense use to the British codebreakers.

The various pinches, which covered a large number of other codes and ciphers, including JN25, came as a total surprise to the British, who asked for a complete catalogue of captured Japanese naval material, most of which they discovered had been retained in Hawaii and Melbourne.

The Admiralty made its displeasure clear and the measures to improve the Japanese naval operations in Kilindini and Bletchley Park in order to make them more independent of the American operation forged ahead. The difficulties of reception in East Africa were to be resolved by a move back to Colombo as soon as circumstances allowed. In the meantime, Jon Cohen and Hugh Denham were sent to Kilindini along with another Japanese-speaker from Captain Tuck's most recent course.

They would be followed by a large number of Wrens in

order to fill the desperate need for more reliable clerical assistants than the Temporary Women Assistants recruited from among the local expatriate community. Their role would be to strip off the ciphers and to operate the Hollerith tabulating machinery.

'We went to Mombasa by landing ship from Merseyside to Takoradi in the Gold Coast,' Cohen recalled. 'Then from there flew to Lagos, spent two weeks in Lagos, which we hated, then by plane to Khartoum and then to Nairobi and finally by train to Mombasa.'

Their arrival coincided with something of a revival for Kilindini. The JN25 code had split, with two separate codebooks and three different methods of encipherment in operation. One of these systems, JN25e11, was available in Kenya in far greater quantities than elsewhere, giving the British codebreakers access to a depth of messages not available to the Americans. For the first time, the Kilindini station managed to exploit the Hollerith tabulating machinery to its full potential. In addition, a new transmitter was set up to allow them direct communications with Bletchley Park and two more Type X cipher machines were introduced to speed up the flow of recoveries.

The new codebreakers had been commissioned as sub-lieutenants in the Royal Navy and had been forced to wear uniform on board the landing ship taking them from Liverpool to West Africa. But when they arrived in Kilindini, Keith, who had been used to the more relaxed atmosphere of Bletchley Park and knew its advantages, told them to revert to civilian clothes, Cohen said. 'Bruce Keith didn't want us to wear uniform because we would then start being ordered to do all the sort of things that would take up time.'

There were three main codebreaking sections at Kilindini, one working on JN40, which consisted of three codebreakers, a pensioner clerk and two locally employed female clerks; a second working on the Fleet Auxillary System, JN11, a derivative of the merchant-shipping code, JN40, which had taken over the most productive traffic; and a third and very much larger section working on JN25 and led by the Dutch naval officer Lieutenant-Commander Leo Brouwer and the veteran Royal Navy codebreaker Lieutenant-Commander George Curnock. This had five codebreakers assisted by three pensioner clerks and seventeen female clerks. All deciphered material was channelled through an intelligence section run by Lieutenant-Commander Neil Barham.

Cohen recalled that he and Denham were set to work on Kilindini's revived JN25 operation under Brouwer and Curnock, rebuilding the codebook.

We did this in different ways. The best, of course, the nicest way is if somebody has been put in the way of stealing or somehow picking up this thing. The most direct way they might have done that was by a copy of the code being left on an island that the Japanese had evacuated. Then you might have received details of the individual code groups from the Americans. But you'd be lucky if you got them all. So what did we do? Well, we might know that a certain type of message at a certain time of day was being sent out from the Commander-in-Chief, or it might fit in with weather, or with some minor battle or engagement that had been going on. So there were these various things that we might expect the Japanese to be talking about and that would be the kind of thing that gave us a clue.

Then there might be patterns in the text of the message. You might find a message that echoed another message that had been sent a long time before and so then you might test if it was right to decode this new message in that way. There were some messages that were sent by a particular station at a certain time of day that were always the same. However strong the warnings sent by the Japanese intelligence people to their juniors that this was insecure, they still broke the rules and did things like send the same message at the same time every day.

The ability of the two new young codebreakers proved the wisdom of Tiltman's decision to implement the six-month Bedford course and impressed the older hands like John MacInnes. 'These two very soon found themselves well in the hurly-burly of translating a mass of messages with an inadequate staff, and rose to the occasion,' he recalled. 'Their experience from April to July 1943, combined with their great ability, made them into translators and book-builders of a standard scarcely reached by later arrivals who did not have to face such a press of work.'

Both at Bletchley and in Kilindini, the new young graduates coming in found it difficult to relate to many of the older pre-war codebreakers, Cohen said.

There were, of course, all sorts in the navy who were recruited as intelligence officers or interpreters or whatever who might not have seemed to be the brightest ones around and, if you can imagine the difference between us in our very early twenties and these other people who were in their forties or fifties, they were senior to us but were not respected by us in the way they should have been. So there was some tension there. But we felt we still had a long way to go and the best people at the game were the ones who taught us how to get on with it. George Curnock in particular was just brilliant at the game, very intelligent. He was a three-ringed commander who had been in the FECB and would 'gin himself up' before work. But he had a very powerful mind and could talk, and sing, irrespective of how many gins he had.

Outside of work, Kilindini was a very relaxed place to be, Cohen recalled.

Mombasa was lovely, a very nice climate. The junior officers' mess was right on the sea front with the roar of the sea hitting the rocks. We were members of the yacht club which was allowed to sail into the harbour. We made an effort to climb Kilimanjaro. Hugh did it and I dropped out 1,000 feet from the top. Then there was the beach. Nowadays, you see Mombasa as a tourist resort but in those days it was unspoilt. Once a week there was a classical music concert, records, of course, up on the ramparts of Fort Jesus, the castle that the Portuguese had built. We all sat out in the tropical night listening to classical records.

The spring and early summer of 1943 saw a gradual change in OP-20-G's attitude towards co-operation on Japanese naval codes and ciphers. Whether this was a result of the strong views being expressed by the Admiralty or the marked increase in the number of useful messages coming out of Kilindini which were not available to the Americans elsewhere is not clear. But at the end of March OP-20-G agreed to institute a weekly US courier service of recoveries and other findings between Washington and Kilindini. Melbourne was still holding back 'crucial material' as late as March but, as signs of a US rethink began to emerge, Fabian was recalled to Washington for discussions.

In May 1943 Bletchley Park reached a groundbreaking co-operation agreement with the US Army. The BRUSA Agreement is widely seen as the predecessor of the post-war UK–USA Accord which continues even now to ensure that British and US signals intelligence operations are very closely co-ordinated. It had not been reached without a great deal of acrimony over the vexed issue of the extent of US Army involvement in the breaking of the German Enigma machine ciphers. But with respect to the Japanese it did little other than to rubber-stamp the willingness of both sides to co-operate fully.

On the naval side, however, despite the apparent thaw in relations between OP-20-G and Bletchley Park, considerable difficulties remained. Joe Redman and Wenger were invited to a series of conferences at Bletchley and the Admiralty during July and August at which the British pushed for better co-operation on Japanese naval matters. The Americans agreed to pass urgent material and all recoveries to the British. The move from Kilindini to Colombo was now only weeks away and Redman promised that the new station could have an American cipher link direct to Melbourne, controlled by a US naval liaison officer. The problems appeared to be over.

Not the least important result of the apparent end to a damaging dispute that had lasted for more than a year was the arrival for the first time at the Admiralty, South-east Asia Command and HQ Eastern Fleet of substantial numbers of US Navy signals intelligence reports of interest to the British.

Another interesting skirmish in the final days of the rows over co-operation involved claims made by a number of British officers that a small Royal New Zealand Navy intercept operation which ostensibly came under Fabian's control was not being given enough 'guidance'. The section was run by a Lieutenant Philpott, assisted by Professor Campbell, Professor of Mathematics at Wellington University, a part-time civilian Japanese interpreter and two women assistants, 'both of whom were above average ability and one of whom knew quite a bit of Japanese'. Interception, DF and radio-fingerprinting were carried out by New Zealand Wrens at a number of sites in the South Pacific, extending as far as Suva in Fiji, and despite its small size and apparent lack of assistance or direction from Melbourne the section was remarkably productive.

New Zealand was not the only Commonwealth country to do what it could to intercept Japanese naval communications. The Canadian signals intelligence organization, the Examination Unit, whose main target was diplomatic and commercial traffic, also intercepted Japanese naval communications, including JN25 material picked up at its intercept site in Esquimalt. The Examination Unit received assistance with decoding from Bletchley Park, which stationed a senior codebreaker in Ottawa on a permanent basis to control operations, but its naval intercepts were co-ordinated by OP-20-G, albeit with a similar lack of control and guidance to that exercised by FRUMEL over the New Zealand operation.

There was also an 'unofficial' intercept operation in

Mauritius, which was set up and run entirely of his own volition by Edward Twining, later Baron Twining and a member of the tea family, who was the island's chief censor and information officer. His civilian staff worked under the cover of the colony's censorship department, and although the extraordinary size of his organization led to local criticism that they were a waste of public money and were engaged in everything from censoring letters to 'fixing the prices of cabbages', their true purpose appears never to have been suspected.

The main codebreakers were a local Mauritian civil servant, a botanist from the colony's agricultural department who had studied Japanese, a former headmaster's secretary who had 'a crossword-puzzle mind' and a trained chemist who came in on a part-time basis. There were a number of clerical assistants, described by Twining as being recruited from 'good Mauritian families who, if their standard of intelligence is not high, are keen, hardworking, sound and adequate', and the intelligence passed to London, which was deemed by the Admiralty to be 'of considerable value', was enciphered before transmission by wives of local British officials.

That the operation, codenamed CHESOR, was never compromised is all the more remarkable given that, in Twining's words, the eighty intercept operators were 'mainly drawn from the colonial community and are an undisciplined lot of ragamuffins. We possess no disciplinary powers except dismissal, which in most cases is undesirable.' Order was kept by force of Twining's personality and a daily bonus of between three and five rupees for turning up to work and satisfactory conduct while there.

At Bletchley Park, Hut 7 was expanding rapidly as more and more staff from the Italian naval section moved across to work on Japanese material and new recruits arrived, many of them Wrens like Rosemary Calder, who recalled being put to work in the Japanese Navy traffic analysis section which was run by the Cambridge historian Sir John Plumb.

I was interviewed by Jack Plumb, who told me, 'we analyse traffic'. I had no idea what this meant. I had this picture in my mind of people sat on camp stools by the side of the road counting lorries and gun carriages. I spent most of my time at BP attached to the room of which Angus Wilson the famous novelist was head. We considered ourselves to be a small, exclusive group who were all given scope for initiative and intelligence despite the bulk of the work being of a repetitive clerical nature. Any of us could do any of the jobs in the office. It was a very democratic place. Wrens mixed up with civilians. We might as well have not been in uniform. We were having a marvellous time. It was like being back at college.

Angus was a great darling who spoilt us all and we spoilt him in return. He called us all Ducky and he had this special friend called Bentley Bridgwater who took over the traffic analysis section from Jack Plumb and later went on to become Secretary of the British Museum. Angus was known to be very brilliant but crazy. He had at least one nervous breakdown before I got there and was still going to Oxford to see a psychiatrist, writing all his dreams down. But he was very good-natured most of the time and if he started getting agitated, we would just give him a copy of *Vogue* or *Tatler* and he could go off and sit down by the lake flicking through it and come back as happy as a sandboy.

Anne Petrides, another of the young Wrens in Hut 7, worked on an index of merchant-shipping movements.

I joined naval section at BP the day after my eighteenth birthday 'celebrated' at the WRNS training centre at Mill Hill on 31 May 1944 and was flung into the work of cataloguing ships, entering brief notes on their cards about the decoded signals as they came to us from the translations. Most of their warships had been sunk by then and we were dealing with *maru* – merchant ships.

The naval officers in my office included Gorley Putt and 'Shrimp' Hordern, brother of Michael Hordern, the actor.

As a very young girl I was petrified to be left all alone at lunchtime, in four interconnecting rooms – and in fact justifiably so, as a senior officer from the Admiralty phoned and said, 'Can we go over . . . ?', followed by a burble of words. He came back in clear language and was outraged to find that not only had no-one seen fit to tell me which button to press for the scrambler but that no 'duty officer' was present.

A regular visitor from 'down the passage', usually on quieter night watches, was Angus Wilson. His first book of stories was said to have originated in a series of sessions he had with a psychiatrist. I believe the men cracked more easily under the strain, whereas girls found it easier to have a crying breakdown. We Wrens were extremely spoilt in our accommodation, nothing but the best country houses in the area, including Woburn Abbey, while the ATS lived in barracks at the back of the park. I started out at Wavendon House. Then I lived at Stockgrove Park. It had been rather knocked about by the 51st Highland Division which had been there before us. I remember dances attended by locally billeted GIs and drinking draught cider. Very heady.

The authorities at Bletchley Park also continued to rely on the Oxbridge old-boy network to talent-spot new recruits. Norman Scott was reading Mathematics at Brasenose College, Oxford, when his tutor Theodore Chaundy, who had himself spent some time at Bletchley Park early in the war, recommended him for work on Japanese codes. Scott was assigned to Hut 7 to work on the relatively new JN11:

There were two familiar faces in the group: Patrick Taylor had been at Brasenose with me and I knew Harry Field from New College. I also recall meeting Hugh Foss, the head of Hut 7. Apparently, he had been in the code and cipher-breaking business for many years. As a 'break-in' guru, his talents were not those needed for the exploitation of partially cracked ciphers. It was not long before all of us working on JN11 moved to the Japanese naval block to become part of Commander McIntyre's group which already dealt with JN25 and other Japanese naval codes and ciphers.

Most of my working time was spent in a long, narrow upper-floor room with one door to the corridor. This accommodated all of us except our sub-section chiefs Brian Augarde and John English. Both were lieutenants in the Army Intelligence Corps. Immediately opposite our door was an equally large room for the JN11 translators headed by an army captain. His chief assistant was a Bedford-trained RAF sergeant named Harris-Jones. He would walk over with his needs for missing portions of a partly deciphered message and leave us with helpful suggestions on how we might tackle the blank stretches on our worksheets.

JN11 was similar to the JN25 code used by the Japanese Fleet proper. However, it was much simpler to use. (Merchant Navy wireless operators could not be trained as well as their counterparts in the Imperial Navy.) When I joined the team many of the JN11 code groups and stretches of the first book of additive tables had already been identified. Looking at our worksheets, one could see the human factor in play. It was easier for the sender to use the right-hand page of the random-number books to copy out the additive groups below those in his encoded message. Very few messages exceeded 100 groups. To save turning the page, the encipherer would start at or near the top-left of the page. Positions 90, 01, 10 and 11 were very popular. Finally, if there are three books to choose from, it can be expected that the first book will be used more often.

As messages came in and had their starting positions determined, they would be copied out by hand on to wide sheets of fifty columns with three or more vertical spaces between each message. At the top of each column would be the additive, if known. If it were known, it would be added to each enciphered group in the column to yield the underlying code group. Beneath that code group would be its meaning in Japanese if this meaning were known. The

247

number of messages under each column heading was known as 'depth'.

The most common first code group of a message was 7879, meaning *hatsu*, 'from'. After that, 4276 meaning *maru*, 'merchant ship' could be hypothesized in the next few columns. Then there were pairs like 2269 for 'open bracket' which would lead to a search of following columns for 0328, meaning 'close bracket'. If *hokui*, 'North', showed up, one could search for *tookei*, 'East', to follow. Then there were the Japanese grammatical suffixes *ha* (nominative case), *wo* (accusative case), *no* (genitive). The group 5566 for *shuushifu*, meaning 'full-stop', often followed the 'from so & so' opening.

Like JN25, the JN11 code had a built-in error check. The sum of the four figures would be divisible by three with one over, and this helped the codebreakers to check that their calculations were correct, Scott said.

For instance, on a depth of three, hypothesizing 4276 as one of the underlying code groups would yield acceptable code groups by chance in only one in nine tries. As more of the code group meanings were established, even arithmetically acceptable code groups whose meaning was still undetermined could be doubted as a valid solution for the additive.

Very much a part of the scene were the young women who performed, manually, a great deal of the work. As I recall, all but two Wrens were civilians from the London area. They copied out new messages on to the single set of 600 wide sheets, each with fifty columns. They wrote in additives received from the US Navy team in Washington and applied them to the enciphered groups in the column. They kept our codebooks up-to-date as new meanings came from the translators across the hall and from Washington. If and when these tasks were all completed, they would 'drag' commonly used code groups through wide stretches of unbroken messages where some depth existed. The process of discovering the 30,000 additive

248

groups was akin to stripping away the disguise which hid all the code groups in any one column. Consequently the process itself was known as 'stripping'. This led, of course, to the term 'stripper' for a person who did it. Our hard-working helpers declared it a great pity that they could not tell their families and friends that they worked at Bletchley Park as strippers.

Olive Humble, one of the Temporary Women Assistants drafted in to work as 'strippers', was put into another sub-section of Hut 7. She had been called up in early 1943 for the WRNS but there were no places and she found herself sent off instead to the Foreign Office as a civil servant.

So in February 1943 I arrived at BP and was escorted to the Billeting Office by an armed soldier, to my great consternation. I had never left home before, having worked in an insurance office in the City when I left school. I was suitably impressed with my new surroundings, until I saw the Mansion, which no-one can say is beautiful to the eye.

I was parcelled off to a Commander Thatcher, a fierce naval man who put the fear of God into me. He informed me that I was in the Japanese naval section, which confused me even further, that from then on I would not be allowed to leave the Park other than through death or disablement, that if I said one word of what I or anyone else was doing, even to my nearest and dearest, I would get thirty years without the option. He stood over me while I digested the Official Secrets Act and dutifully signed it.

My billet was in Bedford – the lady of the house was not a willing billeter, and for the few months I was there she made my life miserable. I was turned out in the evenings as I was in the way, and so roamed round Bedford, which was manned by the American Army Air Force. I was petrified. Later I made a friend in another part of my section and we joined forces and went to another billet, again in Bedford, to a Mr and Mrs Buick, who had two children. They were completely and absolutely magnificent, never probed, always there for us.

So many of the people working at Bletchley Park were now women that Edward Travis had set up a 'Women's Committee' to advise him on 'all questions affecting women at the War Station' and to ensure 'the promotion of the well-being of all the women working at the War Station'. The committee included representatives of all three women's services plus Foreign Office civil servants, and its chairman, a Miss J. V. Wickham, was available at all times to offer advice and help to 'any civilian woman who is in difficulty of any kind'.

Olive was put to work on the JN40 merchant-shipping code broken in Kilindini.

One half was manned by a host of civilian women, who seemed to be dealing with coloured flimsy sheets of paper. I never did know what they did. The other half of the room was manned by the navy, and there we went. I was put on to three shifts immediately, the civvies were always on days, and I found myself sitting at a table with six to eight Wrens. In the centre of the room was the boss, Major W. E. Martin. He was older than us, of course, and looked after his youngsters like a benevolent father. At the other end were three or four navy boys. All were young and bright, and I was quite happy, as I had really wanted to join the Wrens.

We put the five-figure blocks, typed on flimsy paper, into clear English letters from pads, and constructed clear messages, such as, '*Otaru maru* leaving Manila at 0200 hrs for Singapore arrives such and such.' These messages were then passed to Major Martin, who I suppose with hindsight passed them on. We didn't know what was happening in any other part of the section: the need-to-know syndrome was very much to the fore. One thing I regret deeply. I was an only child, and on my first day home my father at dinner said, 'What do you do at the Foreign Office?' I replied, 'I cannot tell you. Sorry. Please don't ask me again.' And he didn't; nor did my mother at any time. She died in the early 1960s and he in 1976, before I realized the silence had been lifted.

One of the young civilian women working in the other part of Major Martin's section was Elizabeth Ross.

I was conscripted after one year at Oxford University read- ing Medicine, along with a friend, Felicity Berryman. We were both sent to Hut 7 to work on the JN40 merchant- shipping code. It changed every month and once you had broken it you could set up the grids for the next month. A lot of the messages were positions, endless positions in latitude and longitude, sightings of ships. When there was a 'rush' on we were occasionally sent to work on JN25, which was a nice change and was presided over by the Cambridge mathematician Septimus Wall. There was always great competition with the Americans on JN25. If we got some way in there was always a feeling that we shouldn't tell them this time: 'We can get there first. Don't let them know about this one.' That was always the joke, of course. We always did tell them but we always felt that we did terribly well without the machinery and vast amounts of manpower they had.

Like other Bletchley Park employees, we never spoke to anyone, even people in the neighbouring offices, about what we did. It was extraordinary. You might have friends in the next office, but you would meet them outside or in the canteen. You would never visit them in the office. We were billeted first in London Road, Bedford, and travelled in to BP in the army transport – very basic buses with wooden seats. After a few months we managed to move to a self-catering billet at Stony Stratford in an old coaching inn with wobbly floors. This was a wonderful improvement.

We were on twenty-four-hour shifts throughout our time at BP. There was no weekly day off as far as I remem- ber but we were entitled to a long weekend every month and there was sometimes a bit of free time when the shifts changed over, especially if you didn't bother going to bed after the night shift. Days off we spent in one of two ways. We either hitched along Watling Street to London – the marvellous lorry drivers always picked us up and the roads

251

were empty of all other traffic, except military vehicles, because of petrol rationing – or we bicycled to meet friends in Oxford – sometimes spending a night. But we seem to have been valiant bikers because sometimes we'd return the same day. We went via Buckingham but never learned the names of the villages because no notices or signposts were allowed to be displayed for fear of helping the enemy in case of an invasion or spy drop.

Olive Humble also remembered cycling to various places on her days off.

The social life at BP was for me rather mixed, as being on shift work did curtail it to a certain extent. When I did get enough time off, between shifts, I would remain in Bedford, sometimes with a Wren, whose name I have forgotten but who introduced me to Mozart. She would drag me into her favourite music shop, and we would land in the booths and listen to records. My recollection of hearing *Eine Kleine Nachtmusik* for the first time is still very vivid.

I met some odd characters there. One was a very brainy lad, who could only work well while under the influence of whisky, so the caring FO provided him with a bottle a day or equivalent, until he broke and was taken away. I remember passing him in the corridors, always dressed in a pin-stripe suit, papers under his arm, muttering to himself, and a strong smell of malt wafting by with him. Another bright specimen divested himself of all his clothing and galloped round the lake with the army in hot pursuit, cheered on by us spectators on the banks, and the Wrens rowing lustily on the lake.

17

RETURN TO COLOMBO

The move from Kilindini to Colombo began in August 1943, the advance party arriving in Ceylon on 1 September 1943. Keith had wanted a site up-country away from the city, where reception was expected to be better. But he was overruled by the Chief of Intelligence Staff for HQ Eastern Fleet, who insisted the codebreakers should be within easy reach of headquarters. The intercept station and codebreaking operation had to be set up on the only available site at the Anderson Golf Course, just six miles from the Colombo HQ.

This was hardly the ideal site for intercepting radio traffic, stuck between a railway line and a main road, directly under the flightpath of aircraft flying into the Racecourse Aerodrome and far too close to a 33,000-volt high-tension electricity supply. As a result, radio reception was nowhere near as good as it could have been. Nevertheless, it was far better than at Kilindini and the codebreakers were soon swamped with JN25, JN11 and JN40 intercepts to work on.

The intercept operators at Anderson were kept extremely busy, not only noting down the messages passing between the Japanese naval stations but controlling an extensive Allied DF system which ranged from South Africa to India and on to Australia, recalled Paul Longrigg, one of the operators.

The main receiving room at Anderson consisted of about a hundred receiver bays. Radio communications between all the main Japanese bases in South-east Asia were covered continuously at Anderson. Each operator was assigned an enemy radio channel to monitor and took down all the traffic it passed.

Occasionally, a Jap mobile unit would come up on one of these channels, to indicate very briefly and quickly to the shore station that it wanted to pass traffic on another previously assigned channel. The mobile would then immediately switch to this new frequency and send its traffic as rapidly as possible. When this occurred the control room at Anderson became a pandemonium of activity. When it happened on more than one channel simultaneously (as it often did) everything turned into a veritable 'madhouse'.

The enemy frequency on which the main traffic was to be passed had to be monitored. Sometimes these channels were known, and sometimes they were not, in which case a frantic search of the most likely part of the spectrum had to be made.

Once the signal was intercepted it was fed over a 'guard channel' to all the DF outstations in the network, Longrigg said.

The operator at each of the DF stations had one earphone tuned to Anderson's guard channel, while the other earphone was tuned to the enemy signals picked up on a local receiver at the outstation. When the two signals matched the operator immediately took a bearing on the enemy unit with a radio goniometer, a device that electronically moves a search antenna through 360 degrees. The skill of the DF operator lay mainly in his ability to tune his receiver quickly to match the signals on Anderson's guard channel, and also in his ability to take accurate bearings with the goniometer.

The various bearings allowed the position of the

Japanese ship or submarine to be plotted on the map, but the DF operators had only a very brief period of time in which to get their bearing. 'All of this activity had to be done extremely rapidly,' explained Longrigg, 'for the enemy did not linger around when transmitting traffic, knowing that he was being listened to and, in all probability, his position being determined. Some transmissions would last for only a matter of seconds, but such was the efficiency of Anderson's organization that enemy locations were very often determined from such short periods of traffic.'

Anderson was centred on a long, narrow, single-storey building built in a rectangle with wings coming off the centre. 'It was specially built for the purpose,' said Jon Cohen. 'You came in at one end and then at right angles there was one very large unit going off and then another one.'

Each section was located next to the section handling the next stage in the production process. Intercepted messages were recorded in the central wireless telegraphy watchroom on standard white message forms specially designed to fit the needs of every section in the production process. These then passed from one room to the next.

'The whole process was absolutely continuous,' said Cohen.

It got better because as the Japanese got weaker and their positions were overrun by Americans, Australians or whatever it became more and more easy to get cribs, breaking into the cipher without having to work away at it. In Mombasa there were only about four or five people working on book-building. When we got to Colombo they came out in wodges of about three at a time. We had an enormous mechanical computer or tabulating machine which we used for storing our information. There was a firm called Hollerith, which had some kind of contract with the navy, and they had a very large office with an enormous mechanical computer, rods going through. A lot of the work was filed away, what data you had about a certain code group. We would collect a depth of messages with that particular group in it so that when you felt you might have a conjecture to test you hoicked it out and saw what context it had come in.

There were huts on the camp itself for the junior ranks but initially officers and civilians were based elsewhere.

I lived in a junior officers' mess on the sea front. Then more and more people came out and a mess was set up for junior officers. But I wasn't keen to move out of this lovely place on the sea. The people out there were very hospitable, the planters or whatever, so we were invited to join the tennis club and the yacht club. There were parties, what you would expect with a lot of Wrens. It was difficult to get any transport so we did a lot of cycling, including one or two leaves spent cycling in the bush visiting ancient ruins that had been built by Sinhalese kings. Sri Lanka is a very beautiful island and we did quite a lot of sightseeing.

Large numbers of Wrens were sent out to assist the codebreakers, not just on the Hollerith machinery, which was housed in a separate long hut running parallel to the main building, but as intercept operators, traffic analysts, cipher strippers and in identifying types of traffic from call signs and preambles. They were sent first to Bletchley Park to be trained, recalled Dorothy Robertson, who lived in the 'Wrennery' at Woburn Abbey while being taught traffic analysis.

After breakfast every morning, several coaches awaited us Wrens at the front door of the mansion and we were driven to Bletchley Park. There were many huts in the grounds, each one dealing with top-secret work, about which none of us knew anything. We simply knew that our own hut was used for instruction on analysis of Japanese naval messages so that in Ceylon we could gain 'inference' from them. We had two instructors: one, a brilliant young homosexual called Angus Wilson. He used to mince into the room wearing, in those days, outrageous clothes in all colours; he chain-smoked; his nails were bitten down to the quick and he had a rather hysterical laugh.

The Wrens were then sent out in batches on convoys to Colombo, travelling out into the Atlantic, through the Mediterranean and then into the Indian Ocean via the Suez Canal, Robertson said.

The other ships in our convoy always seemed far away and I know that we must have had several submarine scares, as we often zigzagged en route, but life was so exciting with only some sixty Wrens and forty female army nurses on board and five to six thousand servicemen. We really had a marvellous time. The OC troops had to ration the men daily to meet us, so we had different batches up on B Deck every day, with dancing on deck at night.

One of my clearest recollections is that of waiting in our convoy to enter the Suez Canal. It was gloriously hot and sunny and the sea had that smooth greenish tinge all round. We were up on B Deck with lots of the lads, looking over the side watching ship movements and generally wondering what was going to happen next, when we began to notice that a lot of landing craft seemed to be moving towards us filled with men in white helmets. I shall never forget, as they came alongside, far below, one helmet looked upwards at us on deck and emitted a loud cry: 'Gee! Dames!' Whereupon the whole flotilla of landing craft looked up and bawled: 'Gee! Dames!' We girls simply fled down to our cabins and locked ourselves in. Over the following days, the Yanks were also rationed to meet us, but somehow or other they seemed to appear here and there on our deck in spite of this, and, I must say, they were often very amusing, and, of course, terrible flirts. Our British lads were absolutely furious and used to surround us, four or five to one Wren, as an anti-Yank bodyguard.

In Colombo we were stationed at Kent House in Flower Road, a large house once privately owned, now a

Wrennery for several hundred. The compound was filled with lots of whitewashed huts with thatched palm-leaf, or *cadjan*, roofs, providing sleeping quarters for up to 500 Wrens. The big house was the mess. Concrete paths led from it to all the huts, so that one had dry feet in the heavy rains. Alongside the paths were planted lines of brilliant zinnias and I remember how beautiful they looked at night under the lights.

Our work was done some miles away in the jungle at Anderson Wireless Telegraphy Station and, as ever, we worked in naval watches, or shifts, all round the clock. To go on duty, we had to congregate under a huge banyan tree in the compound where two or three naval buses or trucks waited to take us out to Anderson. Our drivers were locals and pretty rum characters, too. One, a skinny, scruffy, devilish chap, used to take a swig at his arak bottle before revving up and driving us, one toe on the gas, hurtling through the jungle.

On watch, we petty officers shared a room with several others: a Royal Navy commander; two sub-lieutenants; three Admiralty civilians; and two Malay seamen who had escaped from Singapore on a raft with the naval commander. We received our 'traffic', or Japanese messages, by messenger from the big wireless watchroom near by, but we never saw the inside of it and they never saw our watchroom either. We had all signed the Official Secrets Act and no-one ever discussed his or her work with anyone else.

There were always plenty of invitations to dances at service messes, so we went out most evenings, when not on duty that is, until we realized that we just could not keep it up any longer and became more selective. Romances blossomed, too, of course. The favourite evening spot was the little nightclub, the Silver Fawn, where we'd be taken for a really glamorous evening's dinner-dancing, the live band playing favourite dance tunes, the lights low, flowers for one's dress, gorgeous food. It was incredibly heady stuff for girls of our age. We were only in our early twenties, and there was usually the knowledge that the boyfriend would be leaving for India or Burma soon, perhaps never to return. There were literally about 1,000 men in Ceylon to a girl, and many of the men had not seen a white girl for months or years. You can imagine how spoilt we were, and we loved it! How different and how naïve we were in those days; one never heard of any misbehaviour and we knew that if any occurred, we'd be sent straight back to Britain. I only ever heard of one Wren who was. We had all been brought up so much more strictly then.

The Japanese belief that to surrender, even in the face of overwhelming odds, was shameful brought a happy welcome bonus for Anderson in the form of a number of Royal Navy sub-lieutenants who had been trained in Japanese in preparation for interrogator duties and had found themselves virtually redundant. Despite the improvement in reception and resources at Colombo, it had become clear by the late summer of 1943 that the end to the problems over co-operation which Bletchley Park believed it had negotiated was in fact little more than a brief respite. By the time the naval codebreakers moved to Anderson, the JN25 codebooks had changed a number of times and the plentiful supplies of easily broken coded messages unavailable elsewhere were no more than a distant memory. The relationship with Melbourne, on which so much hope had been placed, seemed as bad as ever.

Commander Malcolm Saunders, a former head of Bletchley Park's Hut 3 intelligence-reporting section, toured the Allied naval codebreaking centres in the autumn of 1943. He was extremely impressed with the FRUPAC operation at Pearl Harbor. It was a model for a large-scale codebreaking and signals intelligence production unit that was, if anything, more efficient than the system he had helped to set up at Bletchley Park, he said. This was the system that the British should aim for with Colombo.

Saunders was far less impressed with FRUMEL, where Fabian was apparently continuing to block co-operation.

'The liaison with Colombo is not nearly as good as it should be,' Saunders complained. 'This is partly due to bad communications and insufficient staff at each end, but also due to the present lack of productivity of the Colombo unit, and to lack of a clear-cut statement of policy from Washington in this regard. The security aspect is constantly in mind and there is a constant suspicion of "leakage" to the American Military Authorities at Brisbane.'

The dislike of Fabian and his methods was not confined to the British and Australian codebreakers. Some of his own men found him difficult and believed his behaviour acted as a brake on their own operations. 'In November 1943, when I reported to Melbourne, many of the Corregidor team were still serving at the station,' recalled Forrest R. Biard, one of the FRUMEL codebreakers. 'Most of them were pleasant to work with. One most certainly was not.'

Almost all of the 'unpleasantness' at Monterey stemmed from the fact that Fabian was junior to a number of the codebreakers working under him, said Biard.

Three of these officers were captains, while the officer in charge of them was a commander. This could have worked without tremendous friction had the officer in charge and his executive officer been well chosen. But somewhere up the line things went quite amiss. I hasten to add that the crypto-linguist captains who had the misfortune of having to serve under the despotic commander and his equally unfriendly executive officer, both quite junior to these captains, will always have my undying respect. They tolerated the daily and almost hourly insults so frequently given us in the linguistic section by their juniors, yet they still managed to perform their vitally important crypto-linguistical jobs most creditably. The insults some of us had to endure did not add to our ability to perform in that manner. Station Cast did its job and did it well, not because of the officers in charge of the station, but in spite of them.

In an effort to improve the situation Bletchley Park began to push hard for British participation in the dedicated US Navy signals intelligence circuit on which FRUMEL, FRUPAC and OP-20-G exchanged recoveries and discussed codebreaking problems. Harry Hinsley, the senior intelligence reporter within the Bletchley Park naval section, was sent to Washington to negotiate this new link. Travis and Birch also decided to send Hugh Foss to OP-20-G's new headquarters at the Mount Vernon Seminary to work alongside its Japanese codebreaking team. As head of Hut 7, Foss would be in a unique position to assess where each side might be best able to help the other and the posting had the added bonus of helping to solve his domestic problems.

These were so intractable that Foss and his wife Alison had even been offered two Wrens as home helps in an attempt to ensure he could keep his mind totally on the job, his cousin and colleague Elizabeth Browning recalled.

> At first they had a local nanny but the muddle really got her down and she was glad to be called up and become one of the Wrens at the Park. She and I used to have one of the children to stay for a day or two at intervals so as to take some of the pressure off Hugh. After a time, Frank Birch said to me that there had been a conference about Hugh's home problems and they were thinking of transferring him to Washington in order to utilize his abilities more fully. I said I thought it was a most tactful way of improving things and so for a time Hugh was in the States and somehow Alison and the children survived. Nanny and I continued to lend a hand when we could. It was all very Heath Robinsonish but worked out fairly well in the end.

By late 1943, with the Battle of the Atlantic over and OP-20-G bearing the brunt of the attacks on the German Navy's Enigma ciphers, Hut 7 started to get time on Bletchley Park's large bank of Hollerith tabulating machines, drastically improving its ability to break JN25 messages. Hut 7 began to expand rapidly, with new sections being added. As the Allies gained the upper hand and the dislocation of Japanese forces increased, Peter Laslett was put in charge of a group looking for and recording all references in the Japanese messages to changes of codes and ciphers. Laslett, who had gained a first in history at St John's, Cambridge, had joined the Fleet Air Arm. But in mid-1942 he was 'press-ganged' by the navy into learning Japanese.

They sent me to the School of Oriental and African Studies and told us that if we couldn't read Japanese within a year we would be sent back to our ships. I had been on the Murmansk route, which was extremely dangerous, so I learned Japanese under sentence of being drowned. There were one or two of us billeted near Harley Street and we used to walk each morning to SOAS or to the British Museum where we did most of our studying. I had quite a time of it at large in London in bell-bottom trousers.

He was then commissioned and sent to Bletchley Park, where he was put in Hut 7, initially simply concentrating on decoding JN25.

The Japanese codes being book codes, breaking them was no kid's job. We had to look for repeated messages and tried to figure out the sentence structure to work out what the code groups meant. The greatest advantage was just occasionally when the Japanese repeated a message which the Germans had previously passed on a system which our colleagues at Bletchley Park had already broken. But in general it was rather tough and rather unsatisfactory, although it was interesting because the Pacific War was rather active. My great asset, I suppose, was that I was one of the very few people there who had actually served at sea, so I knew the type of terminology that might come up in any given situation. This, of course, was extremely useful in predicting what code groups might be expected to come next.

Isobel Sandison, a Foreign Office civilian who had passed one of the six-month Bedford courses in Japanese, worked in Laslett's section recording the radio references to various codes and ciphers. She was recruited in 1943 from Aberdeen University, where she had studied German.

When I arrived at Bletchley in September I was informed that the end of the German war was in sight and asked if eventually I would be willing to learn Japanese. The first few weeks we spent on general filing, scanning call signs, etc. in the department run by Jack Plumb – 'Dr Plumb's Party' on the door. Eventually the Japanese class began. There were about sixteen, all students or graduates in languages – classics or modern, a mix of naval officers, Wrens and civilians. Our teacher was John Lloyd, ex-Vice-Consul in Tokyo. The language was so different from anything we had encountered before that to begin with it seemed impossible. Working in pairs to help each other, we learned only to read the language – there was no need to be able to speak it convincingly. We practised on captured Japanese documents.

At the end of six months' study we were split up among the different naval intelligence sections. Peter Laslett – my new boss – was a real enthusiast. We were reading, translating and interpreting very specific interceptions to do with codes, codebooks, keeping track of who held them, when they were used and changed. We passed on to the relevant people the information gleaned in what Peter christened 'Japanese Cryptographic References'.

The remarkable atmosphere at Bletchley Park, where rank had very little meaning and people from all walks of life worked together as a close team, made a deep and lasting impression on all the codebreakers. But it was often more like a university campus than a top-secret wartime establishment, Laslett recalled.

Bletchley was a very informal place. It had the atmosphere of a mixture of Oxford and Cambridge High Table. We all had passes but the guards on the gate all knew us, so – although we did show our passes, as a matter of form – they would just wave us in because they knew who we were. Being a careless sort of a fellow, at one point I lost my pass. One of the girls working for me forged me a pass in the name of Rosie Smarty-Pants and for the rest of my time at Bletchley I went past the security gate each day as Rosie Smarty-Pants. It was all informal security. We trusted each other completely. The fact that it worked and the secret was kept for so long is, I think, one of the most remarkable things about Bletchley Park.

18

AN ALLIANCE UNDER THREAT

The last few months of 1943 had brought dramatic improvements for the Colombo codebreakers. Their operations had been bolstered by the improved reception, the dramatic increase in staff and equipment and the promise of direct access to the US recoveries. But at the beginning of December they received worrying news. The new US liaison officer who was to control the link to the Americans was to be Commander Rudi Fabian, who had done so much to block co-operation.

Bruce Keith appealed to Bletchley Park to intervene, but Captain Edward Hastings, who was now in charge of liaison with both the British outstations and Washington, told him that he and his codebreakers would have to learn to live with the belligerent American. 'With reference to the appointment of Fabian as a liaison officer, we must accept the selection made by Admiral Redman,' said Hastings, 'as he particularly dislikes any interference from British authorities and is well aware of the situation.'

Meanwhile, Harry Hinsley had arrived in Washington to negotiate a continuous and comprehensive exchange of information on a dedicated circuit. He had been deliberately picked for the negotiations because he was relatively junior and could therefore talk to his American counterparts at a working level where relations between the two sides were good rather than at a higher administrative level where too many political considerations appeared to come into play. 'A low-level bloke had to be sent in the hope that agreement could be reached on the working level easily and would then get approval upstairs,' said Frank Birch, now a deputy director of Bletchley Park. 'If negotiations started upstairs someone would be bound to pull out the agreement of October 1942 in which we had expressed ourselves as content with strategical intelligence except west of 110° East.'

Hinsley did in the end have to negotiate with Admiral Redman and was distinctly unimpressed, describing him as 'chock-full of grievances largely because he likes grievances for their own sake'. But the two sides agreed to set up a 'comprehensive US–British circuit, to be called the BRUSA Circuit, as early as practicable between Washington, Pearl Harbor, Melbourne, Colombo and GC&CS, incorporating US naval and British circuits at present used for the dissemination of radio intelligence material'.

But the US Navy's reluctance, even at this late stage in the war, to co-operate fully with the British was illustrated by an escape clause which Redman insisted on inserting into the agreement, whereby 'the extent to which radio intelligence information and recoveries can be exchanged between the BRUSA stations will continue to be dependent upon communication and other facilities available and on the need for such an exchange'.

The contrast between relations at Redman's level and those at the cutting edge of the codebreaking operations in OP-20-G and Bletchley Park could not have been starker at this moment. The Japanese Navy used two main cipher machines. The most important was the Coral machine issued to its naval attachés, which the Allied codebreakers were still struggling to break. But in August 1942 a similar machine – known to the Japanese as *97-shiki inji-ki-1 2-gata* and to the Americans as Jade – was introduced for use by the Japanese Navy. Although never popular with the Japanese, it proved easier to crack than Coral and was solved in August 1943 by a team of US Navy codebreakers, including Lieutenant-Commander Francis A. Raven, one of the leading OP-20-G Japanese machine cipher specialists.

The American codebreakers now decided to make a renewed push to break Coral. OP-20-G moved Raven and the Jade system-breakers on to the Japanese naval attaché team, which already included Agnes Driscoll, a veteran machine cipher specialist who had solved the Orange and Red cipher machines for the Americans. It also asked Bletchley Park for any assistance it could give in terms of knowledge gained in the previous attempts.

Coincidentally, the British had already begun to increase their efforts to break the Coral material. The British intercept site at Sarafand in Palestine had been ordered to concentrate on the enciphered traffic, designated JNA20 by the Allies, and the Bletchley Park codebreaking team looking at the Coral machine had been moved into Hut 8, the naval Enigma section, which at the end of 1942 had achieved the impossible in breaking the Shark four-rotor Enigma cipher used by German U-boats in the Atlantic.

The move was 'partly because naval section were very short of space and partly because it was thought that an exchange of ideas might benefit them and us', said Hugh Alexander, the head of the naval Enigma section. In Hut 8 the JNA20 problem could be subjected to extensive examination by some of the best machine cipher specialists in the world, including Alexander himself. The British chess champion, Alexander was a brilliant codebreaker, second only to Tiltman. 'We did quite a large amount of work with the JNA20 party,' he recalled, 'thus starting a profitable association which lasted until well on in 1944.'

The Coral machine resembled its diplomatic counterpart Purple in that it had two typewriters plugged up to a central cipher machine, one for inputting the plain text, the other as output for the enciphered text. The cipher machine comprised three banks of twenty-six telephone stepping switches. The major cryptographic drawback suffered by the Japanese diplomatic machines, the decision to separate six letters off from the other twenty, had been removed, making life more difficult for the codebreakers. But although it had six different possible orders of stepping switches, only three of them were used.

Alexander and the other Hut 8 codebreakers began attacking the Coral machine using methods evolved during the breaking of Enigma. On the German machine the codebreakers had made the assumption – correct far more often than not – that, in the part of the message being studied, the 'fast' rotor of the Enigma machine would not have had the opportunity to move the medium rotor on a notch. The cryptographic effect of both the medium and slow rotors was therefore not changing at all. This reduced the odds to a much more manageable proportion. Since the banks of stepping switches on the Coral machine were designed to simulate the movement of rotors in a conventional machine, the same principle applied.

At the end of September the British began to make real headway and sent a detailed report on their progress to OP-20-G. 'This report really marks the birth of the successful attack on the Coral,' the official US history records. Both the British and the American codebreakers began to move forward rapidly on the basis of the Hut 8 report. They used a number of methods borrowed from the Enigma codebreakers to crack the Coral system, including Yoxallismus, a statistical process originally devised by Leslie Yoxall, one of the Bletchley Park Hut 8 machine cipher experts, to find the plugboard connections on the German Navy's Enigma machine. The US codebreakers also employed a piece of rapid analytic machinery similar in purpose to the Bombe, the machine developed at Bletchley Park by Alan Turing to match the enciphered Enigma traffic against potential cribs. The Rattler was an electronic 'crib-buster' built by a team of engineers from the Massachusetts Institute of Technology who had been drafted into the OP-20-G research section.

By the time Hugh Foss arrived in Washington in January 1944 the Allied codebreakers were closing in. The Americans immediately took the tall, red-bearded eccentric to their hearts, dubbing him 'Lend–Lease Jesus'. With his experience in breaking the earlier Japanese naval attaché machine cipher, known as Orange to the American codebreakers, it seems unlikely that he did not have some form of contribution to make. But the major British input appears to have come from Alexander, who in February flew across to help in the final push and, according to US codebreakers, 'contributed heavily' to what was officially recorded as a joint US–British success. By 11 March, the codebreakers had solved the wiring of the Coral machine and a few messages were read.

Not all the Japanese naval attaché messages used the Coral machine. There were also two codebooks in use. These were superenciphered in much the same way as the main naval and army codes and were broken by Wrens and Foreign Office civilians working in Hut 7 under the supervision of Gordon Flintham, Eric Nave's former assistant on the China Station.

Edith Bennett was a leading Wren working on the naval attaché codebooks. Inspired by her father, who had served for twenty-eight years in the Royal Navy, she had volunteered to go to sea. Instead, she found herself being sent to Bletchley Park with a number of other Wrens.

I wanted to go into boat crew. I imagined myself sitting in the front of a boat and dashing through the waves. None of us had actually heard of Bletchley Park. It was in the middle of the country and I thought, Well, this is a Dickens of a place to send someone who joined the navy.

When we got there we had to sign the Official Secrets Act and it wasn't until we actually got into Hut 7 that we knew what we were going to do. You were told that you couldn't even speak to people in another office. It was completely taboo. Once you came out of the door at Bletchley Park all thought of work had to be forgotten and you didn't discuss it. My mother and father died without knowing what I did there.

The Wrens working on the Japanese material were given

a three-month basic course on the Japanese language and codebreaking. 'It was held in Bletchley Park itself. Hugh Foss was the one who suggested this and he took us for the first lesson. We were shown how to do characters just to put us in the mood, but, of course, it was more important that we knew what the characters were, like shipping, which was *maru*, and *ki*, which was how they denoted an aircraft.'

They first had to strip the additives off the enciphered five-figure messages.

We worked on a particular code called JNA10 and a code called Kuibyshev. This code was very similar to JNA10 but was not on the same codebook and because we could never find any depth to it, Mr Flintham gave it to me to play around with. That was the sort of term they used. It didn't mean play, of course. It meant jolly well try and get something done with it, and I was successful in that I did get a depth of five which was good, because the greater the depth we had the more likely we were to be able to confirm the groups.

We recorded the frequency of groups on what became known as a Dottery. Each time a particular group was used it would be recorded by a dot against it. We used to record the number of times that a particular group had come up and what we thought it meant. When it had appeared twenty-five times with the same meaning, we would draw a little square round it. That was our way of knowing it was a confirmed group. Most times, we didn't get all the message, only parts of it. Then it was sent off to America to see if they could add bits to it. Everything we did was sent to Washington, which was codenamed Susan.

As with all the Wrens at Bletchley Park, they were quartered at nearby country houses. Edith Bennett and her friends were deposited at Woburn Abbey.

We had huts in the courtyard because there were so many of us there. There was one pipe that went through the huts providing hot water for the showers at the end of the block of huts and that was our only heating. We used to go to bed dressed in more clothing than we went out in and the grass used to grow through the floorboards of the huts. I shared a room with one other girl and before we could clean our room out we had to go along with a pair of nail scissors, clipping the grass that was between the floorboards, and all the time we were doing it we were absolutely roaring with laughter.

During our off-duty hours we used to do a fair bit of hitchhiking. Wherever a lorry was going, that's where we would go. It sounds awful to do it now but in those days it was completely safe. We wouldn't go on our own, maybe three or four of us if it was a nice day. Or we even might just walk down the drive to Woburn itself where there used to be a little tea shop. That was sort of high days and holidays, if we could afford to do it. You actually had a tablecloth on the table and a cup and saucer that matched.

A couple of the girls had boyfriends, but I already had a young man. He was in the army, in the Rifle Brigade. We occasionally were invited to the American bases, but I only went once. They used to come and fetch you, but it was such a rough-house. I saw so many goings-on that night, I can tell you. It was all right while the dance was going on, but it was afterwards. It was dark outside and we had GIs trying to stow away on the way home. So I didn't go again. I thought, Golly, that's enough for me.

With D-Day only a few months away, the information that the Allies now obtained from the messages sent back to Tokyo by the Japanese representatives in Berlin was making a major contribution to the planning for Operation Overlord, the invasion of Europe. Most Japanese diplomatic messages were now sent by radio. They were intercepted in Britain by the Foreign Office interception stations at Brora, Sandridge and Whitchurch; at British embassies in the neutral countries; and at various points in Asia and Australasia, including Canberra, where a number of RAANs worked, and at the Abbottabad and

271

Bangalore stations in India. The Royal Canadian Navy also intercepted diplomatic material at Winnipeg and Point Grey, Vancouver.

Among the more important diplomatic intercepts in the run-up to D-Day was a detailed report by Oshima Hiroshi on a tour he made in November 1943 of the German defences in northern France. One of the US codebreakers working on the Purple messages later recalled the excitement of working through the night and into the next day on Oshima's detailed rundown of the Atlantic Wall:

> When I picked up the first intercept I was not sure what I had because it was not part one. But within a few hours the magnitude of what was at hand was apparent. I remained on duty throughout much of the day, continuing to translate along with colleagues who had pitched in to complete the work. I was too electrified to sleep. In the end we produced what was veritably a pamphlet, an on-the-ground description of the north French defences of 'Festung Europa', composed *dictu mirabile* by a general.

The gaps in Oshima's report were more than filled in by Colonel Ito Seiichi, the Japanese Military Attaché who had made his own tour of the entire German coastal defences, sending a massive thirty-two-part report back to Tokyo. The reports reassured the Allies that Hitler remained convinced that the main thrust of the invasion was to be along the Pas de Calais.

Bill Sibley was one of the interpreters translating the Japanese Military Attachés' messages.

> I was recruited from Balliol (I was a classicist, at the end of my first year) for the second Japanese-language course at Bedford, which began in September 1942. We were summoned to a five-minute one-to-one interview with John Tiltman, having been pre-selected by the Master of Balliol, A.D. Lindsay. I then went to Bletchley in the spring of 1943 and was set to work as a translator on the Japanese military attaché code until the end of the war,

272

Headquarters of the joint US-Australian-British Central Bureau codebreaking organization at 21 Henry Street, Brisbane. Australian War Memorial negative number P0125/05/01

Members of the American contingent to Central Bureau in September 1943. Seated in the front row from right to left are Joe Richard, who broke the Water Transport Code, known as 2468; Zach Halpin, the head of the IBM tabulating machine operation; Larry Clark, the veteran of Rowlett's Purple Section who advised Richard during the break into 2468; Colonel Abe Sinkov, the head of the bureau's codebreakers; and Hugh S. Erskine, who was in charge of the translation branch. Joseph F. Richard

Joe Richard after receiving the Legion of Merit for his work breaking the Water Transport Code.
Joseph E. Richard

Wilfrid Noyce, the British cryptographer based at the Wireless Experimental Centre, Delhi, who broke the Water Transport Code at the same time as Richard. Noyce, a leading mountaineer, is pictured during the preparations for the first successful ascent of Everest in 1953.

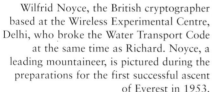

Central Bureau tents on the Eagle Farm racecourse at Ascot Park, Brisbane.

The Monterey flats in Melbourne, which were originally acquisitioned to house Eric Nave's Special Intelligence Bureau and were eventually taken over by Joe Fabian's US Navy FRUMEL operation. National Archives, Washington DC

Captain Joe Rochefort, the eccentric US codebreaker sacked as head of the US Navy's Pearl Harbor cryptanalysis centre for proving his superiors wrong. National Security Agency

Members of the Women's Royal Australian Naval Service (WRANS) working in the General Index at FRUMEL. National Archives, Washington DC

The WRANS barracks at Fleet Radio Unit, Melbourne (FRUMEL).
National Archives, Washington DC

Three WAAAF Japanese intercept operators at the rear of the Central Bureau, Henry Street headquarters. Sergeant Joy Linnane is centre. Australian War Memorial, negative number P0123/09/08

(*Front row, right to left*) Lieutenant-Colonel Norman Webb, senior British officer at Central Bureau; Colonel Mik Sandford, head of the Australian contingent; and Wing-Commander Roy Booth, senior RAAF officer, pictured during a liaison visit to WEC Delhi. Australian War Memorial, negative number P1443/71/23

The headquarters of No. 1 Wireless Unit, RAAF, at Stuart Creek, ten miles west of Townsville, Queensland. The building looks like a farmhouse, but only the tanks and steps are real; the rest of the features are painted on to the reinforced concrete walls. Australian War Memorial, negative number P1443/71/03

The entrance to the HMS Anderson Royal Navy intercept and codebreaking base near Colombo, Ceylon. © Public Record Office, HW4/3

Peter Budd and other Royal Navy wireless operators inside their 'banda' at HMS Anderson. Peter Budd

The makeshift canteen for 'C' (Indian) Special Wireless Group in Meiktila, Burma.
Dennis Underwood

The Central Bureau forward operations base at San Miguel, in the Philippines.
Australian War Memorial, negative number P1443/71/58

The first twelve British army codebreakers sent to Central Bureau, April 1944. (*Back row, left to right*) Brian Warmington, Cyril James, Rupert Fenn, Michael Webster, Bernard Billingham, Bennie Polack. (*Seated, left to right*) Donald Fletcher, Peter Hall, Barry Smallman, John Smart, Hugh Melinsky. (*Front*) Ray Eddols. Hugh Melinsky

Royal Navy wireless operator Peter Budd controlling a direction-finding site. Peter Budd

Vice-Admiral Lord Louis Mountbatten, Supreme Allied Commander South-East Asia, celebrating with members of the Special Liaison Unit in Kandy after the victory over the Japanese. Ken Kelsey is holding a glass, to Mountbatten's immediate left. © Ken Kelsey

The Bletchley Park liaison team in Washington, 1945. (*Left to right*): Peter Laslett, Barron Chalkley, William Bodsworth, Philip Howse, Kevin O'Neil and Molly Darby. National Archives, Washington DC

apart from a period of a few months when I was seconded to work on the Japanese naval attaché cipher.

Our work began after the real cryptographers had done their work and identified where in relation to the double substitution cipher 'keys' individual messages were located. The texts on which we worked were provided for us by 'key-breakers' who were not trained in the language, and whose task was to 'break' the keys used in the messages, relying on acquired familiarity with the frequencies of the bigrams in which the messages were composed before being enciphered.

We lived an introverted existence, insulated from the real world. Our masters did occasionally send us words of encouragement, but I can't recall that at our level we were ever told of any examples of our work having produced any positive results. Nobody knew what was going on in the rest of the place. It was a funny life, very funny, particularly the secrecy, and the oddity of some of the people. There was one famous professor of English who used to read about three detective novels a day. He used to walk around the grounds reading them.

In early May the Japanese Naval Attaché in Berlin made his own tour of the German defences. Sent in the newly broken Coral JNA20 cipher, his report was easily read by the Allies. It was more authoritative than that of Oshima, whose pro-German tendencies led him to accept unquestioningly what he was told. Rommel, who had been appointed to lead the main force resisting an invasion, intended 'to destroy the enemy near the coast, most of all on the beaches, without allowing them to penetrate any considerable distance inland,' the Naval Attaché said. 'As defence against airborne operations, he plans to cut communications between seaborne and airborne troops and to destroy them individually.'

The report gave detailed appraisals of the German dispositions and intentions and, worryingly for the Allies, said Normandy was regarded as a prime target and was being reinforced. This trend was confirmed by a report from Oshima of a meeting with Hitler at which the Führer had told him that the British were expected to establish an initial bridgehead in Normandy before launching the main front against the Pas de Calais.

It was this information that enabled the British to use the so-called double-cross agents to refine Fortitude, the D-Day deception operation, to weaken the defences in Normandy by reinforcing Hitler's suspicions of a second front. MI5 had turned the majority of Nazi agents who were sent to Britain – the rest were jailed or hanged – and was using them to feed back disinformation to the Abwehr, German military intelligence.

The double-cross agents built up the impression that the Normandy landings would be a feint. The real assault was to be mounted on the Pas de Calais by the 1st United States Army Group, a completely fictitious organization created with false reports from the double agents, dummy invasion craft planted in east coast ports and mobile wireless vehicles travelling around south-east England broadcasting messages from a number of different locations to fool the German radio interception units.

But although the information relating to German preparations for the Allied invasion of Europe was the most high-profile material obtained from the breaking of Coral, the Japanese Naval Attaché also gave far greater detail of German technical developments than Oshima or Ito. He had close contact with the chief of the German Naval Operations Division and through him the Allies heard the first details of the new, faster U-boats under development for the German Navy just a few weeks after Coral was broken. He also provided the precise specifications of the new Arado 234 and Messerschmitt ME-163 jet aircraft that were being introduced for the Luftwaffe.

Professor R. V. Jones was in charge of British scientific intelligence during the war and received much of his information from Bletchley Park.

The Japanese attachés even sometimes had with them men who were specifically termed 'Scientific Intelligence

Officers' to assist them in gathering information about their ally. We watched their activities with interest, and could say, for example, that the Germans had supplied early forms of German radars, listening receivers for sub-marines and guided anti-shipping bombs, although we noted a reluctance to let the Japanese have the latest models. We also learned details of Japanese developments in airborne radar as they revealed them to the Germans. We were thus able to throw a useful sidelight on Japan, and one of my officers was posted for a time to Lord Mountbatten's command in South-east Asia.

Evidence of Japanese scientific abilities was also collected by a small Japanese commercial section co-located with the diplomatic sections in London's Berkeley Street and headed after his return from Kilindini by Captain Harry Shaw. Encoded and plain-text messages between Japanese companies and their offices abroad were intercepted at a number of interception sites around the world, including Edward Twining's Mauritius operation and the Canadian naval base at Point Grey, Vancouver.

While co-operation between the Bletchley Park and OP-20-G sections dealing with the Japanese naval attaché material remained good, there were, even at this late stage of the war, still clear signs of tension over the sharing of information on JN25. The new BRUSA network linking Colombo with Hawaii and Melbourne came into force on 27 June 1944, three weeks after the D-Day invasion. But even as it did, Colonel Tim O'Connor, who had replaced Geoffrey Stevens as Chief UK Liaison Officer in Washington, was complaining to Frank Birch that he had difficulty per-suading the Americans to agree to 'any new departure which will mean the US helping Great Britain to take a greater share in the Pacific War'.

The response from Birch revealed just how close the British had come to ditching co-operation with the Americans over the US Navy's reluctance to co-operate, a decision that would have had immense implications for the future of the close exchange of intelligence between the two countries. The US attitude was 'no doubt the real reason for the general impression we get that whereas our co-operation is whole-hearted – almost too naïvely so – the Americans are co-operative with considerable reservations,' Birch told O'Connor. He added:

> OP-20-G's reluctance at times to go out of their way to meet our requests is due, to quote your own letter, to OP-20-G's feeling 'that they lead the Allies in the Naval cryptographic effort in the Japanese war' and that 'GC&CS should begin by filling in the gaps which OP-20-G has been unable to fill in and only begin to duplicate OP-20-G's work when there is labour and coverage to spare'.
>
> American caginess in the past has constituted a grave threat to our relations with them because Admiralty very categorically refused to be dependent on USA for Japanese intelligence. The lack of US intelligence supply to CinC Eastern Fleet led the British to consider ditching the Americans on the Japanese side. That could have been done; it still could be done. The test is the BRUSA Circuit. If the Americans play ball and circulate all their available intelligence, as the British will theirs, all is well.

In the end, after some initial caution by the US sites and a number of communication problems, the BRUSA Circuit did begin to work. But even then, while most of the material produced in Hawaii was swapped with Anderson, barely two-fifths of that emanating in Washington found its way to Colombo. Nevertheless, this was a great improvement on the previous situation. As a result, the productivity of the Royal Navy codebreakers improved markedly and the Americans began to see more reason to co-operate. Japanese suspicions that the Allies might be able to read JN25, heightened by injudicious use of signals intelligence by some US commanders, had led to security improvements that made it increasingly difficult to break.

In his tirade against OP-20-G's reluctance to co-operate

fully with the British on naval codes, Birch pointed out that the gaps in the Allied ability to break the Japanese naval codes were 'appallingly wide and, as far as JN25 is concerned, widening dangerously'. The tensions were beginning to show on both sides to the point where, in a moment rich in irony, Fabian complained to Admiral Somerville that material was being 'deliberately held back' from him by the Colombo codebreakers.

During the summer Bletchley Park began to throw an increasing amount of resources into the JN25 problem. Hugh Alexander was appointed to head naval section IIJ, the department attempting to break the main Japanese naval systems JN11 and JN25. His transfer to Hut 7 was a measure of the priority which Bletchley Park now attached to improving its record against the Japanese naval codes.

By late summer Bletchley Park was so concerned by the situation that Tiltman had also been called in to look at the problem. 'The loss of JN25 over so long a period has deprived us of about 60 per cent of strategic intelligence and Naval Air Order of Battle is becoming rapidly out of date,' one BP codebreaker complained. Recent signals from Colombo seemed to indicate that the codebreakers would soon be back on top of the problem, he said, but co-operation with Washington was apparently still not all that could be expected. 'We are suffering considerably from not knowing at present how current is information in OP-20-G because of the paucity of intelligence from their end of BRUSA.'

Alexander flew to Washington in August in order to try to co-ordinate a joint attack and found that OP-20-G was struggling as much as Bletchley Park, although clearly less willing to admit it. But there was now a recognition in Washington that they needed the British contribution. During a visit to Colombo, Admiral Redman finally agreed to a direct link between the British outstation and OP-20-G. Bruce Keith was in little doubt as to the motive behind this. 'The large increase in Anderson's output was the main reason for the Americans reversing their previous refusal to accord direct communication,' he said. Colombo was now able both to intercept and to decode very many intercepts that were simply not available elsewhere.

In October 1944 Travis flew to Washington to put his signature to an updated agreement that, while maintaining the OP-20-G control over Japanese naval signals intelligence, at last offered genuine co-operation between the two sides.

19

OPERATION CAPITAL

The Japanese, who were determined to cut the Burma Road and isolate Chiang Kai-shek's Chinese Nationalist forces from supplies, had overwhelmed the British forces in Burma by the end of May 1942. Despite a limited British counter-offensive and the highly publicized but somewhat overrated efforts of Orde Wingate's Chindits, they were still very much in control of the country as 1943 came to a close.

Allied plans for a major campaign in Burma designed to divert Japanese forces that might otherwise be directed against MacArthur's drive northwards towards the Philippines were delayed by political arguments between the British and American commanders. The abrasive US general 'Vinegar Joe' Stilwell, deputy to Lord Mountbatten, the Supreme Allied Commander South-east Asia, refused point-blank to countenance any campaign which had as its ultimate aim the retaking of other British colonies, principally Malaya.

Eventually they agreed a more limited offensive under the command of the British general Bill Slim aimed purely at driving the Japanese out of Burma. Operation Capital was to begin in the dry season of early 1944. The Chindits would penetrate deep inside Burma to capture Indaw ahead of the advancing Allied forces. Stilwell's Chinese Nationalist troops were to invade from the north, aiming to capture the strategically important town of Myitkyina. Stilwell was to be supported by a Chindit-style US special forces unit which became known as Merrill's Marauders after its commander, Brigadier-General Frank D. Merrill. Meanwhile, the British and Indian forces of 15 Indian Corps were to advance down the Arakan region along Burma's western coast, capturing the ports of Maungdaw and Akyab. The main thrust would then come through central Burma, with the rest of Slim's 14th Army pushing across the Chindwin River towards Indaw and then south towards Mandalay.

The primary signals intelligence support for these operations was to come from the British via Bletchley Park and, more particularly, its outposts in India controlled from Delhi by the Wireless Experimental Centre, which, alongside its codebreaking operation, had eighty-eight radio sets intercepting Japanese communications twenty-four hours a day at various sites across India.

The 1943 Bletchley Park conference, which allocated responsibility for breaking the different Japanese high-grade military codes to various Allied signals intelligence centres, had given Arlington Hall overall control of breaking the General Army Administrative Code 7890. But the latter was nevertheless exploited by C Branch, the codebreaking division of the WEC, which had a staff of around two hundred.

Michael Kerry, a young RAF pilot-officer, was trained in Japanese and codebreaking in the relaxed and rarefied atmosphere at the School of Oriental and African Studies and Bletchley Park before being sent out to the WEC. It was something of a culture shock.

The trouble with the WEC was that it was much more militaristic than BP. It was such a contrast. Four of us went out in June 1944, all of us RAF officers. We were equipped for the Boer War with drainpipe shorts and pith helmets. So we bought some new khaki shorts, which were fine, and some new hats which as it later turned out were not. We arrived at the WEC and were shown into Peter

Marr-Johnson's office. He said he didn't like the RAF and he liked them even less improperly dressed, and he told us to get out. We puzzled over this and eventually realized that the new tan hats we had bought were in fact 'Bombay bowlers' as worn by Indian civil servants.

Despite being in the RAF, Kerry was put to work on high-level army codes.

I was sat opposite Wilfrid Noyce, the mountaineer, who was a very nice chap but had a very battered face. He had fallen off a number of mountains and must have had India-rubber bones. A great character in the section was Hugh Lloyd-Jones who became Regius Professor of Greek at Oxford. We worked on army messages, mainly using the 7890 code and carrying daily reports of strengths of things like weapons, rations, sickness. It was quite hard at times working with indistinct photographs of captured code-books in a temperature of 117 degrees. There was no air-conditioning and an Indian woman was employed purely to sit by a great big woven straw door, called a *khaskhas tatti*, throwing handfuls of water over it every few seconds to keep the temperature down.

Unlike the Royal Navy, which had shown no qualms about dispatching Wrens to the far corners of the Empire, both the army and the RAF had been extremely protective of their female services and there were very few ATS and WAAF personnel posted abroad. So in complete contrast to Bletchley Park there were not many women around, Kerry recalled.

A friend of mine who took his sex life very seriously pursued an Indian servicewoman but that was it and I can't remember very much drinking or alcohol at all. When we weren't working on anything current we worked normal daytime hours and at six o'clock you went off to your little bungalow, you each had a bearer, and he served you with tea. Once a week, every Wednesday, we had a curry lunch and took little horse carts or *ghari* into Delhi to have tea.

By late 1943 the BRUSA agreement had ensured complete co-operation on military codes between the British and the US Army. The WEC had a direct link to Arlington Hall via its resident US Liaison Officer and indirect links via a relatively large Signal Intelligence Service analytical and intercept unit, Station 8, also based in New Delhi.

It also had direct dedicated signals intelligence chatlines to Bletchley Park and to Central Bureau in Brisbane, over which it could discuss recoveries, as well as direct contact with its two main outstations, the Western Wireless Signal Centre in Bangalore, where, owing to seasonal difficulties with reception in Delhi, much of the interception was now taking place, and the Eastern Wireless Signal Centre at Barrackpore, near Calcutta. It was the intelligence and codebreaking operation in Barrackpore, known for cover reasons as Intelligence School 'C', which provided the immediate signals intelligence needs of Slim's 14th Army, the main force involved in the invasion of Burma, with the assistance of a number of mobile Special Wireless Sections.

Air intelligence operations were covered by the Tactical Air Intelligence Section (TAIS) based at Comilla, the headquarters of both 14th Army and the 3rd Tactical Air Force, and by a number of RAF wireless units. The section had its own intelligence and codebreaking operation quite separate from Delhi and Bangalore which provided detailed information on the traffic of Japanese aircraft into and out of airfields in Burma. The 3rd Tactical Air Force detailed a squadron of USAAF Lightning long-range fighters to react to TAIS intelligence and the US pilots enjoyed 'spectacular' success during a series of snap sweeps of enemy territory, shooting down 135 enemy aircraft and destroying a number of others on the ground, thereby ensuring Allied air superiority at a crucial point in the offensive.

One of the codebreakers sent to the Wireless Experimental Centre at Anand Parbat to keep track of the heavily depleted Japanese Army Air Force was Alan Stripp, a young Intelligence Corps subaltern who had worked on army air codes in the Bletchley Park military section. Stripp recalled his arrival at the WEC.

At the bottom of the hill, further away from the road, was the lower camp where we lived in rows of standard-issue Public Works Department bungalows. In each were ten or so rooms opening off the long front veranda with 'bathrooms' behind; these were cubicles with a canvas bath and a 'thunderbox'. Majors and above had two rooms. In hot weather we often moved our beds on to the veranda, never forgetting the obligatory mosquito-net. The rule was to wear long sleeves and long trousers as an anti-malarial precaution after twilight, though most people preferred shorts and short sleeves during the day.

My servant or 'bearer' was Abdul Hamid, a cheerful and resourceful man who looked after me and my possessions devotedly. He must have been born about the time his notorious namesake the Sultan of Turkey died. I settled in and walked up the stony track to the security area, where I was issued with a pass and introduced to a roomful of people informally presided over by Hugh Lloyd-Jones. The room was square and high, and had a huge old-fashioned fan in the ceiling which revolved just fast enough to give a gentle breeze without swishing our papers on the floor or disturbing the fat pigeon who sat on the blade and spent most of his life placidly going round and round. When the fan stopped he stayed there, giddy or not.

Stripp was initially put to work translating decoded messages in a code designated 6633, a variant of the Army Air General Purpose Code 3366 which was in widespread use within the Burma area.

I soon moved from Lloyd-Jones's room to Robin Gibson's, where we were concerned not so much with routine translation as with tougher problems: messages which could not

283

be dealt with because the keybook or substitution table had been changed, or the indicator lost, or because either the Japanese operator or our own had slipped up. Such messages could play havoc with shift-working, especially when a badly mangled message seemed to contain urgent information; it continued to go round and round in your head long after you had given it up as hopeless. Sometimes light would dawn, or at least a promising line of attack would suggest itself, some hours later, and mean an unexpected return in someone else's shift to try it out.

The 6633 and other signals broken by us and by other Allied centres, and worked up into joint intelligence summaries, produced by late 1944 a virtually complete order of battle for the JAAF. It showed not only where almost every *hikoo-sentai* (air regiment, nominally of forty-eight fighters or thirty-six bombers, plus one aircraft for the commanding officer) was stationed, but how many of those aircraft were serviceable, what type they were, where they had served since 1942, where their base unit in Japan was, and often what the full name of the commanding officer was.

Japanese Navy Air Force transmissions were covered in Ceylon. Two RAF wireless units, 357 WU and 370 WU, were attached to the Royal Navy's codebreaking centre in Colombo – where they were known collectively as RAF Anderson – and a separate naval air codebreaking section was set up within the navy codebreaking base under Commander E. H. M. Colegrave.

The navy air operational codes, JN165 and JN166, were broken by Eric Nave's section in Central Bureau, allowing advanced warning of air raids and providing important intelligence on Japanese naval convoys. With the Allies now firmly in the ascendant, the Japanese Navy was forced to provide air cover for any convoy in reach of Allied bases. The escort aircraft provided daily positions of the convoys. As the dangers the convoys were exposed to became greater, it became normal practice to shelter overnight in safe anchorages, and these too were always faithfully reported by the escort aircraft, Nave recalled.

> I found a few messages from planes to base which fell into no known pattern and were unreadable at first sight. However, experience in this field was a most valuable thing, and identifying first a few numerals, I found the aircraft was reporting to base its position. It was a valuable discovery to read: 'Have taken up position over convoy,' with latitude, longitude, course and speed given. Almost invariably I could get sufficient of the whole message to be able to give this to our US Navy contact. This situation provided a rich field of operation for the US submarines of which they made good use.

The naval air transport codes were also easily read. Security on these frequencies was very slack with large amounts of operator chatter often referring in clear to facts that had been encoded elsewhere. Frequent cribs were also provided by the common use of different systems; for example, two aircraft might be flying to Truk at around the same time, one from Japan using the latest code and the other from some more remote location such as Rabaul which was still having to use the old code. The main Japanese meteorological station would then have to provide the same weather details for one aircraft in the old code, the details of which were familiar to the Allied codebreakers, and for the other aircraft in the new code, which until this point had not been broken.

The codebreakers working on army air systems at Bletchley Park were part of the military section. Bob Biggs was one of those transferred across to Japanese codes as the war in Europe began to wind down.

> I was called up into the Royal Army Service Corps in December 1941 and eventually found myself sent to Bletchley Park. I had been to grammar school but I had never gone to university. I certainly wasn't one of the geniuses you always hear about. But I think at that stage they were just looking for people with a reasonable

amount of intelligence, common sense and a good memory, and that I did have. I worked first in the Italian section, then on the Balkans and from mid-1944 I was in the Japanese army air section. We were dealing with two codes – 3366 and 6633 – both four-figure reciphered codes using the same book but different methods of recipherment.

The only way first to decipher and then to decode these messages was to collect a batch of messages each of which had the same indicator number. These were then written out, one underneath the other, on large sheets of graph paper to form a depth. It was essential that the code groups of every message were lined up in the columns because the break would be done vertically.

There were six of us, the others from the Intelligence Corps, and we were known jokingly as 'strippers' because our main task was to find the cipher and then strip it off the codebook groups column by column. I knew no Japanese at all when I started but it is possible to do the sort of work I was doing without knowing how to read, write or speak any foreign language. My previous experience as an assistant in the Italian and Yugoslav sections had taught me to look for a proforma message such as a strength report, stock returns, rations incident, casualties or sick report, or even a weather forecast.

The Japanese codebooks had code groups for special instructions such as open and close brackets, full stops, figures 0–9, and Latin alphabet *romaji* letters to spell out proper or place names. We would start off by deducting the code group for, say, an open bracket from each of the four-figure groups of one of the messages in turn to produce a potential cipher additive figure. By deducting that additive figure from all of the groups in the same column, you might be lucky enough to find another common code group and expose further clues as to what might precede or follow that particular group. In any event, if you found the position of an open bracket then it is obvious you must look for the close bracket. It was known that brackets would enclose figures, which meant you had ten chances of finding out what each of those figures was. By perseverance and patience you would now be creating a jigsaw-like pattern across the sheet, which allowed you to predict more code or additive groups.

If individual letters appeared in any of the messages you might be fortunate enough to recognize what they were spelling out and so be able to complete a run of breaks. Although much of this work could be done without any knowledge of the language, it was, of course, essential for a linguist to be available to interpret words and phrases or guess at the meanings of the Japanese text. The completed graph sheets were then translated into plain English by the linguists and were passed to the officers of the watch to be sorted into priority and distributed for any action deemed necessary. The cipher groups were recorded on a master sheet and newly identified code groups were put into the master codebook.

Bernard Keeffe was one of the Japanese linguists working in the army air section, having been one of the bright young schoolboys recruited when John Tiltman set up his language course.

I had won a scholarship in Classics to Clare, Cambridge, and was invited to take a test to see if I was apt to take the Japanese course. We were given crosswords to solve and some basic words in Japanese to see if we could recognize them and deduce their meaning in different contexts. There was also some simple substitution ciphering. I was accepted and called up at the age of eighteen to undergo six weeks' basic training in Bury St Edmunds before being transferred to Bedford – a brief but painful and revealing experience of the idiocy of army life. The NCOs knew nothing of our destination but assumed these potential officers (POs) were something special. If we did anything wrong – didn't get the body-locking pin, 'the ladies' delight', on the Bren gun in the right place – 'Call yourself a f***ing PO' – we found ourselves on a charge. Unfortunately, I developed bronchial pneumonia from lying in the snow on an exercise and missed the delight of the passing-out parade.

The Japanese course was held in a large house in De Parys Avenue, Bedford. We lived in digs. As you entered the house the Japanese course was on the left and a code-breaking course on the right. We knew each other, of course; one of the code-boys was Robert Pitman, a passionate lefty who turned into a right-wing columnist for the *Daily Express*. But even at that stage it was remarkable that we didn't discuss each other's activities. I was interested in music and had started solo singing as a baritone at school. Bedford was like musical heaven because the BBC Symphony Orchestra had been evacuated there, giving broadcasts from Bedford School Hall or from the Corn Exchange, and added to that there were shows by Glenn Miller and his US Army Air Force Band.

At the end of his course, Keeffe was sent to the army air section, where his boss was Alexis Vlasto. By the time he arrived at Bletchley the capture of a codebook had eased the difficulties faced by the codebreakers, who nevertheless still had to identify the indicator and strip off the additive cipher.

We were working on the order of battle of the Japanese naval air force, collating tedious reports of aircraft damage, how many were transferred, say, from 'Kuara Rumpuru' [Kuala Lumpur] to 'Shingaporu' [Singapore], how many sorties had been flown – rarely anything dramatic in itself, but giving the analysts material to keep in touch with the changing situation. We worked from clumsily photographed copies of the four-figure codebook, which I believe had been captured by the Americans. They were nothing like modern copies but stiff photos in a ring binder.

Like all other members of the British Army, Keeffe was quartered in the Shenley Road Barracks.

This was commanded by Colonel Fillingham – quite mad, probably too much even for the Durham Light Infantry, who no doubt gladly shot him off to what the rest of the army regarded as a nuthouse. He was not allowed into BP and wasn't told what was going on. He took out his frustration on us; he hated the sight of long-haired intellectuals and used to stop them and give them sixpence to get a haircut. He organized boxing – I was put into the ring with someone six inches taller and just about survived. Then he started cross-country runs before breakfast. I shall never forget the sight of Staff Sergeant Asa Briggs, future professor and historian of the BBC, trying to keep up with less portly young blades.

BP was an astonishing community. I was born to a poorish family in Woolwich. My father was a clerk in the local Co-op society, my family descendants of illiterate Irish immigrants who fled the famine in 1849. I shall never forget the impact of arriving in BP; it was a microcosm of the highest intellectual life. I discovered there was a lively opera group run by James Robertson, later Music Director of Sadlers Wells. I sang with an orchestra for the first time as the Gardener in *The Marriage of Figaro* and the Constable in Vaughan Williams's *Hugh the Drover*. Soon after I arrived I organized lunchtime concerts in the Assembly Hall outside the main gate. There were many professional musicians: Captain Daniel Jones, the doyen of Welsh composers; Lieutenant Ludovic Stewart, violinist; Jill Medway, a singer who later married Vlasto; Captain Douglas Jones (later Craig), singer and later company manager at Glyndebourne. There was a choir conducted by Sergeant Herbert Murrill, future Head of Music at the BBC. Working with me on the army air codes was Lieutenant Michael Whewell, bassoonist, and later producer in charge of the BBC Symphony Orchestra. There was a great deal of bed-hopping, the odd pregnancy and post-war divorces. All that was much easier for the civilians who lived in outlying villages; we had to make do with the Wrens in whatever nest we could find.

Despite the presence of the Japanese Army air sub-section in the Bletchley Park military section, a separate Japanese air sub-section was set up as part of Hut 10, the RAF section, in October 1943, following the Italian surrender. It dealt not with the high-grade four-figure codes like 3366 but with lower-grade three-figure material and collation of both army and naval air intelligence. The section was made up largely of the old Italian air sub-section and headed by Joe Hooper, one of the young graduates who had been recruited by GC&CS in the years immediately prior to the war and the move to Bletchley. Hooper had been given a watching brief over Japanese air codes and ciphers, in addition to his responsibilities as head of the Italian air section, ten months earlier.

Margaret Daly, a twenty-year-old WAAF sergeant, was moved from the German air section to be his PA. 'I typed his reports out for him. I remember typing out this great order of battle chart of the Japanese Army Air Force. Joe used to walk up and down dictating. He had tremendous mental control and never hesitated. He was a marvellous boss, very considerate and very good with people. He must have been around thirty and married but he was very popular with all the girls. There were quite a few of them swooning over him.'

Hooper's deputy was Brin Newton-John, an RAF officer whose daughter Olivia would later become a famous pop star. Newton-John was transferred to the Japanese operation from Hut 3, the section dealing with intelligence gathered from the German Enigma ciphers. The German influence led to the intelligence-reporting process being known as 'melding', from *melden*, the German verb 'to report'. The intelligence reporters were known as 'melders'.

The melders were split into two separate watches. The 'J' Watch handled the current material decoded at Bletchley Park while the 'M' Watch processed the less immediate material coming in from the outstations and Washington, carefully checking it against an index of previously produced material to extract every scrap of new intelligence.

Margaret Robertson was just twenty and two years into a history course at Aberdeen University when she was called up, sent as a Foreign Office civilian to Bletchley Park and put to work on the 'M' Watch.

I was called a melder, which meant I was given a pile of already decoded messages, scraps of this and that. If they showed any Japanese troops had moved, I had to write it up and hand it over. I was straight from university and for a while I had a WAAF officer called Margaret Pellow looking after me, checking I had got it right. We did it day after day after day. We didn't ever feel there was anything of moment because the messages were very much out of date. They were just trying to keep up with where units were.

The melders researched the background of any information that came up in their reports in a large index which contained details extracted from all previous messages, recalled Ann Lavell, a WAAF indexer.

We used to get the decrypted messages and index every minute detail therein so that a higher form of life than us, the melders, could consult the cards and decide with their help whether to include any given message they had to deal with in their intelligence reports. There were about nine or ten of us, some of us WAAFs and some civilians. We lived in Block F, right down at the bottom of the main corridor – the Burma Road – and right down at the bottom of the last spur on the left – so we were in the very corner of the whole BP perimeter, the boundary fence dividing us from what was then a stud farm. Thereby hangs a tale, quite a drama in our humdrum lives.

One evening one of the WAAFs put her in-tray (choc-a-bloc with top-secret documents waiting to be indexed) on the window ledge and went off to dinner. While she was away somebody did the blackout but failed to close the window, and a considerable wind sprang up and whisked away most of the contents of the basket, whirling some of them off over the perimeter fence, and some of them all over the place inside the fence. Major panic ensued – we were all conscripted to charge outside and retrieve what we could (lucky it wasn't raining), some going right outside into the stud farm and combing the field there.

When we had retrieved what appeared to be all there were, the question remained – had everything been found? The lost documents were all items in three or four series of reports, all of course numbered; so the only way to check that all had come safely home was to locate all the numbers in all the series. That was a huge task because items could be almost anywhere in the section – in various baskets, in the index, and in the melders' room – and it took Barbara de Grey, Nigel de Grey's daughter who was head of the section – together with the unfortunate WAAF who was the main cause of it (tearfully fearing that she would be posted away from BP in disgrace), and a handful of helpers – the whole night to satisfy the demands of security. I'm afraid I didn't join that stage of the fun, but slunk off home to bed in the RAF camp which adjoined the park.

20

DEFEAT INTO VICTORY

The increased value of the codebreakers' efforts to the campaign in Burma led to serious concerns at Bletchley Park over the security of the material emanating from its outposts on the Indian sub-continent. Signals intelligence had produced little of any interest to the military in India until the middle of 1943 and the need for total security was therefore not properly understood among some of those receiving the Ultra reports. There were also concerns over the large numbers of Indian staff employed. Many of the Indian servicemen and women working as intercept operators were excellent. But substantial numbers of their frontline colleagues had deserted to the Japanese-backed Indian National Army and some of the locally employed staff clearly had no understanding of the need for secrecy.

'There was a fruit stall outside the secure perimeter at the WEC,' recalled Michael Kerry. 'One day to our amazement his fruit was all wrapped in pieces of secret documents. The Indian who was supposed to destroy the confidential waste had decided it would make more sense to give it to the fruit wallah to wrap his fruit.'

Partly in order to improve security, a Special Liaison Unit (SLU) was set up in Delhi in early 1944 to pass the intelligence gathered by the codebreakers on to Slim. The SLUs had first emerged during the Battle for France in 1940 and were designed to provide Ultra intelligence

293

swiftly and securely to commanders in the field. They were made up of communications experts to link the unit to the codebreaking centres plus intelligence officers provided by MI6, who passed the Ultra material on to the commanders. Their role was to control the use of high-grade signals intelligence strictly to ensure that only those who had been indoctrinated knew of its existence. They also had to enforce the regulations on its use, making sure that it was never acted upon without a secondary source being available, and to liaise with the codebreakers on any queries from commanders. Two other SLUs were set up, one at Comilla to pass the signals intelligence to Slim and the other at Mountbatten's headquarters in Peradeniya four miles west of Kandy.

Frederick Winterbotham, the MI6 officer in charge of the SLUs, flew to Comilla to discuss the arrangements with Slim himself.

General Slim's HQ was in a large old Indian house, its spacious grounds covered with scented shrubs and shady trees and a small tented camp in a sunken garden. Beneath the house lived father, mother and three baby mongoose who kept the snakes away both from the house and our tents, which was a comforting thought.

The type of Ultra information received from the Japanese was much the same as that received from the German Army in Europe, operational and movement orders, strength returns and locations of Japanese formations which not only formed useful targets for the air but gave General Slim a complete order of battle of the Japanese forces.

Ken Kelsey was posted to the Kandy SLU in mid-1944 as a twenty-one-year-old RAF sergeant cipher operator.

Mountbatten's HQ was situated in the Botanical Gardens in Peradeniya. Its proud boast was that it contained a specimen of every species of tree in the world. Whether this is true or not I do not know, but it was a wonderful environment in which to work.

All the SLU personnel were RAF and technically responsible to air intelligence in Whitehall. This gave us certain privileges – we could not be put on a charge; we were excused all fatigue and guard duties and the like; and it was our *duty* to avoid capture. We had two means of receiving signals, a teleprinter link from Colombo and a radio link from our Special Communications Unit receiving signals from the Wireless Experimental Centre in Delhi, which was essentially Bletchley Park overseas. It would come in Type X cipher in five-letter groups and we would decipher it on a strip of plain-language text which would then go to Mountbatten.

The shifts were very, very onerous. We worked eight hours on, then sixteen hours off, followed by sixteen hours on and eight hours off, and when you went off to sleep you had these five-letter groups going through your mind all the time. We tried to swap shifts between ourselves to get a full twenty-four hours off occasionally but then you just had to work longer shifts when you came back.

Our living quarters were in a rubber plantation two or three miles away. Wherever I went in the Far East the toilet arrangements were uniformly abysmal. Snakes used to collect in the pit beneath our thunderboxes, and we were advised to take a razor blade with us in case we were bitten. We were then supposed to ask a fellow squatter to take the blade, slice open the bite and suck the venom out! You can imagine the ribald comments which greeted this advice. However, Lord Louis's loo at the HQ was immaculate. It possessed a flush toilet, decent toilet paper, a mirror, a strip light and a shelf on which were perfumes and lotions. I used to like the night shift, for at around 3 a.m. when there was never a soul about I would slip across to his quarters and avail myself of all the facilities. You can have no idea of the extent to which my morale was lifted by these few but precious visits.

As the 14th Army prepared for its thrust through central Burma, the codebreakers warned that the Japanese had reinforced their troops in the region with four divisions and appeared to be preparing an attack of their own. On 6 March the Japanese 15th Army crossed the Chindwin River on a broad front heading for the two small towns of Kohima and Imphal, centres for Assam's tea industry before the war but now home to the British frontline garrisons. Inspired by Slim's leadership, and sustained by occasional airlifts, the British and Indian troops stood firm through eighty days of siege and some of the bitterest fighting on any front of the war.

Slim's determination that his men should not yield to the Japanese was built on the detailed knowledge of the Japanese position that was being fed to him by the code-breakers. Winterbotham recalled:

> Some of the most interesting signals had been those show-ing the shortages of rations and equipment. General Slim told me that the intelligence from Ultra about the Japanese forces had been invaluable throughout the campaign, but the real triumph had been the information which led up to the final attack by the Japanese at Imphal and Kohima. It had become very evident from Ultra that the Japanese supply position was desperate and that their attack was being planned in order to capture the 14th Army supply depots, so as to keep the Japanese Army in business. Ultra had also shown that the Japanese Air Force in the area had dwindled so as to be practically useless. It was these two factors which determined the plan to allow the Japanese attack to spend itself while the 14th Army formed a defensive box around their bases at Imphal and Kohima while General Stratemeyer, commanding the Eastern Air Command, was able to supply the 14th Army from the air with men and materials, without the menace of Japanese fighter aircraft.

Imphal was relieved on 22 June 1944, and shortly after-wards, their supply lines cut by the monsoon and ravaged by disease, the Japanese were forced to withdraw. Of the 85,000 troops in the enemy invasion force, less than a quarter were still fit to fight. But despite these difficulties and their lack of air support, their retreat was typically stubborn. The 14th Army pursued the Japanese back across the Chindwin, setting up bridgeheads on the eastern bank of the river and regrouping in anticipation of a renewed advance, once the monsoon came to an end, on the central Burmese town of Meiktila. The codebreakers were providing Slim with a wealth of information on the retreating Japanese forces. 'Evidence was now coming in to me daily of the extent of the Japanese defeat, of their losses in tanks, guns, equipment, and vehicles, and of the disorganization of their higher command,' the British commander said.

One of the key reasons for the Japanese defeat was the air superiority enjoyed by the Allies, in part at least due to the ability of the codebreakers to predict Japanese air raids. The Bletchley Park air section had broken a three-figure reciphered army air-to-ground code, *kuuchi renraku kanji-hyoo 2-goo*, known to the British as BULBUL. By the late summer of 1944 it was clear that this would provide vital tactical intelligence and should be worked on in India rather than Bletchley.

Traffic from the army air operational flying units based around Meiktila was particularly valuable, allowing the Japanese air section to produce detailed intelligence on all their activities. 'It is thought that this is the first time that the complete correspondence of a number of stations on a particular network and in a particular cipher has become readable,' Joe Hooper said in a report to Arlington Hall. 'The correspondence is actually that of the operational flying units in the region reporting aircraft movements; revised unit dispositions before operations; accounts of operations; fuel stock on advanced airfields; Japanese air losses and claims; and DF data.'

An agreement was reached with the WEC that BULBUL should be taken over by the outstations in India while Bletchley Park concentrated on the high-grade four-figure codes. Although good progress had been made at Bletchley on rebuilding the BULBUL codebook, the capture of a book and some additive sheets from a Japanese aircraft shot down over India made the task of reading it even easier, and by November many of the messages were being intercepted, decoded and sent out as finished intelligence within the space of ninety minutes.

Michael Kerry was one of the codebreakers assigned to the BULBUL codes.

> When we started reading things regularly, five of us went down to Comilla. We travelled by train and had to change railway lines in Calcutta. The two different lines were on either side of the Hooghly River and I have this very vivid memory of the five of us with fifteen porters solemnly trudging across the Howrah Bridge to get to the other station.
>
> There was an interception unit at Comilla and we joined that and we read quite a lot. The Japanese bombers used to be kept safely down in Bangkok and then when there was a full moon they were moved forward to Mingaladon air base in Rangoon.

The codebreakers were able to monitor the flight from Bangkok to the Burmese capital and to give warning of the impending air raids. 'On one occasion, we got wind in advance that a raid was going to take place and passed the information on. Most of the time, we had no way of knowing if what we did was a pennyworth of use but in this particular instance the nightfighters got the lot and all night we could hear Mingaladon air base calling for its lost children.'

The allocation of the various high-level army codes had been firmed up during a conference at Arlington Hall in early 1944 and by the autumn the only Japanese military codes being worked on at Bletchley Park apart from JMA were: the Army Air Force General Purpose Code, designated 3366; its Burma area variant 6633; and the Air Safety Service Code, *koku hoan angoo-sho No. 1*, designated 3636.

Since Bletchley Park was now the central authority for

the Allied codebreakers on all Japanese Air Force codes and ciphers it made sense that they should all be concentrated under one roof. So the military section's army air experts were transferred over to Hooper's Japanese air section. Among those working there was Tony Flew, a linguist who had been due to go to Oxford on a scholarship before becoming involved in a tug-of-war between the university and RAF intelligence.

Some time in 1942 while I was doing a couple of turns at Oxford the word went out for applications to study East European languages. I won one of the scholarships. But before I could get my RAF service deferred I got my call-up papers. There was then a bit of argy-bargy over whether or not I should be allowed to go on to study Russian and in the end there was this curious auction between the university and the RAF which suggested other languages I might study instead. We eventually settled on Japanese and I then spent a year at the School of Oriental and African Studies. I was very much the odd bod. I was in civilian clothes and all the rest of my course were in uniform.

He was initially posted to the Inter-Services Topographical Department based at the New Bodleian in Oxford, collecting topographical intelligence on Japan, but in June 1944 was sent to Bletchley Park.

By now, I was a flying officer. There was a whole lot of us, I would guess around ten, deciphering material that had been sent to us from elsewhere. Alexis Vlasto was in charge. We used captured army air force codebooks, heaven knows how we had ever captured them, to decipher four-figure army air force traffic and then translate it. It wasn't all plain sailing, I must say. You often found that there was a corrupt group and you had to work out what it might have been. We sent the translated messages on and they were radioed out to advance units. The army air force messages were also being deciphered at Comilla

299

and it might seem more sensible to do it there closer to the front line, but the medical situation being what it was it was remarkably more efficient to do it at BP, where none of us ever reported sick, or much less frequently, at least.

Flew was billeted in Bedford and as a result took no part in the Bletchley social life. 'By the time we got back to the billets there wasn't much time to go anywhere, the occasional trip to the pub or to see a film. Despite what you sometimes hear, food in the canteen at Bletchley was nothing to complain about. We had different-coloured tickets issued to us for each day as vouchers for our meals. As you can imagine, we quickly broke the code to get extra food.'

The Japanese air section received its material from India, Colombo, Arlington Hall, OP-20-G and from three set positions of its own at the RAF intercept site at Chicksands Priory in Bedfordshire. Bletchley Park's high productivity on Japanese air codes had led to a dramatic increase in size, with nearly 250 people working on the army air material and a much smaller number, around 75, on the navy air operation which during the latter part of 1944 was severely hampered by the frequent changes to JN25 and the continuing lack of assistance from the US Navy codebreakers.

Slim's 14th Army began crossing the Chindwin in mass at Sittaungom on 19 November. That night W. C. Smith was just leaving the Wireless Experimental Centre when he was called back in. 'Perhaps the most exciting moment was to come off duty at 2215 hours one night, only to be told to go back immediately and to discover from enemy sources that one and a quarter hours earlier our forces had crossed the Chindwin,' Smith recalled. 'I expect some wag said, "We have to learn it from the enemy." '

By the end of January the American and Chinese forces forming the northern thrust of Operation Capital had reopened the Burma Road and were pushing forward into central Burma. The British 15th Corps on the left flank had captured Akyab and the main force of 14th Army in the centre was preparing for a final showdown with the enemy. As a result of the lack of resistance to 14th Army's advance on the Irrawaddy, Slim was expecting the Japanese commander, General Kimura Hoyotaro, to counter-attack as the main British force crossed the river.

He devised a brilliant deception plan, leaving a dummy 4th Corps headquarters communicating with one division which continued to push forward towards the river north of Mandalay, the old royal capital of Burma, where the Japanese expected the British to cross. Meanwhile, the real 4th Corps cut south, behind 33rd Corps on its right flank, to cross the river 100 miles south of Mandalay. It then drove northwards to encircle the Japanese, who were swiftly driven out of the two main towns of Mandalay and Meiktila.

The Allied troops were supported by a number of mobile army and RAF intercept units during the advance into Burma. Dennis Underwood was posted from Abbottabad to join 'C' (Indian) Special Wireless Group which was attached to Slim's tactical headquarters at Monywa on the Chindwin River.

After a lengthy rail and river-boat journey across India to Comilla we were put through a short and sharp battle course, having been warned that if we got sunburn we would be put on a charge – this despite the fact we had come from the North-West Frontier! The temperature was 100 degrees Fahrenheit and we were out in the blazing sun, very lightly dressed, but at any event my fair skin did not burn.

We then flew into Monywa. The unit was in tented accommodation, six to a tent. I found the makings of a *charpoy*, propped it on some empty boxes and that was home. We were working on lower-level traffic using low-powered transmitters. The set room was a large tent and we lived under canvas. We were much better off than one or two of our smaller units who were somewhat nearer the fighting and living in far worse conditions. There weren't many of us British other ranks and most of the unit consisted of Indian operators who were extremely good. We worked four- or five-hour shifts which was quite enough in the hot and sweaty conditions; after that your concentration went.

Off duty we swam in the Chindwin River, which was within walking distance. As it was the dry season, it was quite low and only about 400 yards across with a pleasant sandy beach and a sunken river-boat to play around and dive off. While we did this we got our clothes washed by some of the local population who were happy to be paid in cigarettes.

As the Japanese retreated we moved south and flew the unit with all its equipment to Meiktila. The aircraft we went in was very heavily loaded and on trying to take off the pilot was unable to get the tail plane to lift. So he came to a halt, came back and asked us all to move forward up to the front of the plane on top of all the equipment. Then he tried again. This time he made it but was not able to get very high. Fortunately, we were over the central Burmese plain and so we staggered on to Meiktila.

The Special Wireless Groups were fairly large operations with around 300 men and a dozen officers. Smaller Special Wireless Companies, around a third of the size, were attached to each of 14th Army's three corps, and similar-sized units were with the rear elements at Shillong, Imphal, Chittagong and Cox's Bazaar. Each unit had an Intelligence Corps Wireless Intelligence Section alongside it to interpret and analyse the intercepts and to carry out basic codebreaking. The RAF had 355 WU at Calcutta; 367 WU in Cox's Bazaar; 368 WU with TAIS in Comilla; and 358 WU attached to Slim in Meiktila. Underwood said:

Our leisure time was again spent swimming in a large lake near by. It had small fresh-water crabs in it, although they never seemed to bite. Our drinking water came from this lake and it was rumoured that Japanese dead had been dumped in it. I never saw any but the drinking water had to be heavily treated and had an appalling taste. Snakes were plentiful; we suspected the heavy shelling had disturbed all their usual habitats and it was not unusual to find a cobra in the tent. Fortunately, they seemed as scared of us as we were of them but mosquito-nets were tucked in more securely here than anywhere else I got to. This had been the scene of very heavy fighting and dead Japanese were only a little below the surface where dugouts had been bulldozed over. Our latrine had a dead Japanese mounting guard over it and, as the body had been booby-trapped, no-one wanted to move it.

The capture of Mandalay allowed motorized elements of 4th Corps to push forward along the central railroad while 33rd Corps advanced down the bank of the Irrawaddy and 15th Corps at Akyab prepared to hop down the coast to make an amphibious landing, south of Rangoon. The monsoon rains began just as the British troops converged on the Burmese capital. On 2 May an RAF Mosquito pilot flying over the city saw a message written by PoWs on the roof of Insein Jail announcing: 'JAPS GONE.' He landed his aircraft at Mingaladon air base and walked into the city centre where he visited the British PoWs and assured himself that the Japanese had indeed withdrawn. He then commandeered a sampan and sailed down the Rangoon River to meet the forward elements of the amphibious force and cheekily announced that the Burmese capital had been captured by the RAF.

Slim's Special Wireless Group now moved down to Rangoon by road with his headquarters, Underwood recalled.

We had an overnight stop when a small party of escaping Japanese went through the middle of our temporary camp. I suppose they came upon us by accident and decided their safest way was through as we couldn't fire on them because our own people were just the other side.

In Rangoon we occupied houses that would have been the homes of Westerners before the war and life was much better. We even had running water and crude showers. But with the arrival of the monsoon season life became much grimmer; constant damp, always sweaty, plagued with prickly heat, message pads sticking to hands and wrists. The lightning would blow the fuses in the antennae feeds so that we lost our stations – better than having the sets burned out, though.

Standard dress was more or less anything we fancied. Our warrant officer preferred drawers cellular, jungle green, fastened with a safety pin at the front, with sandals made locally from old vehicle tyres. Most of us wore something similar. The Quartermaster ran out of plimsolls as we wore them out so quickly playing badminton on an old tennis court and we had to play barefoot. We swam in a proper pool at what had been a club for Europeans, called, I think, the Konkine Club. Here the water was rarely changed and was a pea-green colour, as well as being very warm, so we found another natural pool and used that. Leeches were a problem but the free cigarette ration came in very handy again for getting rid of them by touching them with the hot end to make them release their grip.

We obtained a lot of our food locally by exchanging army rations for chickens, ducks etc. (no doubt strictly illegal) and we also purchased salad items from a nearby Chinese market gardener. Some time after we reached Rangoon we managed to travel on leave to Ootacamund in the Nilgiri Hills in southern India. This was accomplished by a typical service wangle as strictly speaking no leave was being allowed. The Adjutant arranged a posting to a sister unit outside Calcutta and on reporting there we were given our leave passes and travel documents.

As there was no normal route out of Burma we left by going to the airstrip and hitching a lift out. We had hoped that someone might be going to Calcutta but we could only manage to find an aircraft returning empty to Chittagong after bringing in supplies to Rangoon. On arrival we reported to the local railway transport officer and moved into a transit camp. It was two or three days before we got places on a train to Calcutta and I remember that one evening we went to a sort of circus performance (in a ring but with no animals): there were acrobats, jugglers, dancers and a clown.

Eventually we reached Calcutta and another transit camp to await a place on a train to Madras and then on to Ootacamund. This was a tented camp on what was (and is again, I think) the racecourse. We had to conserve our money but managed a visit to the Lighthouse Cinema (popular because it was air-conditioned) and declined the attentions of young Indians who wanted to provide us with their sisters. Not that we weren't interested, but the fear of disease kept us on the straight and narrow.

21

MACARTHUR RETURNS

By the beginning of 1944, army and air force codebreakers at Bletchley Park, Brisbane and Delhi were able to read the mainline army air and water transport systems without difficulty. But, despite David Mead's break into the indicator system of the Japanese Army Administrative Code, Arlington Hall had suffered a setback when the Japanese introduced a new codebook and false addition squares like those for the Japanese military attaché code.

But help was at hand. The Japanese forces in northern New Guinea were now pulling troops back to defend Madang, the next major base facing MacArthur. When the 20th Division withdrew from Sio, it was unable to take all its codebooks with it so they had to be destroyed. The division's chief signals officer should have ensured they were burned. But they were dumped in a metal chest in a deep water-filled pit. When US Army engineers began searching the area with mine detectors, they found the metal crate and demolitions experts were called in, only to find that it was full of codebooks.

The captured codebooks were for the Army General Administrative System, 7890, and its derivative systems: the Army Ordnance System, 2345; the North Pacific System, 5555; the South-west Pacific System, 7777; and the old Philippines System, 6666, which was now used by all cut-off units in an attempt to protect the other systems against being compromised by capture. The codebooks were sent immediately to Central Bureau, Joe Richard recalled.

I remember when the chest arrived at our hut in Ascot Park, Brisbane. We had just moved from the Henry Street House to the fenced-in small park, just across the suburban railway from the Eagle Farm racetrack where our enlisted men were now in wooden-floored tents. Our hut, Hut 7, had two new kitchen stoves for making tea, an important ritual in Australia. Colonel Sinkov and some other officers immediately took the captured codebooks and started to dry them out in the ovens of these stoves. Everyone seemed to be busy drying additive books. I had one. It was sopping wet. I had it on the edge of a table with a desk fan blowing on it. I and others were taking turns holding a small one-bar electric heater close to it. As I recall there was more than one copy of each book so we could package one copy of everything and send them by officer courier to Arlington Hall.

The Allied codebreakers were now able to read all the mainline Japanese Army systems – in the case of the 6666 code until the end of the war – and the Japanese seemed unaware of the 'pinch'. The codebooks were minus their covers which under Japanese signals security regulations were supposed to be handed in as 'proof of burning' and Central Bureau even monitored the 20th Division's chief signals officer insisting that all its codebooks had been completely destroyed. The bureau's translators were overwhelmed with deciphered messages and MacArthur appealed personally to Washington on their behalf for assistance. Amid the beginnings of a rapprochement between the US Army and Navy codebreakers, two of FRUMEL's top Japanese linguists, Lieutenant-Commanders Forrest R. 'Tex' Biard and Tom Mackie, were sent to Brisbane to help translate the backlog. Biard said:

The first morning at work remains one of the most memorable events of my entire life. As I remember it, the Central Bureau was on the outskirts of Brisbane in a wooded section into which temporary screened wood huts had been placed. According to one post-war author, it had been the location of a rather famous bordello that was run by an equally famous madam. As to the authenticity of this tale I cannot comment. But it was nice to have our hut and the surrounding area well shaded by the heavy growth of eucalyptus trees, for the summer sun in Brisbane is quite hot. The bureau was well fenced and quite adequately guarded. We were escorted to the codebreaking section in what I will call the 'hut', which was one of only three buildings I entered while working at the bureau. The other two were the mess hall and the latrine. We were not introduced to anyone outside the group of fifteen or so working directly with us. All our new cohorts were very pleasant and most co-operative and we truly liked them, but they needed help very quickly and badly.

The US Army codebreakers had been working their way through the pile of decoded messages in date–time order. Biard and Mackie decided it would be more productive to work from the top, looking for the most interesting and current messages.

Tom and I took the top two messages and started to read. Neither of us said a word for a minute or two but very soon I leaned over to see what Tom had, and he leaned my way to see what I was reading. Both of us had eyes as big as mill wheels. It was almost unbelievable. Mackie and I stumbled all over the words in our haste to tell our hosts that we had just read two parts of a thirteen-part message that was hotter and more explosive than Vesuvius. The message was the work of one 'Staff Officer Izumi'. He was reporting to his area commander on the decisions being made at a conference of high-level officers of both the Imperial Army and the Imperial Navy on the general situation in the New Guinea, Bismarck Archipelago,

308

Admiralty Islands and Solomon Islands areas. The purpose of this conference was to decide what could be done about the ever-worsening situation for them in these regions to the north and north-east of Australia.

The thirteen-part message, dated 19 January 1944, gave precise details of the Japanese plans for the region. They were reinforcing Wewak and the Madang–Hansa Bay area in anticipation of MacArthur's next move forward but defences at Hollandia further west were weak. Other messages and traffic analysis of Japanese radio communications allowed Central Bureau to provide MacArthur with detailed information on the Japanese order of battle along the northern New Guinea coast. He decided on the strength of this new information to drop plans to work his way along the coast and to concentrate his attack on the defensively weak Hollandia, isolating the Japanese at Wewak and Madang and allowing them to be picked off later.

Meanwhile, Nimitz was leading a far-reaching campaign to recapture the islands of the central Pacific. Operation Galvanic had begun in November 1943 with the seizure of the Gilberts and was followed by the invasion of the Marshall Islands in late January and Eniwetok three weeks later. Informed by the US Navy codebreakers of a build-up of ships and aircraft of the Combined Fleet at Truk, the main Japanese naval base in the Caroline Islands, Admiral Marc Mitscher's Fast Carrier Force swept ahead of the advance to carry out a Pearl Harbor-style attack. Admiral Koga Mineichi, Yamamoto's successor, was warned of the impending attack by his own signals intelligence units and managed to get most of his ships out of Truk. But fifty merchant vessels and more than three hundred aircraft remained when the US force arrived on 17 February. It destroyed 200,000 tons of Japanese shipping; some 200 aircraft; plus 2 cruisers and 3 destroyers that had failed to flee in time. But more importantly, Truk was no longer a safe haven for the Japanese Navy which withdrew behind the protection of the Marianas to the Philippines Sea.

As a result of the codebooks found at Sio, Central Bureau had built up a good picture of the Japanese defences along the New Guinea coast from their own forward base at Saidor to Wakde. The RAAF's No. 1 Wireless Unit had moved forward from Port Moresby to Nadzab in the Markham Valley in February 1944 from where it monitored a steady build-up of enemy aircraft being ferried into Hollandia. Although the Japanese air base was relatively poorly defended, the Japanese were keeping the bulk of their aircraft there because it was outside the known range of the US P-38 Lightning fighters that would have to escort any bombing raid. But General Kenney's Lightnings, unbeknown to the Japanese, had been modified with the addition of wing tanks that would extend their range beyond Hollandia. Beginning at the end of March and continuing for the next three weeks, his 5th Air Force carried out a series of raids that destroyed the vast bulk of the Japanese aircraft, many of them on the ground.

Despite the sustained bombardment of Hollandia, the messages intercepted by Central Bureau showed that the Japanese still saw the Hansa Bay–Madang area as the most likely focus of MacArthur's next ground attack. Secure in this knowledge, he landed two divisions at Hollandia, at the same time seizing the airstrip at Aitape in order to provide continued air support. The move was a brilliant use of Ultra that left an entire Japanese army totally encircled at the cost of very few casualties.

Signs that the Japanese were attempting to reinforce their beleaguered New Guinea garrisons came initially in naval intercepts referring to the imminent formation of a large convoy and the anticipated arrival of an infantry division. These were hardened up by water transport messages decoded at Central Bureau which announced that two infantry divisions, the 32nd and 35th, were on their way to New Guinea via the Philippines aboard the 'TAKE' convoy.

The submarine USS *Jack* intercepted the convoy off Luzon in late April, sinking one transport vessel. As the convoy moved towards New Guinea there was a plethora of messages in both naval and army codes describing its route and make-up. At the beginning of May, Central Bureau decoded water transport messages indicating that there were 12,784 troops in nine transport vessels, escorted by seven other ships. The messages gave precise speeds and directions for the route, revealed that the convoy was due to split into two parts on 7 May north of Halmahera, and provided the scheduled positions for noon on 2 and 9 May. The day before the convoy was due to separate, the submarine USS *Gurnard* waited for it in the Celebes Sea 100 miles off Menado. In the space of ten minutes three troop transports were sunk and, despite the rescue by other ships of a large number of troops, 4,000 had drowned.

All the time the codebreakers were looking for pinches that would help them in their work. When Central Bureau intercepted a message reporting that the *Yoshimo maru*, a Japanese merchantman sunk in Aitape Harbour, had an additive book for the Army General Purpose Systems on board, General Akin sent down divers to recover the cipher book. It was found in a metal box lodged behind a ladder in the burned-out ship. The whole operation was supervised personally by Akin, Joe Richard recalled.

He requisitioned an aircraft and had the box flown back to Brisbane. When opened it was found to contain an additive book we didn't have but in a very charred condition and with the number groups unreadable. Our photographic officer, a graduate chemist called Robert Holmes, devised a method for reading the numbers. He took a surgeon's scalpel and flaked off a page. Then he laid it on some cotton padding on a table and sat two soldiers alongside each other. One dipped a cotton bud in neat alcohol and then gently touched two groups on the additive page with it, making them instantly readable for long enough for the other soldier to copy them down. Since there were 50,000 additives on 500 pages, plus the page co-ordinates, you can see this was a lot of work.

In the wake of his capture of Hollandia, the islands of Wakde, Biak and Noemfor soon fell to MacArthur's troops. Meanwhile, 55 Australian Wireless Section, which had moved to Finschhafen in February 1944, followed the fighting to Hollandia, from where it intercepted a large number of reports about the 18th Army's preparations for a counter-attack. Using the newly captured additive groups, Central Bureau deciphered detailed messages about enemy intentions. The 18th Army was marching through the jungle from Madang towards Aitape, intent on recapturing it. The codebreakers read operational orders in the mainline Army General Administrative Code giving full details of the Japanese plans. The attack was repelled and the remnants of the Japanese forces were pushed back into the jungle where with neither supplies nor reinforcements their numbers steadily dwindled.

During the course of 1944 Bletchley Park reinforced the British contingent at Central Bureau with a number of young army and RAF officers who had passed through Captain Tuck's six-month Japanese course. Hugh Melinsky, who had been recruited on Tiltman's behalf by his tutor at Christ's College, Cambridge, arrived in April 1944 and was put to work on the naval air desk, part of Eric Nave's air–ground section

What Captain Nave did not know about codebreaking was not worth knowing. He had a sixth sense which enabled him to sniff out a meaning in what looked to me like a jumble of letters or numbers. He gave me a collection of messages with some words already translated and told me to do the rest. I learned the hard way, for six weeks. Captain Nave received messages from several wireless units. This was useful because if one version of a message contained gaps or faults another version might put these right. The greater the quantity of material available the better was the chance of breaking the code.

Apart from the cribs, the most helpful tool to the army

codebreakers was the use of stereotyped reports, Melinsky recalled.

Many messages were routine and followed the same pattern; for example, weather reports gave the place and time of origin, the general weather, the temperature, the amount of cloud, the wind direction and speed and perhaps the further outlook. In addition, the uncoded messages or traffic from or to the aircraft might very well give a clue to one or several groups in a coded message.

Brisbane was not all work. There was a club for servicemen where the lady in charge arranged for my friend Donald Fletcher and me to meet an Australian family at the cinema on a Saturday evening, and they took us home with them to spend the night. We slept on the veranda under mosquito-nets. The next morning their two daughters and son, about our age, took us for a long walk through the bush despite a temperature of ninety degrees. In the afternoon we went for a car ride to some beautiful spots and tasted strange fruit like avocados, custard apples and passion fruit. In the evening we were joined by two American friends of theirs and had a grand party. The parents took us back to the camp rather late.

There were so many kind and hospitable families that I could have gone out almost every evening. They loved to hear about England, the bombing and the rationing, and they offered to send food parcels to our parents by post. There were also concerts, a ballet and dances, though army boots were unkind to one's partner's toes. I had to go and buy a pair of shoes, which were not rationed as in England.

Claude Lanacaster Jr, a US Army codebreaker from North Carolina, flew out on the same flight from San Francisco as another group of British Army codebreakers.

I was twenty years old when I was called to active duty. I had enlisted in the Signal Corps in 1942 after a year and a half at University of North Carolina at Chapel Hill. I took my training at Vint Hill Farms, about thirty-five miles from Washington, DC. We were there for about six months and then one group was sent to England and the other group went to Australia.

At Central Bureau we worked in a frame building about 40 foot × 40 foot, like one of the huts at Bletchley Park. It was divided into three sections; one section had Captain Nave and the Australian Army's Captain Jury, who was the oldest in the building and a former teacher at the University of Adelaide. There were also two young British Japanese translators, Geoff Spencer and Hugh Melinsky.

We received Japanese intercepts and one of my jobs was to work on the estimated times of arrival and departure of the aircraft and sometimes the naval traffic. I would keep Captain Nave's book of messages up to date as to the particular whereabouts of these aircraft. Sometimes we would receive plain-text Japanese messages advising of their sightings of Allied ships and aircraft and once in a while they were careless enough to give their latitude and longitude as well as the time of observation. This type of intelligence was usually sent immediately to General MacArthur's HQ which was located about five miles away in downtown Brisbane. Captain Nave was all business. I sat about twenty feet from him for one and a half years but I didn't know until after the war what a well-known crypt-analyst he was and his past accomplishments.

As MacArthur prepared to return to the Philippines, Melinsky was sent to the RAAF's 2 Wireless Unit, which was based near Darwin, monitoring naval air traffic, alongside 3 Wireless Unit, which had responsibility for army air communications. There were about sixty men in Melinsky's unit, all Australians.

They received me politely but were somewhat puzzled by this strange young Pommie who had dropped in from nowhere.

The operational part of the unit was at the top of a hill and consisted of three large lorries with a canvas awning stretched between two of them. Under this I and four or five others worked at tables, with the wireless sets in one lorry and the Intelligence Officer in the other. The third lorry contained generators for providing the electricity. Airmen brought me messages which the operators had picked up listening to Japanese aircraft, and I did my best to decode and translate them. The other traffic consisted of all the other signals sent out by the planes and their bases, and this was carefully examined and collected.

We had a teleprinter link to Brisbane and every message we received was sent down to Captain Nave. Life was very busy when I arrived, with over a hundred messages a day. I started work at eight in the morning, had breaks for lunch and tea and then went back till nine or ten at night. I had a corporal to help me and later two airmen as well. I did not have a day off for three and a half months. The commonest messages were weather reports, which were valuable to us for forecasts. The most exciting were those from and to aircraft escorting convoys and giving their positions. Every evening I sent to Captain Nave a list of code groups which I thought I had broken, together with their meanings, and every morning I received back from him a list confirming them if they were right, correcting them if they were wrong, and giving me additional ones.

The US advance across the central Pacific had meanwhile reached the strategically important Marianas Islands, where Japanese naval messages intercepted by FRUPAC in Hawaii and US Navy ship-borne radio intelligence units would prove vital. One message decoded at Pearl Harbor revealed the exact locations of Japanese submarines forming a defensive patrol line west of the islands. A new 'hunter-killer' group of destroyer escorts was sent to attack the Japanese submarines, destroying five as a direct result of the intelligence supplied by FRUPAC. There was one drawback to this US success. The Japanese realized it could only have come from signals intelligence of some sort and changed their procedures, making life harder for the traffic analysts.

315

The landings by US Marines on Saipan, the first of the Marianas to be attacked, triggered the last large-scale carrier battle of the Second World War. The Japanese 1st Mobile Fleet, including nine aircraft carriers, aimed to squeeze the US 5th Fleet between itself and the land-based air power on the island of Guam. But the Japanese movements were monitored by FRUPAC and the radio intelligence units on board USS *Indianapolis*, *Hornet* and *Yorktown*, allowing the US Navy aircraft to anticipate the Japanese aerial attacks. Only one small group of twenty Japanese aircraft managed to get through, the rest being shot down in a victory so overwhelming that it became known as 'The Great Marianas Turkey Shoot'.

At the end of 1943, Central Bureau had placed liaison officers at MacArthur's forward headquarters at Port Moresby and the headquarters of 6th Army at Finschhafen. An advanced echelon of Central Bureau was sent to New Guinea in August 1944 to join the forward headquarters which was on its way to a new base at Hollandia, recalled Geoff Ballard, the Central Bureau Liaison Officer.

> When we reached Hollandia and drove up to our camp at GHQ, we were overwhelmed by the majestic scene all around us. For sheer, awesome grandeur, this place had no parallel and for us, on our hill at GHQ, it was like being suspended in mid-air. To the north, an immense valley, sweeping up to the Cyclops Mountains with their shapely peaks and girdle of clouds; below us Lake Sentani, of shining mother of pearl, and strewn with green islets like small boats on the surface. In the midst of this grand architecture of nature were the man-made wonders of the US engineers. Within the space of three months they had built two towns – one for GHQ and the other for the 7th Fleet HQ – and to approach them from the valley beneath they had built a highway eight kilometres long.

Back in Brisbane, the size of Central Bureau had

increased considerably and had 1,350 staff, 772 of them Americans, including a large Women's Army Corps contingent, 558 Australians, many of whom were members of the AWAS or the WAAAF, 20 British Army and 4 RAF interpreters, and 2 Royal Canadian Air Force codebreakers.

The bureau was divided into eight separate branches, but in terms of intelligence work there were five main branches. B Branch was 'solution', comprising the various codebreaking sections. It was led by Abe Sinkov, who dealt with high-grade army systems, and Eric Nave, who was in charge of attacking the codes used for air–ground communications. It also included Professor Thomas Room, who was in charge of a section breaking meteorological codes and ciphers providing advanced warning of Japanese targets. E Branch was traffic analysis, under Captain Stan Clark, one of the Australian officers. G Branch was 'machine procedure', the IBM tabulating machine operation based in the three-car garage of 21 Henry Street and controlled by Major Zach Halpin of the US Army. H Branch was translation, under another American officer, Major Hugh S. Erskine. I Branch was general intelligence and liaison, reporting as before solely to the Australian authorities.

The bureau also controlled nearly 3,400 intercept operators, including several hundred women. The forward elements were now 53 Australian Wireless Section, 111th, 125th and 126th Signal Radio Intelligence Companies, US Army, all based in Hollandia, 1 Wireless Unit RAAF based on the island of Biak, off the north-west coast of New Guinea, and 112th Signal Radio Intelligence Company, US Army, which was based in the Solomon Islands.

When the invasion of the Philippines began with the assault on Leyte, on 20 October, General Akin ordered Ballard to make arrangements for an Australian mobile intercept unit to accompany the first landings. The Australian operators were regarded as being more experienced than their American counterparts. A new RAAF mobile intercept unit, 6 WU, was formed, based on a small nucleus drawn from the 1 WU personnel based on Biak, and supplemented by operators sent from 4 WU in Brisbane. General Akin also took a small detachment from the Central Bureau advanced echelon, comprising five Australians and one of the British codebreakers, Peter Hall, with him in the first assault.

The landings on Leyte sparked the Battle of Leyte Gulf, the largest and the last major naval battle of the Second World War and the first phase of the *Shoo* (Victory) operations launched by Japan as a final attempt to defend the homeland. Naval Ultra was useful but not decisive in the Allied victory. This was largely due to the superior air power of the US Navy and Admiral Kurita Takeo's decision to withdraw just as he had the chance to destroy the 7th Fleet task group protecting the invasion force.

The RAAF intercept unit was operational throughout the journey to Tacloban in Leyte, and was able to report that the convoy had been sighted by enemy aircraft. Once on the ground, the Australian operators soon located the enemy air–ground frequencies and passed warnings of attacks to the US air controllers. They also intercepted details of Japanese convoys attempting to reinforce the Japanese troops on Leyte and were credited with responsibility for the sinking of seventeen ships, including the complete destruction of a convoy of Japanese transports attempting to reinforce Ormoc on the western coast of Leyte. A dozen Japanese naval aircraft escorted the convoy in a concentrated effort to protect it, but it was their radio signals, intercepted by the Australian operators, that sealed the convoy's fate. A mile from Ormoc it was attacked by 347 US aircraft. All five troop transports and four escorting destroyers, including the *Shimakaze*, the fastest ship in the Japanese fleet, were sunk. The only Japanese soldiers to survive were the few who managed to swim to shore.

Other intelligence garnered from the airwaves by 6 WU included: the location of convoys moving along the Indochina coast; enemy sightings of Allied shipping and task forces operating in the area; air base activity and movements of Japanese aircraft; movements of enemy air formations and high-ranking officers; serviceability reports for enemy airfields; and enemy weather reports. But the most ominous was the creation of a Japanese 'Special Attack Unit' of *kamikaze* suicide pilots at the Clark Air Base on Luzon, the most northerly of the main Philippines islands. The Australian intercept operators were able to plot the flight patterns of the aircraft and volunteer pilots coming in from Japan via Formosa. Many were shot down before they even reached their air base.

The Australian operators and codebreakers, together with their British companions, aroused the curiosity of the war correspondents attached to the US forces, who reported that MacArthur appeared to be accompanied by a small 'Foreign Legion'.

Back in Brisbane, Central Bureau was also benefiting from the Japanese disarray in the face of overwhelming US military and naval force. The enemy's attempts to co-ordinate the activities of their army and navy air units were providing Eric Nave with large numbers of cribs for the naval air codebook. A Japanese army air unit was co-operating with the Japanese naval aircraft searching for Allied convoys, he said.

> The army air unit reported all sightings back to the base in a three-figure code with simple substitution spelling table apparently devised for the purpose. This was most valuable as in addition to being very easy to read these reports had to be re-enciphered in the naval air book for passing to naval air units. These Allied convoy sightings, reports, involving the most carefully prepared section of the book with a vast variety of groups for ship types, courses, etc., were the most difficult to break. However, with the aid of these cribs and the grid system for positions, our information was complete.

In early November MacArthur's GHQ moved to Tacloban, Geoff Ballard recalled.

I was ordered to set up my office in a tumbledown bowling-alley, which was surrounded by a sea of mud. It at least had the merit of a certain isolation. We put up our board by the door which now read 'Forward Echelon, Central Bureau' to distinguish it from the Advance Echelon, still at Hollandia. Going to the office was quite an adventure, first stepping along the duckboards over the mud and water, and, once inside, stepping over the alleys to the one level area where we had our tables. Just across the road was the 'Big House' where, every evening, we would see General MacArthur, corn-cob pipe in mouth, pacing the long balcony and now and again waving to children in the street below.

The production of Ultra by Central Bureau had continued to expand to the point where Japanese plans and strategy became known to us as soon as they had been formulated and communicated for action to their own forces. Accordingly, it was vital for this intelligence to be available to GHQ at every stage of its planning because its own operations were largely based upon it. As a consequence, my liaison duties assumed a still more intensive role and most days saw an exhausting round of intelligence briefings and discussions not only at GHQ but at the 7th Fleet HQ and aboard the command ship USS *Arkansas* moored in Tacloban Harbour. My visits to the *Arkansas* were a special experience. The technical gadgetry in the operations room had all the elements of that in a science-fiction laboratory, particularly of illuminated screens with intelligence items moving constantly upwards upon them.

The capture of the Marianas island of Guam, and the new-found willingness of the US Navy and Army codebreakers to co-operate, allowed the creation of an advanced joint signals intelligence operation. The level of inter-service co-operation was remarkable by US standards. Radio Analysis Group, Forward Area, or RAG-FOR, had more than 600 army codebreakers and a similar number of navy codebreakers working alongside each other under the command of a US Navy officer and fed by army and navy intercept operators. It was located far closer to Tokyo than any other Allied static intercept site and was in operation and fully integrated with the US and British sites via the BRUSA Circuit by December 1944. The US Navy element of RAGFOR effectively replaced FRUMEL, which with the battle now having moved far forward of Melbourne was stripped of most of its US personnel and handed over to the Australians.

22

THE ATOMIC BOMB

For several months the Allied codebreakers had been monitoring the build-up of Japanese troops in the Philippines as part of the *Shoo* campaign, the last-ditch defence of the empire. A combination of messages decoded by Central Bureau and the Japanese military attachés' 'Tokyo Circular' had revealed that a quarter of a million Japanese troops were defending Luzon, the largest and most heavily populated island in the Philippines.

The Japanese general Yamashita Tomoyuki, known as the 'Tiger of Malaya' for his role in masterminding the fall of Singapore, believed the Americans would be at their most vulnerable on the island. By December 1944 it was clear that the attempts to reinforce Leyte had significantly reduced his forces on Luzon. When the Central Bureau codebreakers caught him bemoaning the state of the Japanese defenders, MacArthur decided he must strike now or risk further Japanese reinforcements causing serious disruption to the fulfilment of his promise to liberate the Philippines.

As the US troops fought their way across Leyte and MacArthur prepared for the assault on Luzon, the Australian and British 'Foreign Legion' based at Tacloban was joined by two US Army intercept units which also came under the control of Central Bureau. The 111th and 125th Signal Radio Intelligence Companies covered mainline army and army air systems, radioing the results back to the codebreakers in Hollandia and Brisbane for decryption.

Central Bureau's army air 'solution' section moved to Leyte where the RAAF intercept operators of 6 Wireless Unit had been augmented by a detachment from 4 Wireless Unit to cover naval air traffic. The codebreakers were able to monitor times and targets of planned enemy air raids, details of Japanese attempts to move reinforcements into the region, flights carrying high-ranking personalities and details of weather reports.

When the first US troops came ashore at Dagupan in the Lingayen Gulf they were joined by a detachment of 6 Wireless Unit and their American counterparts from 112th Signal Radio Intelligence Company. The Allied intercept operators hit the beaches within twenty minutes of the first assault but while the RAAF operators were soon at work, their US counterparts were waylaid by army commanders who inexplicably put them to work as a shore party, unloading ammunition, fuel and other supplies for the US troops. It was a week before they were released for their proper duties but eventually they rejoined the RAAF 'Foreign Legion' who had commenced intercept operations at San Miguel, the new site picked out for Central Bureau's forward elements.

The ability of the Central Bureau codebreakers to produce useful intelligence was hampered at the beginning of February by a change in the Army General Administrative System codebook which deprived them of a key source of intelligence. Worse, since the Japanese High Command had by now decided that the Philippines were bound eventually to fall to superior US resources, Yamashita's forces were no longer being reinforced and the water transport messages provided little intelligence of any value. But gradually the codebreakers began to rebuild the book, and during the battle for Okinawa in April, a near complete cryptographic library, including the new codebook, was captured, ensuring that they were able to read all the main Japanese Army messages immediately for several weeks and without major difficulty until the end of the war.

Both Central Bureau and the Royal Navy codebreakers in Colombo provided small radio intelligence or 'Y' units on the American model for the ships of the recently formed British Pacific Fleet and the US Navy's 5th Fleet. The units, which comprised two officers and fourteen intercept operators, monitored air–ground frequencies in order to warn of any impending Japanese attacks on the Allied ships. The most successful of these parties was that led by Colombo's Lieutenant John Silkin (later a senior Labour Party politician and Environment Secretary in the British Government) during the assault on Okinawa. Silkin's party was on board HMS *King George V*, the same ship that had brought the first Purple machine across the Atlantic to Britain. Although lacking the experience and knowledge of the known frequencies enjoyed by their US counterparts, they provided an accurate, up-to-date picture of the enemy air activity in the region which was vital in ensuring that the British ships did not fall victim to the increasingly desperate Japanese *kamikaze* attacks. 'We were dealing with a beaten and disorientated enemy, whose sole power of retaliation lay in his suicide bombers,' Silkin said in his report of the operation. 'These last hopes were foiled, largely by the watch kept by Y parties.'

The invasion of Okinawa saw the Japanese Navy's final attempt to take the battle to the Americans when the Imperial Naval General Staff ordered the super-battleship *Yamato* to lead a force of one cruiser and six destroyers in a suicidal attack on the US ships supporting the invasion force. But the entire Japanese plan was decoded by the US Navy codebreakers in Hawaii and the 'unsinkable' *Yamato* was sent to the bottom of the ocean by US carrier aircraft along with her cruiser and four destroyers.

The Royal Navy codebreakers at Colombo were given more autonomy over their operations with the creation of their own unit, HMS Anderson, and Hugh Alexander was sent out to revitalize their operations against the key codes JN25 and JN11.

A number of the Bletchley Park 'Hut 7' codebreakers had already been posted to Colombo, among them Norman Scott, and they were to play a crucial role in the sinking of one of the last big ships available to the Japanese Navy, the heavy cruiser *Haguro*. Scott was working on JN11, which in a sign of the drastic improvement wrought at Colombo was now solved as quickly by the British as by the Americans, if not more quickly, and had become their most important source of intelligence.

Most of us at Bletchley Park and at Anderson knew what was needed to do our jobs, but little else. We realized that our efforts could shorten the war but we rarely knew just how. There was, however, one instance where I could see that my personal effort had directly contributed. Towards the end of May 1945 the senior translator on duty came over with a very current, but scantily readable message on JN25. He explained to me that the Japanese were anxious to get a supply convoy from Singapore to the garrison and airfield in the Andaman Islands. It was known that a Japanese cruiser of the *Haguro* class was involved in this relief operation. This message was expected to lay out the plans. So I buckled down to work. Including the new message, I recollect a depth of three or four on the mostly unsolved worksheet. The translator alternately phoned HQ's intelligence section with more scraps of the message and then suggested words which I could try in the still unsolved columns.

At 8 p.m. the relief translators came on watch, but no cryptanalyst. Apparently there was a big party going on in the mess. I can remember taking a few minutes' break in the canteen at the station for a mug of tea and a sandwich. Then it was back to the grind and slog. From 2 a.m. to 8 a.m. the designated cryptanalyst on duty was myself. However, we now began to make significant progress. By about 5 a.m. the intelligence people were no longer calling every ten minutes. I drank more tea in the comparative cool of the pre-dawn hours. Until the evening of that day, no noisy party in the mess could have disturbed my sleep after being on watch for twenty of the previous twenty-four hours.

Some three or four days later the local press printed a naval communiqué which gave the news that a flotilla of British destroyers had sunk a Japanese cruiser in the Indian Ocean. Not long after a DSO was awarded to the flotilla commander and a DSC to one of the destroyer commanders. Over the years more details of this naval action have come to light. It seems that the four British destroyers had enjoyed sufficient lead time to practise their tactics. Contact was first made at night by radar. The destroyers were then able to spread out and approach within range of the cruiser's heavier guns from four directions simultaneously. Amid much ensuing confusion, the *Haguro* was finally sunk by gunfire and torpedoes.

The sinking of the *Haguro,* and the contributions played by Anderson in providing intelligence on the Japanese Navy's movements and intentions during the attacks on the Philippines, Okinawa and Rangoon, led to a congratulatory telegram from Bletchley Park and a morale-boosting visit to the station from Mountbatten himself, during which the Supreme Allied Commander South-east Asia told the Royal Navy codebreakers they were worth 'ten divisions'.

Bletchley Park was not just sending codebreakers to Colombo to help them to improve their efforts against JN25. Peter Laslett was posted to Washington, where he worked in the OP-20-G Communication Annex on Michigan Avenue and saw no sign of the disagreements over co-operation that had soured relations at senior levels.

The American effort was much more substantial and much better supported. But they hadn't the same experience of codebreaking as some of the people at Bletchley Park so their facility of breaking it was not really commensurate with the effort they were putting in. My main job was to explain to the Americans how we did it. I heard rumours of bad relations at a higher level, but my relationships with the people actually attacking the codes were good. I was conscious that the Americans thought the British had made a right balls of the war and, of course, conversely, we thought the Americans had. But the use of our material was of less importance to us. We were only interested in rebuilding the book. If we could get a third of the code groups in a book recovered before it was changed that was what gave us satisfaction. A half was virtually impossible, but a third was good.

Meanwhile, back at Bletchley Park, with the war in Europe over, one of the most secret locations in the country was about to become the focus of a radio programme to be broadcast across the length and breadth of the country. The amount of musical talent congregated at Bletchley had come to the attention of the producers of a popular BBC Home Service music programme, Bernard Keeffe recalled. 'Alec Robertson turned up in June 1945 with a BBC Outside Broadcast van and recorded a selection of our music-making for a special edition of *Music Magazine*. I made my first broadcast as soloist in Vaughan-Williams's Mass in G minor. The Japanese War was still on and yet, in an extraordinary breach of security, the most secret establishment in the country was introduced to the world on the Home Service on a Sunday morning.'

The rather erudite goings-on at the British codebreaking centre were in complete contrast to events in the Far East. Bitter fighting was continuing on Okinawa and the Philippines where the Advanced Echelon of Central Bureau had now moved to San Miguel, supported by the army air codebreakers, the RAAF's 5 and 6 Wireless Units, a detachment of 4 Wireless Unit and the 111th, 125th and 126th Signal Radio Intelligence Companies.

The rest of 4 Wireless Unit was taking part in the operations to recapture Borneo. Accompanied by the young British Army intelligence officers Tony Carson and Hugh Melinsky, they had landed on the island of Labuan, north-west of Borneo, early on 10 June, Melinsky recalled.

At precisely eight o'clock the morning calm was shattered as every warship opened up with its big guns firing on to the Japanese coastal defences. The peaceful shore beneath its swaying palms shook and leapt, and dark columns of dirt rose and fell, to be replaced by another and yet another until the whole shore became a grey swirling mass punctuated by orange points of explosions.

Then the assault began. The small landing-craft which had been huddling round the transport ships like chicks round a hen slowly drew away into formation heading for the shore. On the stroke of nine o'clock the barrage stopped and a few minutes later the first wave of soldiers was lost to sight in the smoke and debris of the plantations. The rattle of rifle and machine-gun fire echoed across the water of the bay as further waves of troops moved in, and soon the larger landing-ships nosed clumsily up the beach to disgorge tanks and lorries, guns and ammunition. I retired below for a drink of iced water . . .

The ops tent was soon up and working, the messages started coming in, and we did our usual job of decoding and translating them and sending the results to Captain Nave in Brisbane, though now by wireless. The local battle went on for ten days, of which we were well aware because we had a battery of large guns, twenty-five pounders, firing shells over our heads against a cave where the surviving enemy were gathered. One night a hundred or so of them broke out and made their way to the beach by way of the airfield. Their officers used their swords and the men their bayonets because they had run out of ammunition, and several Australians and Americans were killed and wounded before the Japanese were finally overcome. They must have passed very near our tents.

The operations met little resistance and by the middle of June virtually the whole of Central Bureau, including most of the elements that had so far been left behind in Brisbane, were being moved forward to San Miguel. Eric

Nave was deemed to be unfit for the tropics and left in charge of a rear detachment where he continued to work on the naval air codes that were giving away the details of Japanese convoy movements.

In a letter home to his young wife, Geoff Day described Central Bureau's arrival at its new base.

> San Miguel is only a village. The nearest town is Tarlac, some seven miles away and the capital of the province. The district around here is cultivated mainly for sugar plantations but also for the inevitable rice fields. At the moment, we are temporarily camped in a paddy field, dry fortunately, but just like a ploughed field. We had to sleep on it for our first night, not too comfortably either, as you can imagine, but after that we were presented with canvas cots. Our washing facilities consist of dipping in water from a running stream and to take a shower one has to strip off in the open. There is no danger from enemy aircraft here but there are still quite a number of Japs around. Last week, 100 were killed in the San Miguel area. We have a range of mountains to our east and one to the west. There are still a fair number of Japs in the eastern range trying to get access to the west where they believe they can escape to the sea. Unfortunately we are in the middle and thus are subject to infiltration tactics the whole time. We have protection from the Philippine Guerrilla Army who prowl around constantly, especially at night. It pays to answer their challenge pretty quickly.

Hugh Melinsky was sent to San Miguel from Labuan followed later by the rest of 4 Wireless Unit.

> We were on the edge of a large sugar plantation where they brewed alcohol from the sugar-cane. It was good to see ordinary people around the place again, and we were particularly glad because the Filipinos were willing to wash and iron our clothes for us at a small charge, and I felt very smart as a result. I met up again with a number of friends, including Peter Hall, who had been with 6 Wireless Unit

since it arrived in the Philippines on the day after the first landings. General MacArthur was making his plans for the final invasion of Japan on the southern island of Kyushu and we were told that we were going to be the only non-American unit involved. I never did understand why his staff were so dissatisfied with the work of the equivalent American units.

By now, the ability to read the mainline army codes captured at Okinawa and the regular 'Tokyo Circular' sent to Japanese military attachés in the embassies abroad was providing chilling reading. The determination with which the Japanese defences were being built up on the home islands, the surprising number of troops the Japanese High Command could still call on, the presence of several thousand aircraft that were being prepared for suicide attacks and the proven willingness of the Japanese elsewhere to fight to the last man gave the Allies pause for thought as they prepared to invade Japan.

Since March, General Curtis LeMay had been directing a series of devastating raids on the Japanese mainland. Flying from the Marianas, 1,500 miles south of Tokyo, and escorted by fighter aircraft based on the recently captured island of Iwo Jima, the US bombers had launched a series of low-level fire-bomb attacks on Japanese cities. On the night of 9–10 March a total of 1,667 tons of incendiary bombs were dropped on Tokyo, in the most devastating single air raid ever launched. Sixteen square miles of the city's mainly wooden and paper residential districts were razed to the ground and upwards of 84,000 people, many of them women and children, killed.

The Allies were by now aware that a sizeable faction within the Japanese Government would be prepared to sue for peace, but the Ultra signals intelligence from the mainline army and navy codes showed that, despite such horrific losses, the Japanese military remained determined to fight on.

The only man capable of bringing the Japanese Army to heel was the Emperor himself. On 12 July the codebreakers intercepted a Purple message from the Japanese Foreign Minister Togo Shigenori to Japan's Ambassador in Moscow ordering him to pass on to the Russians an urgent plea for peace from Emperor Hirohito. The message was sent just days before the Potsdam Conference at which Stalin was to meet Churchill and Harry Truman, the new US President. 'His Majesty the Emperor, mindful of the fact that present war daily brings greater evil and sacrifice upon peoples of all belligerent powers, desires from his heart that it may be quickly terminated,' it said. 'But so long as England and United States insist upon unconditional surrender in Great East Asian War, Empire has no alternative but to fight on with all its strength for honour and existence of Motherland. His Majesty is deeply reluctant to have any further blood lost among people on both sides and it is his desire, for welfare of humanity, to restore peace with all possible speed.'

Truman was already on his way to Potsdam when Hirohito's peace approach was decoded. Allied intelligence had advised that if the Emperor ordered the Japanese armed forces to surrender they would obey but that if 'unconditional surrender' meant the Emperor must lose his throne and be treated as a war criminal, the Japanese would fight to the last man. As a result the Combined Chiefs of Staff had urged on their respective governments a modification of the term 'unconditional surrender' to make it clear that the Emperor would be allowed to stay in place.

Four days after the Emperor's message was intercepted, the first atomic bomb was tested at a site in the New Mexico Desert. For reasons which remain inexplicable, the final declaration of the Potsdam Conference made no attempt to clarify the terms of surrender and, despite an acceptance by both America and Britain that the Emperor would have to be retained in order to control post-war Japan, no attempt was made privately to reassure the Japanese that he would not be forced to stand down. America and Britain issued an ultimatum to Japan. If there was not an immediate and unconditional surrender, it would lead to 'the inevitable and complete destruction of the Japanese armed forces and . . . the utter devastation of the Japanese homeland'.

Lacking any assurances over the future of their Emperor, the Japanese were never likely to surrender. At 8.15 on the morning of 6 August 1945, a B-29 bomber of the USAAF's 509th Composite Group dropped an atomic bomb on the south-western Japanese port of Hiroshima, flattening two-thirds of the city. Three days later a second bomb exploded over the port of Nagasaki, destroying the bulk of the city. Although the Allies put the number killed in the two attacks at around 120,000, Japanese sources have argued convincingly that it was double that number. Whatever the figure for those killed immediately, the appalling long-term effects of radiation on successive generations make it impossible to come to a final death toll. Peter Laslett recalled the events of August 1945:

My most vivid memory of the whole war was sitting in the Annex on a hot Washington night and decoding this Japanese naval message reporting that the *genshi bakudan*, the atomic bomb, had been dropped on Hiroshima. The Japanese had not referred to an atomic bomb in traffic before so I believe I was the first person to decode and translate the words that night. It was a terrible shock. As far as I recall, it didn't give any casualty figure but it must have given me some sort of evidence of the devastation. The sense of disaster was very clear.

Even before the news that the atomic bomb had been dropped on Hiroshima was officially announced, the messages arriving in Bletchley Park provided a frightening vision of what had happened, recalled Rosemary Calder. 'I was on a day watch by myself and all this stuff came in and it was total gibberish,' she said. 'I didn't know the bomb had been dropped but you could tell from the disruption of all the messages that something terrible had happened. You could just feel the people standing there screaming their heads off.'

Later messages were more specific. An army air message to the chief of staff of the General Army Air Command in Tokyo deciphered at Bletchley Park gave one of the first descriptions of the now familiar mushroom cloud associated with the atomic bomb: 'There was a blinding flash and a violent blast – over the city centre, the flash and burst were almost simultaneous but in the vicinity of the airfield the blast came two or three seconds later – and a mass of white smoke billowing up into the air.'

The dropping of the atomic bombs and the Soviet Union's invasion of Manchuria on 9 August led the Japanese Government to sue for peace. Only then were they informed of the precise terms of the unconditional surrender under which they would not only be allowed to keep their Emperor but were assured that the four main islands would remain part of Japan. Had such an offer been made two weeks earlier the war would almost certainly have been ended without recourse to the atomic bombs.

On 14 August Jack Grafing, a US Navy intercept operator, was on duty at the Adelaide River interception site south of Darwin.

I copied the first message in Japanese plain language I had ever heard. It was Emperor Hirohito's message to his troops to lay down their arms. After the Japanese surrender we closed the station at Adelaide River. I heard a long time later that our group was a key link in the information-gathering, and I do recall receiving some kind of a unit citation after I had returned home. At that time everything was still top secret, and since I was out of the navy, they could not tell me much about what it was for.

Around the world, the codebreakers and intercept operators working on the 'Japanese problem' had become redundant. Julie Lydekker was a WAAF who had been working on the index in the Japanese air section at Bletchley Park and had been sent to Washington to show the Americans how to set up a similar operation.

Washington was another world after the austerity and grind of Britain in 1945. For the first time in four years there was no weekend work, but wonderful opportunities for sightseeing, concerts and marvellous food. I had never seen one-inch fillet steaks and real cream ices like the ones that were normal fare there. Nothing could have been more of a contrast to Bletchley and its one cinema, tatty café and local pubs. On VJ Day Washington was vibrating with excitement, tempered with relief that the war with Japan was over. Everyone with a car converged on the White House with their hands firmly pressed on their horns, making an unbelievable cacophony which went on all day and was followed in the evening by a stunning firework display.

Olive Humble was on leave from the Hut 7 naval section when Japan surrendered.

I came back to Bletchley Park two days later to find all the civilians had shipped out. I was sent to the fearsome Commander Thatcher, who lectured me again about keeping my mouth shut for all time, had to re-sign the Official Secrets Act, and was threatened with the thirty years and/or firing squad if I went off the straight and narrow. I was then given a month's salary, a total of £3, plus or minus a few shillings, and I said farewell to the navy, and to Major M, who gave me a glowing reference, including words like 'National Importance'. Then I received the Foreign Office one, which was even better: 'employed on important and highly specialized work of a secret nature. The Official Secrets Act precludes any information in connection with these duties.' Heady stuff, even better than navy cocoa!

The Wrens based at HMS Anderson were soon to be sent home. But not before being enlisted to help with what one of them described as 'the most moving and satisfying job in my whole life'. Thousands of prisoners of war released from camps across the Far East were being brought back to Britain, stopping off in Colombo on their way home, recalled Dorothy Robertson.

Among many others, I worked in a mock-up Post Office hut where three of us sorted mail for any incoming ex-PoWs and helped any of them who wanted to send a message home. It was hard to remain dry-eyed when a lad would open and read the first letter he had had from home for several years, from a mother, wife or sweetheart; one chap read out to me: 'She says, "I am still waiting," ' as he broke down and wept.

There were civilians, too, some very emaciated indeed; I remember an elderly looking gentleman, who could perhaps have been much younger than he appeared, shuffling along in jungle-made shoes, tied with jungle creepers, and a similar wide-brimmed hat; he and his friends were pathetically polite and grateful for the smallest favour that we were only too glad to show them. We were all very moved and felt immensely humble in the presence of the PoWs who had suffered so much and for so long.

Life afterwards in post-war Britain was really grey and cheerless and one felt sorry for those who had not enjoyed any of the fun and colour and excitement that we had had. There were innumerable shortages, and ration cards and clothing coupons were to continue for some time yet. People had gone through a ghastly time, but the knowledge that we, incredibly, had won this six-year war when at times this seemed impossible was everything. It truly was a David and Goliath story.

In truth, the real Goliath had been America. Hirohito and Yamamoto had recognized before the war began that the might of American resources would beat the Japanese in the end, and so it did. But the assistance given by the codebreakers was immense. The influence exerted by Ultra on the war in the Far East and Pacific only rarely matched its effect on the European War. Nevertheless, historians have argued that it shortened both by around two years, saving many lives on both sides of the conflict. Yet it is impossible to make this claim with regard to the war in the Far East without also accepting that the difficulties placed in the way of co-operation, both with the British and their own military, by elements within the US Navy must have cost lives, the majority of them American.

Counter-factual history can be a dangerous thing. Wars are by their very nature full of mistakes that lead to unnecessary loss of life. But the effects of the rows over co-operation and the refusal of FRUMEL to share their material with Central Bureau were not momentary mistakes. They were the result of a sustained and deliberate policy based only partly on security concerns. It was clearly also motivated by a desire to ensure that the US Navy's signals intelligence hierarchy received the credit for any successes.

The codebreakers themselves should be absolved from any blame for this policy. Its architects and proponents were administrators, some of whom had little respect for those who achieved the successes, as demonstrated most clearly by the appalling treatment meted out to Joe Rochefort. The Pearl Harbor codebreaking operation that he put in place was one of the most efficient operating anywhere and, irrespective of its effect on the war, the breaking of the Yamamoto operational orders prior to the Battle of Midway was a truly spectacular success. Only very rarely were the Allied codebreakers able to decode more than stereotypical JN25 traffic; reading Yamamoto's complicated operational orders was therefore an amazing cryptographical achievement.

Rochefort, who retired from the navy in 1953, never did receive the Distinguished Service Medal that Admiral Nimitz had recommended him for in the wake of Midway, but it was belatedly awarded to him posthumously in 1986.

Frank B. Rowlett, who broke the Purple diplomatic cipher machine, one of the greatest codebreaking achievements of the war, was awarded the US Legion of Merit and the Order of the British Empire in 1946. He continued to work as a codebreaker with the National Security Agency, the American post-war signals intelligence agency, until his retirement in 1965. He died in 1998.

The leading British codebreaker John Tiltman, the pioneer in breaking the Japanese superenciphered codes and the man who broke JN25, stayed with GC&CS when it changed its name at the end of the war to the Government Communications Headquarters (GCHQ). He had already been appointed OBE in 1930 and Commander of the British Empire in 1944. He was awarded the US Legion of Merit in 1946 and appointed Commander of the Order of St Michael and St George in 1954. The extent of his codebreaking abilities can be discerned less from the honours he was awarded than from the fact that he was, exceptionally for a civil servant, allowed to continue working at GCHQ until his seventieth birthday. But even then he transferred to NSA, where he worked as a codebreaking troubleshooter for a number of years. He died in Hawaii in 1982.

Hugh Alexander was awarded an OBE at the end of the war and initially returned to his pre-war post as Director of Research at the John Lewis chain of department stores. But he evidently missed codebreaking and rejoined GCHQ. He was appointed Commander of the British Empire in 1955 and Commander of the Order of St Michael and St George in 1970. When he finally retired in 1971 he was two years past the standard civil service retirement date and as with Tiltman, NSA made determined efforts to recruit him as a codebreaking *éminence grise*. He turned them down in favour of a retirement writing about chess. He died in 1974.

Eric Nave, the Australian codebreaker whose work on Japanese codes and ciphers provided the early start for the British, was appointed OBE in 1946 and later joined the Australian Security Intelligence Organization. His reputation was damaged in 1991 by an ill-fated attempt to publish his memoirs which fuelled the conspiracy theories over Pearl Harbor. It is now clear from a copy held in the Australian War Memorial that James Rusbridger, his co-author on *Betrayal at Pearl Harbor*, distorted the original to make it conform to his own conspiracy theories. Nave died in 1993.

Hugh Foss, who worked with Nave to break the original Japanese naval attaché machine cipher, and almost certainly the original Red diplomatic machine cipher, retired to Scotland after the war. He died in 1971. Agnes Driscoll, who broke the same ciphers for the Americans, ended the war as OP-20-G's Principal Cryptanalyst. She went on to work for the NSA and retired in 1959. She died in 1971.

Francis A. Raven, the US Navy machine cipher specialist who broke Jade and worked on Coral with Alexander, received a Legion of Merit. He too worked for NSA after the war, winning a number of further awards for his work, and retired in 1974. He died in 1983.

Joseph E. Richard, who broke the Water Transport Code, the first of the mainline army superenciphered codes to be broken, while he was based at Central Bureau, also served with the NSA for many years, latterly as a member of the same cryptanalysis consultancy team as Tiltman. He retired in 1973. Wilfrid Noyce, who broke the same code simultaneously at the Wireless Experimental Centre, Delhi, worked as a master first at Malvern and then Charterhouse before becoming a full-time poet and author. He was a member of the team that made the first successful assault on Everest in 1953 and was killed climbing in the Pamir Mountains of Soviet Central Asia in 1962.

These codebreakers were, of course, only the most prominent of the many thousands of men and women who intercepted or decoded Japanese messages during the Second World War. The historians' estimate that the actions of all these men and women shortened it by two years and the countless lives they must have saved in so doing remain the most fitting testament to their remarkable achievements.

APPENDIX

BREAKING THE JAPANESE SUPERENCIPHERED CODES

The process used to break the Japanese superenciphered codes like JN25 can perhaps best be demonstrated by taking a notional example and working through it to 'strip' off the additive cipher in the same way that the codebreakers did. Remember in a superenciphered code, the originator encoded the message into a series of five-figure code groups using the codebook and then enciphered the encoded message by adding a series of five-figure groups, taken from an additive/cipher book, to the encoded groups. It is this additive/cipher that the codebreakers needed to strip off to reveal the encoded message underneath.

The first step was to go through all the available Japanese messages in the system the codebreakers were trying to crack, sorting them according to the 'indicator' groups. These were the groups inserted into each message, sometimes at the beginning, or more often in a predetermined position, which told the Japanese receiving station the starting point of the sequence of five-figure groups fron the additive/cipher book that had been added to the already encoded message in order to encipher it.

The codebreakers looked for a number of messages with the same starting points, or with starting points that were close to each other. For the sake of example, let us say we are lucky enough to find five messages that fit the bill, the first 12 groups of which are shown in the following table:

Table 1

00300 78389 89535 87019 49073 38472 91259 86989 38094 38898 66585 89960

00303 30962 49517 75834 29851 43682 42742 43467 40719 15673 06409 54277

00301 27755 98185 29481 03559 60851 33868 56611 92166 30082 12600 85741

00306 87033 67676 18443 16011 86097 12379 57368 00502 37078 76809 14376

00304 57508 66911 89708 63482 24236 98011 96177 72072 90160 89094 28736

For the sake of clarity, in the example shown in table 1, the starting points for the five-figure messages the codebreaker is trying to decipher have been sent 'in clear' at the beginning of the message. Each is using different but overlapping parts of page 3 of the additive/cipher book, indicated by the fact that they all commence with the figures 003. The 'indicator' for the first message is 00300. This means that the additive sequence in use begins on Page 3, first line, first column, i.e. the first additive group at the top of that page – the Japanese having numbered the columns and lines from 0-9 rather than from 1-9. The second starts with page 3, line 0, column 3, i.e., the fourth group on the page.

The codebreakers would then write the messages out on a large sheet of graph paper, known as a worksheet. The messages were aligned so that each group in any one column had been enciphered using the same additive group. On our worksheet we can line up the first group of message two (30962) underneath the fourth group of message one (49073), knowing that both these groups were enciphered using the fourth additive group on page 3 of the cipher book. Every subsequent group in message two will now appear underneath a counterpart in message one that was enciphered using the same additive. The third begins with line 0, column 1, i.e., the second group on the page, so its first group is lined up under the second group of message one – and so on. If we now line up our messages so that all the groups in each column have been enciphered using the same additive group, they look like table 2 below. It would probably be easier to understand if you copy out this example so that you can work on top of it, stripping the additive off as we go along, just as the codebreakers did. You will need to leave a space at the top for the additive groups we recover plus two lines between each row of figures so you can fill in the codegroups and any original text we recover.

Table 2

00300 78389 89535 87019 49073 38472 91259 86989 38094 38898 66585 89960

00303   30962 49517 75834 29851 43682 42742 43467 40719

00301   27755 98185 29481 03559 60851 33868 56611 92166 30082 12600

00306   87033 67676 18443 16011 86097

00304   57508 66911 89708 63482 24236 98011 96177

The number of groups using the same additive/cipher group that can be lined up under each other in the vertical columns is referred to as the 'depth'. The more depth there is on the worksheet, the easier it should be to break the messages. In table 2, there is a depth of two groups from the second column onwards, the second group in message one (89535) and the first group in message three (27755) having been enciphered using the same additive/cipher group – i.e., the second group in line one of page three of the additive/cipher book. This grows to a more useful depth of three by the fourth; a depth of four by the fifth group; and a much more healthy depth of five from the seventh group onwards.

Sometimes, the codebreakers would be lucky enough to know from previously broken messages what the sequence of additive groups for the given starting point would be. But if they were starting from scratch, which was frequently the position, the first task was to begin hypothesising possible codegroups to match up to individual enciphered groups until they could make them fit. By subtracting the known code group from the enciphered group, they produced an additive group, which could then be subtracted from all the enciphered groups in the same column to produce potential codegroups. If other known codegroups began appearing in the correct positions, the codebreakers would know they were on the right track. There were a number of key codegroups that the codebreakers would look for. These involved words that might be expected to appear more frequently than others, the first being *hatsu*, the Japanese word for 'from', which appeared at the start of most messages to indicate who was originating the message. Depending on the station sending the message, the likely originator might also be known. The next codegroup after the group giving the originator would be *shuushifu*, the Japanese word for 'fullstop'.

We can begin to try some of these entry devices out, starting with *hatsu*. It would be best to start with the first enciphered group of message four, in the seventh column, since that column has a depth of five. The advantage of starting with a depth of five is that if either of the already recovered codegroups for *hatsu* works then we can begin stripping off the additive from all five codegroups in the column, with the possibility that some of those codegroups may already have been recovered, giving us yet more ways in. There would be a number of five-figure JN25 codegroups for a common word like *hatsu*. But let us say there are just two – 58743 and 78225 – and that we have already recovered both from the breaking of previous messages. Note that the sums of all the figures in each of these codegroups, as with every five-figure JN25 codegroup are divisible by three. This was the garble check for the Japanese operators. If having deciphered the message they found that any of the codegroups they were left with were not divisible by three, they knew that either the message had been sent or taken down incorrectly, or that their sums were wrong and they had to start again. But equally this garble check also turned out to be an invaluable tool for the codebreakers. If, having stripped off the additive groups, they were left with any codegroups that were not divisible by three, they knew they too had got something wrong.

So let us try the first of our *hatsu* codegroups: 58743. We subtract it from the first enciphered group of message four: 87033, using the Fibonacci non-carrying system, which for ease of use was common to all additive systems. Each digit is treated separately, so if we subtract 8 from 7 we get 9 and do not carry any figures over to the next digit. Similarly if we were to add 8 to 7 we would get 5 rather than 15. Subtracting the codegroup 58743 from the enciphered group 87033 we come up with a possible additive group for column four of 39390. This suggests codegroups for that column, less subtracting the additive group from the enciphered group and working from top to bottom, of 57699; 90561; 04578. Our hypothesised codegroup 58743; and 50418, the arithmetic using the non-carrying Fibonacci system looks like this:

Table 3

86989	29851	33868	87033	89708
−39390	−39390	−39390	−39390	−39390
=57699	=90561	=04578	=58743	=50418

The last group of the seventh column is in the third position of the fifth message, precisely where we might expect to see *shuushifu*. Because this is a codegroup that we see all the time, it has already been recovered from breaking of previous messages as 50418, giving us the confirmation we need that our additive group is correct.

Table 4

Additive								39390			

Message	00300	78389	89535	87019	49073	38472	91259	86989	38094	38898	66585
Codegroup								57699			
Text								?			

Message	00303			30962	49517	75834	29851	43682	42742	43467
Codegroup						90561				
Text						?				

Message	00301	27755	98185	29481	03559	60851	33868	56611	92166	30082
Codegroup						04578				
Text						?				

Message	00306					87033	67676	18443	16011
Codegroup					58743				
Text					From				

Message	00304				57508	66911	89708	63482	24236	98011
Codegroup					50418					
Text					Stop					

We could now try one of the two *hatsu* codegroups on the other two messages, but that would be away from the main depth and give us less chance of a breakthrough. So put it to one side for the moment. If we try the *shuushifu* codegroup 50418 instead, we only have one group to worry about and therefore may have more luck. Hypothesising it for the third group of message two, 75834 – remember you subtract the potential codegroup from your enciphered group – produces an additive group for that column of 25426 while in the third group of message four, 18443, it gives us an additive group of 68035. Now we subtract these new additive groups from the enciphered groups to come up with the other codegroups in those respective columns. Some of those will not have been previously recovered but equally some well known codegroups can now be filled in. In this case, we know from previously broken messages that 76883 is *'maru'* (the suffix used after the name of each ship); that 84717 is 'supplies'; that 45435 is 'begin'; that 34131 is 'good'; that 41595 is 'Commander-in-Chief'; and that 66201 is 'radio silence'. None of the other codegroups from which the additive groups have been stripped have been previously recovered. Our worksheet now looks like this:

Table 5

Additive						25426	39390		68035	
Message	00300	78389	89535	87019	49073	38472	91259	86989	38094	38898 66585
Codegroup						76833	57699		70863	
Text						*maru*	?		?	
Message	00303			30962	49517	75834	29851	43682	42742	43467
Codegroup						50418	90561		84717	
Text						Stop	?		Supplies	
Message	00301	27755	98185	29481	03559	60851	33868	56611	92166	30082
Codegroup						45435	04578		34131	
Text						Begin	?		Good	
Message	00306					87033	67676	18443	16011	
Codegroup						58743			50418	
Text						From			Stop	
Message	00304				57508	66911	89708	63482	24236	98011
Codegroup						41595	50418		66201	
Text						C-in-C	Stop		Radio Silence	

We are not going to be able to strip the first four groups of message one and the first two groups of message three at this stage so it is easier to move along the worksheet to give us more of the potentially breakable body of the messages. Table 6 moves along the worksheet so the fourth column of the previous example is now at the extreme left.

Table 6

	1	2	3	4	5	6	7	8	9	10	11	12
Additive			25426	39390		68035						
Message	49073	38472	91259	86989	38094	38898	66585	89960	11940	98702	28983	29024
Codegroup			76833	57699		70863						
Text			*maru*	?		?						
Message	30962	49517	75834	29851	43682	42742	43467	40719	15673	06409	54277	71073
Codegroup			50418	90561		84717						
Text			Stop	?		Supplies						
Message	29481	03559	60851	33868	56611	92166	30082	12600	85741	42130	07701	98001
Codegroup			45435	04578		34131						
Text			Begin	?		Good						
Message			87033	67676	18443	16011	86907	12379	57368	00502	37078	
Codegroup			58743			50418						
Text			From			Stop						
Message		57508	66911	89708	63482	24236	98011	96177	72072	90160	89094	28736
Codegroup			41595	50418		66201						
Text			C-in-C	Stop		Radio Silence						

Let us now return to the two possible codegroups for *hatsu*, in the first enciphered groups of messages two and five. If we start with the codegroup for *hatsu* we have already used, 58743, and subtract it from the first enciphered group in message five, 57508, we get an additive group of 09865. When this is subtracted from the groups in this column, it produces codegroups of 39617; 40752; and 04794 respectively. There is a problem here. The Japanese operators' garble check ensures that the sum of the figures in all codegroups is divisible by three. Codegroups 40752 and 04794 conform to this rule, but group one does not. Either it has been taken down incorrectly by the intercept operator or 58743 is not the codegroup in use. If we try the other *hatsu* codegroup, 78225, instead, and subtract it from the first enciphered group in message five we get an additive group of 89383. When this is subtracted from the other enciphered groups in this column, it produces codegroups of 59199; 60234; and 24276 respectively, all of which fit the garble check, which has now become a useful codebreaking check. If we try both *hatsu* codegroups on the first enciphered group of message two, only the 58743 codegroup passes the garble check. Our example now looks like this:

Table 7

Additive	82229	89383	25426	39390		68035						

Message	49073	38472	91259	86989	38094	38898	66585	89960	11940	98702	28983	29024
Codegroup	67854	59199	76833	57699		70863						
Text	?	?	*maru*	?		?						

Message	30962	49517	75834	29851	43682	42742	43467	40719	15673	06409	54277	71073
Codegroup	58743	60234	50418	90561		84717						
Text	From	?	Stop	?		Supplies						

Message	29481	03559	60851	33868	56611	92166	30082	12600	85741	42130	07701	98001
Codegroup	47262	24276	45435	04578		34131						
Text	?	?	Begin	?		Good						

Message			87033	67676	18443	16011	86907	12379	57368	00502	37078
Codegroup		58743		50418							
Text		From		Stop							

Message	57508	66911	89708	63482	24236	98011	96177	72072	90160	89094	28736
Codegroup	78225	41595	50418		66201						
Text	From	C-in-C	Stop		Radio Silence						

Unfortunately, none of the resultant codegroups has been recovered from previously broken messages. But we are beginning to make headway with the last of the messages on our worksheet, message number five. We know it is from the Commander-in-Chief (C-in-C), and that it is talking about radio silence. The most likely codegroups to be used with radio silence are those for 'begin' and for 'end'. Since we know that the stations concerned had not previously been maintaining radio silence, they cannot be ending it. So 'begin' seems the most likely option. If we try the codegroup for 'begin', 45435, with that enciphered group, we get an additive group of 28057 and when we subtract that from the other enciphered groups in the same column, every one fits the garble check. We also get another recovery in column five of message three, where 38664 is known to be the codegroup for 'until further notice'.

Table 8

Additive	82229	89383	25426	39390	28057	68035						

Message	49073	38472	91259	86989	38094	38898	66585	89960	11940	98702	28983	29024
Codegroup	67854	59199	76833	57699	10047	70863						
Text	?	?	*maru*	?	?	?						

Message	30962	49517	75834	29851	43682	42742	43467	40719	15673	06409	54277	71073
Codegroup	58743	60234	50418	90561	25635	84717						
Text	From	?	Stop	?	?	Supplies						

Message	29481	03559	60851	33868	56611	92166	30082	12600	85741	42130	07701	98001
Codegroup	47262	24276	45435	04578	38664	34131						
Text	?	?	Begin	?	Until F/N	Good						

Message			87033	67676	18443	16011	86907	12379	57368	00502	37078
Codegroup			58743	49629	50418						
Text			From	?	Stop						

Message		57508	66911	89708	63482	24236	98011	96177	72072	90160	89094	28736
Codegroup		78225	41595	50418	45435	66201						
Text		From	C-in-C	Stop	Begin	Radio Silence						

With all those codegroups in place, an interesting possibility emerges. It appears that the text in message five may be being repeated in message three. The most likely reason for this would be that the Commander-in-Chief's message is being passed on to a station further on down the line. We can test our theory on message five, providing us with two more potential additive groups and allowing us to extend the fifth message, and the stream of additive groups, still further. When we do so we find that the garble checks are working out. It is clear that yet again we are on the right track.

Table 9

Additive	82229	89383	25426	39390	28057	68035	60457	62046

Message	49073	38472	91259	86989	38094	38898	66585	89960	11940	98702	28983	29024
Codegroup	67854	59199	76833	57699	10047	70863	06138	27294				
Text	?	?	*maru*	?	?	?	*maru*	?				

Message	30962	49517	75834	29851	43682	42742	43467	40719	15673	06409	54277	71073
Codegroup	58743	60234	50418	90561	25635	84717	83010	88773				
Text	From	?	Stop	?	?	Supplies	For	?				

Message	29481	03559	60851	33868	56611	92166	30082	12600	85741	42130	07701	98001
Codegroup	47262	24276	45435	04578	38664	34131	70635	50664				
Text	?	?	Begin	?	Until	Good	?	With				
					F/N							

Message			87033	67676	18443	16011	86907	12379	57368	00502	37078	
Codegroup			58743	49629	50418	56664	24051					
Text			From	?	Stop	Assist	?					

Message		57508	66911	89708	63482	24236	98011	96177	72072	90160	89094	28736
Codegroup		78225	41595	50418	45435	66201	38664	34131				
Text		From	C-in-C	Stop	Begin	R/	Until	Good				
						Silence	F/N					

What we might now do is look at the sequence of additive groups that we have recovered to see if it matches any known sequences. If it does, this will make our job much easier.

With luck, we will be able to continue stripping off the additive cipher by 'piggy-backing' two groups along at a time in each message. As we move along the worksheet, a number of already recovered codegroups are appearing in the messages. None are anywhere near as complete as message five. But by good fortune, a number of previously recovered codegroups are appearing in the repetition sequence in message three. The codegroups 83302 ('your') and 02633 ('mission') fill in the major remaining gaps and, although it cannot be confirmed, established Japanese practice leads us to guess that the unrecovered codegroup 70635 is probably 'luck'.

Not only have we successfully stripped additive cipher to uncover the codegroups underneath but we have also decoded an important message indicating that a major operation is imminent. While that information is being sent out in the form of an intelligence report, the worksheet, now looking like Table 10, will be handed on to other codebreakers who will attempt to use other messages and knowledge of Japanese procedure to break the so far unrecovered codegroups, building up the codebook for future use. The string of additive groups will also be recorded so that when the same indicator groups appear again, the codebreakers dealing with those messages have a much easier time.

Table 10

```
Additive   82229 89383 25426 39390 28057 68035 60457 62046 02447 40506 06790 26102


Message    49073 38472 91259 86989 38094 38898 66585 89960 11940 98702 28983 29024
Codegroup  67854 59199 76833 57699 10047 70863 06138 27294 19503 58206 22293 53922
Text         ?     ?   maru    ?     ?     ?    maru    ?   Special Escort and    ?


Message    30962 49517 75834 29851 43682 42742 43467 40719 15673 06409 54277 71073
Codegroup  58743 60234 50418 90561 25635 84717 83010 88773 13236 66903 58587 55971
Text        From    ?   Stop    ?     ? Supplies For    ?     ?     ?     ?     ?


Message    29481 03559 60851 33868 56611 92166 30082 12600 85741 42130 07701 98001
Codegroup  47262 24276 45435 04578 38664 34131 70635 50664 83304 02634 01011 72909
Text         ?     ?   Begin  (R/   Until Good (Luck) With  Your Mission  ?     ?
                          Silence) F/N


Message                87033 67676 18443 16011 86907 12379 57368 00502 37078
Codegroup              58743 49629 50418 56664 24051 10932 17862 04812 11976
Text                    From    ?   Stop Assist  ?     ?     ?     ?     ?


Message    57508 66911 89708 63482 24236 98011 96177 72072 90160 89094 28736
Codegroup  78225 41595 50418 45435 66201 38664 34131 70635 50664 83304 02634
Text        From C-In-C Stop Begin   R/   Until Good (Luck) With  Your Mission
                                   Silence F/N
```

This is of course only a demonstration exercise and it was rarely this easy, although even so note how few codegroups are recovered. But we have used only a limited number of the possible means used to break into the Japanese superenciphcrd codes.

NOTES

CHAPTER 1

Pages 23–8 Interviews with John Burrows, Hettie Cox (née Marshall), Geoff Day, Joan Dinwoodie (née Sprinks), Lillie Feeney (née Gadd), Phil Puttick and Rene Watson (née Skipp) conducted September 1999–April 2000; unpublished memoirs of Geoff Day; Attiwell, Kenneth, *The Singapore Story* (Frederick Muller, London, 1959); Elphick, Peter, Singapore, *The Pregnable Fortress: A Study in Deception, Discord and Desertion* (Hodder & Stoughton, London, 1995); Elphick, Peter and Smith, Michael, *Odd Man Out: The Story of the Singapore Traitor* (Hodder & Stoughton, London,1993); Simson, Ivan, *Singapore: Too Little, too Late: Some Aspects of the Malayan Disaster in 1942* (Leo Cooper, London, 1970).

CHAPTER 2

Page 29 History of codebreaking up to end of First World War see PRO HW3/15; Andrew, Christopher, *Secret Service: The Making of the British Intelligence Community* (William Heinemann, London, 1985); Smith, Michael, *New Cloak, Old Dagger* (Victor Gollancz, London, 1996).

Page 30 Clarke on setting up of GC&CS from PRO HW3/1; HW3/3; HW3/16.

Page 30 Background to setting up of GC&CS from PRO HW3/33.

Pages 30–1 Denniston on early days of GC&CS from Denniston, A.G., The Government Code and Cipher School between the Wars (*Intelligence and National Security*, Vol. 1, No. 1, 1986).

Page 31 Curzon from Jeffery, Keith (ed.), The Government Code and Cypher School: A Memorandum by Lord Curzon (*Intelligence and National Security*, Vol. 1, No. 3, 1986).

Pages 30–2 Denniston on interception of diplomatic cables from Denniston, The Government Code and Cipher School between the Wars.

Pages 31–2 Senate subcommittee investigates British arrangement with American cable companies from NARA RG457, SRH-012; Rusbridger, James and Nave, Eric, *Betrayal at Pearl Harbor: How Churchill Lured Roosevelt into War* (Michael O'Mara, London, 1991).

Page 33 Denniston on early days of Japanese codebreaking from Denniston, The Government Code and Cipher School between the Wars.

Pages 32–3 Clarke on early days of Japanese codebreaking PRO HW3/1; HW3/3; HW3/16.

Page 33 Denniston on Maine and Hobart-Hampden from Denniston, The Government Code and Cipher School between the Wars.

Pages 33–4 British interception of Japanese ciphers during the 1921 Washington Conference from PRO HW14/15; Denniston, The Government Code and Cipher School between the Wars.

Pages 34–5 Clarke on Curzon and Sinclair from PRO HW3/1; HW3/3; HW3/16.

Page 36 Japanese language explanation courtesy of Hilary Jarvis.

Page 36 Clark on difficulties experienced by Royal Navy wireless telegraphists attempting to read Japanese Morse from PRO HW3/1; HW3/3; HW3/16.

Pages 36–7 Problems recruiting Japanese interpreters from PRO HW3/55.

Page 37 Navy sends officers to Japan for cryptographic section and shortage of Japanese-speaking naval officers from PRO ADM116/2349.

Page 37 Nave details and quotes from Nave, Eric, *An Australian's Unique Naval Career*, Unpublished Memoir, Australian War Memorial, MSS 1183; National Australian Archives (Melbourne) MP 1049, 1997/5/196.

Page 38 Clarke on Nave from PRO HW3/1; HW3/3; HW3/16.

Page 38 Nave already working on Japanese messages from National Australian Archives (Melbourne) MP 1049, 1997/5/196 (I am grateful to Joe Straczek for drawing my attention to this file).

Pages 38–9 Admiralty instructions from National Australian Archives (Melbourne) MP 1049, 1997/5/196.

Pages 39–40 Nave progress and assistance of Flintham from Nave, *An Australian's Unique Travel Career*.

Pages 42–3 Codebreaking techniques from Smith, Michael, *Station X: The Codebreakers of Bletchley Park* (Channel 4 Books, London, 1998); Rowlett, Frank, *The Story of Magic: Memoirs of an American Cryptologic Pioneer* (Aegean Park Press, Laguna Hills, 1998).

Page 44 Parlett from Denniston, The Government Code and Cipher School between the Wars.

Page 44 Nave recalled from Nave, *An Australian's Unique Naval Career*; PRO FO366/978.

CHAPTER 3

Page 45 Nave arrives in London from Nave, *An Australian's Unique Naval Career*.

Pages 45–6 Background from Best, Antony, *Britain, Japan and Pearl Harbor: Avoiding War in East Asia* (Routledge, London, 1995); Elphick, Peter, *Far Eastern File: The Intelligence War in the Far East 1930–1945* (Coronet, London, 1997).

Page 46 Nave progress on codes from Nave, *An Australian's Unique Naval Career*; PRO FO366/978.

Pages 46–7 Introduction of new Japanese naval code and Nave return to Far East from Nave, *An Australian's Unique Naval Career*.

Page 47 Manchuria Incident and effect on interception from PRO HW3/1; HW3/3; HW3/16; Elphick, *Far Eastern File*.

Page 47 Red forms from National Australian Archives (Melbourne) MP 1049, 1997/5/196.

Page 48 Return of Nave to London and exchange with Shaw from PRO FO366/978; Nave, *An Australian's Unique Naval Career.*

Pages 48–9 Singapore spy scandal from PRO ADM223/495.

Page 50 Dickens's concern from PRO ADM223/495; Elphick, *Far Eastern File.*

Pages 50–1 Rutland from Nave, *An Australian's Unique Naval Career*; Elphick, *Far Eastern File.*

Pages 51–2 Dickens quotes from PRO ADM223/495.

Pages 52–3 Japanese naval attaché machine cipher broken by Foss and Strachey from Nave, *An Australian's Unique Naval Career.*

Page 53 US break of Orange from Stafford, L.F., *History of Japanese Cipher Machines*, NARA RG 457 HCC 2344.

Pages 53–4 Meeting of Y Committee and decision to set up naval codebreaking centre in Hong Kong from HW3/33; ADM223/495; HW4/24; HW4/25; Nave, *An Australian's Unique Naval Career*. Overseas signals intelligence coverage at this time was divided between the British and Indian armies and the Royal Navy with the British Army taking responsibility for 'the Near East, including Arabia; Persia; Turkey and South Russia'; the Indian Army was responsible for the Indian sub-continent and Burma; and the Royal Navy covered the Far East.

Page 54 Request for more staff for opening of Hong Kong Bureau from PRO FO366/1004.

Pages 54–8 Organization and operations of FECB from PRO HW4/24; HW4/25; ADM233/494; HW3/102; AIR20/374; National Australian Archives (Melbourne) MP1185 2021/5/529; MP1185/8 1945/2/6.

Pages 59–61 Tiltman from Tiltman, John H., *Some Reminiscences*, NARA RG457 OD4632; Erskine, Ralph, Brigadier John H. Tiltman: One of BP's Finest (forthcoming, in *Global Intelligence Monthly*).

CHAPTER 4

Page 62 Denniston on recruitment of language experts from Denniston, The Government Code and Cipher School between the Wars; PRO FO366/978.

Pages 62–3 Kennedy from Ferris, John, From Broadway House to Bletchley Park: The Diary of Captain Malcolm D. Kennedy, 1934–1946 (*Intelligence and National Security*, Vol. 4, No. 3, July 1989).

Page 63 Shaw on drop copies, diplomatic telegrams and interception from PRO HW4/25.

Page 64 Denniston on Maine from Denniston, The Government Code and Cipher School.

Page 64 Kenworthy on co-option of Metropolitan Police unit from PRO HW3/163 and C.L. Sinclair Williams, unpublished personal account of Kenworthy's wartime work with Bletchley Park and the Metropolitan Police Intercept Unit.

Pages 65–6 Red machine from Kelley, Steve, *Big Machines: The Relative Cryptographic Security of the German Enigma, the Japanese PURPLE, and the US SIGABA/ECM Cipher Machines in World War II* (Joint Military Intelligence College, Washington, 1999); Deavours, Cipher, and Kruh, Louis, *Machine Cryptography and Modern Cryptanalysis* (Artech, London, 1985).

Pages 66–7 Kenworthy progress on Red machine from Johnson, John, *The Evolution of British Sigint: 1653–1939* (HMSO, Cheltenham, 1997) and PRO HW3/163.

Page 67 American attack on Red machine and methods of approach from Rowlett, Frank, *The Story of Magic: Memoirs of an American Cryptologic Pioneer* (Aegean Park Press, Laguna Hills, 1998); Alvarez, David, *Secret Messages: Codebreaking and American Diplomacy* (University Press of Kansas, Lawrence, 2000). Professor Alvarez suggests that US files stating that the US codebreakers broke Red in October 1936 must be wrong, since the same files contain decrypts of messages dating from November 1934. But, as Rowlett explains, this is because they went back over old intercepts, decoding them.

Page 68 Clarke and Cooper on British decision to ignore

German codes from PRO HW3/1 and HW3/83.

Page 68 Information on Oshima from PRO WO208/4703; WO106/5606; Boyd, Carl, *Hitler's Japanese Confidant: General Oshima Hiroshi and Magic Intelligence, 1941–1945* (University Press of Kansas, Lawrence, 1993).

Page 69 British military intelligence analysis of Oshima BJs from PRO WO106/5530.

Pages 70–2 Kennedy from Kennedy Papers, University of Sheffield Library, quoted by kind permission of the School of East Asian Studies.

Page 72 Sir Eric Drummond and Sujimura from PRO FO371/21183; FO371/21176; FO371/20279.

Page 73 Secretary on Foss from various interviews with Barbara Eachus (née Abernethy) October–December 1999.

Page 74 Browning on Foss from Hawken, Elizabeth, *Recollections of Bletchley Park*, her unpublished memoirs kindly provided to the author by her daughter Miss S. C. J. Hawken.

CHAPTER 5

Pages 75–6 Background on China Incident, Rape of Nanking, Chamberlain and US attitude from Elphick, Peter, *Far Eastern File: The Intelligence War in the Far East 1930–1945* (Coronet, London, 1997); Best, Antony, *Britain, Japan and Pearl Harbor: Avoiding War in East Asia* (Routledge, London, 1995).

Pages 76–7 Tiltman on military codes from Tiltman, *Some Reminiscences*; Erskine, Brigadier John H. Tiltman.

Page 78 Sinclair and purchase of Bletchley Park from Smith, *Station X*.

Page 79 Tiltman gets Hong Kong to take over military codes and takes Marr-Johnston and Stevens to Hong Kong from Tiltman, *Some Reminiscences*; PRO HW4/25.

Page 79 Number of RAF operators at Stonecutters from PRO AIR20/374.

Page 79 De Grey on RAF move to Hong Kong from PRO HW3/102.

Page 79 Nave return and breaking of cipher from Nave, *An*

Australian's Unique Naval Career; PRO HW4/25; HW14/48.

Page 80 Setting up of commercial section from Denniston, The Government Code and Cipher School between the Wars.

Page 80 Introduction of Type B from Friedman's Preliminary Report on the Solution of the B Machine, NARA RG457 OD2344; Rowlett, *The Story of Magic*. The main capitals were Washington, Berlin, London, Paris, Moscow, Rome, Geneva, Brussels, Ankara, Shanghai and Peking.

Page 81 Nave and Dockyard Code from Nave, *An Australian's Unique Naval Career*; HW14/48; Tiltman from Tiltman, *Some Reminiscences*; Erskine, Brigadier John H. Tiltman.

Pages 81-2 Abernethy on Clarke and Tiltman from various interviews and conversations with Barbara Eachus (née Abernethy).

Pages 82-3 Tiltman break of JN25 from Johnson, *The Evolution of British Sigint*; Erskine, Brigadier John H. Tiltman; PRO ADM223/496; HW4/25. See Budiansky, Stephen, Too Late for Pearl Harbor, *US Naval Institute Proceedings*, December 1999 for a description of how the Americans broke JN25 in the autumn of 1940, more than a year after Tiltman.

Page 83 Kennedy on move to BP from Ferris, From Broadway House to Bletchley Park.

Page 84 FECB move to Singapore from PRO HW4/24; HW4/25; ADM233/494.

Page 85 DF network from PRO HW4/26; Smith, *Station X*.

Page 85 Nave marriage from Nave, *An Australian's Unique Naval Career*.

Page 85 Burnett to Singapore with JN25 recoveries from PRO HW4/25.

Page 85 Break of new Dockyard Code from PRO HW14/48.

Page 86 Recruitment of new staff from PRO HW4/25.

Page 86 Status of General Code/Cipher (JN25) from PRO HW4/25.

Pages 86-7 Training of Wrens from correspondence and interview with Joan Dinwoodie (née Sprinks) 19 November 1999.

Pages 87-8 Training on *kana* Morse from correspondence and interview with Kirk Gill, November 1999; HW4/26.

Pages 86–8 Wrens joining the FECB from correspondence and interview with Joan Dinwoodie (née Sprinks).

CHAPTER 6

Page 89 Background from Calvocoressi, Peter, Wint, Guy and Pritchard, John, *The Penguin History of the Second World War* (Penguin, London, 1999); Best, *Britain, Japan and Pearl Harbor*; Elphick, *Far Eastern File*.

Pages 89–90 Malcolm Kennedy from Ferris, From Broadway House to Bletchley Park.

Page 90 Introduction of Type B machine from Rowlett, *The Story of Magic*.

Page 91 Harry Shaw on attempted pinch of Type B machine from PRO HW4/25.

Pages 91–2 Operation of Type B machine from NARA RG457 OD3679; Rowlett, *The Story of Magic*; Deavours, Cipher and Kruh, Louis, *Machine Cryptography and Modern Cryptanalysis*; Kelley, Steve, *Big Machines* (I am extremely grateful to Steve Kelley for his assistance and to Robert J. Hanyok for providing me with details of the OD3679 file).

Pages 93–8 Breaking of Type B/Purple machine from Friedman's Preliminary Report on the Solution of the B Machine, NARA RG457 OD2344; Rowlett, *The Story of Magic*.

Page 93 Friedman background from Clarke, Ronald, *The Man Who Broke Purple* (Weidenfeld & Nicolson, London, 1977).

Page 93 Rowlett background from Rowlett, *The Story of Magic*.

Page 99 Oshima return to Berlin from Boyd, *Hitler's Japanese Confidant*.

Pages 99–103 Co-operation with Americans see PRO HW14/45 (this file contains a copy of the undertaking signed by Currier not to reveal to anyone other than Safford what he had received from the British and an exchange of messages about the initial difficulty the Americans had understanding the British paper model of Enigma due to a missing document which was later found to have been mislaid in Washington); PRO HW4/25; ADM223/297; ADM199/1477; Currier, Prescott, My Purple Trip to England in 1941 (*Cryptologia*, Vol. 20, No. 3, 1996);

Currier, Prescott, NSA Oral History OH-38-80 (November 1980); author's various conversations with Barbara Eachus (née Abernethy); Erskine, Ralph, Churchill and the Start of the Ultra–Magic Deals (*International Journal of Intelligence and Counterintelligence*, Vol. 10, 1997); Erskine, Ralph, The Holden Agreement on Naval Sigint: The First BRUSA? (*Intelligence and National Security*, Vol. 14, No. 2, Summer 1999); Best, *Britain, Japan and Pearl Harbor.*

CHAPTER 7

Page 104 Full exchange with the Americans from PRO HW4/25; HW14/45; Erskine, Churchill and the Start of the Ultra–Magic Deals; Erskine, The Holden Agreement on Naval Sigint.

Pages 105–6 British progress on JN25 from PRO HW4/25; ADM223/297.

Page 105 Barham on Japanese error in changing JN25 code-book and not additive or indicator systems from PRO ADM223/496.

Page 105 Details of British recoveries handed over to Americans from Stinnett, Robert B., *Day of Deceit: The Truth about FDR and Pearl Harbor* (Free Press, New York, 1999).

Page 106 Co-operation with Dutch from PRO HW4/25; HW14/18.

Page 106 Nave to Australia from Nave, *An Australian's Unique Naval Career.*

Page 106 Co-operation with Australians PRO HW4/25; HW4/27; HW4/28; HW4/29; National Australian Archives (Melbourne) MP1185 2021/5/529; MP1185/8 1945/2/6; Nave, *An Australian's Unique Naval Career.*

Page 106 Wylie to Australia from PRO HW4/25; National Australian Archives (Melbourne) MP1185 2021/5/529; MP1185/8 1945/2/6.

Page 107 Wylie to New Zealand from National Australian Archives (Melbourne) MP1185 2021/5/529; MP1185/8 1945/2/6.

Page 107 Australian facilities from National Australian

361

Archives (Melbourne) MP1185 2021/5/529; MP1185/8 1945/2/6; Nave, *An Australian's Unique Naval Career*; Central Bureau Technical Records, Part A: Organisation.

Page 108 Shaw/Nave exchange agreement from PRO HW4/25; ADM223/296.

Page 108 Shaw on modalities of exchange agreement with US codebreakers from PRO HW4/25.

Page 109 Subsequent progress in co-operation with the Americans from PRO HW4/25; Budiansky, Too Late for Pearl Harbor.

Page 109 Use of tabulating machines from PRO HW4/25; HW14/18. (Although by this stage Hollerith punch-card tabulators were being used constantly at Bletchley Park, the British codebreakers in Singapore were sceptical at the usefulness of such equipment until Burnett saw it in operation in Corregidor. Hollerith equipment was subsequently sent to Singapore but was never installed because of a lack of power and insufficient trained personnel).

Page 109 Anglo-American army co-operation in Far East from PRO HW4/25.

Pages 109–11 Sprinks and Gamlin from author's correspondence and interview with Joan Dinwoodie (née Sprinks); Gamlin, George, The Y Group at Kranji, Singapore, up to the Surrender to the Japanese, in Hugh Skillen (ed.), *The Enigma Symposium 1998* (Hugh Skillen, Pinner, 1998).

Pages 111–12 FECB capabilities against Japanese Navy from PRO HW4/25; WO208/892.

Page 111 Introduction of radio-fingerprinting from PRO HW18/89; Elphick, *Far Eastern File*.

Page 112 Direction of Japanese intelligence southwards from PRO WO208/896.

Page 112 Background on Japanese political situation from Best, *Britain, Japan and Pearl Harbor*; Calvocoressi, Wint and Pritchard, *The Penguin History of the Second World War*.

Pages 112–13 Military Attaché in Stockholm and War Office reaction from PRO WO208/896.

Page 113 Warning to Japanese diplomats in London to be ready to leave at a moment's notice from PRO ADM223/792.

Page 113 Intercepts of Matsuoka talks and first indication of Hitler turning on Stalin from PRO WO208/896; Boyd, *Hitler's Japanese Confidant*.

Pages 113–14 German–Japanese military co-operation from PRO WO208/896.

Page 114 Oshima and the codebreakers' predictions of Barbarossa from Boyd, *Hitler's Japanese Confidant*; Hinsley, F.H., *British Intelligence in the Second World War* (revised abridged edition) (HMSO, London, 1994); Smith, *Station X*.

Pages 114–15 Oshima messages revealing German attempts to draw Japan into war with Russia from Boyd, *Hitler's Japanese Confidant*.

Page 115 Singapore Consul-General messages suggesting attack on Malaya from PRO WO208/896.

Page 115 Imperial Conference details from Calvocoressi, Wint and Pritchard, *The Penguin History of the Second World War*.

Page 116 Purple message on occupation of Indochina from PRO ADM199/1474; ADM223/792; WO208/896.

Pages 116–17 Reaction in Britain to occupation of Indochina from PRO WO208/896; Ferris, From Broadway to Bletchley Park.

Page 117 American decision to impose stiff trade embargoes from Best, *Britain, Japan and Pearl Harbor*; Calvocoressi, Wint and Pritchard, *The Penguin History of the Second World War*; Keegan, John, *The Second World War* (Viking, New York, 1990).

CHAPTER 8

Page 118 Oshima on German progress on Eastern Front from PRO HW1/259; WO208/896; Boyd, *Hitler's Japanese Confidant*.

Pages 118–19 Hitler unhappy with Japanese attitude to war and promises to join Japan in war against US with Churchill comment from PRO HW1/25.

Page 119 Churchill visit to BP from PRO HW3/16.

Page 119 Tojo failure to railroad Cabinet into war from Keegan, *The Second World War*; Calvocoressi, Wint and

Pritchard, *The Penguin History of the Second World War.*

Page 120 Oshima irritation at being kept in the dark from PRO HW1/32.

Page 120 Denniston comments on US codebreaking from PRO HW14/45.

Page 121 Codebreakers' report on early Japanese fleet reorganization from PRO ADM223/321; ADM223/496.

Page 122 Collapse of Konoye Government and appointment of Tojo as PM from Keegan, *The Second World War*; Calvocoressi, Wint and Pritchard, *The Penguin History of the Second World War*; Best, *Britain, Japan and Pearl Harbor.*

Pages 122–3 Japanese consular messages on intelligence reporting and efforts of Japanese Consul-General in Singapore from PRO ADM223/321; HW4/30; HW1/235; HW1/303.

Page 122 Oshima suggestion of synchronizing Japanese attack on Malaya with German invasion of Britain from PRO ADM223/321.

Page 123 FECB tracking of Japanese Navy and start of move south from PRO ADM223/494.

Page 123 Kennedy on indications of Japanese attack from Diary of Malcolm Kennedy, Kennedy Papers, University of Sheffield.

Page 123 *Asamu maru* to be last Japanese ship to call at Singapore from PRO ADM223/321.

Page 123 Arrival of RAF unit in Singapore from PRO HW4/25.

Page 123 Yamamoto/Terauchi agreement from Parker, Frederick D., *Pearl Harbor Revisited: United States Navy Communications Intelligence, 1924–1941* (United States Cryptologic History, Series IV, World War II, Vol. 6) (National Security Agency, Fort George G. Meade, 1994); Parker, Frederick, D., The Unsolved Messages of Pearl Harbor (*Cryptologia*, Vol. 15, No. 4, October 1991).

Page 123 FECB continued tracking of Japanese naval vessels south from PRO ADM223/494.

Page 124 Japanese Embassy in London told to await coded Winds message from PRO HW1/303; ADM223/321; HW1/240.

Page 124 Yamamoto messages from Parker, *Pearl Harbor Revisited*; Parker, The Unsolved Messages of Pearl Harbor.

Pages 124–5 Barham on intelligence covering a wide field from JN25 from PRO ADM223/496.

Page 125 FECB reports conversion of liners as destroyers from PRO ADM223/494.

Page 125 'Hypo' traffic analysis report on formation of task force and confirmation from FECB from Parker, *Pearl Harbor Revisited*; Parker, The Unsolved Messages of Pearl Harbor; PRO ADM223/494.

Page 125 Japanese messages intercepted but not deciphered from Parker, *Pearl Harbor Revisited*; Parker, The Unsolved Messages of Pearl Harbor.

Page 126 Breakdown of talks from Best, *Britain, Japan and Pearl Harbor*; Calvocoressi, Wint and Pritchard, *The Penguin History of the Second World War*.

Page 126 Oshima told from PRO HW1/288.

Page 126 Japanese missions ordered to destroy codes and ciphers from PRO HW1/290; HW1/294; HW1/296; ADM223/321.

Page 126 Rowlett memory of destruction order from Boyd, *Hitler's Japanese Confidant*.

Page 127 Oshima message on Hitler determination to declare war on US from PRO HW1/312; Boyd, *Hitler's Japanese Confidant*.

Page 127 Call sign change from Parker, *Pearl Harbor Revisited*; Parker, The Unsolved Messages of Pearl Harbor.

Page 127 British uncover composition and objectives of Japanese special task force from PRO ADM223/494.

Page 127 Thai wish that Japan draw Britain into pre-emptive strike from PRO ADM223/321; HW1/244; HW1/277.

Page 128 Operation Matador and Force Z from Calvocoressi, Wint and Pritchard, *The Penguin History of the Second World War*; Elphick, *Far Eastern File*.

Page 128 JN25 additive change from PRO HW4/25.

Page 128 Oshima negotiates secret agreement with Germany and Italy from PRO ADM223/321.

Page 129 British on full alert from PRO HW4/25 and Ferris, From Broadway to Bletchley Park.

Page 129 Winds alert message intercepted at Hong Kong from

PRO HW4/25.

Page 130 Messages intercepted but not deciphered from Parker, *Pearl Harbor Revisited*; Parker, The Unsolved Messages of Pearl Harbor.

Page 130 Kennedy reaction to attack on Pearl Harbor from Diary of Malcolm Kennedy, Kennedy Papers, University of Sheffield.

Pages 130–1 Nave on Japanese radio deception from Nave, *An Australian's Unique Naval Career*.

Page 131 Destruction of British aircraft and capital ships from PRO HW4/25; Elphick and Smith, *Odd Man Out*.

Page 131 Reaction to loss of *Prince of Wales* at BP from Ferris, From Broadway to Bletchley Park.

Pages 131–2 Loss of stations in Penang, Kuching and Hong Kong from PRO HW4/27; HW4/28; HW4/29; ADM223/494.

Page 132 Bennett capture from Elphick, *Far Eastern File*.

Page 132 Various evacuations of FECB staff and families from PRO HW4/25.

Page 132 Norman Webb background from Ballard, Geoffrey, *On Ultra Active Service: The Story of Australia's Signals Intelligence Operations during World War II* (Spectrum, Richmond, Victoria, 1991); Elphick, *Far Eastern File*.

Pages 132–3 Cooper recollections on Japanese naval air messages from PRO HW4/30.

Page 133 Captured air–ground codebook from Central Bureau Technical Records, Part C: Army Air–Ground Communications.

Page 133 Churchill quote from Churchill, Winston S., *The Second World War*, Vol. IV, *The Hinge of Fate* (Cassell, London, 1951).

CHAPTER 9

Pages 134–5 Departure from Singapore and arrival in Colombo from PRO HW4/25 and interviews with Joan Dinwoodie (née Sprinks) and Lillie Feeney (née Gadd).

Page 135 Hollerith equipment goes missing from PRO HW4/25.

Pages 135–6 Purple machine goes missing from Erskine, Ralph, When a Purple Machine Went Missing: How Japan

Nearly Discovered America's Greatest Secret (*Intelligence and National Security*, Vol. 12, No. 3, July 1997).

Page 136 Final evacuation of Singapore codebreakers to Java from PRO HW4/25; HW4/30; unpublished memoirs of Geoff Day kindly made available to the author by Mr Day.

Page 137 Hypo codebreakers ordered to work on JN25 from Benson, Robert Louis, *A History of US Communications Intelligence during World War II* (United States Cryptologic History, Series IV, World War II, Vol. 8) (National Security Agency, Fort George G. Meade, MD, 1997).

Pages 137-8 Advance of American codebreakers and British problems from PRO HW4/25.

Pages 137-8 Activities of US codebreakers from Benson, *A History of US Communications Intelligence during World War II*; Jacobsen, Phillip H., *The Codebreakers* (http://www.microworks.net/pacific/intelligence); Prados, John, *Combined Fleet Decoded: The Secret History of American Intelligence and the Japanese Navy in World War II* (Random House, New York, 1995).

Pages 137-8 MacInnes on Colombo's limited operations against JN25 from PRO HW4/25.

Pages 138-40 Rochefort biography supplied by Phillip H. Jacobsen. Rochefort quotes from *Cryptolog, the Journal of the US Naval Cryptologic Veterans Association* published on its website at http://www.usncva.org/clog/index.html. See also Lord, Walter, *Incredible Victory* (Harper & Row, New York, 1967).

Page 140 Darwin raid from Cain, Frank, Sigint in Australia during the Pacific War, in Alvarez, David (ed.), *Allied and Axis Signals Intelligence in World War II* (Frank Cass, London, 1999).

Page 140 Background on progress of war in Far East from Elphick, *Far Eastern File*; Prados, *Combined Fleet Decoded*; Davidson, Edward and Manning, Dale, *Chronology of World War Two* (Cassell, London, 1999); Dupuy, R. Ernest, and Dupuy, Trevor N., *The Encyclopedia of Military History* (Macdonald & Jane's, London, 1974).

Pages 140–1 US codebreakers move to Melbourne from Benson, *A History of US Communications Intelligence during World War II*; Jacobsen, *The Codebreakers*; Prados, *Combined Fleet Decoded*; Chamberlin, Vince, The FRUMEL – Australia May 1942 (*NCVA Cryptolog*, Vol. 9, No. 1, Fall 1982); Biard, Forrest R., *Wartime Melbourne – Heaven or Hell* (*NCVA Cryptolog*, Vol. 19, No. 1, Winter 1998); Nave, *An Australian's Unique Naval Career*.

Pages 141–2 WRANS component at Moorabbin from Gascoine, Nourma, Memories of Moorabbin United States Naval Wireless Telegraphy W/T Station (*NCVA Cryptolog*, Vol. 9, No. 4, Spring 1983) (originally published in the ex-WRANs' magazine *Ditty Box*, October 1978).

Page 142 Setting up of Central Bureau from Central Bureau Technical Records, Part A: Organisation; Ballard, *On Ultra Active Service*; NARA RG457 OD3431.

Page 143 Special Intelligence Bureau and role of Arthur Cooper from Nave, *An Australian's Unique Naval Career*.

Page 144 Nave's early involvement with Central Bureau from Ballard, *On Ultra Active Service*; Nave, *An Australian's Unique Naval Career*.

Pages 144–5 Australian intercept operators from unpublished memoirs of Geoff Day.

Pages 144–5 Journey to Darwin and atmosphere there from the unpublished memoirs of Geoff Day and Ballard, *On Ultra Active Service*.

Page 145 Work of 51 Section from Central Bureau Technical Records, Part J: Field Sections; Defence Signals Directorate obituary of Ralph Thompson; Ballard, *On Ultra Active Service*.

Page 146 Joy Roberts memories from papers held by her husband Geoff Day.

Pages 146–7 Further details of their romance from the unpublished memoirs of Geoff Day.

Pages 147–9 Work of WAAAF operators from correspondence with Joy Linnane.

CHAPTER 10

Page 150 Bletchley Park Japanese section from PRO HW14/30; Hawken, *Recollections of Bletchley Park*.

Page 150 Flowerdown from Denham, Hugh, Bedford–Bletchley–Kilindini–Colombo in F.H. Hinsley and Alan Stripp (eds), *Codebreakers: The Inside Story of Bletchley Park*; letter from Juliet Tasker (née MccGwire) dated 17 February, 2000.

Page 151 Reorganization of Bletchley Park and move of diplomatic section back to London from Smith, *Station X*; diary of Malcolm Kennedy, Kennedy Papers, University of Sheffield.

Page 151 Colombo recruitment of Temporary Women Assistants and Brouwer from PRO HW4/25.

Page 151 Shaw on Brouwer from PRO HW4/25.

Pages 151–2 Tiltman and course from Tiltman, *Some Reminiscences*; interview with Jon Cohen, December 1999.

Pages 152–3 Tuck from interview with Maurice Wiles; interview with Jon Cohen; Denham, Bedford–Bletchley–Kilindini–Colombo; Stripp, Alan, *Codebreaker in the Far East* (Frank Cass, London, 1989).

Page 155 RAF course from Tiltman, *Some Reminiscences*; PRO HW14/27.

Pages 155–6 Rochefort recruitment of bandsmen and quotes from *Cryptolog, The Journal of the US Naval Cryptologic Veterans Association*.

Pages 156–7 US courses from PRO ADM223/496; HW4/31; correspondence with Phil Jacobsen, December 1999.

Pages 157–8 Tiltman visit to USA and agreement on coverage and data exchange from PRO HW14/46 and HW14/31.

Page 157 Progress of Colombo from PRO HW4/25.

Pages 158–62 Barham description of how to break JN25 from PRO ADM223/496; additional information from Denham, Bedford–Bletchley–Kilindini–Colombo; NARA RG457 OD3645.

Pages 162–5 Colombo interception of message indicating Japanese activity in Indian Ocean and subsequent attack on Ceylon from PRO HW4/24; HW4/25; Denham, Bedford–

Bletchley–Kilindini–Colombo; Prados, *Combined Fleet Decoded*; Elphick, *Far Eastern File*; interviews with Lillie Feeney (née Gadd) and Joan Dinwoodie (née Sprinks).

CHAPTER 11

Pages 166–7 Move to Kilindini and resultant problems from PRO HW4/24; HW4/25; interview with Joan Dinwoodie (née Sprinks).

Pages 167–78 Role of codebreakers in the Battles of the Coral Sea and Midway from Parker, Frederick D., *A Priceless Advantage: US Navy Communications Intelligence and the Battles of Coral Sea, Midway, and the Aleutians* (United States Cryptologic History, Series IV, World War II, Vol. 5) (National Security Agency, Fort George G. Meade, MD, 1993); Prados, *Combined Fleet Decoded*; Jacobsen, *The Codebreakers;* correspondence with Phillip H. Jacobsen, December 1999 to February 2000; Holmes, W.J., *Double-edged Secrets: US Naval Intelligence Operations in the Pacific during World War II* (Annapolis, MD, US Naval Institute Press, 1979); PRO HW4/25.

Pages 175–6 Rochefort interviews from *NCVA Cryptolog, The Journal of the US Naval Cryptologic Veterans Association.*

Pages 177–8 Newspaper leak of codebreakers' Midway triumph from PRO HW14/47; HW14/61; HW4/24; Parker, *A Priceless Advantage*; Japanese order change to back-up codes from HW14/48; I am grateful to Phillip H. Jacobsen for drawing my attention to the Japanese communications history *Operational History of Japanese Naval Communications – December 1941–August 1945* and for supplying extracts from it.

Pages 179–80 Treatment of Rochefort from Benson, *A History of US Communications Intelligence during World War II*; Jacobsen, *The Codebreakers*.

CHAPTER 12

Pages 181–4 Japanese naval section at Bletchley Park during 1942 from interview with Jon Cohen; Denham, Bedford–Bletchley– Kilindini–Colombo; Browning from

Hawken, *Recollections of Bletchley Park*.

Pages 184–5 Kilindini problems from PRO HW4/25.

Page 184 Fabian attitude towards Nave and co-operation with the British from PRO HW4/25; Maneki, Sharon A., *The Quiet Heroes of the Southwest Pacific Theater: An Oral History of the Men and Women of CBB and FRUMEL* (United States Cryptologic History, Series IV, World War II, Vol. 7) (National Security Agency, Fort George G. Meade, MD, 1996); Benson, *A History of US Communications Intelligence during World War II*.

Page 185 OP-20-G July signal on progress made with JN25c from PRO HW14/47.

Pages 185–7 Disagreement within Kilindini and with Bletchley Park over future of British efforts to read JN25 from PRO ADM223/496; HW4/25; HW14/40; HW14/61.

Pages 186–7 Breaking of JN40, JN167 and JN152 from PRO HW14/57; HW14/58; HW4/25; Denham, Bedford–Bletchley–Kilindini–Colombo; Eachus on counter-productive FBI pinch from interview with Joe Eachus, December 2000.

Pages 188–9 Negotiation of Holden agreement and its subsequent effects from Erskine, The Holden Agreement on Naval Sigint; Erskine, Churchill and the Start of the Ultra–Magic Deals; PRO HW14/55; HW4/24; HW4/25; ADM223/496; Benson, *A History of US Communications Intelligence*.

Pages 189–91 Birch on lack of US co-operation and British willingness to go its own way PRO HW3/93; HW14/142.

Page 191 Bruce Keith replacement of Shaw from PRO HW4/25.

Pages 191–2 Keith views on way forward from PRO ADM223/496.

Pages 193–4 Burnett complaints and DNI rejection from PRO ADM223/496.

Page 194 Laird on Fabian from PRO ADM223/494.

CHAPTER 13

Page 195 Background to MacArthur/King disagreements from Drea, Edward J., *MacArthur's Ultra: Codebreaking and the War*

371

against Japan, 1942–1945 (University Press of Kansas, Lawrence, 1992); Dupuy and Dupuy, *The Encyclopedia of Military History.*

Pages 196–8 Breaking of JMA from Tiltman, *Some Reminiscences*; HW14/49.

Page 197 Messages about Burma Railroad from Lewin, Ronald, *The Other Ultra* (Hutchinson, London, 1982).

Page 197 Japanese military section set up in May 1942 from PRO HW3/102; HW3/156.

Pages 198–9 Interviews and correspondence with Maurice Wiles and William Sibley; Wiles, Maurice, Japanese Military Codes in Hinsley and Stripp, *Codebreakers.*

Page 199 Japanese military attachés forced to use old books because new ones had not arrived from PRO HW14/142.

Page 199 'Tokyo Circular' from PRO HW3/156; HW3/157.

Pages 199–200 Tiltman in India from Tiltman, *Some Reminiscences.*

Page 200 Pre-war Indian signals intelligence sites from PRO HW3/90; HW3/102.

Pages 199–202 WEC from PRO HW3/90; HW3/102; Smith, W.C., *Wireless Experimental Centre, Hill of Happiness, Anand Parbat, Delhi 1943–6* (The Rose and the Laurel, Ashford, 1986). See also Stripp, *Codebreaker.*

Page 202 WE code broken from PRO HW4/25.

Pages 203–4 WEC outposts from PRO HW3/102; NARA RG457 OD3645.

Page 203 Beckhough on WEC outposts from Beckhough, Harry, *Secret Communications: The Hidden Sources of Information through the Ages, from the Sumerians to the Cold War* (Minerva Press, London, 1995).

Pages 203–6 Abbottabad information from correspondence with Dennis Underwood, December 1999; correspondence and conversation with Dorothy Ratcliffe April 1999 and January 2000. See also Brighty, Roy, Teaching Japanese Morse to the Royal Indian Air Force, in Skillen, Hugh (ed.), *The Enigma Symposium 1997* (Hugh Skillen, Pinner, 1997); Cartwright, Richard L., *They Did Not Fail* (New Millennium, London,

1997); Stripp, *Codebreaker*; Stripp, Alan, Japanese Army Air Force Codes, in Hinsley and Stripp, *Codebreakers*.

Pages 206–7 Setting up of Central Bureau and general organization from Technical Records of Central Bureau, Part A: Organisation; PRO HW3/102; HW14/142; Drea, *MacArthur's Ultra*.

Pages 207–8 Early difficulties with high-grade army ciphers from correspondence with Joseph E. Richard.

CHAPTER 14

Pages 209–10 Fabian on lack of co-operation between FRUMEL and Central Bureau from Maneki, *The Quiet Heroes*.

Page 210 Fabian burning document from Drea, *MacArthur's Ultra*.

Page 210 Fabian arguments for no co-operation with Central Bureau from Benson, *A History of US Communications Intelligence*.

Page 210 Value of navy messages for military codebreakers from PRO HW3/102; HW14/142.

Page 211 Naval air traffic predominant off north-east Australia from NARA RG457 OD 3431.

Page 211 De Grey on creation of black market with 7th Fleet from PRO HW3/102. This black market mirrored the position in other areas where overzealous security prevented those who should have received Ultra material from receiving it, most notably those involved in the British double-cross system where German agents arriving in Britain were played back to their controllers. See Smith, Michael, *Foley: The Spy Who Saved 10,000 Jews* (Hodder & Stoughton, London, 1999).

Page 211 Sandford passing material to FRUMEL with no return from Benson, *A History of US Communications Intelligence*; BP concerns and attempts to intervene from PRO HW3/102.

Page 211 Richard on Nave's usefulness to Central Bureau from correspondence with Joseph E. Richard.

Page 212 Diplomatic unit using former British Consuls from National Australian Archives A6923/3 37/401/425.

CHAPTER 15

Page 224 Difficulties with JN25f from PRO HW14/68; Prados, *Combined Fleet Decoded*.

Page 224 Battle of Bismarck Sea from Drea, *MacArthur's Ultra*; Prados, *Combined Fleet Decoded*.

Page 224 Ultra codeword introduced for all high-level signals intelligence in September 1942 from PRO HW14/52.

Page 225 Description of Lasswell at work from Holmes, *Double-edged Secrets*.

Page 225 Gill Richardson on low-level Yamamoto message from Maneki, *The Quiet Heroes*.

Page 225 W.E. 'Nobby' Clarke on 51 Wireless Section interception of low-level Yamamoto message from *CB News: The Journal of the Central Bureau Intelligence Corps Association*, September 1997.

Pages 225–6 Yamamoto shootdown from Drea, *MacArthur's Ultra*; Prados, *Combined Fleet Decoded*.

Pages 226–7 Contribution of Central Bureau, 55 Wireless Section and No. 1 Wireless Unit to New Guinea campaign in second half of 1943 from Central Bureau Technical Records, Part A: Organisation, Part H: Traffic Analysis, and Part J: Field Sections; Ballard, *On Ultra Active Service*.

Page 228 David Mead on breaking indicator system for main Japanese Army Administrative Code 7890 from Mead, David, The Breaking of the Japanese Army Administrative Code (*Cryptologia*, Vol. 18, No. 3, July 1994).

Page 229 Tiltman calls UK conference to co-ordinate attacks on Japanese high-level code systems from PRO HW3/102; Central Bureau Technical Records, Part A: Organisation.

Pages 229–30 Expansion of Bletchley Park Japanese military section in May 1943 from PRO HW3/102; HW3/156.

Pages 230–2 Gladys Sweetland memories from interview dated 1 February 2000.

Page 232 Details of 3366 code from PRO HW3/102; Drea, Edward J., Were the Japanese Army Codes Ever Secure? (*Cryptologia*, Vol. 19, No. 2, April 1995).

Page 232 Central Bureau early work and difficulties from Central Bureau Technical Records, Part A: Organisation, and

Part G: Mainline Army Systems.

Page 232 Bletchley break from Drea, Were the Japanese Army Codes Ever Secure?; Stripp, *Codebreaker*.

Pages 232–4 Maurice Wiles memories from interview, 22 December 1999. See also Wiles, Japanese Military Codes, in Hinsley and Stripp, *Codebreakers*.

Pages 233–4 Elsie Hart memories from interview with Elsie Griffin, 1 February 2000.

Page 234 Material used by Japanese military intelligence section from PRO HW3/156.

Pages 235–7 Betty Vine-Stevens on paraphrasing and colleagues in Japanese military section from correspondence and interviews with Betty Webb (née Vine-Stevens), July 1999 to January 2000.

Page 237 Maurice Wiles on competition with Arlington Hall from interview, 22 December 1999.

CHAPTER 16

Page 238 Discovery of undisclosed US collection of pinches from PRO HW14/55; HW14/58; HW14/61.

Pages 238–9 Reinforcement of Kilindini and decision to move back to Colombo from PRO ADM223/496; HW4/25; interview with Jon Cohen.

Page 239 Kilindini revival from PRO HW4/25; HW1/61; ADM223/496.

Page 239 Cohen and Denham's journey to and arrival in Kilindini from interview with Jon Cohen; Denham, Bedford–Bletchley–Kilindini– Colombo.

Pages 239–40 Codebreaking organization at Kilindini PRO HW4/25; ADM223/496.

Pages 240–2 Cohen work from interview with Jon Cohen; PRO HW4/25.

Page 242 Improvement in OP-20-G attitude to Kilindini from PRO HW14/68; HW14/70; HW14/71; HW14/73.

Page 242 Fabian still holding material back and recall to Washington from PRO ADM223/496.

Page 242 BRUSA Agreement from Benson, *A History of US Communications Intelligence*.

Page 242 Meetings with Redman, Wenger and promise of new cipher link/US liaison officer at Colombo from PRO HW14/74; ADM223/497; Benson, *A History of US Communications Intelligence*.

Page 243 Eastern Fleet starts receiving US Navy intelligence from PRO ADM223/496.

Page 243 New Zealand Navy signals intelligence operation from PRO ADM 223/494; ADM223/497; HW14/74. A New Zealand Army codebreaking and interception unit was formed in 1942. It was part of the Army Signal Company based at Nairnville Park, Ngaio, Wellington, and had an intercept site at Johnsville in a building that for security reasons was made to look like an old farm shed. The staff included members of the New Zealand Women's Army Auxiliary Corps. Material was sent to Central Bureau and at least one New Zealand Army Japanese interpreter/codebreaker was sent to Central Bureau to work. See Lord, Cliff, The New Zealand Y Service in WW2, in Skillen, Hugh (ed.), *The Enigma Symposium 1995* (Hugh Skillen, Pinner, 1995).

Page 243 Canadian signals intelligence operation from PRO HW14/47; NAC RG24 Vol. 3806, 1008, 75.20. A Canadian Army intercept unit, No. 1 Special Wireless Group, comprising 300 Royal Canadian Signals and Canadian Intelligence Corps personnel was sent to Australia in early 1945 to take over air defence and mainline army intercepts tasks from 51 Australian Wireless Section, thereby allowing Australian intercept operators to be posted into the forward zones (Yolleck, Ben Y., Canadian Walkabout, *Ink Emma Ink, Magazine of the Australian Special Wireless Group*, 1960).

Page 244 Mauritius signals intelligence operation from PRO ADM223/297.

Pages 244–5 Calder on Hut 7, Angus Wilson from correspondence and conversations with Rosemary Merry (née Calder), July 1999, February 2000.

Pages 245–6 Ann Petrides on Hut 7 from letter to author, 20 November 1999.

Pages 246–9 Norman Scott on Hut 7 and Colombo from Scott,

Norman, Solving Japanese Naval Ciphers 1943–45 (*Cryptologia*, Vol. 21, No. 2, April 1997). I am grateful to Mr Scott for permission to use extracts from this article.

Pages 249–50 Olive Humble on Hut 7 from letter to author from Olive Hirst (née Humble), 11 July 1999.

Page 250 Women's Committee from PRO HW14/139.

Pages 251–2 Elizabeth Ross on Hut 7 from correspondence and conversations with Elizabeth Davis (née Ross).

CHAPTER 17

Page 253 Return to Colombo, setting up of Anderson station and problems there PRO HW4/24; HW4/25.

Pages 253–5 Interception and DF operations at Anderson from Longrigg, Paul, *HMS Anderson and Far Eastern Direction Finding Network in World War II*, unpublished memoir kindly provided by the TEL(S) 1942–1945 Association.

Page 255 Description of operations complex at Anderson from interview with Jon Cohen; PRO HW4/3.

Page 255 Production process at Anderson from PRO HW4/24; HW4/25.

Pages 255–6 Cohen on details of set-up at Anderson from interview with Jon Cohen.

Page 256 Large numbers of Wrens sent out to assist the codebreakers from PRO HW4/25.

Pages 256–9 Robertson from correspondence with Dorothy Smith (née Robertson).

Page 259 Influx of Royal Navy Japanese interpreters from PRO HW14/25.

Pages 259–60 Saunders on US sites and Fabian refusal to cooperate from PRO ADM223/496.

Page 260 Biard on Fabian from Biard, Forrest R., *Wartime Melbourne – Heaven or Hell* (*NCVA Cryptolog*, Vol. 19, No. 1, Winter 1998).

Page 261 Hinsley sent to Washington PRO HW3/93; Benson, *A History of US Communications Intelligence*.

Page 261 Foss sent to Washington from Nave, *An Australian's Unique Naval Career*; PRO HW14/142.

Page 261 Browning on Foss home problems from Hawken, Elizabeth, *Recollections of Bletchley Park*.

Page 261 Hut 7 access to tabulating machinery from PRO HW14/142.

Pages 262–4 Laslett from interview with Peter Laslett, 17 February 2000.

Pages 263–4 Sandison on language course, cryptographic references from letter from Isobel Sandison.

Pages 263–4 Laslett from interview with Peter Laslett, 17 February 2000.

CHAPTER 18

Page 265 Row over Fabian's appointment as USLO Colombo from PRO HW14/90; HW14/92; HW14/142.

Pages 265–6 Hinsley trip from PRO HW3/93; HW14/142; Benson, *A History of US Communications Intelligence*.

Pages 266–8 Joint Anglo–American attack on Coral/JNA20 from PRO HW14/50; HW14/67; HW25/1; NARA RG457 SRH206; RG457 HCC Nr 4424; Hinsley, F. H., *British Intelligence in the Second World War* (abridged edition) (HMSO, London, 1993); Deavours and Kruh, *Machine Cryptography and Modern Cryptanalysis*; Prados, *Combined Fleet Decoded*. I am particularly grateful to Ralph Erskine for material which he very kindly shared with me on Hugh Alexander's involvement in the break into the Coral/JNA20 cipher.

Page 268 Use of the Rattler in the attack on Coral from Burke, Colin, Automating American Cryptanalysis 1930–45: Marvellous Machines, a Bit too Late, in David Alvarez (ed.), *Allied and Axis Signal Intelligence in World War II* (Frank Cass, London, 1999).

Pages 269–71 Work on JNA10 by Edith Bennett and other Wrens from interviews and correspondence with Edith Becker (née Bennett) between May 1999 and April 2000.

Pages 271–3 Interception of Japanese diplomatic messages from PRO HW4/25; HW4/29; HW14/33; HW14/38; HW14/47; HW14/58.

Pages 272–3 Codebreaker's recollection of breaking the Oshima Atlantic Wall message from Boyd, *Hitler's Japanese Confidant*.

Page 272 Japanese Military Attaché message from Hinsley, *British Intelligence in the Second World War* (abridged edition); Boyd, *Hitler's Japanese Confidant*.

Pages 272–3 Sibley on JMA section from correspondence with Bill Sibley, July 1999 and January 2000.

Page 273 Naval Attaché's own report from PRO HW1/2768.

Page 273 Oshima regarded as too gullible from PRO WO208/4703; ADM223/792. After the fall of Germany, Oshima was interned in the United States before being sent back to Japan where he was jailed for life by a war crimes tribunal. He was paroled in December 1955 and died at the age of eighty-nine in June 1975, still unaware that many of the messages he sent back to Japan from wartime Germany had been read by the Allies (Boyd, *Hitler's Japanese Confidant*).

Page 274 Double-cross operations from Smith, *Foley*.

Pages 274–5 Value of Naval Attaché scientific material from ADM223/792; Lewin, *The Other Ultra*; Jones, R.V., *Most Secret War: British Scientific Intelligence 1939–1945* (Coronet, London, 1979).

Page 275 GC&CS commercial section from HW14/38; NARA RG24 Vol. 3806; RG457 OD883.

Pages 275–6 Birch on co-operation difficulties and possibility of break with Americans from PRO HW3/93 and HW14/142.

Page 276 Early difficulties with BRUSA Circuit from PRO HW3/157.

Page 276 Japanese improvement of JN25 security and concerns over possible Allied break from Prados, *Combined Fleet Decoded*.

Page 277 Fabian complaint that material withheld from him from Somerville Diary, 17 July 1944, Somerville Papers, Churchill College, Cambridge.

Page 277 Hugh Alexander brought in to head Bletchley Park JN25 operation from PRO HW14/120; HW25/1.

Page 277 Concern over loss of JN25 for long period from PRO HW14/142.

Page 277 Alexander goes to Washington from information supplied by Ralph Erskine.

Page 277 Redman agrees direct link between Colombo and OP-20-G and Travis signs updated agreement from PRO HW4/24; HW4/25; Benson, *A History of US Communications Intelligence*.

CHAPTER 19

Pages 279–80 Background to opening of Burma campaign and arguments over its prosecution from Slim, Field Marshal Viscount, *Defeat into Victory* (Pan, London, 1999); Dupuy and Dupuy, *The Encyclopedia of Military History*; Wheal, Elizabeth-Anne and Pope, Stephen, *The Macmillan Dictionary of the Second World War* (Macmillan, London, 1989).

Page 280 Sigint support for Burma campaign from PRO HW3/102; HW14/71; HW14/73.

Page 280 WEC working on both 7890 and 3366 from NARA RG457 OD815; interview with Sir Michael Kerry, 15 February 2000.

Pages 280–1 Kerry memories from interview with Sir Michael Kerry, 15 February 2000. Sir Michael was subsequently HM Procurator General and Treasury Solicitor.

Page 282 WEC links with Americans and Station 8 from PRO HW3/102; NARA RG457 OD3645.

Page 282 WWSC and EWSC operations from PRO HW3/102; HW3/156.

Page 282 Poor reception in Delhi leads to transfer of coverage to Bangalore from NARA RG457 OD883.

Page 282 Comilla operations PRO HW3/102; HW3/156; NARA RG457 OD3401.

Pages 283–4 Stripp from Stripp, *Codebreaker*; Hinsley and Stripp, *Codebreakers*.

Page 284 Japanese Navy Air Force transmissions covered in Ceylon from PRO HW3/102; HW4/25.

Pages 284–5 Usefulness of Japanese naval air convoy and meteorological reports from Nave, *An Australian's Unique Naval Career*; Central Bureau Technical Records, Part B: Naval Air–Ground Communications.

Pages 285–7 Bob Biggs on military codebreaking at Bletchley Park from correspondence with Bob Biggs, January and February 2000.

Pages 287–9 Bernard Keeffe on army air section, military training and general life at Bletchley Park from correspondence with Bernard Keeffe, August 1999.

Page 290 Separate air section set up under Hooper from PRO HW3/102; HW3/157; HW14/64.

Page 290 Daly on Hooper interview with Margaret Gethen (née Daly), 23 February 2000.

Page 290 Newton-John from PRO HW3/157.

Page 290 'Melding' from PRO HW3/157.

Page 291 Robertson on 'melding' from letter from Margaret Robertson (née Melvin).

Pages 291–2 Lavell on air section from correspondence with Ann Cunningham (née Lavell), July 1999.

CHAPTER 20

Page 293 Security problems at WEC from PRO HW3/165; interview with Sir Michael Kerry, 15 February 2000.

Pages 293–5 Setting up of SLUs from PRO HW3/165; Winterbotham, *The Ultra Secret* (Weidenfeld & Nicolson, London, 1974); interview with Ken Kelsey, 24 February 2000.

Pages 295–6 Background to start of Burma campaign from Keegan, *The Second World War.*

Pages 296–7 Progress of campaign from Slim, *Defeat into Victory.*

Pages 297–8 Predicting of Japanese air raids and transfer of BULBUL coverage to India from PRO HW14/142; HW3/102; Central Bureau Technical Records, Part C: Army Air–Ground Communications, and Part A: Organisation.

Page 298 Kerry on Comilla operations from interview with Sir Michael Kerry, 15 February 2000.

Page 298 Arlington Hall conference and military codes worked on and broken at Bletchley Park from PRO HW3/157; HW14/142; Drea, Were the Japanese Army Codes Secure?

Page 299 Transfer of military air section staff to Japanese air section under Hooper from PRO HW3/102; HW14/142.

Pages 299–300 Flew memories from interview with Professor Anthony Flew, 22 October 1999.

Page 300 Japanese air section resources and effect of loss of JN25 coverage from PRO HW14/92; HW14/115; HW14/142.

Page 300 W. C. Smith on 14th Army crossing of Chindwin River from Smith, *Wireless Experimental Centre.*

Page 301 Capture of Mandalay from Slim, *Defeat into Victory.*

Pages 301–2 Underwood memories from correspondence with Dennis Underwood, December 1999.

Page 302 Mobile intercept operations from PRO HW14/64; NARA RG457 OD3645.

Page 303 Capture of Rangoon from Slim, *Defeat into Victory.*

Pages 302–5 Underwood memories from correspondence with Dennis Underwood, December 1999.

CHAPTER 21

Page 306 Arlington Hall difficulties with 7890 from NARA RG457 Boxes 827 and 828.

Page 306 Sio pinch of codebooks Central Bureau Technical Records, Part A: Organisation; Correspondence with Joseph E. Richard, 19 February 2000; PRO HW3/156. Since Bletchley Park was now in charge of providing Allied designations for all enemy code and cipher systems, British descriptions of these systems have been used.

Page 307 Richard memories from correspondence with Joseph E. Richard, 19 February 2000.

Page 307 Allied ability to read mainline army codes to end of war from Central Bureau Technical Records, Part G: Mainline Army Systems.

Pages 307–8 Biard and Mackie sent to help translate army backlog from Biard, Forrest R., The Pacific War through the Eyes of Forrest R. 'Tex' Biard (*Cryptolog*, Vol. 10, No. 2, Winter 1989).

Page 309 MacArthur use of the Central Bureau intelligence from mainline army codes from Drea, *MacArthur's Ultra.*

Page 309 Naval intelligence and Operation Galvanic from Jacobsen, *The Codebreakers*; Prados, *Combined Fleet Decoded*; Dupuy and Dupuy, *The Encyclopedia of Military History.*

Page 310 No. 1 Wireless Unit monitoring of Japanese aircraft being ferried into Hollandia and US raids from Central Bureau Technical Records, Part J: Field Sections; Drea, *MacArthur's Ultra.*

Pages 310–11 Landings at Hollandia and attacks on TAKE convoy from Drea, *MacArthur's Ultra.*

Pages 311–12 *Yoshimo maru* pinch from Central Bureau Technical Records, Part G: Mainline Army Systems; Central Bureau Technical Records, Part A: Organisation; correspondence with Joseph E. Richard, 19 February 2000.

Page 311 Interception of Japanese plans to retake Aitape from Drea, *MacArthur's Ultra.*

Page 312 British reinforcement of Central Bureau from PRO HW3/102; Melinsky, Hugh, *A Code-breaker's Tale* (Lark's Press, Dereham, 1998).

Pages 312–13 Melinsky memories from Melinsky, *A Code-breaker's Tale.*

Pages 313–14 Lanacaster memories from correspondence with Claude Lanacaster Jr, 29 January 2000.

Pages 314–15 Melinsky memories from Melinsky, *A Code-breaker's Tale.*

Page 315 Battle for the Marianas from Prados, *Combined Fleet Decoded*; Jacobsen, *The Codebreakers.*

Pages 315–16 Advanced echelon of Central Bureau to New Guinea from Central Bureau Technical Records, Part A: Organisation; Ballard, *On Ultra Active Service.*

Page 316 Ballard memories from Ballard, *On Ultra Active Service.*

Page 316 Structure and manning of Central Bureau from Central Bureau Technical Records, Part A: Organisation; PRO HW3/102.

Pages 316–17 Deployment of interception units from Central Bureau Technical Records, Part J: Field Sections; Ballard, *On Ultra Active Service.*

Page 317 Battle of Leyte Gulf from Prados, *Combined Fleet Decoded*.

Pages 318–19 Australian intercept operations and intelligence gathered from Central Bureau Technical Records, Part J: Field Sections.

Page 319 Japanese Special Attack Unit from Melinsky, *A Codebreaker's Tale*.

Page 319 'Foreign Legion' from Ballard, *On Ultra Active Service*.

Page 319 Nave on army air code from Central Bureau Technical Records, Part B: Naval Air–Ground Communications; CB News, September 1999.

Pages 319–20 Ballard on move to Tacloban, expanded production of Ultra by Central Bureau, US technology from Ballard, *On Ultra Active Service*.

Page 320 RAGFOR and improved US Army/Navy and BRUSA co-operation from Benson, *History of US Communications*; PRO ADM223/297.

CHAPTER 22

Page 322 Build-up of Japanese troops on Philippines from Drea, *MacArthur's Ultra*.

Page 322 Central Bureau Technical Records, Part J: Field Sections; Drea, *MacArthur's Ultra*.

Page 322 Australian intercept operators joined by US units from Central Bureau Technical Records, Part J: Field Sections; Drea, *MacArthur's Ultra*.

Page 323 Central Bureau's army air 'Solution' section move to Leyte and increase in RAAF intercept operators at 6 Wireless Unit from Central Bureau Technical Records, Part J: Field Sections; Central Bureau Technical Records, Part A: Organization.

Page 323 Intercept units go ashore at Dagupan and move to San Miguel from Central Bureau Technical Records, Part J: Field Sections.

Page 323 Changes in army codebooks hamper codebreakers from Central Bureau Technical Records, Part G: Mainline Army Systems.

Page 324 Ship-borne Y units from PRO ADM223/494; ADM223/495; HW4/25; Ballard, *On Ultra Active Service*.

Page 324 Okinawa and last-ditch Japanese naval battle from Prados, *Combined Fleet Decoded*.

Page 324 Creation of HMS Anderson, streamlining of code-breaking operation and Alexander contribution from PRO HW4/24; HW4/25.

Pages 325–6 Scott memories from Scott, Solving Japanese Naval Ciphers 1943–45.

Page 325 JN11 solved quicker by British from PRO HW4/25.

Page 326 Mountbatten visit from interview with Ken Kelsey; PRO HW14/142; Denham, Bedford–Bletchley–Kilindini–Colombo, Hinsley and Stripp, *Codebreakers*.

Page 326 Laslett on Washington operation from interview with Peter Laslett, 17 February 2000.

Page 327 Keeffe on BBC outside broadcast from Bletchley Park from letter from Bernard Keeffe, 22 July 2000.

Pages 327–8 Central Bureau Philippines operations from Central Bureau Technical Records, Part J: Field Sections.

Page 328 Melinsky memories from Melinsky, *A Code-breaker's Tale*.

Pages 328–9 San Miguel operations from correspondence with Geoff Day; Melinsky, *A Code-breaker's Tale*; Ballard, *On Ultra Active Service*.

Page 330 Strength of Japanese forces known from 'Tokyo Circular' from PRO HW3/156; HW3/157.

Page 330 US air raids on Japan from Wheal and Pope, *The Macmillan Dictionary of the Second World War*.

Pages 330–1 Emperor's peace plea to Moscow intercepted from PRO HW14/107.

Pages 331–2 Decision to drop the atomic bomb from Alperovitz, Gar, *The Decision to Use the Atomic Bomb and the Architecture of an American Myth* (Knopf, New York, 1995).

Page 332 Laslett memory of message referring to the bomb from interview with Peter Laslett, 17 February 2000.

Page 332 Calder memory of message referring to the bomb from correspondence and conversations with Rosemary Merry (née

Calder), July 1999 and February 2000.

Page 333 Army air message detailing effects of the bomb from Drea, *MacArthur's Ultra*.

Page 333 Grafing on surrender message from correspondence with Jack Grafing.

Pages 333–4 Lydekker memories of VJ Day from letter from Julie Lydekker.

Page 334 Olive Humble on last days of Bletchley Park from letter from Olive Hirst (née Humble), 11 July 1999.

Page 334 Wrens at HMS Anderson help PoWs before being sent home from correspondence with Dorothy Smith (née Robertson), February and April 1999.

Page 336 Rochefort information kindly supplied by Phil Jacobsen.

Page 336 Rowlett information from Rowlett, *The Story of Magic*.

Page 337 Tiltman from Erskine, *Brigadier John H. Tiltman*.

Page 337 Alexander information from Milner-Barry, Sir Stuart, C.H.O'D. Alexander – a Personal Memoir, in Harry Golombek and William R. Hartson, *The Best Games of C.H.O'D. Alexander* (OUP, Oxford, 1976).

Page 337 Nave information from Nave, *An Australian's Unique Naval Career*; Rusbridger and Nave, *Betrayal at Pearl Harbor*.

Page 338 Hugh Foss information from Hawken, *Recollections of Bletchley Park*.

Page 338 Agnes Driscoll information from Robert Hanyok, Still Desperately Seeking 'Miss Agnes' (*NCVA Cryptolog* Vol. 18, No. 5, 1997).

Page 338 Raven information kindly supplied by Phil Jacobsen.

Page 338 Joseph E. Richard information from correspondence with Joseph E. Richard, December 1999 to April 2000.

Page 338 Wilfrid Noyce information from *The Concise Dictionary of National Biography* (OUP, Oxford, 1995).

BIBLIOGRAPHY

Aldrich, Richard J., *Intelligence and the War against Japan: Britain, America and the Politics of Secret Service* (CUP, Cambridge, 2000)

Alperovitz, Gar, *The Decision to Use the Atomic Bomb and the Architecture of an American Myth* (Knopf, New York, 1995)

Alvarez, David (ed.), *Allied and Axis Signals Intelligence in World War II* (Frank Cass, London, 1999)

Alvarez, David, *Secret Messages: Codebreaking and American Diplomacy, 1930–1945* (University Press of Kansas, Lawrence, 2000)

Andrew, Christopher, *Secret Service: The Making of the British Intelligence Community* (William Heinemann, London, 1985)

Attiwell, Kenneth, *The Singapore Story* (Frederick Muller, London, 1959)

Ballard, Geoffrey, *On Ultra Active Service: The Story of Australia's Signals Intelligence Operations during World War II* (Spectrum, Richmond, Victoria, 1991)

Bamford, James, *The Puzzle Palace* (Sidgwick & Jackson, London, 1983)

Beckhough, Harry, *Secret Communications: The Hidden Sources of Information through the Ages, from the Sumerians to the Cold War* (Minerva Press, London, 1995)

Benson, Robert Louis, *A History of US Communications Intelligence during World War II: Policy and Administration* (United States Cryptologic History, Series IV, World War II, Vol. 8) (National Security Agency, Fort George G. Meade, MD, 1997)

Best, Antony, *Britain, Japan and Pearl Harbor: Avoiding War in East Asia* (Routledge, London, 1995)

Biard Forrest R., The Pacific War through the Eyes of Forrest R. 'Tex' Biard (*NCVA Cryptolog*, Vol. 10, No. 2, Winter 1989)

Biard, Forrest R., Wartime Melbourne – Heaven or Hell (*NCVA Cryptolog*, Vol. 19, No. 1, Winter 1998)

Bleakley, Jack, *The Eavesdroppers* (AGPS Press, Canberra, 1991)

Boyd, Carl, *Hitler's Japanese Confidant: General Oshima Hiroshi and MAGIC Intelligence, 1941–1945* (University Press of Kansas, Lawrence, 1993)

Budiansky, Stephen, Too Late for Pearl Harbor (*US Naval Institute Proceedings*, December 1999)

Calvocoressi, Peter, Wint, Guy and Pritchard, John, *The Penguin History of the Second World War* (Penguin, London, 1999)

Cartwright, Richard L., *They Did Not Fail* (New Millennium, London, 1997)

Chamberlin, Vince, The FRUMEL – Australia May 1942 (*NCVA Cryptolog*, Vol. 9, No. 1, Fall 1987)

Chitty, Jean, *Kent House Colombo: Letters from a Wren, May 1944 to November 1945* (Belhaven, Lymington, 1994)

Clarke, Ronald, *The Man Who Broke Purple* (Weidenfeld & Nicolson, London, 1977)

Clayton, Anthony, *Forearmed: A History of the Intelligence Corps* (Brassey's, London, 1993)

Currier, Prescott, NSA Oral History OH-38-80 (November 1980)

Currier, Prescott, My Purple Trip to England in 1941 (*Cryptologia*, Vol. 20, No. 3, 1996)

Davidson, Edward and Manning, Dale, *Chronology of World War Two* (Cassell, London, 1999)

Deavours, Cipher and Kruh, Louis, *Machine Cryptography and Modern Cryptanalysis* (Artech, London, 1985)

Denniston, A. G., The Government Code and Cypher School between the Wars (*Intelligence and National Security*, Vol. 1, No. 1, 1986)

Denniston, Robin, The Professional Career of A. G. Denniston, in Kenneth Robertson (ed.), *British and American Approaches to Intelligence* (Macmillan, London, 1987)

Denniston, Robin, Diplomatic Eavesdropping, 1922–1944: A New Source Discovered (*Intelligence and National Security*, Vol. 10, No. 3, 1995)

Denniston, Robin, *Churchill's Secret War* (Sutton Publishing, Stroud, 1997)

Drabble, Margaret, *Angus Wilson: A Biography* (Minerva, London, 1996)

Drea, Edward J., *MacArthur's Ultra: Codebreaking and the War against Japan, 1942–1945* (University Press of Kansas, Lawrence, 1992)

Drea, Edward J., Were the Japanese Army Codes Ever Secure? (*Cryptologia*, Vol. 19, No. 2, April 1995)

Dupuy, R. Ernest and Dupuy, Trevor N., *The Encyclopedia of Military History from 3500 BC to the Present* (Macdonald & Jane's, London, 1976)

Elphick, Peter, *Singapore: The Pregnable Fortress: A Study in Deception, Discord and Desertion* (Hodder & Stoughton, London, 1995)

Elphick, Peter, *Far Eastern File: The Intelligence War in the Far East 1930–1945* (Coronet, London, 1997)

Elphick, Peter and Smith, Michael, *Odd Man Out: The Story of the Singapore Traitor* (Hodder & Stoughton, London, 1993)

Erskine, Ralph, Churchill and the Start of the Ultra–Magic Deals (*International Journal of Intelligence and Counterintelligence*, Vol. 10, 1997)

Erskine, Ralph, The First Naval Enigma Decrypts of World War II (*Cryptologia*, Vol. 11, 1997)

Erskine, Ralph, When a Purple Machine Went Missing: How Japan Nearly Discovered America's Greatest Secret (*Intelligence and National Security*, Vol. 12, No. 3, 1997)

Erskine, Ralph, The Holden Agreement on Naval Sigint: The First BRUSA? (*Intelligence and National Security*, Vol. 14, No. 2, Summer 1999)

Erskine, Ralph, Brigadier John H. Tiltman: One of BP's Finest (forthcoming, *Global Intelligence Monthly*)

Ferris, John, From Broadway House to Bletchley Park: The Diary of Captain Malcolm D. Kennedy, 1934–1946

(*Intelligence and National Security*, Vol. 4, No. 3, July 1989)

Filby, P. W., Floradora and a Unique Break into One-time Pad Ciphers (*Intelligence and National Security*, Vol. 10, No. 3, 1995)

Gascoine, Nourma, Memories of Moorabbin United States Naval Wireless Telegraphy W/T Station (*NCVA Cryptolog*, Vol. 9, No. 4, Spring 1983)

Hawken, Elizabeth, *Recollections of Bletchley Park* (unpublished memoir, 1994)

Hillier, Jean, *No Medals in This Unit* (Jean Hillier, Mundulla, 1996)

Hinsley, F. H., *British Intelligence in the Second World War* (revised abridged edition) (HMSO, London, 1994)

Hinsley, F. H. and Stripp, Alan (eds), *Codebreakers: The Inside Story of Bletchley Park* (OUP, Oxford, 1993)

Hinsley, F. H., Thomas, E. E., Ransom, C. F. G. and Knight, R. C., *British Intelligence in the Second World War*, Vols I–III (HMSO, London, 1979–1984)

Holmes, W. J., *Double-edged Secrets: US Naval Intelligence Operations in the Pacific during World War II* (Annapolis, MD, US Naval Institute Press, 1979)

Jacobsen, Phillip H., *The Codebreakers* (http://www.microworks.net/pacific/intelligence/index.htm)

Jarvis, Sue, Japanese Codes (*Bletchley Park Reports*, No. 6, July 1997)

Jeffery, Keith (ed.), The Government Code and Cypher School: A Memorandum by Lord Curzon (*Intelligence and National Security*, Vol. 1, No. 3, January 1986)

Johnson, John, *The Evolution of British Sigint: 1653–1939* (HMSO, Cheltenham, 1997)

Jones, R. V., *Most Secret War: British Scientific Intelligence 1939–1945* (Coronet, London, 1979)

Kahn, David, *The Codebreakers: The Story of Secret Writing* (Weidenfeld & Nicolson, London, 1966)

Keegan, John, *The Second World War* (Viking, New York, 1990)

Keegan, John (ed.), *Who's Who in World War II* (Routledge, London, 1995)

Kelley, Steve, *Big Machines: The Relative Cryptographic*

Security of the German Enigma, the Japanese PURPLE, and
the US SIGABA/ECM Cipher Machines in World War II
(Joint Military Intelligence College, Washington, 1999)

Lewin, Ronald, *The Other Ultra* (Hutchinson, London, 1982)

Lord, Walter, *Incredible Victory* (New York, Harper & Row,
1967)

Maneki, Sharon A., *The Quiet Heroes of the Southwest Pacific
Theater: An Oral History of the Men and Women of CBB
and FRUMEL* (United States Cryptologic History, Series IV,
World War II, Vol. 7) (National Security Agency, Fort
George G. Meade, MD, 1996)

Marder, Arthur J., *Old Friends, New Enemies* (OUP, Oxford, 1981)

Mead, David, The Breaking of the Japanese Army
Administrative Code (*Cryptologia*, Vol. 18, No. 3, July 1994)

Melinsky, Hugh, *A Code-breaker's Tale* (Lark's Press, Dereham,
1998)

Milner-Barry, Sir Stuart, C. H. O'D. Alexander – a Personal
Memoir, in Harry Golombek and William R. Hartson, *The
Best Games of C. H. O'D. Alexander* (OUP, Oxford, 1976)

Nave, Eric, *An Australian's Unique Naval Career* (unpublished
memoir, Australian War Memorial, MSS 1183)

Page, Gwendoline, *Growing Pains: A Teenager's War* (The Book
Guild, Lewes, 1994)

Parker, Frederick D., The Unsolved Messages of Pearl Harbor
(*Cryptologia*, Vol. 15, No. 4, October 1991)

Parker, Frederick D., *A Priceless Advantage: US Navy
Communications Intelligence and the Battles of Coral Sea,
Midway, and the Aleutians* (United States Cryptologic
History, Series IV, World War II, Vol. 5) (National Security
Agency, Fort George G. Meade, MD, 1993)

Parker, Frederick D., *Pearl Harbor Revisited: United States Navy
Communications Intelligence, 1924–1941* (United States
Cryptologic History, Series IV, World War II, Vol. 6) (National
Security Agency, Fort George G. Meade, MD, 1994)

Prados, John, *Combined Fleet Decoded: The Secret History of
American Intelligence and the Japanese Navy in World War
II* (Random House, New York, 1995)

Richelson, Jeffrey T. and Ball, Desmond, *The Ties That Bind* (Unwin Hyman, Boston, 1990)

Rowlett, Frank, *The Story of Magic: Memoirs of an American Cryptologic Pioneer* (Aegean Park Press, Laguna Hills, 1998)

Rusbridger, James and Nave, Eric, *Betrayal at Pearl Harbor: How Churchill Lured Roosevelt into War* (Michael O'Mara, London, 1991)

Scott, Norman, Solving Japanese Naval Ciphers 1943–45 (*Cryptologia*, Vol. 21, No. 2, April 1997)

Simson, Ivan, *Singapore: Too Little, Too Late: Some Aspects of the Malayan Disaster in 1942* (Leo Cooper, London, 1970)

Skillen, Hugh, *Spies of the Air Waves* (Skillen, Pinner, 1989)

Slim, Field Marshal Viscount, *Defeat into Victory* (Pan, London, 1999)

Smith, Bradley, *The Ultra–Magic Deals: And the Most Secret Relationship 1940–1946* (Presidio Press, Novato, CA, 1993)

Smith, Michael, *New Cloak, Old Dagger* (Victor Gollancz, London, 1996)

Smith, Michael, *Station X: The Codebreakers of Bletchley Park* (Channel 4 Books, London, 1998)

Smith, W. C., *Wireless Experimental Centre, Hill of Happiness, Anand Parbat, Delhi 1943–6* (The Rose and the Laurel, Ashford, 1986)

Stripp, Alan, *Codebreaker in the Far East* (Frank Cass, London, 1989)

Tiltman, Brigadier John H., *Some Reminiscences* (NARA RG457 OD4632)

Weintraub, Stanley, *Long Day's Journey into War, December 7, 1941* (Plume, New York, 1992)

West, Nigel, *GCHQ: The Secret Wireless War 1900–86* (Weidenfeld & Nicolson, London, 1986)

Wheal, Elizabeth-Anne and Pope, Stephen, *The Macmillan Dictionary of the Second World War* (Macmillan, London, 1989)

Winterbotham, Frederick, *The Ultra Secret* (Weidenfeld & Nicolson, London, 1974)

INDEX

397

IN HARM'S WAY
by Doug Stanton

A harrowing, adrenaline-charged account of America's worst naval disaster.

On 30 July 1945 the USS *Indianapolis* was torpedoed in the South Pacific by a Japanese submarine. Of a crew of 1196 men an estimated 300 were killed upon impact; nearly 900 sailors were cast into the Pacific Ocean, where they remained, undetected by the Navy, for nearly five days. Battered by a savage sea, they struggled to stay alive, fighting off sharks, hypothermia and dementia. By the time rescue arrived, all but 321 men had died (four more would succumb to wounds in military hospitals).

Interweaving the stories of three survivors – the captain, the ship's doctor and a young marine – Doug Stanton has brought this incredible human drama to life in a narrative that is at once immediate and timeless. The definitive account of a little-known chapter in Second World War history, *In Harm's Way* is destined to become a classic.

'A powerfully written account of a nightmare at sea, one of the most poignant tragedies and injustices of World War II'
Mark Bowden, author of *Black Hawk Down*

'Doug Stanton...writes carefully and judiciously, with a sense of timing and an eye for the right detail, to make this the most frightening book I've ever read'
Stephen E. Ambrose

0 593 04740 0

NOW AVAILABLE FROM BANTAM PRESS

TOMORROW TO BE BRAVE
by Susan Travers

'Wherever you go, I will go too'

These were the words Susan Travers spoke to General Koenig, the Commander of the Free French and the Foreign Legion in North Africa during the Second World War, and the man with whom she was in love.

Her words were about to be tested to the limit. It was early Spring 1942, and under the pitiless desert sky the great siege of Bir Hakeim was about to begin. Surrounded for fifteen days and nights by Rommel's Afrika Korps, outnumbered ten to one, pounded by Stuka and Heinkl bombers, Susan, the General and the thousand soldiers seemed doomed. Then, one moonless night, the French made an audacious bid for freedom. Speeding across the minefields of no-man's-land towards Rommel's deadly Panzer tanks, her foot hard on the accelerator, Susan led the convoy of men and vehicles away from Bir Hakeim. Hailed as the heroine of the night, she was awarded the Military Medal and the Legion d'Honneur.

Tomorrow To Be Brave is the story of Susan Travers's amazing life, from her childhood in England, her growing–up in the South of France, to her decision to join the Free French, and her time as a regular serving officer in the Foreign Legion – the only woman ever to achieve this. It is a tale of exceptional courage, and also a passionate love story, as Susan Travers risked everything for the country and for the man she loved so well.

'A striking account of an extraordinary life'
The Times

0 552 14814 8

THE YAMATO DYNASTY
The secret history of Japan's imperial family
by Sterling and Peggy Seagrave

'Reads like a political thriller. It is essential reading'
Sunday Times

The Yamato Dynasty takes us behind the walls of privilege and tradition and reveals, in uncompromising detail, the true nature of the Japanese imperial family – a dynasty until now shrouded in myth and legend – and the powerful shoguns and financiers who control the throne from the shadows.

Sterling and Peggy Seagrave bring to light new evidence that points at the implicit involvement of Hirohito, and other members of the imperial family's inner circle, in the war crimes of the Second World War. Moreover, and shockingly, the American occupying force after the war were aware of this but deliberately protected Japan's élite family to guard US investments in Japan and prevent Japan's fall into communism. The Seagraves here supply documentary evidence that General MacArthur and his men ensured that the major war crimes witnesses would completely exonerate Hirohito from all culpability in war crimes and shift the blame to others.

They also reveal for the first time the full scale of *Kin No Yuri*, 'Golden Lily', the looting operation that removed many billions of dollars' worth of gold, platinum, diamonds, art, religious artefacts and other treasures from a dozen occupied countries during the war, and the fate of these hidden assets after 1945.

'A highly controversial book that cannot fail to have a lasting impact upon Japanese national politics, the way Japanese view themselves, and the way the rest of the world views them'
Martin Booth, *Sunday Times*

0 552 14709 5

THE PAST IS MYSELF
by Christabel Bielenberg

'It would be difficult to overpraise this book. Mrs Bielenberg's experience was unique and her honesty, intelligence and compassion makes her account of it moving beyond words'
The Economist

Christabel Bielenberg, a niece of Lord Northcliffe, married a German lawyer in 1934. She lived through the war in Germany, as a German Citizen, under the horrors of Nazi rule and allied bombings. *The Past is Myself* is her story of that experience, an unforgettable portrait of an evil time.

'This autobiography is of exceptional distinction and importance. It deserves recognition as a magnificent contribution to international understanding and as a document of how the human spirit can triumph in the midst of evil and persecution'
The Economist

'Marvellously written'
Observer

'Nothing but superlatives will do for this book. It tells its story magnificently and every page of its story is worth telling'
Irish Press

'Intensely moving'
Yorkshire Evening News

0 552 99065 5

A SELECTED LIST OF NON–FICTION TITLES AVAILABLE FROM CORGI AND BANTAM BOOKS

40664 7	CHE GUEVARA	Jon Lee Anderson	£12 99
99065 5	THE PAST IS MYSELF	Christabel Bielenberg	£7.99
13337 X	THE PROVISIONAL IRA	Patrick Bishop & Eamonn Mallie	£6.99
14750 8	BLACK HAWK DOWN	Mark Bowden	£5.99
50650 1	BOUND FEET AND WESTERN DRESS	Pang–Mei Natasha Chang	£6.99
81303 X	THE RAINBOW PALACE	Tenzin Choedrak	£7.99
99091 4	ANIMALS IN WAR	Jilly Cooper	£6.99
50582 3	BONES OF THE MASTER	George Crane	£6.99
14465 7	CLOSE QUARTER BATTLE	Mike Curtis	£6.99
14239 5	MY FEUDAL LORD	Tehmina Durrani	£5.99
13928 9	DAUGHTER OF PERSIA	Sattareh Farman Farmaian	£6.99
12833 3	THE HOUSE BY THE DVINA	Eugenie Fraser	£8.99
14760 5	THE CUSTOM OF THE SEA	Neil Hanson	£5.99
14185 2	FINDING PEGGY: A GLASGOW CHILDHOOD	Meg Henderson	£6.99
14164 X	EMPTY CRADLES	Margaret Humphreys	£6.99
13356 6	NOT WITHOUT MY DAUGHTER	Betty Mahmoody	£5.99
40936 0	THE HIDDEN CHILDREN	Jane Marks	£5.99
12419 2	CHICKENHAWK	Robert C. Mason	£7.99
13953 X	SOME OTHER RAINBOW	John McCarthy & Jill Morrell	£6.99
14127 5	BRAVO TWO ZERO	Andy McNab	£6.99
40814 3	THE HAREM WITHIN	Fatima Mernissi	£5.99
81335 8	THE FULL MONTEZUMA	Peter Moore	£6.99
14288 3	BRIDGE ACROSS MY SORROWS	Christina Noble	£5.99
14607 2	THE INFORMER	Sean O'Callaghan	£6.99
81302 1	LA PRISONNIERE	Malika Oufkir & Michele Foutissi	£6.99
81195 9	SORROW MOUNTAIN	Ani Pachen and Adelaide Donnelley	£6.99
40805 4	DAUGHTERS OF ARABIA	Jean P Sasson	£5.99
14709 5	THE YAMATO DYNASTY	Sterling and Peggy Seagrave	£7.99
14814 8	TOMORROW TO BE BRAVE	Susan Travers with Wendy Holden	£6.99
50554 9	RED CHINA BLUES	Jan Wong	£7.99